CLEOPATRA

A Great Improvisation: Franklin, France, and the Birth of America

Véra (Mrs. Vladimir Nabokov)

Saint-Exupéry: A Biography

CLEOPATRA

A Life

STACY
SCHIFF

LITTLE, BROWN AND COMPANY

New York Boston London

932.021
Sch

Little, Brown and Company
Hachette Book Group
237 Park Avenue, New York, NY 10017
www.hachettebookgroup.com

First Edition: November 2010

Maps by George W. Ward

Little, Brown and Company is a division of Hachette Book Group, Inc. The
Little, Brown name and logo are trademarks of Hachette Book Group, Inc.

Library of Congress Cataloging-in-Publication Data
Schiff, Stacy.
  Cleopatra / by Stacy Schiff. — 1st ed.
     p. cm.
  Includes bibliographical references and index.
  ISBN 978-0-316-00192-2 — 978-0-316-12044-9 (large print)
  1. Cleopatra, Queen of Egypt, d. 30 B.C.   2. Queens—Egypt—Biography.
3. Egypt—Kings and rulers—Biography.   4. Egypt—History—332–30 B.C.   I. Title.
DT92.7.S35 2010
932'.021092 — dc22
  [B]   2010006988

10   9   8   7   6   5   4   3   2   1

RRD-IN

Book design by Fritz Metsch

Printed in the United States of America

Finally, for Max, Millie, and Jo

Contents

CONTENTS

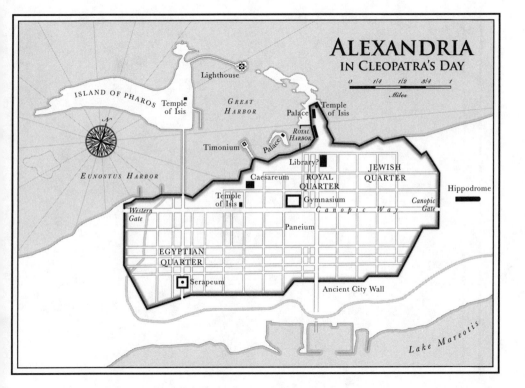

ALEXANDRIA
IN CLEOPATRA'S DAY

0   1/4   1/2   3/4   1
Miles

Lighthouse

ISLAND OF PHAROS   Temple of Isis

GREAT HARBOR

Temple of Isis

Palace

ROYAL HARBOR

Timonium   Palace

EUNOSTUS HARBOR

Library?

Caesareum

JEWISH QUARTER

ROYAL QUARTER

Hippodrome

Temple of Isis

Gymnasium

Canopic Way

Canopic Gate

Western Gate

Paneium

EGYPTIAN QUARTER

Serapeum

Ancient City Wall

Lake Mareotis

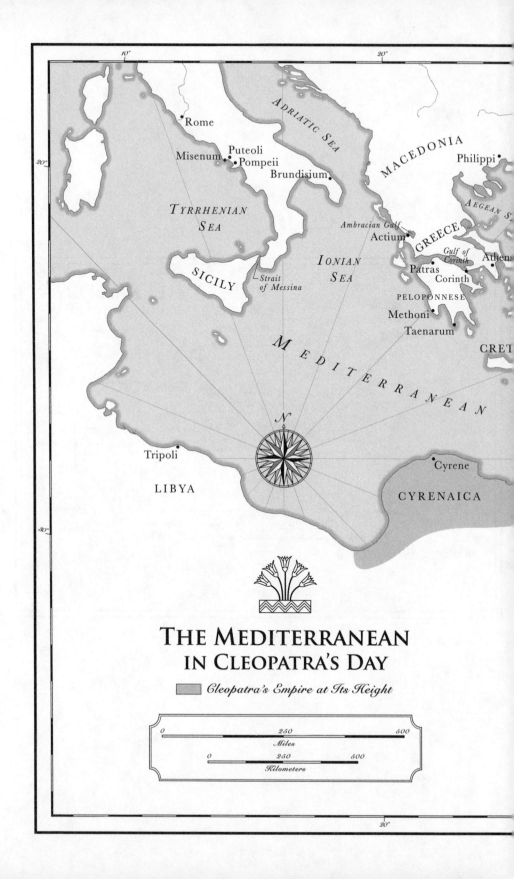

THE MEDITERRANEAN
IN CLEOPATRA'S DAY

Cleopatra's Empire at Its Height

0   250   500
Miles

0   250   500
Kilometers

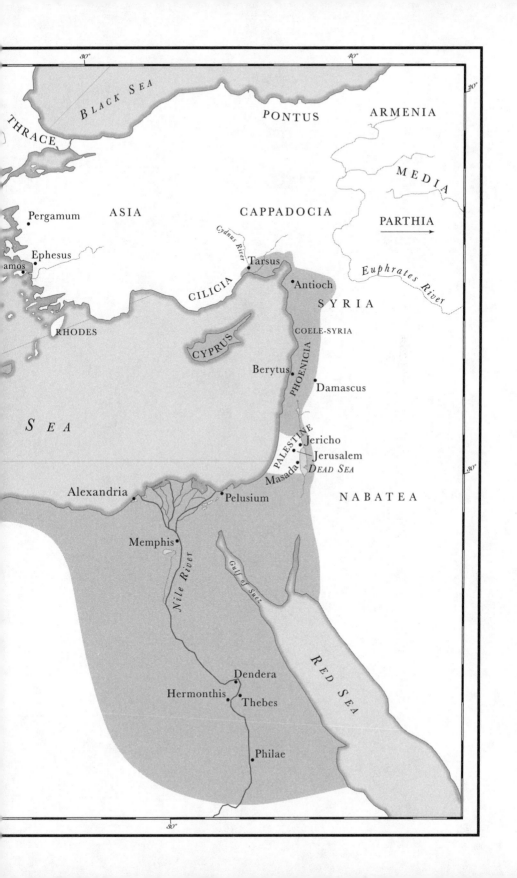

CLEOPATRA

THAT EGYPTIAN WOMAN

"Man's most valuable trait is a judicious sense of what not to believe."
— EURIPIDES

AMONG THE MOST famous women to have lived, Cleopatra VII ruled Egypt for twenty-two years. She lost a kingdom once, regained it, nearly lost it again, amassed an empire, lost it all. A goddess as a child, a queen at eighteen, a celebrity soon thereafter, she was an object of speculation and veneration, gossip and legend, even in her own time. At the height of her power she controlled virtually the entire eastern Mediterranean coast, the last great kingdom of any Egyptian ruler. For a fleeting moment she held the fate of the Western world in her hands. She had a child with a married man, three more with another. She died at thirty-nine, a generation before the birth of Christ. Catastrophe reliably cements a reputation, and Cleopatra's end was sudden and sensational. She has lodged herself in our imaginations ever since. Many people have spoken for her, including the greatest playwrights and poets; we have been putting words in her mouth for two thousand years. In one of the busiest afterlives in history she has gone on to become an asteroid, a video game, a cliché, a cigarette, a slot machine, a strip club, a synonym for Elizabeth Taylor. Shakespeare attested to Cleopatra's infinite variety. He had no idea.

If the name is indelible, the image is blurry. Cleopatra may be one of the most recognizable figures in history but we have little idea of what she actually looked like. Only her coin portraits—issued in her lifetime, and which she likely approved—can be accepted as authentic. We remember her too for the wrong reasons. A capable, clear-eyed sovereign, she knew how to build a fleet, suppress an insurrection, control a currency, alleviate a famine. An eminent Roman general vouched for her grasp of military affairs. Even at a time when women rulers were no rarity she stood out, the sole female of the ancient world to rule alone and to play a role in Western affairs. She was incomparably richer than anyone else in the Mediterranean. And she enjoyed greater prestige than any other woman of her age, as an excitable rival king was reminded when he called, during her stay at his court, for her assassination. (In light of her stature, it could not be done.) Cleopatra descended from a long line of murderers and faithfully upheld the family tradition but was, for her time and place, remarkably well behaved. She nonetheless survives as a wanton temptress, not the last time a genuinely powerful woman has been transmuted into a shamelessly seductive one.

Like all lives that lend themselves to poetry, Cleopatra's was one of dislocations and disappointments. She grew up amid unsurpassed luxury, to inherit a kingdom in decline. For ten generations her family had styled themselves pharaohs. The Ptolemies were in fact Macedonian Greek, which makes Cleopatra approximately as Egyptian as Elizabeth Taylor. At eighteen Cleopatra and her ten-year-old brother assumed control of a country with a weighty past and a wobbly future. Thirteen hundred years separate Cleopatra from Nefertiti. The pyramids—to which Cleopatra almost certainly introduced Julius Caesar—already sported graffiti. The Sphinx had undergone a major restoration, a thousand years earlier. And the glory of the once great Ptolemaic Empire had dimmed. Cleopatra came of age in a world shadowed by Rome, which in the course of her childhood extended its rule to Egypt's borders. When Cleopatra was eleven, Caesar reminded his officers that if they did not make war, if they did not obtain riches and rule others, they were not Romans. An Eastern sovereign who waged an epic battle of his own against Rome articulated what would become Cleopatra's predicament differently: The Romans had the temperament of wolves. They hated the great kings. Everything they possessed they had plundered. They intended to seize all, and would "either destroy everything or perish in the attempt." The implications for the last remaining wealthy country in Rome's sphere of influence were clear. Egypt had distinguished itself for its nimble negotiating; for the most part, it retained its autonomy. It had also already embroiled itself in Roman affairs.

For a staggering sum of money, Cleopatra's father had secured the official designation "friend and ally of the Roman people." His daughter would discover that it was not sufficient to be a friend to that people and their Senate; it was essential to befriend the most powerful Roman of the day. That made for a bewildering assignment in the late Republic, wracked by civil wars. They flared up regularly throughout Cleopatra's lifetime, pitting a succession of Roman commanders against one another in what was essentially a hot-tempered contest of personal ambition, twice unexpectedly decided on Egyptian soil. Each convulsion left the Mediterranean world shuddering, scrambling to correct its loyalties and redirect its tributes. Cleopatra's father had thrown in his lot with Pompey the Great, the brilliant Roman general on whom good fortune seemed eternally to shine. He became the family patron. He also entered into a civil war against Julius Caesar just as, across the Mediterranean, Cleopatra ascended to the throne. In the summer of 48 BC Caesar dealt Pompey a crushing defeat in central Greece; Pompey fled to Egypt, to be stabbed and decapitated on an Egyptian beach. Cleopatra was twenty-one. She had no choice but to ingratiate herself with the new master of the Roman world. She did so differently from most other client kings, whose names, not incidentally, are forgotten today. For the next years she struggled to turn the implacable Roman tide to her advantage, changing patrons again after Caesar's murder, ultimately to wind up with his protégé, Mark Antony. From a distance her reign amounts to a reprieve. Her story was essentially over before it began, although that is of course not the way she would have seen it. With her death Egypt became a Roman province. It would not recover its autonomy until the twentieth century.

Can anything good be said of a woman who slept with the two most powerful men of her time? Possibly, but not in an age when Rome controlled the narrative. Cleopatra stood at one of the most dangerous intersections in history: that of women and power. Clever women, Euripides had warned hundreds of years earlier, were dangerous. A Roman historian was perfectly happy to write off a Judaean queen as a mere figurehead and — six pages later — to condemn her for her reckless ambition, her indecent embrace of authority. A more disarming brand of power made itself felt as well. In a first-century BC marriage contract, a bride promised to be faithful and affectionate. She further vowed not to add love potions to her husband's food or drink. We do not know if Cleopatra loved either Antony or Caesar, but we do know that she got each to do her bidding. From the Roman point of view she "enslaved" them both. Already it was a zero-sum game: a woman's authority spelled a man's deception. Asked how she had obtained her influence over Augustus, the first Roman emperor, his wife purportedly replied that she had done so "by being scrupulously chaste herself, doing gladly whatever pleased him, not meddling with any of his affairs, and, in particular, by pretending neither to hear of nor to notice the favorites that were the objects of his passion." There is no reason to accept that formula at face value. On the other hand, Cleopatra was cut from very different cloth. In the course of a leisurely fishing trip, under a languid Alexandrian sun, she had no trouble suggesting that the most celebrated Roman general of the day tend to his responsibilities.

To a Roman, license and lawlessness were Greek preserves. Cleopatra was twice suspect, once for hailing from a culture known for its "natural talent for deception," again for her Alexandrian address. A Roman could not pry apart the exotic and the erotic; Cleopatra was a stand-in for the occult, alchemical East, for her sinuous, sensuous land, as perverse and original as its astonishment of a river. Men who came in contact with her seem to have lost their heads, or at least to have rethought their agendas. She runs away even with Plutarch's biography of Mark Antony. She works the same effect on a nineteenth-century historian, who describes her, on meeting Caesar, as "a loose girl of sixteen." (She was rather an intensely focused woman of twenty-one.) The siren call of the East long predated Cleopatra, but no matter; she hailed from the intoxicating land of sex and excess. It is not difficult to understand why Caesar became history, Cleopatra a legend.

Our view is further obscured by the fact that the Romans who told Cleopatra's story very nearly knew their ancient history too well. Repeatedly it seeps into their accounts. Like Mark Twain in the overwhelming, overstuffed Vatican, we sometimes prefer the copies to the original. So did the classical authors. They conflated accounts, refurbishing old tales. They saddled Cleopatra with the vices of other miscreants. History existed to be retold, with more panache but not necessarily greater accuracy. In the ancient texts the villains always wear a particularly vulgar purple, eat too much roasted peacock, douse themselves in rare unguents, melt down pearls. Whether you were a transgressive, power-hungry Egyptian queen or a ruthless pirate, you were known for the "odious extravagance" of your accessories. Iniquity and opulence went hand in hand; your world blazed purple and gold. Nor did it help that history bled into mythology, the human into the divine. Cleopatra's was a world in which you could visit the relics of Orpheus's lyre, or view the egg from which Zeus's mother had hatched. (It was in Sparta.)

History is written not only by posterity, but for posterity as well. Our most comprehensive sources never met Cleopatra. Plutarch was born seventy-six years after she died. (He was working at the same time as Matthew, Mark, Luke, and John.) Appian wrote at a remove of more than a century; Dio of well over two. Cleopatra's story differs from most women's stories in that the men who shaped it—for their own reasons—enlarged rather than erased her role. Her relationship with Mark Antony was the longest of her life, but her relationship with his rival, Augustus, was the most enduring. He would defeat Antony and Cleopatra. To Rome, to enhance the glory, he delivered up the tabloid version of an Egyptian queen, insatiable, treacherous, bloodthirsty, power-crazed. He magnified Cleopatra to hyperbolic proportions so as to do the same with

5

his victory—and so as to smuggle his real enemy, his former brother-in-law, out of the picture. The end result is a nineteenth-century British life of Napoleon or a twentieth-century history of America, were it to have been written by Chairman Mao.

To the team of extraordinarily tendentious historians, add an extraordinarily spotty record. No papyri from Alexandria survive. Almost nothing of the ancient city survives aboveground. We have, perhaps and at most, one written word of Cleopatra's. (In 33 BC either she or a scribe signed off on a royal decree with the Greek word *ginesthoi*, meaning, "Let it be done.") Classical authors were indifferent to statistics and occasionally even to logic; their accounts contradict one another and themselves. Appian is careless with details, Josephus hopeless with chronology. Dio preferred rhetoric to exactitude. The lacunae are so regular as to seem deliberate; there is very nearly a conspiracy of silences. How is it possible that we do not have an authoritative bust of Cleopatra from an age of accomplished, realistic portraiture? Cicero's letters of the first months of 44 BC—when Caesar and Cleopatra were together in Rome—were never published. The longest Greek history of the era glosses over the tumultuous period at hand. It is difficult to say what we miss most. Appian promises more of Caesar and Cleopatra in his four books of Egyptian history, which do not survive. Livy's account breaks off a century before Cleopatra. We know the detailed work of her personal physician only from Plutarch's references. Dellius's chronicle has vanished, along with the raunchy letters Cleopatra was said to have written him. Even Lucan comes to an abrupt, infuriating halt partway through his epic poem, leaving Caesar trapped in Cleopatra's palace at the outset of the Alexandrian War. And in the absence of facts, myth rushes in, the kudzu of history.

The holes in the record present one hazard, what we have constructed around them another. Affairs of state have fallen away, leaving us with affairs of the heart. A commanding woman versed in politics, diplomacy, and governance; fluent in nine languages; silver-tongued and charismatic, Cleopatra nonetheless seems the joint creation of Roman propagandists and Hollywood directors. She is left to put a vintage label on something we have always known existed: potent female sexuality. And her timing was lousy. Not only was her history written by her enemies, but it was her misfortune to have been on everyone's minds just as Latin poetry came into its own. She survives literarily in a language hostile to her. The fictions have only proliferated. George Bernard Shaw lists among his sources for *Caesar and Cleopatra* his own imagination. Plenty of historians have deferred to Shakespeare, which is understandable but a little like taking George C. Scott's word for Patton's.

To restore Cleopatra is as much to salvage the few facts as to peel away the encrusted myth and the hoary propaganda. She was a Greek woman whose history fell to men whose futures lay with Rome, the majority of them officials of the empire. Their historical methods are opaque to us. They seldom named their sources. They relied to a great extent on memory. They are by modern standards polemicists, apologists, moralists, fabulists, recyclers, cut-and-pasters, hacks. For all its erudition, Cleopatra's Egypt produced no fine historian. One can only read accordingly. The sources may be flawed, but they are the only sources we have. There is no universal agreement on most of the basic details of her life, no consensus on who her mother was, how long Cleopatra lived in Rome, how often she was pregnant, whether she and Antony married, what transpired at the battle that sealed her fate, how she died.* I have tried here to bear in mind who was a former librarian and who a Page Sixer, who had actually set eyes on Egypt, who despised the place and who was born there, who had a problem with women, who wrote with the zeal of a Roman convert, who meant to settle a score, please his emperor, perfect his hexameter. (I have relied little on Lucan. He was early on the scene, before Plutarch, Appian, or Dio. He was also a poet, and a sensationalist.) Even when they are neither tendentious nor tangled, the accounts are often overblown. As has been noted, there were no plain, unvarnished stories in antiquity. The point was to dazzle.

*Even the fiction writers cannot agree about Caesar and Cleopatra. He loves her (Handel); he loves her not (Shaw); he loves her (Thornton Wilder).

I have not attempted to fill in the blanks, though on occasion I have corralled the possibilities. What looks merely probable remains here merely probable—though opinions differ radically even on the probabilities. The irreconcilable remains unreconciled. Mostly I have restored context. Indeed Cleopatra murdered her siblings, but Herod murdered his children. (He afterward wailed that he was "the most unfortunate of fathers.") And as Plutarch reminds us, such behavior was axiomatic among sovereigns. Cleopatra was not necessarily beautiful, but her wealth—and her palace—left a Roman gasping. All read very differently on one side of the Mediterranean from the other. The last decades of research on women in antiquity and on Hellenistic Egypt substantially illuminate the picture. I have tried to pluck the gauze of melodrama from the final scenes of the life, which reduce even sober chroniclers to soap opera. Sometimes high drama prevails for a reason, however. Cleopatra's was an era of outsize, intriguing personalities. At its end the greatest actors of the age exit abruptly. A world comes crashing down after them.

WHILE THERE IS a great deal we do not know about Cleopatra, there is a great deal she did not know either. She knew neither that she was living in the first century BC nor in the Hellenistic Age, both of them later constructs. (The Hellenistic Age begins with the death of Alexander the Great in 323 BC and ends in 30 BC, with the death of Cleopatra. It has been perhaps best defined as a Greek era in which the Greeks played no role.) She did not know she was Cleopatra VII for several reasons, one of which is that she was actually the sixth Cleopatra. She never knew anyone named Octavian. The man who vanquished and deposed her, prompted her suicide, and largely packaged her for posterity was born Gaius Octavius. By the time he entered Cleopatra's life in a meaningful way he called himself Gaius Julius Caesar, after his illustrious great-uncle, her lover, who adopted him in his will. We know him today as Augustus, a title he assumed only three years after Cleopatra's death. He appears here as Octavian, two Caesars remaining, as ever, one too many.

Most place names have changed since antiquity. I have followed Lionel Casson's sensible lead in opting for familiarity over consistency. Hence Berytus is here Beirut, while Pelusium—which no longer exists, but would today be just east of Port Said, at the entrance to the Suez Canal—remains Pelusium. Similarly I have opted for English spellings over transliterations. Caesar's rival appears as Pompey rather than Gnaeus Pompeius Magnus, Caesar's deputy as Mark Antony rather than Marcus Antonius. In many respects geography has changed, shorelines have sunk, marshes dried, hills crumbled. Alexandria is flatter today than it was in Cleopatra's lifetime. It is oblivious to its ancient street plan; it no longer gleams white. The Nile is nearly two miles farther east. The dust, the sultry sea air, Alexandria's melting purple sunsets, are unchanged. Human nature remains remarkably consistent, the physics of history immutable. Firsthand accounts continue to diverge wildly.* For well over two thousand years, a myth has been able to outrun and outlive a fact. Except where noted, all dates are BC.

---

*As they have done since time immemorial. "And the endeavor to ascertain these facts was a laborious task, because those who were eyewitnesses of the several events did not give the same reports about the same things, but reports varying according to their championship of one side or the other, or according to their recollection," grumbled Thucydides, nearly four hundred years before Cleopatra.

DEAD MEN DON'T BITE

"It's a godsend, really lucky, when one has so few relations."
— MENANDER

THAT SUMMER SHE rallied a band of mercenaries, at a desert camp, under the glassy heat of the Syrian sun. She was twenty-one, an orphan and an exile. Already she had known both excessive good fortune and its flamboyant consort, calamity. Accustomed to the greatest luxury of the day, she held court two hundred miles from the ebony doors and onyx floors of home. Her tent amid the scrub of the desert was the closest she had come in a year. Over those months she had scrambled for her life, fleeing through Middle Egypt, Palestine, and southern Syria. She had spent a dusty summer raising an army.

The women in her family were good at this and so clearly was she, accomplished enough anyway for the enemy to have marched out to meet her. Dangerously close at hand, not far from the seaside fortress of Pelusium, on the eastern frontier of Egypt, were 20,000 veteran soldiers, an army about half the size of that with which Alexander the Great had crossed into Asia three centuries earlier. This one was a formidable assembly of pirates and bandits, outlaws, exiles, and fugitive slaves, under the titular command of her thirteen-year-old brother. With him she had inherited the throne of Egypt. She had shunted him aside; in return he had banished her from the kingdom over which they were meant to rule jointly, as husband and wife. Her brother's army controlled

Pelusium's redbrick walls, its massive twenty-foot, semicircular towers. She camped farther east, along the desolate coast, in a smoldering sea of amber sand. A battle loomed. Her position was hopeless at best. For the last time in two thousand years Cleopatra VII stands offstage. In a matter of days she will launch herself into history, which is to say that faced with the inevitable, she will counter with the improbable. It is 48 BC.

Throughout the Mediterranean a "strange madness" hung in the air, ripe with omens and portents and extravagant rumors. The mood was one of nervous exasperation. It was possible to be anxious and elated, empowered and afraid, all in the course of a single afternoon. Some rumors even proved true. Early in July Cleopatra heard that the Roman civil war—a contest that pitted the invincible Julius Caesar against the indomitable Pompey the Great—was about to collide with her own. This was alarming news. For as long as Cleopatra could remember, the Romans had served as protectors of the Egyptian monarchs. They owed their throne to that disruptive power, which in a few generations had conquered most of the Mediterranean world. Also as long as she could remember, Pompey had been a particular friend of her father's. A brilliant general, Pompey had for decades piled up victories, on land and sea, subduing nation after nation, in Africa, Asia, and Europe. Both Cleopatra and her estranged brother, Ptolemy XIII, were in his debt.

Days later Cleopatra discovered that the chances of being murdered by someone who owed you a favor were every bit as good as the chances of being murdered by a member of your immediate family. On September 28, Pompey appeared off the coast of Pelusium. He had been routed by Caesar. Desperate, he cast about for a refuge. He thought logically enough of the young king whose family he had supported and who was deeply beholden to him. No request he might make could in good faith be denied. The three regents who essentially ruled for young Ptolemy— Theodotus, his rhetoric master; Achillas, the bold commander of the royal guard; and Pothinus, the eunuch who had nimbly parlayed his role as childhood tutor into that of prime minister—disagreed. The unexpected arrival presented them with a difficult decision, which they hotly debated. Opinions differed. To cast off Pompey was to make an enemy of him. To receive him was to make an enemy of Caesar. Were they to eliminate Pompey, he could offer no assistance to Cleopatra, to whom he was well disposed. Nor could he install himself on the throne of Egypt. "Dead men don't bite" was the irrefutable counsel of Theodotus, the rhetoric teacher, who—having proved by simple syllogism that they could afford neither to befriend nor offend Pompey—delivered the line with a smile. He dispatched a welcoming message and a "wretched little boat" for the Roman. Pompey had not yet set foot on shore when, in the shallow waters off Pelusium, in full view of Ptolemy's army and of the miniature king in his purple robes, he was stabbed to death, his head severed from his body.*

Caesar would try later to make sense of that savagery. Friends often turn into enemies in time of disaster, he conceded. He might equally well have noted that at times of disaster enemies reinvent themselves as friends. Ptolemy's advisers beheaded Pompey most of all to curry favor with Caesar. What better way to endear themselves to the undisputed master of the Mediterranean world? By the same logic the three had simplified matters for Cleopatra. In the Roman civil war—a contest of such searing intensity that it seemed less an armed conflict than a plague, a flood, a fire—she now appeared to have backed the losing side.

Three days later Julius Caesar ventured ashore in the Egyptian capital, in pursuit of his rival. He arrived in advance of the bulk of his troops. A great metropolis, Alexandria was home to malicious wit, dubious morals, grand larceny. Its residents talked fast, in many languages and at once; theirs was an excitable city of short tempers and taut, vibrating minds. Already it was in ferment, unrest this second flash of imperial red exacerbated. Caesar had been careful to modulate his joy in his victory and continued to do so. When Theodotus presented him with Pompey's three-day-old severed head, Caesar turned away in horror. He then burst into tears. A few may even have been genuine; at one time Pompey had

---

*Ptolemy XIII surveyed the murder from the beach but for his part in it earned a permanent place in Dante's ninth circle of hell. He keeps company with Cain and Judas.

been not only his ally but his son-in-law. If Ptolemy's advisers felt the gruesome welcome would hold Caesar off, they were wrong. If Caesar thought that Pompey's murder constituted a vote in his favor, he too was mistaken, at least so far as the Alexandrians were concerned. Riots greeted him onshore, where no one was less welcome than a Roman, especially one bearing the official trappings of power. At best Caesar would interfere with their affairs. At worst he had conquest in mind. Already Rome had restored an unpopular king who—to make matters worse—taxed his people to pay off the debt for that restoration. The Alexandrians did not care to pay the price for a king they had not wanted in the first place. Nor did they care to become Roman subjects.

Caesar installed himself securely in a pavilion on the grounds of the Ptolemies' palace, adjoining the royal dockyards, in the eastern part of the city. The skirmishing continued—roars and scuffles echoed loudly down the colonnaded streets—but in the palace he was safe from all disturbance. He sent hastily for reinforcements. And having done so, he summoned the feuding siblings. Caesar felt it incumbent upon him to arbitrate their dispute, as a decade earlier he and Pompey had together lobbied for their father. A stable Egypt was in Rome's best interest, the more so when there were substantial debts to be paid. As Caesar had himself recently suggested to his rival, it was time for the warring parties "to put an end to their obstinate behavior, abandon armed struggle, and not risk their luck any further." Cleopatra and her brother should have mercy on themselves and on their country.

The summons left Cleopatra with some explaining to do, as well as some calculating. She had every reason to plead her case promptly, before her brother's advisers could undermine her. His army effectively blocked her from Egypt. Although Caesar had requested he disband it, Ptolemy made no effort to do so. To move her own men west, through the golden sand, toward the border and the high towers at Pelusium, was to risk an engagement. By one account she made contact with Caesar through an intermediary, then, convinced she had been betrayed (she was unpopular with the palace courtiers), she determined to plead her case herself.

Which left her to puzzle out how to slip past enemy lines, across a well-patrolled frontier, and into a blockaded palace, covertly and alive. Cleopatra's reputation would come to rest on her gift for pageantry, but in her first and greatest political gamble the challenge was to make herself inconspicuous. By modern standards too hers was a curious predicament. To make her mark, for her story to begin, this woman had to smuggle herself back into the house.

Clearly there was some deliberation. Plutarch tells us that "she was at a loss how to get in undiscovered" until she—or someone in her entourage; she, too, had confidants—hit on a brilliant ruse. It would have required a dress rehearsal. And it called for several exceedingly skilled accomplices, one of whom was a loyal Sicilian retainer named Apollodorus. Between the Sinai peninsula, where Cleopatra was camped, and the palace of Alexandria, where she had grown up, lay a treacherous marshland, thick with mites and mosquitoes. That swampy flat protected Egypt from eastern invasions. It took its name from its ability to devour whole armies, which the heavy sands did with "malevolent cunning." Ptolemy's forces controlled the coast, where Pompey's body rotted in a makeshift grave. The surest and simplest route west was then neither through the muddy pools of Pelusium nor along the Mediterranean, where Cleopatra would have been exposed to view and to a strong opposing current. It made more sense to detour south, up the Nile to Memphis, afterward to sail back to the coast, a trip of at least eight days. The river route was not without its dangers either; it was heavily trafficked and carefully surveyed by customs agents. Along the turbid Nile Cleopatra presumably sailed, with a strong wind and a host of mosquitoes, in mid-October. Ptolemy's advisers meanwhile balked at Caesar's request. How dare a Roman general summon a king? The lower-ranking party should call on the higher, as Caesar well knew.

So it was that Apollodorus silently maneuvered a tiny two-oared boat into Alexandria's eastern harbor and under the palace wall just after dusk. Close to shore all was dark, while from a distance the city's low-lying coast was illuminated by its magnificent, four-hundred-foot-tall lighthouse, a wonder of the ancient world. That blazing pillar stood a half mile from Cleopatra, at the end of a man-made causeway, on the island of Pharos. Even in its glow she was nowhere to be seen, however. At some point before Apollodorus docked his boat, she crawled into an oversize sack of hemp or leather, in which she arranged herself lengthwise. Apollodorus rolled up the bundle and secured it with a leather cord, slinging it over his shoulder, the only clue we have as to Cleopatra's size. To the gentle lap of the waves he set out across the palace grounds, a complex of gardens and multicolored villas and colonnaded walkways that spread over nearly a mile, or a quarter of the city. It was an area that Apollodorus—who certainly had not rowed from the desert alone but may have masterminded his queen's return—knew well. On his shoulder, Cleopatra rode through the palace gates and directly into Caesar's quarters, rooms that properly belonged to her. It was one of the more unusual homecomings in history. Many queens have risen from obscurity, but Cleopatra is the only one to have emerged on the world stage from inside a sturdy sack, the kind of bag into which one customarily stuffed rolls of papyrus or transported a small fortune in gold. Ruses and disguises came readily to her. On a later occasion she would conspire with another woman in peril to make her escape in a coffin.

We do not know if the unveiling took place before Caesar. Either way it is unlikely that Cleopatra appeared "majestic" (as one source has it) or laden with gems and gold (as another purports) or even marginally well coiffed. In defiance of the male imagination, five centuries of art history, and two of the greatest plays in English literature, she would have been fully clothed, in a formfitting, sleeveless, long linen tunic. The only accessory she needed was one she alone among Egyptian women was entitled to wear: the diadem, or broad white ribbon, that denoted a Hellenistic ruler. It is unlikely she appeared before Julius Caesar without one tied around her forehead and knotted at the back. Of Cleopatra's "knowledge of how to make herself agreeable to everyone," we have, on the other hand, abundant evidence. Generally it was known to be impossible to converse with her without being instantly captivated by her. For this audience, the boldness of the maneuver—the surprise appearance of the young queen in the sumptuously painted halls of her own home, which Caesar himself could barely penetrate—proved in itself an enchantment. Retrospectively, the shock appears to have been as much political as personal. The jolt was that generated when, in a singular, shuddering moment, two civilizations, passing in different directions, unexpectedly and momentously touch.

Celebrated as much for his speed as for his intuition, Julius Caesar was not an easy man to surprise. He was forever arriving before expected and in advance of the messengers sent to announce him. (He was that fall paying the price for having preceded his legions to Egypt.) If the greatest part of his success could be explained "by his rapidity and by the unexpectedness of his movements," he was for the rest rarely disconcerted, armed for all contingencies, a precise and lucid strategist. His impatience survives him: What is *Veni, vidi, vici*—the claim was still a year in the future—if not a paean to efficiency? So firm was his grasp of human nature that he had at their decisive battle that summer instructed his men not to hurl their javelins but to thrust them into the faces of Pompey's men. Their vanity, he promised, would prove greater than their courage. He was correct: the Pompeians had covered their faces and run. Over the previous decade Caesar had overcome the most improbable obstacles and performed the most astonishing feats. Never one to offend fortune, he felt all the same that it could stand to be nudged along; he was the kind of opportunist who makes a great show of marveling at his sheer good luck. At least in terms of ingenuity and bold decision-making, he had before him a kindred spirit.

In another realm the young Egyptian queen had little in common with the "love-sated man already past his prime." (Caesar was fifty-two.) His amorous conquests were as legendary and as varied as his military feats. On the street the elegant, angular-faced man with the flashing black eyes and the prominent cheekbones was hailed—there was overstatement only on the second count—as "every woman's man and every man's woman." Cleopatra had been married for three years to a brother who was by all accounts "a mere boy" and who—even if he had by thirteen attained puberty, which by ancient standards was unlikely—had been trying for most of that time to dispose of her. Later commentators would write off Cleopatra as "Ptolemy's impure daughter," a "matchless siren," the "painted whore" whose "unchastity cost Rome dear." What that "harlot queen" was unlikely to have had when she materialized before Caesar in October 48 was any sexual experience whatever.

Insofar as the two can be pried apart, survival rather than seduction was first on her mind. As her brother's advisers had amply demonstrated, the prize was Caesar's favor. It was imperative that Cleopatra align herself with him instead of with the family benefactor, whose campaign she had supported and whose headless body lay decomposing on a Mediterranean beach. Under the circumstances, there was no reason to assume Caesar favorably disposed toward her. From his point of view, a young king with an army at his command and the confidence of the Alexandrians was the better bet. Ptolemy had the blood of Pompey on his hands, however; Caesar may have calculated that the price to pay in Rome for allying himself with his countryman's murderers would be greater than the price to pay for assisting a deposed and helpless queen. He had long before grasped that "all men work more zealously against their enemies than they cooperate with their friends." At least initially, Cleopatra may have owed her life more to Caesar's censure of her brother and his distaste for Ptolemy's advisers—they hardly seemed the kind of men with whom one settled frank financial matters—than to any charms of her own. She was also lucky. As one chronicler pointed out, a different man might have traded her life for Pompey's. Caesar could equally well have lopped off her head.

Generally the Roman commander was of a mild disposition. He was perfectly capable of killing tens of thousands of men, equally famous for his displays of clemency, even toward bitter enemies, sometimes toward the same ones twice. "Nothing was dearer to his heart," one of his generals asserts, "than pardoning suppliants." A plucky, royal, well-spoken suppliant doubtless topped that list. Caesar had further reason to take to this one: As a young man, he too had been a fugitive. He too had made costly political mistakes. While the decision to welcome Cleopatra may have been logical at the time, it led to one of the closest calls of Caesar's career. When he met Cleopatra she was struggling for her life. By late fall they both were. For the next months Caesar found himself under siege, pummeled by an ingenious enemy keen to offer him his first taste of guerrilla warfare, in a city with which he was unfamiliar and in which he was vastly outnumbered. Surely Ptolemy and the people of Alexandria deserve some credit for seeing to it that—closeted together for six nerve-wracking months behind hastily constructed barricades—the balding veteran general and the agile young queen emerged as close allies, so close that by early November, Cleopatra realized she was pregnant.

BEHIND EVERY GREAT fortune, it has been noted, is a crime; the Ptolemies were fabulously rich. They were descended not from the Egyptian pharaohs whose place they assumed but from the scrappy, hard-living Macedonians (tough terrain breeds tough men, Herodotus had already warned) who produced Alexander the Great. Within months of Alexander's death, Ptolemy—the most enterprising of his generals, his official taster, a childhood intimate, and by some accounts a distant relative—had laid claim to Egypt. In an early display of the family gift for stagecraft, Ptolemy kidnapped Alexander the Great's body. It had been headed for Macedonia. Would it not be far more useful, reasoned young Ptolemy, intercepting the funeral cortege, in Egypt, ultimately in Alexandria, a city the great man had founded only decades earlier? There it was rerouted, to be displayed in a gold sarcophagus at the center of the city, a relic, a talisman, a recruiting aid, an insurance policy. (By Cleopatra's childhood, the sarcophagus was alabaster or glass. Strapped for funds, her great-uncle had traded the original for an army. He paid for the substitution with his life.)

The legitimacy of the Ptolemaic dynasty would rest on this tenuous connection to the most storied figure in the ancient world, the one against whom all aspirants measured themselves, in whose mantle

Pompey had wrapped himself, whose feats were said to reduce Caesar to tears of inadequacy. The cult was universal. Alexander played as active a role in the Ptolemaic imagination as in the Roman one. Many Egyptian homes displayed statues of him. So strong was his romance—and so fungible was first-century history—that it would come to include a version in which Alexander descended from an Egyptian wizard. Soon enough he was said to have been related to the royal family; like all self-respecting arrivistes, the Ptolemies had a gift for reconfiguring history.* Without renouncing their Macedonian heritage, the dynasty's founders bought themselves a legitimacy-conferring past, the ancient-world equivalent of the mail-order coat of arms. What was true was that Ptolemy descended from the Macedonian aristocracy, a synonym for high drama. As a consequence, no one in Egypt considered Cleopatra to be Egyptian. She hailed instead from a line of rancorous, meddlesome, shrewd, occasionally unhinged Macedonian queens, a line that included the fourth-century Olympias, whose greatest contribution to the world was her son, Alexander the Great. The rest were atrocities.

If outside Egypt the Ptolemies held to the Alexander the Great narrative, within the country their legitimacy derived from a fabricated link with the pharaohs. This justified the practice of sibling marriage, understood to be an Egyptian custom. Amid the Macedonian aristocracy there was ample precedent for murdering your sibling, none for marrying her. Nor was there a Greek word for "incest." The Ptolemies carried the practice to an extreme. Of the fifteen or so family marriages, at least ten were full brother-sister unions. Two other Ptolemies married nieces or cousins. They may have done so for simplicity's sake; intermarriage minimized both claimants to the throne and pesky in-laws. It eliminated the problem of finding an appropriate spouse in a foreign land. It also neatly reinforced the family cult, along with the Ptolemies' exalted, exclusive

---

*They were not alone. By one account, Alexander the Great consulted a famed oracle about his parentage. He had some questions, which is what happens when your mother is said to have mated with a snake. Wisely he left his entourage outside the temple and submitted a bribe in advance: he was, the oracle assured him, the son of Zeus.

status. If circumstances made intermarriage attractive, an appeal to the divine—another piece of invented pedigree—made it acceptable. Both Egyptian and Greek gods had married siblings, though it could be argued that Zeus and Hera were not the most sterling of role models.

The practice resulted in no physical deformities but did deliver an ungainly shrub of a family tree. If Cleopatra's parents were full siblings, as they likely were, she had only one set of grandparents. That couple also happened to be uncle and niece. And if you married your uncle, as was the case with Cleopatra's grandmother, your father was also your brother-in-law. While the inbreeding was meant to stabilize the family, it had a paradoxical effect. Succession became a perennial crisis for the Ptolemies, who exacerbated the matter with poisons and daggers. Intermarriage consolidated wealth and power but lent a new meaning to sibling rivalry, all the more remarkable among relatives who routinely appended benevolent-sounding epithets to their titles. (Officially speaking, Cleopatra and the brother from whom she was running for her life were the *Theoi Neoi Philadelphoi,* or "New Sibling-Loving Gods.") It was rare to find a member of the family who did not liquidate a relative or two, Cleopatra VII included. Ptolemy I married his half sister, who conspired against him with her sons, two of whom he murdered. The first to be worshipped as a goddess in her lifetime, she went on to preside over a golden age in Ptolemaic history. Here too was an unintended consequence of sibling marriage: For better or worse, it put a premium on Ptolemaic princesses. In every respect the equals of their brothers and husbands, Cleopatra's female predecessors knew their worth. They came increasingly to assert themselves. The Ptolemies did future historians no favors in terms of nomenclature; all the royal women were Arsinoes, Berenices, or Cleopatras. They are more easily identified by their grisly misdeeds than their names, although tradition proved immutable on both counts: various Cleopatras, Berenices, and Arsinoes poisoned husbands, murdered brothers, and outlawed all mention of their mothers—afterward offering up splendid monuments to those relatives' memories.

Over the generations the family indulged in what has been termed "an orgy of pillage and murder," lurid even by colorful Macedonian standards. It was not an easy clan in which to distinguish oneself, but Ptolemy IV did, at the height of the empire. In the late third century he murdered his uncle, brother, and mother. Courtiers saved him from poisoning his wife by doing so themselves, once she had produced an heir. Over and over mothers sent troops against sons. Sisters waged war against brothers. Cleopatra's great-grandmother fought one civil war against her parents, a second against her children. No one suffered as acutely as the inscribers of monuments, left to contend with near-simultaneous inaugurations and assassinations and with the vexed matter of dates, as the calendar started again with each new regime, at which time a ruler typically changed his title as well. Plenty of hieroglyph-cutting ground to a halt while dynastic feuds resolved themselves. Early on, Berenice II's mother borrowed Berenice's foreign-born husband, for which double duty Berenice supervised his murder. (She met the same end.) Equally notable among the women was Cleopatra's great-great-aunt, Cleopatra III, the second-century queen. She was both the wife and niece of Ptolemy VIII. He raped her when she was an adolescent, at which time he was simultaneously married to her mother. The two quarreled; Ptolemy killed their fourteen-year-old son, chopped him into pieces, and delivered a chest of mutilated limbs to the palace gates on the eve of her birthday. She retaliated by publicly displaying the body parts. The Alexandrians went wild with rage. The greater astonishment was what came next. Just over a decade later, the couple reconciled. For eight years Ptolemy VIII ruled with two queens, a warring mother and daughter.*

After a while the butchery came to seem almost preordained. Cleopatra's uncle murdered his wife, thereby eliminating his stepmother (and half sister) as well. Unfortunately he did so without grasping that she was the more popular of the pair. He was lynched by a mob after eighteen days on the throne. Which after a two-century-long rampage put an

---

*Given the congested genealogy, Ptolemy VIII was Cleopatra's great-grandfather three times over — and twice her great-great-grandfather.

end to the legitimate Ptolemies, in 80 BC. Especially with an ascendant Rome on the horizon, a successor had to be found quickly. Cleopatra's father, Ptolemy XII, was summoned from Syria, where he had been sent to safety twenty-three years earlier. It is unclear if he was raised to rule, very clear that he was the only viable option. To reinforce his divine status and the link with Alexander the Great, he took as his title "The New Dionysus." To the Alexandrians—for whom legitimacy mattered, despite the crazy quilt of wholly fabricated pedigrees—he had one of two names. Cleopatra's father was either "the bastard" or "Auletes," the piper, after the oboe-like instrument he was fond of playing. For it he seemed to evince as much affection as he did statesmanship, unfortunate in that his musical proclivities were those shared by second-rate call girls. His much-loved musical competitions did not prevent him from continuing the bloodbath of the family history, though only, it should be said, because circumstances left him little choice. (He was relieved of the need to murder his mother, as she was not of royal birth. She was probably a Macedonian courtier.) In any event, Auletes was to have greater problems than interfering relatives.

The young woman holed up with Julius Caesar in the besieged palace of Alexandria was, then, neither Egyptian, nor, historically speaking, a pharaoh, nor necessarily related to Alexander the Great, nor even fully a Ptolemy, though she was as nearly as can be ascertained on all sides a Macedonian aristocrat. Her name, like her heritage, was entirely and proudly Macedonian; "Cleopatra" means "Glory of Her Fatherland" in Greek.* She was not even Cleopatra VII, as she would be remembered. Given the tortured family history, it made sense that someone, somewhere, simply lost count.

The strange and terrible Ptolemaic history should not obscure two things. If the Berenices and Arsinoes were as vicious as their husbands and brothers, they were so to a great extent because they were immensely powerful. (Traditionally they also took second place to those husbands and brothers, a tradition Cleopatra disregarded.) Even without a regnant

---

*Alexander the Great's family included two Cleopatras, his father's last wife and a sister two years Alexander's junior. Both were murdered by family members.

mother, Cleopatra could look to any number of female forebears who built temples, raised fleets, waged military campaigns, and, with their consorts, governed Egypt. Arguably she had more powerful female role models than any other queen in history. Whether this resulted from a general exhaustion on the part of the men in the family, as has been asserted, is unclear. There would have been every reason for the women to have been exhausted as well. But the standouts in the generations immediately preceding Cleopatra's were—for vision, ambition, intellect— universally female.

Cleopatra moreover came of age in a country that entertained a singular definition of women's roles. Well before her and centuries before the arrival of the Ptolemies, Egyptian women enjoyed the right to make their own marriages. Over time their liberties had increased, to levels unprecedented in the ancient world. They inherited equally and held property independently. Married women did not submit to their husbands' control. They enjoyed the right to divorce and to be supported after a divorce. Until the time an ex-wife's dowry was returned, she was entitled to be lodged in the house of her choice. Her property remained hers; it was not to be squandered by a wastrel husband. The law sided with the wife and children if a husband acted against their interests. Romans marveled that in Egypt female children were not left to die; a Roman was obligated to raise only his first-born daughter. Egyptian women married later than did their neighbors as well, only about half of them by Cleopatra's age. They loaned money and operated barges. They served as priests in the native temples. They initiated lawsuits and hired flute players. As wives, widows, or divorcées, they owned vineyards, wineries, papyrus marshes, ships, perfume businesses, milling equipment, slaves, homes, camels. As much as one third of Ptolemaic Egypt may have been in female hands.

So much did these practices reverse the natural order of things that they astounded the foreigner. At the same time they seemed wholly in keeping with a country whose magnificent, life-giving river flowed backward, from south to north, establishing Upper Egypt in the south and

Lower Egypt in the north. The Nile further reversed the laws of nature by swelling in summer and subsiding in winter; the Egyptians harvested their fields in April and sowed them in November. Even planting was inverted: the Egyptian first sowed, then plowed, to cover the seed in loose earth. This made perfect sense in the kind of aberrant kingdom where one kneaded dough with one's feet and wrote from right to left. It was no wonder that Herodotus should have asserted, in an account Cleopatra would have known well, that Egyptian women ventured into the markets while the men sat at home tending their looms. We have ample testimony to her sense of humor; Cleopatra was a wit and a prankster. There is no cause to question how she read Herodotus's further assertion that Egypt was a country in which "the women urinate standing up, the men sitting down."

On another count Herodotus was entirely correct. "There is no country that possesses so many wonders, nor any that has such a number of works that defy description," he marveled. Well before the Ptolemies, Egypt exercised its spell on the world. It boasted an ancient civilization, any number of natural oddities, monuments of baffling immensity, two of the seven wonders of the ancient world. (The capacity for wonder may have been greater in Cleopatra's day but the pyramids were taller too, by thirty-one feet.) And in the intermissions between bloodlettings, largely in the third century and before the dynasty began to wobble under its own depravity late in the second, the Ptolemies had made good on Alexander the Great's plans, establishing on the Nile delta a miracle of a city, one that was as sleekly sophisticated as its founding people had been unpolished. From a distance Alexandria blinded, a sumptuous suffusion of gleaming marble, over which presided its towering lighthouse. Its celebrated skyline was reproduced on lamps, mosaics, tiles. The city's architecture announced its magpie ethos, forged of a frantic accretion of cultures. In this greatest of Mediterranean ports, papyrus fronds topped Ionic columns. Oversize sphinxes and falcons lined the paths to Greek temples. Crocodile gods in Roman dress decorated Doric tombs. "Built in the finest situation in the world," Alexandria stood sentry over a land of fabled riches and fantastic creatures, a favorite enigma to the Roman world. To a man like Julius Caesar, who for all his travels had never before set foot in Egypt, few of its astonishments would have been as great as the quick-witted young woman who had emerged from the traveler's sack.

SHE WAS BORN in 69 BC, the second of three daughters. Two brothers followed, to each of which Cleopatra would, in succession, be briefly joined in marriage. While there was never a particularly safe time to be born a Ptolemy, the first century may have been among the worst. All five siblings met violent ends. Among them Cleopatra distinguishes herself for having alone dictated the circumstances of her demise, no small accomplishment and, in Roman terms, a distinction of some weight. The very fact that she was still alive at the time of Caesar's arrival was testimony to her character. She had clearly been conspiring for a year or more, energetically for months, nearly around the clock over the late summer weeks. Equally significant was the fact that she would outlive her siblings by decades. Neither brother survived adolescence.

Of Cleopatra's mother we have neither glimpse nor echo; she disappears from the scene early in Cleopatra's childhood and was dead by the time Cleopatra was twelve. It is unclear if her daughter knew her any better than do we. She seems to have been one of the rare Ptolemaic women to have opted out of the family melodrama.* Cleopatra V Tryphaena was in any event several decades younger than Auletes, her brother or half brother; the two had married shortly after Auletes ascended to the throne. The fact that his aunt contested his right to the kingship—she went so far as to travel to Rome to press the case against him—is not particularly meaningful, given the family dynamic. It may, however, speak to her political instincts. To many minds Auletes appeared more interested in the arts than in statecraft. Despite a rule that lasted twenty-two years, with one interruption, he would be remembered as the pharaoh who piped while Egypt collapsed.

---

*It is also unclear whether she was Cleopatra's mother, although if Cleopatra were illegitimate it is unlikely that that detail would have escaped her detractors.

Of Caesar's early years virtually nothing is recorded and Cleopatra goes him one better: we have no clues at all. Were her childhood home not today twenty feet underwater or were the climate of Alexandria more forgiving toward ancient papyri, it is unlikely that we would be further enlightened. Childhood was not a big seller in the ancient world, where fate and pedigree were the formative influences. The ancient players tended to emerge fully formed. We can safely assume that Cleopatra was born in the palace of Alexandria; that a wet nurse cared for her; that a household retainer chewed her first foods before placing them in her gummy mouth; that nothing passed her childhood lips that had not first been tasted for poison; that she counted among her playmates a gaggle of noble-born children, known as "foster siblings" and destined to become the royal entourage. Even as she scampered down the colonnaded walkways of the palace, past its fountains and fishponds, or through its lush groves and zoological garden—earlier Ptolemies had kept giraffes, rhinoceroses, bears, a forty-five-foot python—she was surrounded by a retinue. From an early age she was comfortable among politicians, ambassadors, scholars, at ease amid a flock of purple-cloaked court officials. She played with terra-cotta dolls and dollhouses and tea sets and miniature furniture, with dice and rocking horses and knucklebones and pet mice, though we will never know what she did with her dolls and whether, like Indira Gandhi, she engaged them in insurrections and battles.

Along with her older sister, Cleopatra was groomed for the throne; a Ptolemy planned for all eventualities. She made regular trips up the Nile, to the family's harborfront palace in Memphis, to participate in traditional Egyptian cult festivals, carefully stage-managed, opulent processions of family, advisers, and staff. Two hundred miles upriver, Memphis was a sacred city, managed by a hierarchy of priests; death has been said to have been its greatest business. Vast animal catacombs stretched under its center, a magnet for the pilgrims who came to worship and to stock up on miniature mummified hawks and crocodiles at its souvenir stands. At home, these were objects of veneration. On such occasions Cleopatra would have been outfitted in ceremonial dress, though not yet in the traditional Egyptian crown of plumes, sun disk, and cow's horns. And from an early age she enjoyed the best education available in the Hellenistic world, at the hands of the most gifted scholars, in what was incontestably the greatest center of learning in existence: The library of Alexandria and its attached museum were literally in her backyard. The most prestigious of its scholars were her tutors, its men of science her doctors. She did not have to venture far for a prescription, a eulogy, a mechanical toy, a map.

That education may well have exceeded her father's—raised abroad, in northeastern Asia Minor—but would have been a traditional Greek education in every respect, nearly identical to that of Caesar, whose tutor had studied in Alexandria. It was preeminently literary. Letters mattered in the Greek world, where they served additionally as numbers and musical notes. Cleopatra learned to read first by chanting the Greek alphabet, then by tracing letters incised by her teacher on a narrow wooden tablet. The successful student went on to practice them in continuous horizontal rows, later in columns, eventually in reverse order, ultimately in pairs from either end of the alphabet, in capitals and again in cursive. When Cleopatra graduated to syllables it was to a body of abstruse, unpronounceable words, the more outlandish the better. The lines of doggerel that followed were equally esoteric; the theory appears to have been that the student who could decode these could decode anything. Maxims and verse came next, based on fables and myths. A student might be called upon to render a tale of Aesop's in his own words, in simplest form, a second time with grandiloquence. More complex impersonations came later. She might write as Achilles, on the verge of being killed, or be called upon to restate a plot of Euripides. The lessons were neither easy nor meant to be. Learning was a serious business, involving endless drills, infinite rules, long hours. There was no such thing as a weekend; one studied on all save for festival days, which came with merciful regularity in Alexandria. Twice a month all ground to a halt on Apollo's account. Discipline was severe. "The ears of a youth are on his back; he listens when he is beaten," reads an early papyrus. Into that adage the playwright Menander injected cause and effect: "He who is not thrashed cannot be educated." Generations of schoolchildren dutifully inscribed that line on the red wax centers of wooden slates with their ivory styluses.

Even before she graduated to sentences, even before she learned to read, the love affair with Homer began. "Homer was not a man, but a god," figured among the early penmanship lessons, as did the first cantos of the *Iliad*. No text more thoroughly penetrated Cleopatra's world. In an age infatuated with history and calibrated in glory, Homer's work was the Bible of the day. He was the "prince of literature"; his 15,693 lines provided the moral, political, historical, and religious context, the great deeds and the ruling principles, the intellectual atlas and moral compass. The educated man cited him, paraphrased him, alluded to him. It was entirely fair to say that children like Cleopatra were — as a near contemporary had it — "nursed in their learning by Homer, and swaddled in his verses." Alexander the Great was believed to have slept always with a copy of Homer under his pillow; any cultivated Greek, Cleopatra included, could recite some part of the *Iliad* and the *Odyssey* by heart. The former was more popular in Cleopatra's Egypt — it may have seemed a more pertinent tale for a turbulent time — but from an early age she would have known literarily what she at twenty-one discovered empirically: there were days you felt like waging war, and days when you just needed to go home.

On a primary level the indoctrination began with vocabulary lists, of gods, heroes, rivers. More sophisticated assignments followed. What song did the sirens sing? Was Penelope chaste? Who was Hector's mother? The tangled genealogies of the gods would have posed little difficulty to a Ptolemaic princess, next to whose history theirs paled, and with whose theirs intersected; the border between the human and divine was fluid for Cleopatra. (The schoolroom lessons merged again with her personal history in the study of Alexander, the other preeminent classroom hero. Cleopatra would have known his story backward and forward, as she would have known every exploit of her Ptolemaic ancestors.) The early questions were formulaic, the brain fundamentally more retentive. Memorization was crucial. Which gods aid whom? What was Ulysses's route? This was the kind of material with which Cleopatra's head would have been stuffed; it passed for erudition in her day. And it would not have been easy to evade. The royal entourage included philosophers, rhetoricians, and mathematicians, at once mentors and servants, intellectual companions and trusted advisers.

While Homer set the gold standard, a vast catalogue of literature followed. Clearly the rollicking domestic dramas of Menander were a classroom favorite, though it is equally clear that the comic playwright was less read later. Cleopatra knew her Aesop's fables, as she would have known her Herodotus and Thucydides. She read more poetry than prose, though it is possible she knew the texts we read today as Ecclesiastes and 1 Maccabees. Among playwrights Euripides was the established favorite, subtly suited to the times, with his stable of transgressive women who reliably supply the brains of the operation. She would have known various scenes by heart. Aeschylus and Sophocles, Hesiod, Pindar, and Sappho, would all have been familiar to Cleopatra and the clique of well-born girls at her side. As much for her as for Caesar, there was little regard for what was not Greek. She probably learned even her Egyptian history from three Greek texts. Some schooling in arithmetic, geometry, music, and astrology and astronomy (the last two largely indistinguishable) accompanied her literary studies—Cleopatra knew the difference between a star and a constellation, and she could likely strum a lyre—though all were subordinate to them. Even Euclid could not answer the student who had asked what precisely the use for geometry might be.

Cleopatra tackled none of those texts on her own. She read aloud, or was read to by teachers or servants. Silent reading was less common, in public or private. (A twenty-sheet-long scroll of papyrus was both unwieldy and fragile. Reading was very much a two-handed operation: you balanced the scroll in your right hand and rolled the used portion with your left.) Either a grammarian or a retinue of them worked with her on decoding her first sentences, a vexed assignment in a language transcribed without word breaks, punctuation, or paragraphs. For good reason, sight reading was considered an accomplishment, the more so as it was meant to be done with verve and expression, careful enunciation, and effective gestures. At thirteen or fourteen, Cleopatra graduated to the study of rhetoric or public speaking—along with philosophy, the greatest and most powerful art, as her brother's tutor had amply demonstrated on Pompey's arrival. Theodotus may at one time have been Cleopatra's tutor as well. She would have had a dedicated tutor, most likely a eunuch.

The rhetoric master worked the real magic. Though less so for girls, Cleopatra's was a speechifying culture, appreciative of the shapely argument, of the fine arts of persuasion and refutation. One declaimed with a codified vocabulary and an arsenal of gestures, in something of a cross between the laws of verse and those of parliamentary procedure. Cleopatra learned to marshal her thoughts precisely, express them artistically, deliver them gracefully. Content arguably took second place to delivery, "for," noted Cicero, "as reason is the glory of man, so the lamp of reason is eloquence." Head high, eyes bright, voice carefully modulated, she mastered the eulogy, the reproach, the comparison. In terse and vigorous language, summoning a wealth of anecdote and allusion, she would have learned to discourse on a host of thorny issues: Why is Cupid depicted as a winged boy with arrows? Is country or town life preferable? Does Providence govern the world? What would you say were you Medea, on the verge of slaughtering your children? The questions were the same everywhere although the answers may have varied. Some queries—"Is it fair to murder your mother if she has murdered your father?" for one—may have been handled differently in Cleopatra's household than elsewhere. And despite the formulaic quality, history quickly crept into the exercises. Soon students would debate whether Caesar should have punished Theodotus, he of the dead-men-don't-bite coinage. Was Pompey's murder actually a gift to Caesar? What of the question of honor? Should Caesar have killed Ptolemy's adviser to avenge

Pompey, or would doing so suggest that Pompey had not deserved to die?* Would war with Egypt be wise at such a time?

These arguments were to be made with particular and exact choreography. Cleopatra was instructed as to where to breathe, pause, gesticulate, pick up her pace, lower or raise her voice. She was to stand erect. She was not to twiddle her thumbs. Assuming the raw material was not defective, it was the kind of education that could be guaranteed to produce a vivid, persuasive speaker, as well as to provide that speaker with ample opportunity to display her subtle mind and clever wit, in social settings as much as in judicial proceedings. "The art of speaking," it was later said, "depends on much effort, continual study, varied kinds of exercise, long experience, profound wisdom, and unfailing strategic sense." (It was elsewhere noted that this grueling course of study lent itself equally to the court, the stage, or the ravings of a lunatic.)

Cleopatra neared the end of her training just as her father succumbed to a fatal illness, in 51. In a solemn ceremony before Egypt's high priest, she and her brother ascended to the throne, probably late that spring. If the ceremony conformed to tradition, it took place in Memphis, Egypt's spiritual capital, where a sphinx-lined causeway led through dunes of sand to the main temple, with its limestone panthers and lions, its Greek and Egyptian chapels, painted in glowing color and hung with brilliant banners. Amid clouds of incense Cleopatra was fitted with the serpent crowns of Upper and Lower Egypt by a priest in a long linen gown, a panther's skin slung across his shoulder. She took her oath within the sanctuary, in Egyptian; only then was her diadem fitted into place. The new queen was eighteen, Ptolemy XIII eight years younger. Generally hers was a precocious age. Alexander the Great was a general at sixteen, master of the world at twenty. And as was observed later in connection with Cleopatra, "Some women are younger at seventy than most women at seventeen."

---

*Theodotus escaped but was tracked down. By the time he began to figure in classroom discussions he had been crucified.

How she fared is plain to see. The culture was oral. Cleopatra knew how to talk. Even her detractors gave her high marks for verbal dexterity. Her "sparkling eyes" are never mentioned without equal tribute to her eloquence and charisma. She was naturally suited to declaim, with a rich, velvety voice, a commanding presence, and gifts both for appraising and accommodating her audience. On that count she had advantages Caesar did not. As much as Alexandria belonged to the Greek world, it happened to be located in Africa. At the same time, it was in but not of Egypt. One journeyed between the two as today one journeys from Manhattan to America, though with a swap of languages in the ancient case. From the start Cleopatra was accustomed to playing to dual audiences. Her family ruled a country that even in the ancient world astonished with its antiquity. Its language was the oldest on record. That language was also formal and clumsy, with a particularly difficult script. (The script was demotic. Hieroglyphs were used purely for ceremonial occasions; even the literate could decipher them only in part. Cleopatra was unlikely to have been able to read them easily.) It made for a far more demanding assignment than Greek, by Cleopatra's day the language of business and bureaucracy, and which came easily to an Egyptian speaker. While Egyptian speakers learned Greek, it was rare that anyone ventured in the opposite direction. To the punishing study of Egyptian, however, Cleopatra applied herself. She was allegedly the first and only Ptolemy to bother to learn the language of the 7 million people over whom she ruled.

The accomplishment paid off handsomely. Where previous Ptolemies had commanded armies through interpreters, Cleopatra communicated directly. For someone recruiting mercenaries among Syrians and Medians and Thracians that was a distinct advantage, as it was to anyone with imperial ambitions. It was an advantage as well closer to home, in a restive, ethnically diverse, cosmopolitan city, to which immigrants flocked from all over the Mediterranean. An Alexandrian contract could involve seven different nationalities. It was not unusual to see a Buddhist monk on the streets of the city, home to the largest community of Jews outside

Judaea, a community that may have accounted for nearly a quarter of Alexandria's population. Egypt's profitable luxury trade was with India; lustrous silks, spices, ivory, and elephants traveled across the Red Sea and along caravan routes. There was ample reason why Cleopatra should have been particularly adept in the tongues of the coastal region. Plutarch gave her nine languages, including Hebrew and Troglodyte, an Ethiopian tongue that—if Herodotus can be believed—was "unlike that of any other people; it sounds like the screeching of bats." Cleopatra's rendition was evidently more mellifluous. "It was a pleasure merely to hear the sound of her voice," notes Plutarch, "with which, like an instrument of many strings, she could pass from one language to another; so that there were few of the barbarian nations that she answered by an interpreter; to most of them she spoke herself."

Plutarch is silent on the subject of Cleopatra's Latin, the language of Rome, little spoken in Alexandria. Remarkable orators both, she and Caesar certainly communicated in a very similar Greek. But the linguistic divide spoke volumes about the bind in which Cleopatra now found herself, as it did about her legacy and her future. A generation earlier, a good Roman had avoided Greek wherever possible, going so far even as to feign ignorance. "The better one gets to know Greek," went the wisdom, "the more a scoundrel one becomes." It was the tongue of high art and low morals, the dialect of sex manuals, a language "with fingers of its own." The Greeks covered all bases, noted a later scholar, "including some I should not care to explain in class."* Caesar's generation, which perfected its education in Greece or under Greek-speaking tutors, handled both languages with equal finesse, with Greek—by far the richer, the more nuanced, the more subtle, sweet, and obliging tongue—forever supplying

---

*The history parallels that of French on American soil. In colonial America, the language of the dissolute Old World was a vehicle of contagion; where French went, depravity and frivolity were sure to follow. By the nineteenth century, French was the indispensable agent of high culture, fuller of expression, richer of vocabulary, somehow maddeningly superior in its nuance and suppleness. At its edges the admiration bordered on resentment, to which it finally succumbed. An eventful century later, French was outmoded, long-winded, largely irrelevant, an affectation.

the *mot juste*. From the time of Cleopatra's birth, an educated Roman was a master of both. For a fleeting moment it seemed as if a Greek-speaking East and West might just be possible. Two decades later, Cleopatra would negotiate with Romans who were ill at ease in her language. She would play her last scene in Latin, which she certainly spoke with an accent.

An aesthete and a patron of the arts under whom Alexandria enjoyed the beginnings of an intellectual revival, Auletes saw to it that his daughter received a first-rate education. Cleopatra would continue the tradition, engaging a distinguished tutor for her own daughter. She was not alone in doing so. While girls were by no means universally educated, they headed off to schools, entered poetry competitions, became scholars. More than a few well-born first-century daughters—including those not being groomed for thrones—went far in their studies, if not all the way to rigorous rhetorical training. Pompey's daughter had a fine tutor and recited Homer for her father. In his expert opinion, Cicero's daughter was "extremely learned." Brutus's mother was equally well versed in her Latin and Greek poets. Alexandria had its share of female mathematicians, doctors, painters, and poets. This did not mean such women were above suspicion. As always, an educated woman was a dangerous woman. But she was less a source of discomfort in Egypt than elsewhere.* Pompey's beautiful wife, Cornelia, only yards away when her husband's head was hacked off at Pelusium—she had shrieked in horror—had a similar formation to Cleopatra's. She was "highly educated, played well upon the lute, and understood geometry, and had been accustomed to listen with profit to lectures on philosophy; all this, too, without in any degree becoming unamiable or pretentious, as sometimes young women do when they pursue such studies." The admiration was grudging, but it was admiration all the same. Of a Roman consul's wife it was conceded, shortly after Cleopatra introduced herself to Caesar that fall, that for all her dangerous gifts "she was a woman of no mean

---

*The Hellenistic version of pregnant-and-barefoot-in-the-kitchen was a Roman epithet: "She loved her husband, she bore two sons, she kept the house and worked in wool."

endowments; she could write verses, bandy jests, and use language which was modest, or tender, or wanton; in fine, she possessed a high degree of wit and of charm."

TO CAESAR, THEN, Cleopatra was in some ways profoundly familiar. She was also a living link to Alexander the Great, the exquisite product of a highly refined civilization, heir to a dazzling intellectual tradition. Alexandrians had been studying astronomy when Rome was little more than a village. What was reborn with the Renaissance was on many fronts the Alexandria that Cleopatra's forebears had built. Somehow despite the years of savagery and the vacuous Macedonian cultural record, the Ptolemies established in Alexandria the greatest intellectual center of its time, one that had picked up where Athens had left off. When Ptolemy I had founded the library he had set out to gather every text in existence, to which end he made considerable progress. His gluttony for literature was such that he was said to have seized all texts arriving in the city, on occasion returning copies in their stead. (He also offered rewards for contributions. Spurious texts materialized in the Alexandrian collection as a result.) Ancient sources indicate that the great library included 500,000 scrolls, which would appear to be a hopeless exaggeration; 100,000 may be closer to the truth. In any event the collection dwarfed all prior libraries and included every volume written in Greek. Those texts were nowhere more accessible, or more neatly arranged — ordered alphabetically and by subject, they occupied individual cubbies — than in the great library of Alexandria.

Nor were those texts in any danger of collecting dust. Attached to the library, near or within the palace complex, was the museum, a state-subsidized research institute. While teachers elsewhere in the Hellenistic world were held in little esteem — "he's either dead or off teaching somewhere" went the expression; a teacher earned slightly more than an unskilled laborer — scholarship reigned supreme in Alexandria. So did this community of scholars, cosseted by the state, housed tax-free in luxurious quarters, fed in a vast communal dining hall. (Such was true anyway until a hundred years before Cleopatra, when her great-grandfather decided he had had enough of that politically obstreperous class and thinned the ranks, dispersing the best and the brightest across the ancient world.) For centuries both before and after Cleopatra the most impressive thing a doctor could say was that he had trained in Alexandria. It was where you hoped your children's tutor had studied.

The library was the pride of the civilized world, a legend in its lifetime. By Cleopatra's day it was no longer in its prime, its work having devolved from original studies to the kind of manic classifying and cataloguing that gave us the seven wonders of the world. (One bibliographical masterwork catalogued "Those Persons Eminent in Every Branch of Learning," with alphabetical lists of their writings, divided by subject. The study swelled to 120 volumes.) The institution continued all the same to attract the great minds of the Mediterranean. Its patron saint was Aristotle, whose school and library stood as its model, and who had—not incidentally—taught both Alexander the Great and his childhood friend, Ptolemy I. It was in Alexandria that the circumference of the earth was first measured, the sun fixed at the center of the solar system, the workings of the brain and the pulse illuminated, the foundations of anatomy and physiology established, the definitive editions of Homer produced. It was in Alexandria that Euclid had codified geometry. If all the wisdoms of the ancient world could be said to have been collected in one place, that place was Alexandria. Cleopatra was its direct beneficiary. She knew that the moon had an effect on tides, that the Earth was spherical and revolved around the sun. She knew of the existence of the equator, the value of pi, the latitude of Marseilles, the behavior of linear perspective, the utility of a lightning conductor. She knew that one could sail from Spain to India, a voyage that was not to be made for another 1,500 years, though she herself would consider making it, in reverse.

For a man like Caesar, then, highly cultivated, in thrall to Alexander the Great and who claimed descent from Venus, all roads—mythical, historical, intellectual—led to Alexandria. Like Cleopatra his education was first-rate, his curiosity voracious. He knew his poets. He was an omnivorous reader. Though the Romans were said to have no taste for personal luxury, Caesar was, as in so many matters, the exception. Even on campaign he was an insatiable collector of mosaic, marble, and gems. His invasion of Britain had been written down to his fondness for fresh-water pearls. Seduced by opulence and pedigree, he had lingered in Ori-ental courts before, to his lifelong embarrassment. Few charges disconcerted him as did the accusation that he had prolonged his stay in what is today northern Turkey because of his affair with the king of Bithynia. Caesar was of illustrious birth, a gifted orator, and a dashing officer, but those distinctions were meaningless compared to a woman who, however inventively, descended from Alexander, who was in Egypt not only royal but divine. Caesar was very nearly deified in the last years of his life. Cleopatra was born a goddess.

And her looks? While the Romans who preserved her story assure us of Cleopatra's wanton ways, her feminine wiles, her ruthless ambition, and her sexual depravity, few raved about her beauty. That was not for lack of adjectives. Sublime women enter the historical record. Herod's wife was one. Alexander the Great's mother was another. The Sixth Dynasty queen thought to have built the third pyramid was, as Cleopa-tra would have known, "braver than all the men of her time, the most beautiful of all the women, fair-skinned with red cheeks." Arsinoe II — the thrice-married third-century intriguer — was stunning. Beauty had unsettled the world before; the Helen allusion was there for the asking, but only one Latin poet picked up on it, primarily to emphasize Cleopa-tra's bad behavior. Plutarch clearly notes that her beauty "was not in itself so remarkable that none could be compared with her, or that no one could see her without being struck by it." It was rather the "contact of her presence, if you lived with her, that was irresistible." Her personality and manner, he insists, were no less than "bewitching." Time has done bet-ter than fail to wither in Cleopatra's case; it has improved upon her allure. She came into her looks only years later. By the third century AD she would be described as "striking," exquisite in appearance. By the Middle Ages, she was "famous for nothing but her beauty."

As no stone portrait of her has yet proved authentic, André Malraux's quip remains partly true: "Nefertiti is a face without a queen; Cleopatra is a queen without a face." All the same a few matters can be resolved. It would have been surprising had she been anything other than small and lithe, although the men in the family tended toward fat, if not full-fledged obesity. Even allowing for the authoritarian message she intended to broadcast and for cut-rate engraving, coin portraits support Plutarch's claim that she was by no means a conventional beauty. She sported a smaller version of her father's hooked nose (common enough that there is a word for it in Greek), full lips, a sharp, prominent chin, a high brow. Her eyes were wide and sunken. While there were fair-haired, fair-skinned Ptolemies, Cleopatra VII was very likely not among them. It is difficult to believe that the world could have nattered on about "that Egyptian woman" had she been blond. The word "honey-skinned" recurs in descriptions of her relatives and would presumably have applied to her as well, despite the inexactitudes surrounding her mother and paternal grandmother. There was certainly Persian blood in the family, but even an Egyptian mistress is a rarity among the Ptolemies. She was not dark-skinned.

Certainly her face did nothing to undermine her redoubtable charm, her easy humor, or her silken powers of persuasion; Caesar was particular about appearances. For him there were other considerations as well. It had long been clear that the way into Pompey's heart was through flattery, the way into Caesar's through bribery. He spent freely and beyond his budget. One mistress's pearl cost the equivalent of what 1,200 professional soldiers earned in a year. After more than a decade of warfare, he had an army to pay. Cleopatra's father had left an outstanding debt, which Caesar spoke of recouping on his arrival. He would forgive half, which left an astronomical balance of some 3,000 talents. He had extravagant expenses and extravagant tastes, but Egypt had, Caesar knew, a treasury to match. The captivating young woman before him—who spoke so effectively, laughed so easily, hailed from an ancient, accomplished culture, moved amid an opulence that would set his countrymen's teeth on edge, and had so artfully outfoxed an army—was one of the two richest people in the world.

On his return to the palace the other was horrified to discover his sister with Caesar. He stormed out, to throw a temper tantrum in the street.

CLEOPATRA CAPTURES THE OLD MAN BY MAGIC

"A woman who is generous with her money is to be praised; not so, if she is generous with her person."
— QUINTILIAN

VERY LITTLE ABOUT the first century BC was original; mostly it distinguished itself for its compulsive recycling of familiar themes. So it was that when a fiery wisp of a girl presented herself before an adroit, much older man of the world, credit for the seduction fell to her. For some time already that brand of encounter had occasioned the clucking of tongues, as it would for several millennia. In truth it is unclear who seduced whom, just as it is unclear how quickly Caesar and Cleopatra fell into each other's arms. A great deal was at stake on both sides. Plutarch has the indomitable general helpless before the beguiling twenty-one-year-old. He is in two swift steps "captivated" by her ruse and "overcome" by her charm: Apollodorus came, Caesar saw, Cleopatra conquered, a sequence of events that does not necessarily add up in her favor. In his account—it may well derive from Plutarch's, which preceded it by a good century—Dio too acknowledges Cleopatra's power to subjugate a man twice her age. His Caesar is instantly and entirely enslaved. Dio allows, however, for a hint of complicity on the part of the Roman, known to harbor a fondness for the opposite sex "to such an extent that he had his intrigues with ever so many other women—with all, doubtless, who chanced to come his way."

This is to grant Caesar something of a role rather than to leave him defenseless in the hands of a devious, disarming siren. Dio offers too a more elaborate staging. In the palace Cleopatra has time to primp. She appears "in the most majestic and at the same time pity-inspiring guise," a rather tall order. His Caesar is a convert "upon seeing her and hearing her speak a few words," words that Cleopatra surely chose with great care. She had never before met the Roman general and had little idea what to expect. She would have known only that—in a worst-case scenario—it was preferable to be taken prisoner by Julius Caesar than by her own brother.*

By all accounts Cleopatra came easily to some sort of accommodation with Caesar, who was soon enough acting "as advocate for the very woman whose judge he had previously assumed to be." The seduction may have taken some time, or at least longer than the one night of legend; we have no proof that the relationship was immediately sexual. By the clear light of day—if not necessarily the morning after the unorthodox, showstopping arrival—Caesar proposed a reconciliation between Cleopatra and Ptolemy, "on the condition that she should rule as his colleague in the kingdom." This was by no means what her brother's advisers were expecting. They had the upper hand. They assumed that they had signed a pact with Caesar on the beach at Pelusium. Nor were they banking on Cleopatra's unaccountable appearance in the palace.

Young Ptolemy was if anything more surprised to find her there than Caesar had been. Furious to have been outwitted, he resorted to behavior that suggested he very much needed a consort: He burst into tears. In his rage he flew through the gates and into the crowd outside. Amid his subjects, he tore the white ribbon from his head and cast it to the ground, wailing that his sister had betrayed him. Caesar's men seized and returned him to the palace, where he remained under house arrest. It took them longer to quiet the violence in the street, much encouraged in

---

*Neither account was written from living memory. In only one version—a blundering sixth-century AD account—does anyone venture to make the shocking assertion that Caesar might have seduced Cleopatra.

the weeks to come by Pothinus, the eunuch, who had led the move to depose Cleopatra. Her glorious career would have ended here had she not secured Caesar's favor. Assaulted as he was by both land and sea, Caesar might have ended his here as well. He believed he was settling a family vendetta, did not understand that, with two bedraggled and depleted legions, he had incited a full-scale rebellion. Nor does Cleopatra appear to have enlightened him as to her lack of support among the Alexandrians.

Apprehensive, Caesar arranged to appear before the people. From a safe place—it seems to have been an upper-story balcony, or a window of the palace—he "promised to do for them whatever they wished." Here the well-honed rhetorical skills came in handy. Cleopatra may have briefed Caesar on how to appease the Alexandrians but he needed no tutor to deliver a clear, compelling oration, one he typically punctuated with vigorous hand gestures. He was an acknowledged genius in that realm, a pitch-perfect speaker and a lapidary stylist, unsurpassed in the "ability to inflame the minds of his hearers and to turn them in whatever direction the case demands." He made no reference later to his alarm, focusing instead on his negotiation with Ptolemy and asserting that he was himself "particularly anxious to play the part of friend and arbitrator." He appeared to succeed. Ptolemy agreed to a reconciliation, no great concession as he knew that his advisers would fight on regardless. They were at that moment secretly summoning the Ptolemaic army back to Alexandria.

Caesar thereafter convoked a formal assembly, to which both siblings accompanied him. In his high nasal tones, he read aloud Auletes' will. Their father, he pointed out, had plainly directed Cleopatra and her brother to live together and rule in common, under Roman guardianship. Caesar thereby bestowed the kingdom on them. It is impossible not to see Cleopatra's hand in what came next. To prove his goodwill (or, as Dio saw it, to calm an explosive crowd), Caesar went further. He bestowed the island of Cyprus on Cleopatra's two remaining siblings, seventeen-year-old Arsinoe and twelve-year-old Ptolemy XIV. The gesture was significant. The pearl of the Ptolemaic possessions, Cyprus commanded the Egyptian coast. It supplied the Egyptian kings with timber and afforded them a near monopoly on copper. Cyprus also represented a sore spot in Ptolemaic history. Cleopatra's uncle had ruled the island until a decade earlier, when Rome had demanded exorbitant sums from him. He chose poison over payment. His property was collected and carted off to Rome, where it was paraded through the streets. In Alexandria his older brother, Cleopatra's father, had stood by silently, for which craven behavior his subjects had furiously expelled him from Egypt. Cleopatra was eleven at the time. She was unlikely to have forgotten either the humiliation or the revolt.

Caesar succeeded in calming the populace but failed to defuse hostilities so far as Pothinus was concerned. The ex-tutor lost no time in stirring up Achillas's men. The Roman proposal, he assured them, was a sham. Did they not happen to glimpse Cleopatra's long, lovely arm behind it? There is some kind of perverse testimony to be read in the fact that Pothinus—who knew her well, intimately if indeed he had taught her—feared the young woman as much as he did the seasoned Roman. He swore that Caesar "had given the kingdom ostensibly to both the children merely to quiet the people." As soon as he could, he would transfer it to Cleopatra alone. A second danger lurked as well, as indicative of Cleopatra's resolve as of Ptolemy's lack of it. What if—while confined with him in the palace—that devious woman managed to seduce her brother? The people would never oppose a royal couple, even one sanctioned by an unpopular Roman. All would then be lost, insisted Pothinus. He devised a plan, which he evidently shared with too many of his coconspirators. At the banquet held to celebrate the reconciliation, Caesar's barber—there was a reason barbershops served as post offices in Ptolemaic Egypt—made a startling discovery. That "busy, listening fellow," ever inquisitive, learned that Pothinus and Achillas meant to poison Caesar. While they were at it, they plotted Cleopatra's murder as well. Caesar was not surprised: He had been sleeping sporadically and at odd hours to protect himself against assassination attempts. Cleopatra too must have found the nights uneasy, no matter how vigilant her guards.

Caesar ordered a man to dispense with the eunuch, which was done. For his part Achillas focused more intently on what was to become, in Plutarch's understated estimation, "a troublesome and embarrassing war." Caesar had four thousand men, hardly fresh or in any shape to feel invincible. Achillas's force was five times as great and marching toward Alexandria. And no matter what hints Cleopatra may have offered, Caesar had an insufficient grasp of the depths of Ptolemaic guile. Under the young king's name, Caesar dispatched two emissaries with a peace proposal. They were men of stature and experience. Both had served effectively under Cleopatra's father; Caesar had very likely met them earlier in Rome. Achillas— whom Caesar acknowledged to be "a man of remarkable nerve"—read the overture for the weaker hand it was. He murdered the ambassadors before they could so much as deliver their message.

With the arrival of Egyptian troops in the city, Achillas attempted to break into Caesar's quarters. Frantically, under cover of darkness, the Romans fortified the palace with entrenchments and a ten-foot wall. Caesar might well be blockaded, but he did not care to fight against his will. He knew that Achillas was recruiting auxiliary troops in every corner of the country. Meanwhile the Alexandrians established vast munitions factories throughout the city; the wealthy outfitted and paid their adult slaves to fight the Romans. Skirmishes erupted daily. Mostly Caesar worried about water, of which he had little, and food, of which he had none. Already Pothinus had pressed the point by delivering musty grain. As ever, the successful general was the gifted logician; it was essential that Caesar neither be separated from nor vulnerable to Lake Mareotis, south of the city and its second port. That brilliant blue freshwater lake connected Alexandria by canals to Egypt's interior; it was as rich and important as the two Mediterranean harbors. On the psychological front there were additional considerations. Caesar did everything he could to court the young king, as he understood "that the royal name had great authority with his people." To all who would listen he broadcast regular reminders that the war was not Ptolemy's but that of his rogue advisers. The protests fell on deaf ears.

While Caesar tended to supply lines and fortifications, a second plot hatched in the palace, where the atmosphere must already have been strained, at least among the feuding siblings. Arsinoe too had a clever tutor. That eunuch now arranged her escape. His coup suggests either that Cleopatra was negligent (highly improbable under the circumstances), preoccupied with her brother and her own survival, or astutely double-crossed. It is unlikely that she underestimated her seventeen-year-old sister. Arsinoe burned with ambition; she was not the kind of girl who inspired complacency. She clearly had no great faith in Cleopatra, which sentiment she had presumably kept to herself for weeks.* Outside the palace walls she was more vocal. She was a Ptolemy not in thrall to a foreigner, precisely what the Alexandrians preferred. They declared her queen—every sister had now had a turn—and rallied exuberantly behind her. Arsinoe assumed her position at Achillas's side, at the head of the army. In her rooms at the palace, Cleopatra had further reason to believe it wiser to trust a Roman than a member of her own family. This, too, was old news by 48 BC. "One loyal friend," Euripides reminds us, "is worth ten thousand relatives."

IN THE YEAR of Cleopatra's birth, Mithradates the Great, the Pontic king, suggested an alliance to his neighbor, the king of the Parthians.†
For decades Mithradates had hurled insults and ultimatums at Rome, which he felt was systematically gobbling up the world. The scourge was now coming their way, he warned, and "no laws, human or divine, prevent them from seizing and destroying allies and friends, those near them and those far off, weak or powerful, and from considering every government which does not serve them, especially monarchies, as their

---

*We know nothing of Arsinoe's motives, which has not discouraged even the best modern interpreter of the Alexandrian War from speculation: Had she not felt jealous of her older sister's masterful seduction of Caesar, asserts one historian, "She would not have been a woman."

†Parthia is today northeastern Iran. The Pontic kingdom extended from the southern shore of the Black Sea into modern Turkey.

enemies." Did it not make sense to band together? He was unwilling to follow in the mincing steps of Cleopatra's father. Auletes was "averting hostilities from day to day by the payment of money," Mithradates scoffed; the Egyptian king might think himself cunning but was only delaying the inevitable. The Romans pocketed his funds but offered no guarantees. They had no respect for kings. They betrayed even their friends. They would destroy humanity or perish in the process. Over the next two decades they indeed proceeded to dismantle large portions of the vast Ptolemaic Empire, events Cleopatra must have followed closely. Cyrene, Crete, Syria, Cyprus, were long gone. The kingdom she would inherit was barely larger than it had been when Ptolemy I had installed himself on the throne two centuries earlier. Egypt had lost its "fence of client states"; Roman lands now surrounded it on all sides.

Mithradates correctly surmised that Egypt owed its continued autonomy more to mutual jealousies in Rome than to Auletes' gold. Paradoxically, the country's wealth prevented its annexation, a question first broached in Rome, by Julius Caesar, when Cleopatra was seven. Competing interests held the discussion in check. No one faction wished for any other to seize control of so fabulously rich a kingdom, the ideal base from which to overthrow a republic. For the Romans Cleopatra's country remained a perennial nuisance, in the words of a modern historian "a loss if destroyed, a risk to annex, a problem to govern."

From the start Auletes had engaged in a degrading dance with Rome, the indignities of which flavored his daughter's early years. Throughout the Mediterranean, rulers looked to that city to shore up their dynastic claims; it was a haven for kings in trouble. A century earlier Ptolemy VI had traveled there in tatters, to set up house in a garret. Shortly thereafter his younger brother, Cleopatra's great-grandfather, the dismemberer of his son, made the same trip. He displayed scars purportedly inflicted by Ptolemy VI and begged the Senate for mercy. The Romans looked wearily upon the endless procession of applicants, abused or not. They received their petitions and made few decisions. At one point the Senate went so far as to outlaw the hearing of their appeals. There was no reason to adopt a consistent foreign policy. As for the bewildering question of Egypt, some felt that that country would be best transformed into a housing project for Rome's poor.

More recently and more problematically, another of Cleopatra's great-uncles had devised an ingenious strategy to protect himself from his conspiring brother. In the event of his demise, Ptolemy X willed his kingdom to Rome. That testament hung awkwardly over Auletes' head, as did his own illegitimacy, as did his unpopularity with the Alexandrian Greeks. And as his hold on the throne was insecure, he had little choice but to curry favor on the other side of the Mediterranean. That cost him in Roman eyes, where he appeared to be pandering, again in the eyes of his subjects, who did not like their sovereign bowing at foreign feet. Auletes moreover subscribed to the wisdom promulgated by the father of Alexander the Great: any fortress could be stormed, provided there was a way up for a donkey with a load of gold on its back. He consequently found himself trapped in a vicious circle. The donkey loads required Cleopatra's father to tax his subjects more severely, which infuriated the very people whose loyalty he labored so assiduously to buy in Rome.

Auletes knew only too well what Caesar was in 48 discovering first-hand: the Alexandrian populace constituted a force unto itself. The best thing you could say of that people was that they were sharp-witted. Their humor was quick and biting. They knew how to laugh. They were mad for drama, as the city's four hundred theaters suggested. They were no less sharp-elbowed. The genius for entertainment extended to a taste for intrigue, a propensity to riot. To one visitor Alexandrian life was "just one continuous revel, not a sweet or gentle revel either, but savage and harsh, a revel of dancers, whistlers, and murderers all combined." Cleopatra's subjects had no compunction about massing at the palace gates and loudly howling their demands. Very little was required to set off an explosion. For two centuries they had freely and wildly deposed, exiled, and assassinated Ptolemies. They had forced Cleopatra's great-grandmother to rule with one son when she attempted to rule with the other. They had driven out Cleopatra's great-uncle. They had dragged Ptolemy XI from the palace and torn him limb from limb after he had murdered his wife. To the Roman mind, the Egyptian army was no better. As Caesar noted from the palace, "These men habitually demanded that friends of the king be put to death, plundered the property of the rich, laid siege to the king's residence to win higher pay, and removed some and appointed others to the throne." Such were the seething forces that Caesar and Cleopatra could hear outside the palace walls. She knew they harbored no particular affection for her. Their feelings about Romans were equally clear. When Cleopatra was nine or ten, a visiting official had accidentally killed a cat, an animal held sacred in Egypt.* A furious mob assembled, with whom Auletes' representative attempted to reason. While this was a crime for an Egyptian, surely a foreigner merited a special exemption? He could not save the visitor from the bloodthirsty crowd.

What Auletes passed down to his daughter was a precarious balancing act. To please one constituency was to displease another. Failure to comply with Rome would lead to intervention. Failure to stand up to Rome would lead to riots. (Auletes appears not to have been much loved by anyone save Cleopatra, who remained loyal always to his memory, despite the political cost of that loyalty at home.) The dangers were manifold. You could be removed by Rome, as Cleopatra's uncle, the king of Cyprus, had been. You could be eliminated—stabbed, poisoned, exiled, dismembered—by your own family. Or you could be deposed by the disaffected, disruptive populace. (There were variations on those themes as well. A Ptolemy could be hated by his people, adored by the royal courtiers; loved by the people and betrayed by his family; or detested by the Alexandrian Greeks and loved by the native Egyptians, as was Cleopatra.) Auletes would spend twenty years currying favor in Rome only

---

*To the Romans the Egyptian worship of animals was unspeakably primitive and perverse. A second-century Christian took a different view. By comparison with the Greek gods, the Egyptian deities fared well. "They may be irrational animals," conceded Clement of Alexandria, "but still they are not adulterous, they are not lewd, and not one of them seeks for pleasure contrary to its own nature."

to discover that he should have been ingratiating himself at home. When he chose not to intervene in Cyprus he was besieged by his subjects, who demanded he either stand up to the Romans or bail out his brother. Panic ensued. Was this not a cautionary tale for Egypt? Auletes fled to Rome, where he spent much of the next three years negotiating for his restoration. It was to those years that Cleopatra owed Caesar's present visit. While Auletes was by no means universally welcomed in Rome, few — Caesar and Pompey among them — were able to resist a Greek bearing bribes. Many were happy to lend Auletes the money with which to pay those bribes, funds he eagerly accepted. The more numerous his creditors, the more numerous those invested in his restoration.

For much of 57 the hot potato business of the day was how, if at all, to handle the deposed king's appeals. The great orator Cicero furtively worked overtime to walk friends through the thorny matter, a business "bedeviled by certain individuals, not without the connivance of the king himself and his advisers." The question stood at a deadlock for some time. Auletes may have gone down in history as a profligate and a puppet, but in Rome he distinguished himself for tenacity and masterly negotiation, to the dismay of his hosts. He papered the Forum and Senate with flyers. He handed out litters — canopied couches, in which to travel splendidly through the city — to his supporters. The situation was complicated by the rivalries among politicians who vied for the luscious reward of helping him; his restoration amounted to a get-rich-quick scheme. By January 56, Cicero complained that the business had "gained a highly invidious notoriety." It occasioned shouting, shoving, spitting, in the Senate. And the matter only grew more delicate. To prevent Pompey or any other individual from assisting Auletes, a religious oracle surfaced. It warned that the Egyptian king was not to be restored by a Roman army, an act expressly forbidden by the gods. The Senate respected this subterfuge, groaned Cicero, "not for religion's sake, but out of ill will and the odium aroused by the royal largesse."

From Auletes' overseas adventure came another essential lesson for the adolescent Cleopatra. No sooner had Auletes left the country than the eldest of his children, Berenice IV, seized the throne; his stock was so low that the Alexandrians were delighted to exchange him for a teen-aged girl. Berenice enjoyed the support of the native population but suffered from the consort problem, one that would speak to Cleopatra's predicament and that she would address differently. Berenice needed a marriageable co-regent. This was a difficult order, as appropriate, well-born Macedonian Greeks were in short supply. (For some reason it was decided that Berenice should pass over her younger brothers, who would have qualified as kings.) The people chose for her, summoning a Seleucid prince. Berenice found him repellent. He was strangled within days of the union. The next prospect was an ambitious Pontic priest who boasted the only two credentials that mattered: he was hostile to Rome, and he could pass for noble. Installed as co-regent in the spring of 56, he fared better. Meanwhile the Alexandrians had dispatched a delegation of one hundred ambassadors to Rome, to protest Auletes' brutality and prevent his return. He poisoned the group's leader and had the rest assassinated, bribed, or run out of town before they could make their case. Conveniently, no investigation of the massacre—in which Pompey appeared to have been complicit—followed, another tribute to Auletes' generosity.

Roman legions returned Auletes to Egypt in 55. None of them was much enchanted by the dubious assignment, especially as it involved a march through a searing desert, followed by a slog through the quick-sand and fetid lagoons of Pelusium. Aulus Gabinius, the Syrian governor and a Pompey protégé, reluctantly consented to lead the mission, either for legitimate reasons (he feared a government headed by Berenice's new husband); for a bribe nearly equivalent to Egypt's annual income; or at the urging of the eager young head of his cavalry, much in Auletes' thrall. That officer was the shaggy-haired Mark Antony, who was to leave behind a great name on which to capitalize later. He fought valiantly. He also urged Auletes to pardon the disloyal army at the Egyptian frontier. Again sounding a little like an ineffectual dilettante, the king "in his rage and spite" preferred to execute those men. For his part

Gabinius meticulously respected the oracle. He arranged for Auletes to follow safely behind the actual battles so that he could not literally be said to have been restored by an army. The Egyptian king was nonetheless returned to the palace by the first Roman legions to set foot in Alexandria.

Of the reunion with his family we have only a partial account. Auletes executed Berenice. He retaliated at court as well, where he thinned the ranks, confiscating fortunes along the way. He replaced high officials and reorganized the army that had opposed him. At the same time he settled lands and pensions on the troops Gabinius left behind. They transferred their allegiance to Egypt. It was that compelling donkey load again; it paid better to serve a Ptolemaic king than a Roman general. As Caesar later observed, those soldiers became "habituated to the ill-disciplined ways of Alexandrian life and had unlearnt the good name and orderly conduct of Romans." They did so in stunningly short order. In his final moments Pompey had recognized a Roman veteran among his murderers.

Auletes' reunion with his second daughter was presumably of a different flavor. In light of her sister's overreaching, thirteen-year-old Cleopatra was now first in line to the throne. Already she had absorbed a great deal in addition to the training in declamation, rhetoric, and philosophy. Her political education could be said to have been completed in 56; she would draw heavily on this chapter a decade later. To be pharaoh was good. To be a friend and ally of Rome was better. The question was not how to resist that power, like Mithradates, who had made a career of goading, defying, and massacring Romans, but how best to manipulate it. Fortunately, Roman politics were highly personal, due to a clash of senatorial ambitions. With shrewdness it was fairly easy to pit the key players against one another. To an early education in pageantry Cleopatra added a first-class introduction to intrigue. She had been in the palace while Egyptian forces girded against her father on his return. By 48, she was working from a playbook Auletes had handed down to her earlier, and for the second time from a palace under siege. Her alliance with

Caesar was a direct descendant of her father's with Pompey, the greatest difference being that she accomplished in a matter of days what took her father more than two decades.

Five years after the return, Auletes died, of natural causes. He was in his midsixties and had had ample time to prepare his succession. It is possible that, as his eldest surviving daughter, Cleopatra served briefly as his co-regent in his final months, certain that—unlike so many of her ancestors, including Auletes himself—she was actively groomed for the throne. Auletes departed from tradition in leaving the throne to two siblings, which would seem to indicate either that Cleopatra manifested exceptional promise at an early age, that Auletes felt he was heading off a power struggle by appointing the two jointly, or that he believed Cleopatra and Ptolemy XIII inseparable, hardly the case. Most likely father and daughter were particularly close. She went out of her way to acknowledge him, appending "father-loving" to her title and preserving it there, despite a change of consort. One of her first acts would have been to see to the funeral arrangements for her father, a protracted, incense- and unguent-heavy affair, punctuated by offerings, and loud with ritual laments. At eighteen she stepped briskly and vigorously into the role of queen.

Almost immediately she had the chance to embrace the wisdom of her father, who on arrival in Egypt had made a point of paying tribute to the native gods, in small villages and at cult centers. To do so was to secure the devotion of the Egyptian population. They revered their pharaoh as thoroughly as the unruly Alexandrians tested him. A smart Ptolemy dedicated temples to Egyptian gods and underwrote their cult; Cleopatra needed the support, and the manpower, of the indigenous population. Well before her coronation the Buchis bull had died. One of several sacred bulls, he was closely associated with the sun and war gods; his cult thrived near Thebes, in Upper Egypt. Roundly worshipped, the bull traveled by special barge in the company of his dedicated staff. He appeared at public events in gold and lapis. In the open air he was fitted with a net over his face, so as not to be pestered by flies. He lived about twenty years, after which he was replaced by a carefully chosen successor, who bore the singular markings—a white body and a black face—of a sacred animal. Within weeks of Auletes' death, Cleopatra seized the opportunity to shore up a core constituency. In full ceremonial dress she appears to have sailed with the royal fleet six hundred miles upriver toward Thebes, to lead an elaborate, floating procession. All the priests of Egypt converged for that momentous occasion, held during the full moon. Amid a crush of pilgrims, "the Queen, the Lady of the two Lands, the goddess who loves her father," rowed the new bull to his installation on the west bank of the Nile, a strong and unusual vote in support of the native Egyptians. Within the temple sanctuary, amid a throng of officials and white-robed priests, Cleopatra three days later presided over the bull's inauguration. The area was familiar and well disposed to her. As a fugitive in 49, she would take refuge there.

Several times in the early years of her reign she inserted herself into the native cult. She offered assistance as well with the burial of the most important of the sacred bulls, that of Memphis. She contributed to his cult expenses, which were high, and provided generous rations of wine, beans, bread, and oil for his officials. There is no question that the pageantry—and the unusual appearance of a Ptolemy—worked an effect: as she made her regal way up the sphinx-lined causeway to the richly painted temple in 51, Cleopatra "was seen by all." We have the description from a line of hieroglyphics, a ceremonial language with a distinct political purpose, perhaps best described as "boasting made permanent." There is evidence in Cleopatra's first year of her ambition as well. Her brother's name is absent from official documents, where he should have figured as Cleopatra's superior. Nor is he in evidence on her coins; Cleopatra's commanding portrait appears alone. Coinage qualifies as a kind of language, too. It is the only one in which she speaks to us in her own voice, without Roman interpreters. This was how she presented herself to her subjects.

She was less adept at assimilating the lesson of Berenice. Pothinus, Achillas, and Theodotus took poorly to this independent-minded upstart, so intent on ruling alone. They had a formidable ally in the Nile, which refused to cooperate with the new queen. The country's well-being depended entirely on the height of the flood; drought compromised the food supply and the social order. The flood of 51 was poor, that of the following summer little better. Priests complained of shortages that prevented them from performing rituals. Towns emptied as hungry villagers poured into Alexandria. Thieves roamed the land. Prices increased dramatically; the distress was universal. By October 50, when it became clear that drastic measures were in order, Cleopatra's brother was back on the scene. At the end of that month the royal couple jointly issued an emergency decree. They rerouted wheat and dried vegetables from the countryside north. Hungry Alexandrians were more dangerous than hungry villagers; it was in everyone's best interest to appease them. The edict was to be reinforced in the time-honored way: Offenders received a death sentence. Denunciations were encouraged, informants richly rewarded. (A free man received a third of the guilty party's property. A slave obtained a sixth, along with his freedom.) At the same time, Ptolemy XIII and Cleopatra offered incentives to those who remained behind to cultivate the land. Either some oppressing or some coercing took place in those months at the palace as well. The two siblings may have been working in tandem for the good of the country. Or Ptolemy may have been undermining his sister, starving her constituents for the sake of his. Both siblings issued the emergency edict. Cleopatra's name appears second.

Already on treacherous ground, she twice over the next year fell into the trap that had swallowed her father. At the end of June 50, two sons of the Roman governor of Syria arrived in Alexandria, to coax the troops who had restored Auletes to return to the fold. They were needed elsewhere. Those soldiers had no interest in leaving Egypt, where Auletes had amply rewarded them for their service, and where many had started families. They emphatically declined the invitation, by murdering the governor's sons. Cleopatra might have meted out justice herself but opted instead to secure Rome's goodwill with a theatrical flourish: she sent the murderers to Syria in chains, a move she should have known would cost her the support of the army. And she continued to trade one vulnerability for another. Roman requests for military assistance were as common in Alexandria as were requests for dynastic interventions in Rome. They were not universally granted, although Auletes had initially won Pompey's favor by providing him with troops. In 49 Pompey's son made a similar request of Cleopatra, applying for assistance in his father's campaign against Caesar. Cleopatra faithfully offered up grain, soldiers, and a fleet, all at a time of dire agricultural distress. This was most likely her Cyprus. Within months her name disappears from all documentation, and she had fled for her life, to wind up camped in the Syrian desert with her band of mercenaries.

SHORTLY AFTER CLEOPATRA'S October 48 arrival, Caesar moved from the villa on the royal grounds to the palace proper. Each generation of Ptolemies had added to that sprawling complex, as magnificent in its design as in its materials. "Pharaoh" means "the greatest household" in ancient Egyptian, and on this the Ptolemies had delivered. The palace included well over a hundred guest rooms. Caesar looked out at lush grounds dotted with fountains and statuary and guesthouses; a vaulted walkway led from the palace complex to its theater, which stood on higher terrain. No Hellenistic monarchs did opulence better than the Ptolemies, the preeminent importers of Persian carpets, of ivory and gold, tortoiseshell and panther skin. As a general rule any surface that could be ornamented was—with garnet and topaz, with encaustic, with brilliant mosaic, with gold. The coffered ceilings were studded with agate and lapis, the cedar doors with mother-of-pearl, the gates overlaid with gold and silver. Corinthian capitals shimmered with ivory and gold. Cleopatra's palace boasted the greatest profusion of precious materials known at the time.

Insofar as it was possible to be comfortable while under siege, Cleopatra and Caesar were well accommodated. None of the extravagant tableware or plush furnishings of their redoubt detracted, however, from the fact that Cleopatra—virtually alone in the city—was eager for a Roman to involve himself in Egyptian affairs. The rumbles and jeers outside, the scuffling in the street, the whizzing stones, drove that point home. The most intense fighting took place in the harbor, which the Alexandrians attempted to blockade. Early on they managed to set fire to several Roman freighters. The fleet Cleopatra had lent Pompey had moreover returned. Both sides jockeyed for control of those fifty quadriremes and quinqueremes, large vessels requiring four and five banks of rowers. Caesar could not afford to allow the ships to fall into enemy hands if he expected to see either provisions or reinforcements, for which he had sent out calls in every direction. Nor could he hope to man them. He was seriously outnumbered and at a geographic disadvantage; in desperation, he set fire to the anchored warships. Cleopatra's reaction as flames spread over the ropes and across the decks is difficult to imagine. She could not have escaped the penetrating clouds of smoke, sharp with the tang of resin, that wafted across her gardens; the palace was illuminated by the blaze, which burned well into the night. This was the dockyard fire that may have claimed some portion of the Alexandrian library. Nor could Cleopatra have missed the pitched battle that preceded the conflagration, for which the entire city turned out: "And there was not a soul in Alexandria, whether Roman or townsman, except for those whose attention was engrossed in fortification work or fighting, who did not make for the highest buildings and take their place to see the show from any vantage point, and with prayers and vows demand victory for their own side from the immortal gods." Amid mingled shouts and much commotion, Caesar's men scrambled on to Pharos to seize the great lighthouse. Caesar allowed them a bit of plunder, then stationed a garrison on the rocky island.

Also shortly after Cleopatra's arrival, Caesar composed the final pages of the volume we know today as *The Civil War*. About those events he would have been writing in something close to real time. It has been suggested that he broke off where he did—with Arsinoe's defection and

Pothinus's murder—for literary or political reasons. Caesar could not easily discourse on a Western republic in an Eastern palace. He was also at that juncture in his narrative briefly in possession of the upper hand. Just as likely Caesar found himself with less time to write, if not overwhelmed. He was indeed the man who famously dictated letters from his stadium seat, who turned out a text on Latin while traveling from Gaul, a long poem en route to Spain. The murder of the eunuch Pothinus had galvanized the opposition, however. Already it included the women and children of the city. They had no need of wicker screens or battering rams, happy as they were to express themselves with slingshots and stones. Sprays of homemade missiles pelted the palace walls. Battles flared night and day, as Alexandria filled with zealous reinforcements and with siege huts and catapults of various sizes. Triple-width, forty-foot stone barricades went up across the city, transformed into an armed camp.

From the palace Caesar observed what had put Alexandria on the map and what made it so difficult to rule: its people were endlessly, boundlessly resourceful. His men watched in amazement—and with resentment; ingenuity was meant to be a Roman specialty—as the Alexandrians constructed wheeled, ten-story assault towers. Draft animals led those mammoth contraptions down the straight, paved avenues of the city. Two things in particular astonished the Romans. Everything could be accomplished more quickly in Alexandria. And its people were clever copyists of the first rank. Repeatedly they went Caesar one better. As a Roman general recounted later, they "put into effect whatever they saw us do with such skill that it seemed our troops had imitated their work." National pride was at stake on both sides. When Caesar bested the seafaring Alexandrians in a naval battle, they were shattered. Subsequently they threw themselves into the task of building a fleet. In the secret royal dockyard sat a number of old ships, no longer seaworthy. Down came colonnades and the roofs of gymnasiums, their rafters magically transformed into oars. In a matter of days, twenty-two quadriremes and five quinqueremes materialized, along with a number of smaller craft, manned and ready for combat. Nearly overnight, the Egyptians conjured up a navy twice as large as Caesar's.*

Repeatedly the Romans sputtered about the twin Alexandrian capacities for deceit and treachery, which in the midst of an armed conflict surely counts as high praise. As if to prove the point, Ganymedes, Arsinoe's ex-tutor and the new royal commander, set his men to work digging deep wells. They drained the city's underground conduits, into which they pumped seawater. Quickly the palace water proved cloudy and undrinkable. (Ganymedes may or may not have known this to be an old trick of Caesar's, who had similarly annoyed Pompey.) The Romans panicked. Did it not make more sense to retreat immediately? Caesar calmed his men: Fresh water could not be far off, as veins of it reliably occurred near oceans. One lay just beyond the palace walls. As for withdrawal, it was not an option. The legionnaires could not reach their ships without the Alexandrians slaughtering them. Caesar ordered an all-night dig, which proved him correct; his men quickly located fresh water. It remained true, however, that on their side the Alexandrians had great cleverness and plentiful resources, as well as that most potent of motivations: their autonomy was at stake. They had distinctly unfavorable memories of Gabinius, the general who had returned Auletes to the throne. To fail to drive Caesar out now was to become a province of Rome. Caesar could only remind his men they must fight with equal conviction.

He found himself entirely on the defensive, perhaps another reason the account of the Alexandrian War that bears his name was written by a senior officer, based on postwar conversations. Caesar indeed controlled the palace and the lighthouse in the east, but Achillas, Ptolemy's commander, dominated the rest of the city, and with it nearly every advantageous position. His men persistently ambushed Roman supplies. Fortunately for Caesar, if there was one thing he could count on as much as Alexandrian ingenuity it was Alexandrian infighting. Arsinoe's tutor

---

*Their fervor was lost on later Romans. As Dio would write centuries afterward, the Alexandrians were "most ready to assume a bold front everywhere and to speak out whatever may occur to them, but for war and its terrors they are utterly useless."

argued with Achillas, whom he accused of treachery. Plot followed counterplot, much to the delight of the army, bribed generously and in turn more generously by each side. Ultimately Arsinoe convinced her tutor to murder the redoubtable Achillas. Cleopatra knew well what their sister Berenice had accomplished in their father's absence; she had badly blundered in failing to prevent Arsinoe's escape.

Arsinoe and Ganymedes turned out to be no favorites of the people, however. This the Alexandrians made clear as reinforcements approached and as Caesar—despite a forced swim in the harbor and a devastating loss of men—began to feel the war turning in his favor. To the palace came a delegation in mid-January, shortly after Cleopatra's twenty-second birthday. They lobbied for young Ptolemy's release. Already the people had tried unsuccessfully to liberate their king. Now they claimed they were finished with his sister. They yearned for peace. They needed Ptolemy "in order, as they claimed, that they might consult with him about the terms on which a truce could be effected." He had clearly behaved well while under guard. Generally he left no impression of fortitude or leadership, though petulance came naturally to him. Caesar saw some advantages in his release. Were the Alexandrians to surrender, he would need somehow to dispense with this extraneous king; Ptolemy could clearly never again rule with his sister. In his absence Caesar would have better reason to deliver up the Alexandrians to Cleopatra. And were Ptolemy to continue to fight—it is unclear if the rationale here was Caesar's, or attributed to him later—the Romans would be conducting a war that was all the more honorable for being waged "against a king rather than against a gang of refugees and runaway slaves."

Caesar duly sat Cleopatra's thirteen-year-old brother down for a talk. He urged him "to think of his ancestral kingdom, to take pity on his glorious homeland, which had been disfigured by the disgrace of fire and ruin; to begin by bringing his people back to their senses, and then save them; and to trust the Roman people and himself, Caesar, whose faith in him was firm enough to send him to join enemies who were under arms." Caesar then dismissed the young man. Ptolemy made no move to leave; instead he again dissolved into tears. He begged Caesar not to send him away. Their friendship meant more to him even than his throne. His devotion moved Caesar who—eyes welling up in turn—assured him that they would be reunited soon enough. At which young Ptolemy set off to embrace the war with a new intensity, one that confirmed that "the tears he had shed when talking to Caesar were obviously tears of joy." Only Caesar's men seemed gratified by this turn of events, which they hoped might cure their commander of his absurdly forgiving ways. The comedy would not have surprised Cleopatra, well accomplished in the dramatic arts, and possibly even the mastermind behind this scene. It is conceivable that Caesar liberated Ptolemy to sow further dissension in the rebel ranks. If he did so (the interpretation is a generous one), Cleopatra presumably collaborated on the staging.

Fortunately for Caesar and Cleopatra, a large army of reinforcements hurried toward Alexandria. The best help came from a high-ranking Judaean official, who arrived with a contingent of three thousand well-armed Jews. Ptolemy set out to crush that force at nearly the same moment that Caesar set out to join it; he was for some time frustrated by the Egyptian cavalry. All converged in a fierce battle west of the Nile, at a location halfway between Alexandria and present-day Cairo. The casualties were great on both sides, but—by storming the high point of the Egyptian camp in a surprise early-morning maneuver—Caesar managed a swift victory. Terrified, a great number of the Egyptians hurled themselves from the ramparts of their fort into the surrounding trenches. Some survived. It seemed Ptolemy did not; he was probably little mourned by anyone, including his advisers. As his body never materialized, Caesar took special pains to display his golden armor, which did. The magical, rejuvenating powers of the Nile were well known; already it had delivered up queens in sacks and babies in baskets. Caesar did not want a resurrection on his hands, though even his meticulous efforts now would not prevent the appearance of a Ptolemy-pretender later.

With his cavalry Caesar hurried to Alexandria, to receive the kind of welcome he had doubtless expected months earlier: "The entire population of the town threw down their weapons, left their defenses, assumed the garb in which suppliants commonly crave pardon from their masters, and after bringing out all the sacred objects with whose religious awe they used to appeal to their displeased or angry monarchs, went to meet Caesar as he approached, and surrendered to him." Graciously he accepted the surrender and consoled the populace. Cleopatra would have been ecstatic; Caesar's defeat would have been hers as well. She presumably received advance word but would in any event have heard the raucous cheers as Caesar approached on horseback. His legions met him at the palace with loud applause. It was March 27; the relief must have been extreme. Caesar's men had given him more than a decade of service, and on arrival in Alexandria believed the civil war to be over. They had by no means counted on this last, little understood exploit. Nor were they alone in their consternation. Rome had heard nothing from Caesar since December. What was keeping him in Egypt, when all was off-kilter at home? Whatever the reason for the delay, the silence was unsettling. It must have begun to seem that Egypt had claimed Caesar as it had Pompey and—as some would argue—in an entirely different way, it ultimately would.

Why did he stay? There is no convincing political explanation for the interlude, an illogical adventure in the life of a supremely logical man. It remains baffling that the greatest soldier since Alexander, "a prodigy of activity and foresight" on every other occasion, should have been blindsided and sandbagged in Africa. The best that can be said of the Alexandrian War is that Caesar acquitted himself brilliantly in a situation in which he stupidly found himself. For an explanation he cited the northerly winds, "which blew absolutely directly against anyone sailing out of Alexandria." Indeed they would have, though a sentence earlier Caesar acknowledges having sent to Asia for reinforcements, the reinforcements that would ultimately save the day. That mission would have involved an outbound trip. And within weeks the winds were strongly in his favor. Caesar did not back down; even with a depleted, demoralized army, he was not one to turn from danger. He makes no reference himself to Auletes' great debt, a cause for landing if not for remaining. As so often happens, the question comes down to love or money. It is not easy to argue against the former.

In the first place we have Caesar's resounding silence. We leave all kinds of things out of our memoirs and Caesar (and his ghostwriter) omitted a great many, not least of all his personality. Caesar wrote of himself with a stern, clinical detachment and in the third person; his style is so limpid and dispassionate as to appear incontestably true. Which it may well be, though in his account he neither crosses the Rubicon nor sets fire to the Alexandrian library. It is entirely possible that the latter charge was overstated. The dockyard warehouses may alone have gone up in flames, which would have destroyed only grain supplies and a modest number of texts.* Similarly, one of the few places Cleopatra fails to make a dramatic entrance is in Caesar's *Civil War,* where her charms are supplanted by the seasonal winds. For a married man who had been pilloried once for his stay in an Eastern court, for a military genius who made a gross blunder at the side of a queen if not on her behalf, this was not a matter that invited elaboration. In the continuation of Caesar's narrative, Cleopatra appears precisely once. At war's end he bestows the throne of Egypt upon her, because she "had remained loyal to him, and stayed within his lines." Cleopatra goes down in Caesar's history for one reason alone: she was good and obedient.

Certainly the suspicion that there was more to the matter than unfavorable winds and obedient females was in the air. In Rome Cicero lost no time in casting shameful aspersions. Just after Caesar's death, Mark Antony — a curious messenger for this particular message — would protest that Caesar had not tarried in Alexandria "out of voluptuousness." A century later, Plutarch begged to differ: "As to the war in Egypt, some say it was at once dangerous and dishonorable, and noways necessary, but occasioned only by his passion for Cleopatra." (The inconvenient oracle of Auletes' day — prohibiting the restoration of an Egyptian

---

*At the same time it is interesting that the general who continues Caesar's narrative takes such care to emphasize — on his first page and curiously out of context — that the city was fireproof. His assertion contradicts the other early sources, which claim that fire spread from the ships to the docks to the great library. It fails to acknowledge too the masterfully manipulated roofs and beams or the timber barricades of Caesar's account. We are left with a gratuitous apology, and without an offense.

monarch by a Roman army—appears to have been quickly forgotten.)
You could argue that Caesar had no particular affection for Cleopatra,
that the two only happened to find themselves on the same side of a baffling war, but it would be easier to argue that she had no affection for
him. She contributed nothing to that enterprise. Caesar would have been
well served by throwing her over, if only to obtain a temporary truce.
He would have been within his rights at war's end to annex Egypt; Cleopatra must have been very, very persuasive. Pothinus had balked at
repaying the Egyptian debt. Clearly Cleopatra did not. It is difficult to
escape the conclusion that Caesar was to some extent in her sway. Dio
thought that obvious: Caesar handed Egypt to Cleopatra, "for whose
sake he had waged the conflict." He acknowledges a certain embarrassment. At war's end Caesar put Cleopatra on the throne with her remaining brother to defuse Roman anger that he was himself sleeping with
her. To Dio this was "a mere pretence, which she accepted, whereas in
truth she ruled alone and spent her time in Caesar's company." The two
were inseparable. Plutarch felt similarly but expressed himself more subtly. Reading between his lines, he plainly believed Caesar both preoccupied with military matters and in Cleopatra's bed every night. There is as
well the minor matter of the departure date. The Alexandrian War ended
on March 27. Caesar stayed with Cleopatra until mid-June.

THERE WAS REASON to celebrate, all the more so after having been
cooped up behind a thicket of barricades for the better part of six
months. And as every visitor to Hellenistic Egypt had noted, eyes wide,
belly bursting, travel bag groaning, the Ptolemies knew how to entertain. Save that written by a poet who demonized Caesar and had less
affection for Cleopatra, we have no account of her actual postwar banquets. We do know what a Ptolemaic feast looked like. Self-restraint was
not an Alexandrian specialty, and in the spring of 47 Cleopatra had no
cause to embrace it. She had secured the greatest of prizes, for "in view
of Caesar's favor there was nothing that she could not do." He had gone
further out on a limb than had any other Roman for an Egyptian

sovereign. Ptolemy XIII, Pothinus, and Achillas were all dead. Theodotus was in exile, Arsinoe in Roman custody. Caesar had effectively eliminated every one of Cleopatra's rivals to the throne. She reigned supreme, more securely than she had done four years previously, more securely than had any Ptolemy in several generations. She prided herself on her hospitality and knew her guest did as well; Caesar had once thrown his baker into chains for having served substandard bread. He was himself responsible for a fair amount of entertainment inflation. The queen of Egypt had every political reason to impress and please him; personal rapport aside, there would have been a heady admixture of pride, relief, and gratitude. And she had the resources to impress. The Alexandrian War gave Cleopatra everything she wanted. It cost her little.

Even in her exile, a swarm of servants had hovered around Cleopatra, ministering to her comforts. In the spring of 47 that swarm increased to a horde, with the return or appointment of tasters, scribes, lamplighters, royal harpists, masseurs, pages, doorkeepers, notaries, silver stewards, oil keepers, pearl setters. At her side also was a new consort. To satisfy the people's preference for a ruling couple, possibly as well to cover Caesar's tracks, twelve-year-old Ptolemy XIV ascended to the throne. The marriage took place soon after the Alexandrian surrender. We do not know how it was celebrated. From Cleopatra's perspective, one nonentity replaced another. Ptolemy XIV assumed the same title that had been used by his dead brother; he never appeared with his sister on her coins. If he had ambitions or opinions of his own he knew better than to express them now. Surely he had no say in the administration that his sister-wife set about reconstituting. Whether or not Caesar had considered annexing Egypt he had clearly discovered that Cleopatra was in many respects similar to her country: a shame to lose, a risk to conquer, a headache to govern. Some courtiers had remained faithful; among Cleopatra's entourage figured several of her father's advisers. Those who had not did their best quickly to reassess their conduct. So presumably did the Greek aristocracy, which had presented Cleopatra with her strongest opposition.

She had at court a serious handicap, one that Caesar would have done well to observe. As a later Roman leader noted: "For the ruler labors under this special disadvantage as regards his friends, that although he can protect himself from his enemies by arranging his friends against them, there is no corresponding ally on whom he may rely to protect him from these friends." For the most part Cleopatra knew who the ill-wishers were. Matters were murkier concerning her courtiers. She had after all been holed up for months with a Roman, battling a people who wanted no Roman in the house and who had deposed her father for consorting with them. The rules had now changed. There was always a certain amount of rot at court; the war would have been an excuse to clean it out. Those who had opposed Cleopatra paid a heavy price. Those rumored to have done so doubtless paid too. She replaced high officials and eliminated others, confiscating fortunes in the process. There were poisonings and stabbings, not dissimilar from those in which Auletes had engaged upon his restoration. The army alone invited a bloody round of proscriptions. It was by no means a smooth transition.

Around the palace and harbor there was more prosaic work to be done: trenches to be filled, palisades to be dismantled, debris to be cleared, structural damage to be repaired. What emerged was and remained "the first city of the civilized world, certainly far ahead of all the rest in elegance and extent and riches and luxury," as a contemporary traveler put it. Visitors were at a loss to decide if Alexandria's size or beauty was the more imposing. That was before acknowledging its hyperkinetic population. "Looking at the city, I doubted whether any race of men could ever fill it; looking at the inhabitants, I wondered whether any city could ever be found large enough to hold them all. The balance seemed exactly even," effused a native son. Alexandria was studded with an awe-inspiring collection of sculpture, much of it carved of pink or red granite and violet porphyry, all of it pulsing with robust color. To anyone who knew Athens, the Egyptian city felt familiar, crowded as it was with fine Ptolemaic copies of Greek pieces. It was neither the first nor the last place in the world where a decline in power translated into an enormity of symbols; as the Ptolemaic influence diminished, the statuary ballooned, to hyperbolic dimensions. Forty-foot-tall rose granite sculptures of Cleopatra II and Cleopatra III greeted new arrivals in the Alexandrian harbor. At least one colossal hawk-headed sphinx towered over the palace wall. Glossy thirty-foot-long sphinxes guarded the city's temples.

Alexandria's ninety-foot-wide main avenue left visitors speechless, its scale unmatched in the ancient world. You could lose a day exploring it from end to end. Lined with delicately carved columns, silk awnings, and richly painted facades, the Canopic Way could accommodate eight chariots driving abreast. The city's primary side streets too were nearly twenty feet wide, paved with stones, expertly drained, and partially lit at night. From its central crossroads—a ten-minute walk from the palace—a forest of sparkling limestone colonnades extended as far as the eye could see. On the city's western side lived most of its Egyptian population, many of them linen weavers, clustered around the hundred steps that led up to the Serapeum, the third-century temple that dominated the city and housed its secondary library. That rectangular temple—much of it decorated in gold leaf, silver, and bronze—stood on a rocky, artificial hill, surrounded by parks and porticoes. It is one of only three monuments of Cleopatra's day that we can locate with accuracy today. The city's Jewish quarter stood in the northeast, next to the palace. Greeks occupied the fine three-story houses at the center of town. Industry divided neighborhoods as well: one quarter was devoted to the manufacture of perfumes and to the fabrication of their alabaster pots, another to glassworkers.

From east to west the city measured nearly four miles, a wonderland of baths, theaters, gymnasiums, courts, temples, shrines, and synagogues. A limestone wall surrounded its perimeter, punctuated by towers, patrolled at both ends of the Canopic Way by prostitutes. During the day Alexandria echoed with the sounds of horses' hooves, the cries of porridge sellers or chickpea vendors, street performers, soothsayers, moneylenders. Its spice stands released exotic aromas, carried through the streets by a thick, salty sea breeze. Long-legged white and black ibises assembled at every intersection, foraging for crumbs. Until well into the evening, when the vermilion sun plunged precipitously into the harbor, Alexandria remained a swirl of reds and yellows, a swelling kaleidoscope of music, chaos, and color. Altogether it was a mood-altering city of extreme sensuality and high intellectualism, the Paris of the ancient world: superior in its ways, splendid in its luxuries, the place to go to spend your fortune, write your poetry, find (or forget) a romance, restore your health, reinvent yourself, or regroup after having conquered vast swaths of Italy, Spain, and Greece over the course of a Herculean decade.

Given the transporting beauty and rapturous entertainments, Alexandria was not a city into which one sank passively. As a visitor noted, "It is not easy for a stranger to endure the clamor of so great a multitude or to face these tens of thousands unless he comes provided with a lute and a song." Alexandrians embraced their reputation for frivolity. And through the massive portal of the palace hordes of well-wishers and Roman associates thronged at the war's conclusion, gathering in the ivory-paneled entrance hall. With its array of banqueting rooms, that complex could accommodate a vast crowd; its largest hall was furnished with a dazzling collection of couches, sculpted of bronze, inlaid with ivory and glass, works of art unto themselves. Egypt imported its silver but long controlled the greatest gold reserve of the ancient world; the beams of that hall may have been themselves overlaid with gold. It is easy to inflate the city's population, difficult to overstate its magnificence. It taxed the vocabularies even of the ancients. Plenty of wealthy Alexandrian households boasted furniture of Lebanon cedar inlaid with ivory and mother-of-pearl, sophisticated *trompe l'oeil,* and intricate, realistic mosaics. Slabs of caramel-colored alabaster sheathed exteriors. Interior walls shimmered with enamels and emeralds. Where wall decoration yielded to murals, mythological scenes predominated. The quality of the work was an astonishment.

The floor mosaics were in particular worked with a remarkable precision, heavy on geometrics, often three-dimensional in feel, implausibly realistic in their depictions of the natural world. At banquets those intricacies vanished under lush carpets of lilies and roses, with which Egypt was abundantly supplied. "The general rule," gushed one chronicler, "is that no flower, including roses, snowdrops, or anything else, ever completely stops blooming." Strewn in heaps over the floors, they lent the impression of a country meadow, if one littered at meal's end by oyster shells, lobster claws, and peach pits. There was nothing rare about a banquet order for three hundred crowns of roses, or for as many braided garlands. (Roses were crucial, their fragrance believed to prevent intoxication.) Perfumes and unguents were Alexandrian specialties; attendants sprinkled cinnamon and cardamom and balsam perfumes on banqueters' crowns as musicians played or storytellers performed. Fragrance rippled not only from the table but from jewelry, perfumed lamps, soles of shoes; the heavy scents of the oils inevitably flavored the dinner. The wares of the city's other preeminent artisans were on display as well: Tables glinted with silver basins, pitchers, hundreds of candelabra. Blown glass was a Hellenistic invention on which Alexandria had worked its usual magic, gilding the already elaborate lily; the city's glassblowers threaded gold into their work. On the table polychromatic vessels joined silver platters, woven ivory breadbaskets, jewel-encrusted tumblers. The meal itself appeared on gold dishes; at one Ptolemaic feast, the dinner vessels alone were said to have weighed three hundred tons. That tableware showcased both Cleopatra's adaptability and her competitive instinct. When Alexandrian luxury began to make itself felt in the Roman world, Cleopatra renamed her ostentatious tableware. Her elaborate gold and silver place settings became her "ordinary ware."

To one guest a palace dinner itself appeared as a fortune rather than a meal. He gaped at "a silver platter covered with heavy gold plate, and large enough to hold a huge roast piglet lying on its back and displaying its belly, which was full of many delicious items; for inside it were roast thrushes, ducks, and an immense quantity of warblers, as well as egg yolks, oysters, and scallops." Geese were standard fare on the prodigal menus, along with peacocks, oysters, sea urchins, sturgeon, and red mullet, the delicacies of the Mediterranean world. (Spoons were rare, forks unknown. One ate with one's fingers.) Sweet wines—the best came from Syria and Ionia—were spiced with honey or pomegranate. We have no trace of the wardrobe in which Cleopatra presided over these festivities, though we know that she wore plenty of pearls, the diamonds of the day. She coiled long ropes of pearls around her neck and braided more into her hair. She wore others sewn into the fabric of her tunics. Those were ankle-length and lavishly colored, of fine Chinese silk or gauzy linen, traditionally worn belted, or with a brooch or ribbon. Over the tunic went an often transparent mantle, through which the bright folds of fabric were clearly visible. On her feet Cleopatra wore jeweled sandals with patterned soles. Among the greatest hosts in history, the Ptolemies sent their guests stumbling home with gifts. It was not unusual to make off with a place setting of solid silver, a slave, a gazelle, a gold sofa, a horse in silver armor. Excess had put the Ptolemies on the map, where Cleopatra fully intended the dynasty to remain. Such were the "prolonged parties until dawn" of which Suetonius would write later.

The postwar festivities would certainly have included a victory procession, presumably down the Canopic Way. Cleopatra needed to unite her people, to assert her political supremacy, and to cement her claim over her detractors. Alexandria had long been a city of parades and pageantry, displays in which the wealth of the Ptolemies surpassed even the recreational fervor of their subjects. Centuries earlier a Dionysian procession had introduced gilded twenty-foot floats to the city streets, each requiring 180 men to coax it along. Purple-painted satyrs and gold-garlanded nymphs followed, along with allegorical representations of kings, gods, cities, seasons. A center of mechanical marvels, Alexandria boasted automatic doors and hydraulic lifts, hidden treadmills and coin-operated machines. With invisible wires, siphons, pulleys, and magnets the Ptolemies could work miracles. Fires erupted and died down; lights flickered from statues' eyes; trumpets blared spontaneously. For the early procession, the city's ingenious metalworkers outdid themselves: A fifteen-foot-tall statue in a yellow spangled tunic floated through the streets. She rose to her full height, poured offerings of milk, then magically reseated herself, enthralling the crowds. Around her the air was thick with the buzz of anticipation, the murmurs of admiration, the music of flutes. Clouds of incense — essentially moneyed air — settled on the spectators, for whom the burnished wonders continued: golden torch carriers, chests of frankincense and myrrh, gilded palm trees, grapevines, breastplates, shields, statues, basins, gold-adorned oxen. Atop one cart, sixty satyrs trampled grapes, singing as they did so, accompanied by pipers. Vast skins disgorged scented wine into the streets; the air was sweetened first by incense, again by those fragrant streams, a heady combination. Attendants released doves and pigeons over the course of the procession, each with ribbons dangling from its feet. A display of animals was obligatory for the subjects who had traveled to Alexandria and pitched tents for miles around. The third-century procession had included troops of decorated donkeys; elephants shod with gold embroidered slippers; teams of oryxes, leopards, peacocks, enormous lions, an Ethiopian rhinoceros, ostriches, an albino bear, 2,400 dogs. Camels carried loads of saffron and cinnamon. Behind them paraded 200 bulls with gilded horns. Lyre players followed, along with 57,000 infantry and 23,000 cavalry in full armor. Cleopatra would not have had those battalions but would all the same have mustered an extravagant display. The point was to advertise oneself, among monarchs, as "the shrewdest amasser of wealth, the most splendid spendthrift, and the most magnificent in all works." Affluence, power, and legitimacy were inextricably bound together. Especially after the convulsions of the previous decades, it was essential that she confirm her authority.

Caesar may well have stayed to that end. A stable Egypt was as critical to his plans as to Cleopatra's. Nearly alone in the Mediterranean, Egypt produced more grain than it consumed. Cleopatra could single-handedly feed Rome. The reverse was also true; she could starve that city if she cared to. For that reason Caesar was disinclined to install a countryman in Alexandria. A reliable non-Roman was the best solution. It is clear that Caesar trusted Cleopatra as he could not have trusted

Pothinus, equally clear that he had confidence in her ability to rule. Strictly speaking, her Egypt became as of 47 a protectorate with an intimate twist. That arrangement was by no means unorthodox in a century when politics were markedly personal. Hellenistic alliances were regularly ratified with wedding vows. In Rome mercenary marriages were the order of the day, to the dismay of the purists, who railed at that brand of cheap, expedient diplomacy. The more ambitious the politician, the more variegated the marriages. Pompey had wed five times, always for political reasons. Caesar's tumultuous career was closely tied to each of his four wives. Despite an age difference comparable to that between Caesar and Cleopatra, Pompey had married Caesar's daughter, sent to him as a sort of thank-you note.* Relations between the two men soured only when the woman who bound them died, a history that would shortly repeat itself, with far greater repercussions.

Caesar and Cleopatra's relationship was unusual not only for its national differences, but because Cleopatra entered into it of her own will. No male relative forced her hand. To a Roman, that was highly discomfiting. Had her father in his lifetime married her to Caesar (an impossibility on any number of counts), she would have been seen altogether differently. What unsettled those who wrote her history was her independence of mind, the enterprising spirit. The poet Lucan is clear on this point. "Cleopatra has been able to capture the old man with magic," he has Pothinus exclaim, in a broad redefinition of free will. Already in possession of Egypt, she in his account subsequently "whores to gain Rome." Here too there were instructive parallels. The story would later be told of an early Indian monarch, Queen Cleophis. She "surrendered to Alexander but subsequently regained her throne, which she ransomed by sleeping with him, attaining by sexual favors what she could not by force of arms." According to a Roman historian at least, for her degrading

---

*The gift was welcome but the timing was awkward. Julia had been set to marry Quintus Servilius Caepio in a matter of days. He was most displeased. In her place, Pompey offered Caepio his own daughter, although she, in turn, was already engaged to someone else. For the most part Roman women were for horse trading, an idea that—for all their creative family machinations—rarely occurred to the Ptolemies.

behavior Cleophis earned the epithet "royal whore." The story may well be apocryphal, another lurid Roman fantasy about the beguiling East. It may even have been Cleopatra-inflected. But it tells us something of Cleopatra. She was as suspect as Queen Cleophis, though what the Romans mostly seized upon — what inspired backhanded tributes — was her uncanny, occult power.

That an easy rapport if not a great passion developed between Cleopatra and Caesar was unsurprising. Her aplomb and his gamble may have clinched the deal, but their personalities were as neatly matched as their political agendas. They were congenial, charismatic, quick-tongued people, if only one of them would go down in history as having been so seductive as to be dangerous. Cleopatra especially knew how to ingratiate. Where there had been thought to be four kinds of flattery, Plutarch sputtered, always on guard against that noxious brew, "she had a thousand." We have more tributes to the caress of her wit than to Caesar's; his is to be read less in his language than in his innumerable affairs. He was a masterly seducer, with a specialty in aristocratic wives. Both Cleopatra and Caesar manifested the intellectual curiosity that was the trademark of their age, a lightheartedness and a humor that set them apart from their peers, insofar as either had peers. Such an unsociable, solitary thing is power, notes Plutarch; generally those around Caesar and Cleopatra could be relied upon to fawn or plot. Both knew, as Caesar put it, that success came at a price, that "everything that lifts people above their fellows arouses both emulation and jealousy." Theirs was an exclusive brand of social isolation.

Both had daringly crossed lines in their bids for power; both had let the dice fly. Both had as great a capacity for work as for play and rarely distinguished between the two. Caesar answered letters and petitions while attending games. Cleopatra engaged in games for reasons of state. Neither shrank from drama. Both were natural performers, as secure in their ability as in the conviction of their superiority. Much was expected of Cleopatra, who liked to surprise, believed in the *grand geste*, and did not sell herself short. Caesar put a premium on style and admired talent in all its forms; in

Alexandria he was in the constant company of a deft conversationalist, linguist, and negotiator, one who shared his unusual gift for treating new acquaintances as if they were old intimates. There was ample reason on his part for close attention. Cleopatra provided a timely lesson in comportment. Having the year before been declared dictator, Caesar was enjoying his first taste of absolute power. Cleopatra moreover handled matters no woman of his acquaintance had touched. He would have been hard pressed to find a woman in all of Rome who had raised an army, lent a fleet, controlled a currency. As incandescent as was her personality, Cleopatra was every bit Caesar's equal as a coolheaded, clear-eyed pragmatist, though what passed on his part as strategy would be remembered on hers as manipulation. Both were emerging from wars that had nothing to do with issues and everything to do with personalities. They had faced similar difficulties, with similar constituencies. Caesar was no favorite of the Roman aristocracy. Cleopatra was unloved by the Alexandrian Greeks. Their power derived from the common people. The ambitious shine especially in the company of the ambitious; Caesar and Cleopatra came together as might two heirs to legendary fortunes, larger than life and abundantly aware of their gifts, who are accustomed to thinking of themselves in the plural, or writing of themselves in the third person.

IN THE COURSE of one of Cleopatra's banquets, Lucan imagines Caesar quizzing Egypt's high priest. Caesar is a student of a great many subjects, a man of boundless curiosity. His love of exploration was as pronounced as his ambition. He was fascinated by Egyptian lore and culture; in Alexandria he conferred with scientists and philosophers. He has but one request. "There is nothing I would rather know," he pleads, "than the causes of the river which lie hidden through so many ages and its unknown source." If the priest will reveal the source of the Nile, Caesar will abandon warfare. The fervor was understandable. Few mysteries of the ancient world were as compelling; the source of the Nile was the life on Mars of its day. Lucan is the first to mention Caesar and Cleopatra's cruise on the river, 110 years after the fact. He admired neither party and was writing verse; he has been called "the father of yellow journalism" for good reason. All the same he was working from historical sources lost to us today. He is unlikely to have invented the trip. Nor was there reason to believe the postwar cruise any less luxurious, or frantic with entertainments, than the one Shakespeare would ultimately immortalize, still five years in the future. There is better reason to assume Roman historians preferred to remember that journey and forget this one. They made no mention either of Caesar having tarried in Egypt at the war's conclusion.* Had they not closed ranks as they did, Shakespeare might well have written Cleopatra into a different play.

There was ample precedent for a Nile trip. It was traditional to welcome a foreign dignitary with a cruise, to introduce him to the marvel that was Egypt. Two generations earlier a high official went to great lengths to ensure that a Roman senator traveling in Egypt be "received with the utmost magnificence," showered with gifts, entrusted to expert guides, supplied with the pastries and roasted meats with which to feed the sacred crocodiles. Egypt's miles upon miles of grain fields inevitably impressed, even as they made Roman fingers twitch. And burning curiosity aside, there were legitimate state reasons for the excursion. A new ruler traditionally inaugurated his or her reign with a ceremonial journey south. For Cleopatra this amounted to a proprietary tour of her personal estate. Everyone in Egypt worked for her; nearly every resource of the country—its fields, its game, its trees, the Nile and its crocodiles themselves—was hers. From her point of view the cruise was not so much a pleasure trip or a scientific expedition as a state obligation. With it she provided a critical display of Roman military might to her people, a display of Egyptian abundance to Rome. The people of Egypt had supplied her against her brother when she was vulnerable. With Caesar at her side, she returned to them patently invincible.

To journey from Alexandria south was to leave the Greek-speaking for the Egyptian-speaking world, to travel from wine country to beer

---

*One modern historian goes so far as to suggest they expressly covered it up.

country. Here was the culture to which Alexandrians felt themselves superior, where pharaohs were revered and priests held sway. Here Cleopatra's divinity went unquestioned. Even without the Alexandrian pageantry, the agate and the red granite, the monumental past monumentally displayed, the landscape was a wonder. As a later traveler along the same stretch put it, "I gulped down color, like a donkey gorging on oats." Cleopatra introduced Caesar to the world's longest and most spectacular oasis, to the velvety green of the riverbanks, to the hard, black soil of the channel, to the land of red-purple sunsets and amethyst dawns. The two could not have neglected the obligatory stops: the pyramids, which soared above the palms to melt into the haze; the sanctuary and temples of Memphis, where Egypt's high priest would have been on hand to receive them; the three thousand chambers, above and below ground, of the granite and limestone labyrinth; the lakeside shrine of the crocodile gods, where the beasts had been trained to open their jaws on command, and where Caesar may have been as taken by the system of locks and dams, which had reclaimed farmland; the colossi of Memnon, miraculously white against the pale apricot sand, sixty-eight feet tall and visible for miles around. Up the hill behind them, deep in the rock, lay the tombs of the Valley of the Kings. Farther south came the handsome Temple of Isis, decorated and partly built by Cleopatra's father, set on an island among the tossing rapids at Philae.*

More miraculous yet were the accommodations, to which the taste for the colossal extended as well. The idea was to impress as much as to entertain. Cleopatra and Caesar would have left from Lake Mareotis, south of the city, where her pleasure fleet docked. That port could accommodate three-hundred-foot-long royal barges. Their bows were ivory; elaborate colonnades lined the deck, the column shafts of minutely carved cypress. Eighteen-foot gilded statues decorated stern and prow. The ship's hardware was polished bronze, its woodwork embedded with ivory and gold. All was brilliantly painted, including the shipboard col-

*The Sphinx was almost certainly invisible to Caesar and Cleopatra, buried still in sand, as it had been for nearly a thousand years.

lection of royal statuary, which decorated the two floors of living and entertaining quarters. A coffered ceiling covered one banqueting room. Egyptian-style columns decorated another, carved with acanthus leaves and lotus petals in an alternating black and white pattern. Over a third stretched a purple awning, held aloft by arched beams. It was not unusual for a royal barge to include a gym, a library, shrines to Dionysus and Aphrodite, a garden, a grotto, lecture halls, a spiral staircase, a copper bath, stables, an aquarium.

Theirs was no modest procession. A midlevel bureacrat traveled with an entourage of ten, lost as he was without his secretaries and accountants, his baker, his bath attendants, his doctor, his silver steward, his arms master. Cleopatra and Caesar headed south among a swarm of Roman soldiers and Egyptian courtiers. Hospitality during their stay was incumbent on the people and a daunting assignment, especially if, as Appian asserts, a fleet of four hundred ships followed behind. Certainly a multitude of smaller vessels followed their queen's, along a river thick with stone and wine carriers, merchant galleys, police skiffs. It was the people's responsibility to feed and cosset their monarch, to shower gifts upon her, to entertain her retinue, to arrange transportation. This raised all sorts of lodging, security, and provisioning concerns; officials were not above advising subordinates to hide supplies in order to prevent royal requisitioning. That was perfectly reasonable given the demands; one insignificant official called for 372 suckling pigs and 200 sheep. Farmers worked day and night to produce the necessary stores, to ferment beer, stockpile hay, furnish guesthouses, round up donkeys. They did so now in the thick of harvest season. With greater resources and under less complex circumstances, Cicero would be happy to bid Caesar good-bye when he entertained the general and his entourage two years later, at his country estate. He was relieved not to have to ask Caesar to drop by again when next in the neighborhood. "Once is enough," Cicero sighed, having felt less host than quartermaster.

Up the Nile Cleopatra and Caesar sailed in their "floating palace," the wind at their backs. On shore the date trees hung thick with fruit, the palm fronds slightly faded. Beyond the river lay a sea of golden grain; in the trees the bananas glinted yellow. The apricots, grapes, figs, and mulberries were nearly ripe. It was peach season; above their heads, the pigeons visibly paired off. Everything about the landscape before Caesar and Cleopatra reinforced the myths of Egypt's abundance and the river's magical faculties. Renowned throughout the ancient world, the Nile was said to flow with gold; extraordinary powers were ascribed to it. Its water was believed to boil at half the temperature of other waters. Its river creatures attained staggering proportions. Ptolemy II had sent his daughter cases of Nile water when she married into the Syrian royal family, to ensure her fertility. (She was already thirty. It worked.) Egyptian women were known for more efficient pregnancies; it took them less time to produce a baby. They were said as well to have an elevated rate of giving birth to twins, often quadruplets. Goats—which bore two kids elsewhere—were said to bear five in Egypt, pigeons to produce twelve broods rather than ten. The male skull was thought to be stronger in Egypt, where baldness (and comb-overs like Caesar's) were rare. The Nile was believed to have spontaneously generated life; one thing Cleopatra and Caesar did not see were the river creatures of legend, half-mice, half-dirt. Nor presumably did they find serpents with grass sprouting on their backs, or people who lived under turtle shells the size of boats. What they did make out among the tufted papyrus thickets and the lotus plants were herons and storks, hippopotami and eighteen-foot-long crocodiles, an inexhaustible supply of fish, a rarity in Rome. The ancient historians were mistaken about the primordial details, wholly accurate on the subject of Egypt's fecundity. Cleopatra's home was the most productive agricultural land in the Mediterranean, the one in which crops appeared to plant and water themselves.

That had been true since time immemorial, an expression that in Egypt actually meant something. Even in Cleopatra's day there was such a thing as ancient history; somehow the world was older then, thick with legend, swathed in superstition. At her side Caesar could have marveled at twenty-eight centuries of architecture. Already visitors had burgled—

and scrawled graffiti over—the tombs in the Valley of the Kings.*
Already by the spring of 47 one of the seven wonders of the world lay in
ruins. Cleopatra's country had been in the hospitality business long
before the rest of the world so much as suspected gracious living existed.
At the same time, the centuries felt closer than they do to us today. Alexander the Great was further from Cleopatra than 1776 is to our century,
yet Alexander remained always vividly, urgently present. While 1,120
years separated Cleopatra from the greatest story of her time, the fall of
Troy remained a steadfast point of reference. The past was at all times
within reach, a nearly religious awe aimed in its direction. This was
especially true in Egypt, which had a passion for history, and which for
two millennia already had kept a written record. For the bulk of those
years the insular, inaccessible country had changed little, its art barely at
all. There was good reason why Cleopatra's subjects viewed time as a
coil of endless repetitions. Recent events only reinforced that notion.
Ptolemaic advisers had persuaded earlier boy-kings to murder their
immediate families. Previous queens had fled Egypt to muster armies.
Much that could be said of the conquering Romans in 47 could have been
said three centuries earlier of Cleopatra's Macedonian ancestors, a parallel by no means lost on her.

In white linen and a diadem, Cleopatra took part throughout the trip
in religious rituals that were themselves thousands of years old. She
styled herself every bit the living divinity; we do not know how her people displayed their obeisance, but they likely bowed in her presence or
raised a hand in some form of salute. To those who lined up for a view,
on shore and along the causeways, Caesar and Cleopatra represented not
a romance but a sort of magical apparition from another world, the
earthly visitation of two living gods. They made for quite a sight: the
fair-haired, broad-shouldered Roman, a study in hollows and sinews, in
his long purple mantle, with the dark, small-boned queen of Egypt at his
side. Together they visited sacred sites, the monuments of ancient kings,

---

*The most common graffito: "I saw, and I was amazed."

the secondary palaces along the river. Together they were greeted by white-robed priests and cheering crowds. Together they sailed among farmsteads, across a landscape dotted with mud-brick towers and red terraced roofs, past luxuriant orchards and vineyards and golden fields, sphinxes half buried in sand, cliffs of rock-cut tombs. Together they battled the gnats, a seasonal gift of the low river. From a distance they announced themselves with a clatter of oars and the strumming of lyres. In their wake the bite of incense lingered in the sultry air.

Certainly the trip was a vacation compared to the weeks that had preceded it. That it was a debauched pleasure cruise, a lark, a honeymoon, was probably an idea generated by the lavish accommodations. A Roman needed look no further for depravity; by definition the Latin tongue encountered something rotten when it met the word "luxury," which derives from the verb "to dislocate," and which spent thousands of years conjoined with "lascivious." According to Appian, Caesar journeyed up the Nile with Cleopatra "and enjoyed himself with her in other ways as well." From there it was no great leap to the charge that Cleopatra had borne the Roman general off on this folly, one of her design, into the exotic heart of an exotic country, from which he had forcibly to be torn. Cleopatra — or Egypt — tended to have this effect on poor, vulnerable Romans. Her country was itself a tease and a temptation. The itinerary was presumably planned in advance and adhered to, but would not be remembered that way. By later accounts Caesar was reluctant to leave, Cleopatra reluctant to let him go. "She would have detained him even longer in Egypt or else would have set out with him at once for Rome," was Dio's take. Only against his will did Caesar's men coax him back. In Suetonius's version, Caesar has so lost his head over the Egyptian queen that he would have followed her to the Ethiopian frontier had his soldiers not threatened to mutiny. They got their way finally between the rugged cliffs south of modern-day Aswan, where the procession effected an unwieldy about-face.

Dio has Caesar waking slowly to the realization that a delay in Egypt "was neither creditable nor profitable to him" but omits any context for the lull on the river. Caesar had at the time no living children. Nor in the course of three marriages had he fathered a son. On that count Egypt upheld its legendary reputation. In swelling tribute to the fecundity of her land, the one in which flowers bloomed perpetually and wheat harvested itself, Cleopatra was that spring in her last months of pregnancy. She roundly confirmed the myth of the propagative powers of her magnificent country. The two spent somewhere between three and nine weeks on the river and turned back at the first cataract of the Nile. The current carried them gently back to the palace. From Alexandria Caesar set off for Armenia, then in a state of revolt. Late in June Cleopatra gave birth to a half-Roman child, divine on two counts, once as a Ptolemy, again as a Caesar. Here at last was something new under the sun.

THE GOLDEN AGE NEVER
WAS THE PRESENT AGE

Servant: "What excuses shall I make if I am away from the house for a long time?"
Andromache: "You will find no shortage of pretexts. After all, you are a woman."
— EURIPIDES

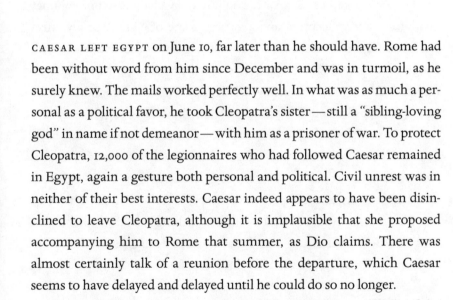

CAESAR LEFT EGYPT on June 10, far later than he should have. Rome had been without word from him since December and was in turmoil, as he surely knew. The mails worked perfectly well. In what was as much a personal as a political favor, he took Cleopatra's sister—still a "sibling-loving god" in name if not demeanor—with him as a prisoner of war. To protect Cleopatra, 12,000 of the legionnaires who had followed Caesar remained in Egypt, again a gesture both personal and political. Civil unrest was in neither of their best interests. Caesar indeed appears to have been disinclined to leave Cleopatra, although it is implausible that she proposed accompanying him to Rome that summer, as Dio claims. There was almost certainly talk of a reunion before the departure, which Caesar seems to have delayed and delayed until he could do so no longer.

Two weeks later Cleopatra went into labor. We know as little of the actual birth as we do of the intimacy that preceded it.* With or without a birthing stool, a team of midwives would have stood at the ready. One

---

*Like so much else in her life—the Nile cruise, the Roman stay, her good faith at Actium—the paternity of this child and the timing of his birth have been contested. His

received the child in a bundle of cloth, securely swaddling him. A second cut the umbilical cord with an obsidian blade. The newborn was to be amply filled with milk, to which end a royal wet nurse was engaged. The requirements for the job were no different from those for a sitter today: The nurse should be congenial and clean. She should "not be prone to anger, not talkative nor indifferent in the taking of food, but organized and sensible." Ideally, she should also be Greek, which was to say educated. Typically she was the lucky wife of a court official; hers was a well-remunerated, prestigious post, several years in duration. To it she brought generations' worth of wisdom. Teething trouble? The standard cure was to feed the child a fried mouse. Excessive crying? A paste of fly dirt and poppy could be counted on to silence the most miserable of infants.

Had she wanted to, Cleopatra could have availed herself of volumes of advice on contraception and abortion, some of it surprisingly effective. Nothing better revealed the conflicting tides of science and myth, enlightenment and ignorance, between which she lived than the literature on birth control. For each valid idea of Cleopatra's age there was an equally outlandish belief. Hippocrates' three-hundred-year-old recipe for inducing miscarriage—jump up and down, neatly touching your heels to your buttocks seven times—made some of the first-century measures look perfectly reasonable. A spider's egg, attached to the body with deer hide before sunrise, could prevent conception for twelve months. This was no stranger (or more effective) than attaching a cat liver to one's left foot, but then it was also asserted that a sneeze during sex worked wonders. In Cleopatra's day crocodile dung was famed for its contraceptive

---

appearance seemed too good and too opportune to be true. Otherwise the skeptics' case rests on Caesar's presumed infertility. Despite a vigorous sex life, he had sired no progeny in thirty-six years. As early as Suetonius the paternity issue was raised; there is a curious silence in the record where one might expect outrage, and, too, an absence of material evidence. That silence can be read equally as affirmation: the birth was so distasteful, the evidence that Cleopatra had hoodwinked Caesar so great, that it was wise to keep the matter quiet. Caesar certainly thought the child his, as did both Antony and Augustus.

powers, as was a concoction of mule's kidney and eunuch's urine. Generally the literature on abortifacients was more extensive than that on contraceptives; the time-tested ingredients for a morning-after pill were salt, mouse excrement, honey, and resin. Long after Cleopatra, it was asserted that the smell of a freshly extinguished lamp induced miscarriage. At the same time, some of the popular herbal remedies of Cleopatra's age proved effective. White poplar, juniper berries, and giant fennel have qualified contraceptive powers. Others — vinegar, alum, and olive oil — remained in use until recently. Early diaphragms existed, of wool moistened with honey and oil. All offered better results than the rhythm method, of dubious benefit to a people who believed that a woman was at her most fertile around the time of menstruation.

As it happened, nothing could better have suited twenty-two-year-old Cleopatra's political agenda than motherhood. And no single act could have secured her future better than bearing Julius Caesar's child. There were a few awkwardnesses, beginning with the fact that each of the new parents was married to someone else. (Technically speaking, Cleopatra had been both widowed and remarried in the course of the pregnancy.) From the Egyptian point of view, Caesar was an imperfect father on two counts: he was neither a Ptolemy nor royal. And from the Roman point of view, there was no advantage whatsoever in broadcasting his paternity, an embarrassment at best. From Cleopatra's perspective, no diplomatic measure could have been as effective as this entirely private one. She had been too preoccupied with her own survival to have given much thought to succession, but she could now expect to be spared the fate of Alexander the Great, who died without an heir. The splendid Ptolemaic dynasty would survive her. Moreover, the child was a boy. The Egyptians were willing to submit to a female pharaoh, but as Berenice IV's messy marital history made clear, a woman needed a male consort, if only as a ballerina does in a Balanchine *pas de deux,* as ornament rather than support. With Caesarion — or little Caesar, as the Alexandrians nicknamed Ptolemy XV Caesar — on her lap, Cleopatra had no difficulty ruling as a female king. Even before he began to babble, Caesarion accomplished a masterly feat. He rendered his feckless uncle wholly irrelevant. Whether Ptolemy XIV realized it or not, his older sister had gained control both of the imagery and the government.

Best of all, Cleopatra's timing was impeccable; she indeed seems to have had help—or great good luck—in producing children precisely when it was most advantageous to do so. Caesarion's birth coincided almost exactly with the early summer rise of the Nile, which psychologically, iconographically, and financially ushered in the season of plenty. Daily anticipation gave way to celebration as the Nile grew turbid and mossy green, then swelled steadily, from south to north. Basket after basket filled with grapes, figs, and melons. The honey flowed abundantly. Cleopatra celebrated the annual feast of Isis at this time, an important, ritual-heavy date on the Egyptian calendar. The tears of that all-powerful goddess were said to account for the rise of the river. Cleopatra's subjects offered her (compulsory) gifts on the holiday, a practice that set off a frenzied competition among her courtiers. Boats arrived at the palace from every corner of Egypt, loaded with fruits and flowers. Caesarion's birth drove home Cleopatra's association with Isis, but on that count Cleopatra took her cue from her most illustrious ancestors, who for 250 years had identified with that ancient goddess. In an age of general longing, she ranked as the greatest deity of the day. She enjoyed nearly unlimited powers: Isis had invented the alphabet (both Egyptian and Greek), separated earth from sky, set the sun and the moon on their way. Fiercely but compassionately, she plucked order from chaos. She was tender and comforting, also the mistress of war, thunderbolts, the sea. She cured the sick and raised the dead. She presided over love affairs, invented marriage, regulated pregnancies, inspired the love that binds children to parents, smiled on domestic life. She dispensed mercy, salvation, redemption. She is the consummate earth mother, also—like most mothers—something of a canny, omnicompetent, behind-the-scenes magician.

Isis appealed equally to both of Cleopatra's constituencies, offering as she did a versatile conflation of two cultures. In a land where many answered to different names in Greek and Egyptian, the goddess served as nation builder and religious icon. Demeter, Athena, Hera, and Aphrodite combined in her person. Her temples dotted Alexandria; her terra-cotta statuette graced most homes. A commanding woman with a distinctly sensual aura, she was a less comfortable presence abroad. Already that powerful enchantress had flustered the more martial Roman world, to which Alexandrian traders had exported her cult. Caesar had himself barred Isis priests from entering Rome. As early as 80 BC, an Isis temple had stood in that city, on the Capitoline Hill. It was destroyed and rebuilt, a history that repeated itself at regular intervals over the course of Cleopatra's lifetime. Such was the popularity of Isis that when the order to dismantle her temples was issued in 50, no workman would pick up an ax to do so. A consul was obliged to strip off his toga and minister the first blows himself.

It is difficult to determine which came first, whether Isis accounted for the supremacy of women in Egypt, or whether the Ptolemaic queens reinforced her eminence.* Certainly she introduced an equality of the sexes. In some accounts, Isis grants women the same strength as men. She was in any event a perfect boon to Cleopatra. To celebrate Caesarion's birth, the new mother ordered coins struck on which he is depicted as Horus, Isis's infant son. (The imagery was conveniently bilingual. It read just as easily as Aphrodite with Eros.) Future events would only reinforce Cleopatra's identification with Isis, into whose role she would step more fully and literally than had any previous Ptolemy. On ceremonial occasions she assumed her guise, appearing in a full, finely pleated linen mantle of iridescent stripes, fringed at the bottom, tightly wrapped from right hip to left shoulder and knotted between the breasts. Under it she wore a snug Greek sheath, or chiton. Corkscrew curls fell around her

---

*Sounding some familiar, inaccurate notes, a historian of Cleopatra's day credited Isis with Egypt's upside-down social hierarchy. In deference to her great wisdoms, claimed Diodorus, the Egyptians had ordained that "the queen should have greater power and honor than the king, and that among private persons the wife should enjoy authority over her husband, the husbands agreeing in the marriage contract that they will be obedient in all things to their wives."

neck. On her head she wore a diadem or, on religious occasions, a traditional pharaonic crown of feathers, solar disk, and cow's horns. Forty-
seven years later the protean Isis would cede her place to a very different
single mother, who appropriated her imagery wholesale.

Motherhood not only enhanced Cleopatra's authority—in her day the
Egyptian queen was more earth mother than femme fatale—but solidi-
fied her links with the native priests, to whom she granted significant
privileges. In this she continued the work of her father. Even while abroad
he had distinguished himself as a prolific builder of temples and had cultivated his relations with the Egyptian clergy. They were central to order
amid the native populace, also intimately engaged with matters of state.
As the temples stood at the center of both religious and commercial life,
there was an interpenetration of the Greek bureaucracy and the Egyptian
hierarchy. The minister of finance might equally supervise the feeding of
the sacred animals. The priest in charge of cult revenues for special occasions might double as a reed merchant. Those with weighty titles at the
Temple of Memphis held equally weighty titles in the world of commerce
and occupied privileged positions at Cleopatra's court. The relationship
was symbiotic: a god on earth, a pharaoh was as necessary to the priests
theologically as were the priests to Cleopatra economically and politically. Priests functioned as lawyers and notaries, the temples as manufac-
turing centers, cultural institutions, economic hubs. You might visit one
to work up a contract, or consult a doctor, or borrow a sack of grain. A
temple could grant refuge within its walls, a right Cleopatra extended in
46 to an Isis shrine, toward the end of her reign to a synagogue in the
southern delta. (It may have represented her half of a bargain. The Jews of
the region were fine soldiers; Cleopatra needed an army at the time.) In
principle, no one granted asylum could be driven or dragged away. It was
where you withdrew when you had had the temerity to organize a strike.
The temples lent money, even, on occasion, to Ptolemies.

It was as well the priests' responsibility to monitor every mood of the
Nile, with which Egypt's fortunes literally rose and fell. The river could
deliver bountiful riches or considerable disaster. A flood of twenty-four

feet induced delirium. Twenty-one feet brought good cheer. Eighteen feet—a season in which the blue-gray sludge clung to the riverbanks and sullenly refused to extend itself over the land—signaled a season of trouble. Such had been the case the previous year, when the Nile appeared to have been as out of joint as the times. As Cleopatra had observed on her clandestine trip to Alexandria, the flood of 48 was disastrous. In the end it measured only seven and a half feet, the lowest rise on record. (With the drought the Egyptian economy had ground to a halt, another reason anti-Roman recruits had been easy to come by that fall.) The river dictated intimate family relations as much as it did national policy. One son signed an agreement with his mother: he was to supply her with specific quantities of wheat, oil, and salt unless the river fell beneath a certain level, at which point she was to do his housekeeping. Many temples had Nilotic measuring columns, monitored secretly and obsessively by their priests. Daily they compared those figures to the previous year's. From them Cleopatra's officials could assess harvests and calculate taxes. Given the mania for measures and comparative data, it makes sense that geometry came of age in Egypt.

The fixation on past performances accounted for the embrace of history as well, although that discipline was less exact. Feeding the people was paramount, a mandate on which Cleopatra prided herself. She depicted herself as the Lady of Abundance for good reason; she stood between her subjects and hunger. Given the rigors of the system, they could manage no reserves. In a crisis Cleopatra had no choice but to authorize distributions from crown warehouses. "There was no famine during my reign" was a popular and gratifying phrase for a monarch to inscribe on his or her temples. Ancient propaganda served the same ends as its modern counterpart, however. There appears to have been little correlation between the alimentary reality and that sunny assertion, as often as not patently false.

BY THE MIDDLE of 47 Cleopatra was free of conspiring court officials and relieved of all antagonistic family members. Civil disturbance was at a minimum. She had her hands full all the same. "Anyone familiar with the wearying work required of kings by all those letters they must read or write would not bother even to pick up a diadem from the ground," an earlier Hellenistic monarch had groaned. And he had no experience of lush Ptolemaic bureaucracy, the natural fruit of an administration-proud, papyrus-rich culture with a planned and centralized economy and an unaccountable passion for records and censuses. The Greek historian Diodorus outlined another first-century sovereign's schedule, some version of which would have been Cleopatra's as well. After being awakened, she waded through sheafs of dispatches from every quarter. Her advisers briefed her on affairs of state. She corresponded with high priests and fellow sovereigns. If they were well, if their public and private affairs proceeded satisfactorily, then—went the formulaic greeting—she was well. She handed down decisions. She dictated memorandums to various scribes and signed off—sometimes with a single, powerful word meaning, "Let it be done"—on others. Only later was she bathed and dressed, perfumed and made up, after which she offered smoky sacrifices to the gods. At some appointed afternoon hour she received callers, on state, temple, and judicial business. Those audiences could be stultifying; they had lulled an earlier Ptolemy to sleep. Cleopatra's responsibilities very nearly rivaled those of Isis: She not only dispensed justice, commanded the army and navy, regulated the economy, negotiated with foreign powers, and presided over the temples, but determined the prices of raw materials and supervised the sowing schedules, the distribution of seed, the condition of Egypt's canals, the food supply. She was magistrate, high priest, queen, and goddess. She was also—on a day-to-day basis and far more frequently—chief executive officer. She headed both the secular and the religious bureaucracies. She was Egypt's merchant in chief. The crush of state business consumed most of her day. And as that early, weary Hellenistic monarch had acknowledged, absolute power consumes absolutely.

A vast, entrenched bureaucracy answered to Cleopatra. On the local level regional clerks and subclerks, village heads, scribes, tax collectors, and police did her bidding. On the national level a chief finance and interior minister, her *dioiketes,* oversaw the functioning of the state, with a horde of subordinates. Close at hand Cleopatra employed personal secretaries, writers of memorandums, an inner circle of advisers, foreign ministers, philosophers. Both Greeks and Greek-speaking Egyptians held those privileged positions, which came with resonant, familial-sounding titles: if you were particularly powerful, you figured among the Order of First Friends, or the Order of Successors. Some of those advisers Cleopatra had known and trusted since her childhood; she retained them from her father's regime. With several—the *dioiketes,* for example—she was in constant contact. She reviewed her secretary's official journal daily.

The administration made for a cumbersome, many-levered piece of machinery. It was founded on two assumptions. It was Cleopatra's role to tax the people, the people's role to fill her coffers. To that end her forebears had inserted controls into every level of every industry; a larger skein of governmental red tape was nowhere to be found. (Caesar could only have been astonished. Rome was at the time bureaucracy-free.) Cleopatra's harvests were the greatest in the Mediterranean world. With them she fed her people, and from them she derived her power. Her officials consequently monitored their every aspect. They distributed the seed. Its equivalent was to be returned at harvesttime. The farmer took a royal oath to do what he said he would do with his planting. You filled your ship only after swearing that you would deliver your goods "unadulterated and without delay." Under Cleopatra and as a consequence of the decades of unrest, shippers traveled with sealed samples, in the company of armed guards. A good-sized Ptolemaic vessel could carry three hundred tons of wheat down the river. At least two such ships made the trip daily—with wheat, barley, lentils—to feed Alexandria alone.

The same punctilious oversight extended to every corner of the economy. The Ptolemaic system has been compared to that of Soviet Russia; it stands among the most closely controlled economies in history. No matter who farmed it—Egyptian peasant, Greek settler, temple priest—most land was royal land. As such Cleopatra's functionaries determined and monitored its use. Only with government permission

could you fell a tree, breed pigs, turn your barley field into an olive garden. All was scrupulously designed for the sake of the record-keeping,
profit-surveying bureaucrat rather than for the convenience of the culti-
vator or the benefit of the crop. You faced prosecution (as did one overly
enterprising woman) if you planted palms without permission. The bee-
keeper could not move his hives from one administrative district to
another, as doing so confused the authorities. No one left his village during the agricultural season. Neither did his farm animals. All land was
surveyed, all livestock inventoried, the latter at the height of the flood
season, when it could not be hidden. Looms were checked to make sure
that none was idle and thread counts correct. It was illegal for a private
individual to own an oil press or anything resembling one. Officials
spent a great deal of time shutting down clandestine operations. (Temples alone were exempt from this rule for two months of every year, at
the end of which they, too, were shut down.) The brewer operated only
with a license and received his barley — from which he pledged to make
beer — from the state. Once he had sold his goods he submitted his profits to the crown, which deducted the costs of raw materials and rents
from his income. Cleopatra was thereby assured both of a market for her
barley and of profits on the brewer's sales. Her officials audited all revenues carefully, to verify that the mulberries and willows and acacia were
planted at the proper time, to survey the maintenance of every canal. In
the process, they were especially and frequently exhorted to disseminate
throughout Egypt the reassuring message that "nobody is allowed to do
what he wishes, but that everything is arranged for the best."

Unparalleled in its sophistication, the system was hugely effective
and, for Cleopatra, hugely lucrative. The greatest of Egypt's industries —
wheat, glass, papyrus, linen, oils, and unguents — essentially constituted
royal monopolies. On those commodities Cleopatra profited doubly. The
sale of oil to the crown was taxed at nearly 50 percent. Cleopatra then
resold the oil at a profit, in some cases as great as 300 percent. Cleopatra's
subjects paid a salt tax, a dike tax, a pasture tax; generally if an item could
be named, it was taxed. Owners of baths, which were private concerns,

owed the state a third of their revenue. Professional fishermen surrendered 25 percent of their catch, vintners 16 percent of their tonnage. Cleopatra operated several wool and textile factories of her own, with a staff of slave girls. She must have seemed divine in her omniscience. A Ptolemy "knew each day what each of his subjects was worth and what most of them were doing."

It was a system that called out for abuse, which call was answered. Ptolemaic fiscal policy occupied a vast hierarchy of people, from the *dioiketes* to managers and submanagers and treasurers and secretaries and accountants. Each stood as ready to arbitrate conflicts as to enrich himself. The opportunities for misconduct were boundless. Their traces survive the glories of Alexandria itself, glories the Ptolemaic machine made possible. Ultimately Cleopatra's officials produced as much resentment as they did graft. As they were themselves often farmers or industrialists, private and public business easily bled into each other. The interests of the general managers and the crown failed to coincide. Those of the government and its customs agents — ever poised to slap a duty on a pillow, a jar of honey, a goatskin bathing costume — never did. Officials at different levels disagreed. And in the thick of the overlapping, otiose bureaucracy, personal opportunities were rarely lost. As the Ptolemaic scholar Dorothy Thompson has pointed out, Cleopatra's family devoted a great deal of time to defining the good official. He should be vigilant, upright, a beacon of goodwill. He should steer clear of dubious company. He was to investigate all complaints, guard against extortion, and — in his tours of inspection — "cheer everybody up and to put them in better spirits." He was also largely a fiction. "We may conclude that it was almost impossible for our good official not to be bad," Thompson avers, upon a survey of the evidence. The temptation was too great, the pay low or nonexistent, the system too hidebound.*

---

*The one exception has been shown to have been the police. Though Greek at the higher level and Egyptian at the lower, they made for an egalitarian force, uncommonly efficient and responsive, on occasion even reprimanding officials. They took the law seriously. They also worked more or less autonomously, considerably relieving the Ptolemies of concerns with "stolen donkeys and assaults on grandmothers."

The list of abuses was impressive. Royal functionaries appropriated lands, requisitioned houses, pocketed monies, confiscated boats, ordered arbitrary arrests, levied illicit taxes. They devised sophisticated extortion rackets. They preyed equally on Greeks and on Egyptians, on temple officials and peasants. Cleopatra intervened regularly between her people and her overzealous officials; even the highest placed among them earned royal rebukes. At one juncture the chief embalmer of bulls complained of harassment. A delegation of farmers appeared before Cleopatra in the spring of 41 to protest a form of double taxation, from which she exempted them in future. Amid the massive flow of papyrus—of reports, petitions, instructions, commands—figured frequent protests and reprimands. Especially over the first years of Cleopatra's reign a volume of grievances poured in. Insubordination, incompetence, and dishonesty may have plagued her at home as well, among the palace doorkeepers, huntsmen, equerries, wine pourers, seamstresses, and servants of the bedchamber.

Even those complaints that did not make their way to Cleopatra in person appealed to her good intentions, her wisdom, her commitment to justice. Like Isis, she was seen as the beneficent guardian of her subjects, as much in her earthly role as in her divine one. Egyptians invoked her name aloud when they suffered indignities or when they sought redress. And though she had plenty of representatives—an official sorted through petitions—there was nothing to prevent an aggrieved party from approaching Cleopatra directly. They did so in droves. The wise queen granted a general amnesty before she moved about the country for audits or religious festivals; to fail to do so was to be greeted by a thousand plaintiffs. The operative philosophy seemed to be: when in doubt, write (or have the village scribe write) a petition. Every brand of misdemeanor and melodrama came Cleopatra's way. Cooks ran off. Workers organized strikes, dodged customs, delivered fraudulent goods. Guards went unpaid. Prostitutes spit on prospective clients. Women attacked the pregnant wives of their ex-husbands. Government officials stole pigs and seized dovecotes. Gangs assaulted tax collectors. Loans went bad. There were tomb robbers and irrigation problems and careless shepherds, doc-tored bills and wrongful arrests. Bath attendants routinely insulted patrons and made off with their clothing. The infirm father complained of his neglectful daughter. The licensed lentil seller—an honest tax-payer—bleated that the pumpkin roasters encroached on his market: they "come early in the morning, sit down near me and my lentils, and sell the pumpkin, giving me no chance of selling lentils." Surely he could prevail upon the authorities for additional time to pay his rent? So preva-lent were tax disputes that Ptolemy II had centuries earlier forbidden lawyers to represent clients in such cases. Exempt as they were from manual labor, must the temple keepers of sacred cats really assist with the harvest? They petitioned.

Cleopatra met regularly with another irritant. When a woman acci-dentally emptied her chamber pot on a passerby and in the ensuing wrangle tore his cloak to shreds and spat in his face, it was fair to assume that ethnic differences were at stake. The same was true when a bath attendant emptied a jug of hot water on a customer and, alleged the cus-tomer, "scalded my belly and my left thigh down to the knee, so that my life was in danger." In a country administered primarily by Greeks and worked primarily by Egyptians, resentment inevitably simmered below the surface. (The spitter and bath attendant were Egyptian, their victims Greek. Probably there were fewer than 500,000 Greeks in the country, the majority of them in Alexandria.) For all its frantic syncretism, for all of Alexandria's cosmopolitanism—to address an Alexandrian was to address an Ethiopian or a Scythian, a Libyan or a Cilician—two parallel cultures remained in place. Nowhere was that more pronounced than in the legal system. A contract in Greek was subject to Greek law, an Egyp-tian contract to Egyptian law. Similarly, an Egyptian woman enjoyed rights not available to her Greek counterpart, answerable always to her guardian. The regulations applied differently. An Egyptian who attempted to depart from Alexandria without a pass sacrificed one third of his property. The Greek who did so paid a fine. In certain ways the two cultures remained separate, just as certain habits—as Cleopatra and

Caesar were to discover—resisted transplant. A Greek cabbage inexplicably lost all flavor when grown in Egyptian soil.

The economy Auletes handed down to his daughter was moreover in tatters. "When we inherited the Republic from our forebears, it was like a beautiful painting whose colors were fading with age," Cicero had moaned a few years earlier. The same was only more true of Cleopatra's Egypt, its glory days firmly behind it. Auletes owed his unpopularity in large part to the onerous taxes he had levied to pay his Roman bill. Cleopatra settled the bill but was left with a depleted treasury. (When word of her father's death reached Rome, the first questions were: who rules Egypt now, and how do I get my money?) By one account Auletes had as well dissipated the family's accumulated fortune. How did Cleopatra fare? In economic affairs she took a determined hand, immediately devaluing the currency by a third. She issued no new gold coins and debased the silver, as her father had done shortly before his death. For the most part hers was a bronze age. She instituted large-scale production in that metal, which had been halted for some time. And she ushered in a great innovation: Cleopatra introduced coins of different denominations to Egypt. For the first time the markings determined the value of a coin. Regardless of its weight, it was to be accepted at face value, a great profit to her.

From there the juries divide as to Cleopatra's financial well-being. When called upon later to offer assistance to Rome, she did not reach deeply into her coffers, proof to some that she was financially constrained. She had a valid reason to prove less than forthcoming, however. She did not intend to comport herself as a Roman puppet. It was argued that Auletes did not have the money to raise a mercenary army in 58, when Cyprus cost him his throne. Somehow Cleopatra had the funds to do so a decade later, when she had been in power for only two years and her brother staged his coup. She stabilized the economy and set the country on a steady course. As the number of her later political suitors implies, she still had significant private treasure. Villages in Upper Egypt prospered. The arts flourished as well. Under Cleopatra the Alexandrians—

their cultural appetite newly whetted—turned out masterpieces of a quality and quantity that had not been seen for a century. The splendid alabaster carvings and gold-laced glass that survive her by no means suggest a bankrupt regime.

How wealthy was she? Into her coffers went approximately half of what Egypt produced. Her annual cash revenue was probably between 12,000 and 15,000 silver talents. That was an astronomical sum of money for any sovereign, in the words of one modern historian "the equivalent of all of the hedge fund managers of yesteryear rolled into one." (Inflation was an issue throughout the century, but it affected Cleopatra's silver less than her bronze currency.) The most lavish of lavish burials cost 1 talent, the prize a king tossed out at a palace drinking contest. A half-talent was a crushing fine to an Egyptian villager. A priest in Cleopatra's day—his post was a coveted one—made 15 talents yearly. That was a princely sum; it was the bail Ptolemy III had posted when he had "borrowed" the official versions of Aeschylus, Sophocles, and Euripides from Athens—and which he sacrificed when he opted not to return those priceless texts. Pirates set a staggering 20-talent ransom on the head of the young Julius Caesar, who, being Caesar, protested that he was worth at least 50. Given a choice between a 50-talent fine and prison, you opted for jail. You could build two impressive monuments for a much-loved mistress for 200 talents. Cleopatra's costs were high, her first years a trial given the uncooperative Nile. But by the most stringent of definitions—that of Rome's wealthiest citizen—she was fabulously well-off. Crassus claimed that no one was truly rich if he could not afford to maintain an army.*

On the level of internal affairs Cleopatra managed uncommonly well. Evidently she handled the flood of petitions effectively. She enjoyed the support of the people. Her reign is notable for the absence of revolts in

---

*On one contemporary list Cleopatra appears as the twenty-second richest person in history, well behind John D. Rockefeller and Tsar Nicholas II, but ahead of Napoleon and J. P. Morgan. She is assigned a net worth of $95.8 billion, or more than three Queen Elizabeth IIs. It is of course impossible accurately to convert currencies across eras.

Upper Egypt, suddenly quiet as it had not been for a century and a half. By the summer of 46, she had reason to believe her kingdom on an even keel, its productivity assured. The Nile rose steadily. She began to issue instructions to trusted chamberlains, to navy officials, to her son's nurses. They assembled a collection of towels, tableware, kitchen utensils, lamps, sheets, rugs, and cushions. With one-year-old Caesarion and a large retinue, Cleopatra prepared to sail to Rome. She took with her secretaries, copyists, messengers, bodyguards, and her brother-husband as well; a wise Ptolemy did not leave a blood relative behind. Whether she traveled for reasons of state or affairs of the heart—or to introduce Caesar to the infant son he had not yet met—is unclear. She may have been waiting for word from Caesar, who had been away from Rome for nearly three years. His return from North Africa, where he brilliantly defeated Pompey's remaining supporters, coincides neatly with Cleopatra's arrival. Two things are abundantly clear. She could not have left Egypt were she not firmly in control of the country. And she would not have dared to set foot in Rome had Julius Caesar not wanted her there.

CLEOPATRA WOULD NOT have undertaken her first trip across the Mediterranean lightly. The voyage was risky at the best of times; on a similar crossing, Herod would be shipwrecked. Josephus, the Jewish-Roman historian who wrote so venomously of Cleopatra, spent a night some years later swimming in the Mediterranean. We have hints that Cleopatra was a nervous sailor. She traveled too both as an institution and an individual, with physicians and philosophers, eunuchs, advisers, seamstresses, cooks, and with a full staff for Caesarion. With her went sumptuous gifts: jars of Nile water, shimmering fabrics, cinnamon, tapestries, alabaster pots of fragrance, gold beakers, mosaics, leopards. She had an image to uphold and every reason to advertise Egypt's wealth. That fall a giraffe made its first appearance in Rome, to electrifying effect. It may well have sailed north with Cleopatra. (The description-defying creature was "like a camel in all respects"—except for its spots, its soaring height, its legs, and its neck.) Presumably Cleopatra made the crossing in a naval galley, most likely a slender, square-rigged, 120-foot trireme, of which there were many in her fleet. A galley was a swift ship, with a crew of about 170 rowers and room for a small group of passengers in the stern. The retinue and gifts followed behind.

However she billed the crossing at home it was by no means a pleasure trip. A Hellenistic monarch ventured abroad with a purpose rather than on a whim.* Nor did Cleopatra slip out of the city quietly, as her father had done. The assembled flotilla made for an extraordinary sight, one that had not greeted Alexandria for at least a generation. There was nothing remotely discreet or economical about it. Crowds gathered on shore to admire the spectacle and to send off their queen, with music and with cheers, amid spicy-sweet clouds of frankincense. Aboard ship she would have heard the commotion until those faces, the spindly palms, the rocky coast, the colossi, the gold roof of the Serapeum, and finally the lighthouse itself faded from view. It is unlikely that Cleopatra had ever before seen that limestone tower with its reflective mirrors from the windward side. Only after a good four hours at sea did the massive statue of Poseidon at its top dissolve completely in the silvery haze.

Before her lay a trip of two thousand miles. At best she could expect to be at sea for a good month. At worst the passage was closer to ten weeks. Rome lay directly northwest of Alexandria, which invited a continual struggle against the prevailing wind. Rather than venturing across the Mediterranean, a naval galley sailed east and north before heading west. It put into port nightly. Space for provisions was limited, and the crew could neither sleep nor eat aboard ship. Villages received advance word of a fleet's arrival; their inhabitants turned out in crowds at the harbor, with water and foodstuffs. In this arduous way Cleopatra journeyed up the coast of the eastern Mediterranean, along the southern shore of Asia Minor, north of Rhodes and Crete, across the Ionian Sea. Beyond Sicily a horizon spread itself out and became the Italian peninsula. She likely traced its western coast, up the gentle Tyrrhenian Sea,

*The good king was advised to stay home. The poor resented his absence, while—obliged to accompany him—the rich felt forced into exile.

gliding along a wild shoreline newly dotted with opulent stone villas. Over the next decade those terraced estates would multiply with such speed that it would be said that the fish felt cramped. Beyond Pompeii she would have enjoyed a view of the bustling port and fine harbor of Puteoli (modern Pozzuoli), where the massive Egyptian grain ships docked. In the harbor she made smoky offerings to the gods, in gratitude for her safe arrival; if Isis was not carved into the prow of Cleopatra's ship, the goddess of navigation stood somewhere on deck. A gangplank ultimately delivered Cleopatra to Europe. From Puteoli she made the three-day trek overland to Rome, by cushioned litter or carriage, along sand and gravel roads, a rough, dusty drive under intense heat. It was in Cleopatra's case also a conspicuous one. A Roman official on a tour of inspection in Asia Minor traveled with "two chariots, a carriage, a litter, horses, numerous slaves, and, besides, a monkey on a little car, and a number of wild asses." And he was an unknown. In the East, baggage trains of two hundred wagons and several thousand courtiers were not unheard of.

At the outskirts of Rome a fragrant dusting of cassis, myrrh, and cinnamon hung in the air. Modest tombs and colossal mausoleums lined both sides of the road, as did shrines to Mercury, the patron saint of travelers. If they had not done so already, Caesar's representatives met Cleopatra outside the city walls and directed her, across a wooden bridge, to his large country estate, on the west bank of the Tiber. With assistance, Cleopatra settled on the southeastern part of the Janiculum Hill, a fine address if by no means as prestigious as those across town, on the opposite hill. In Caesar's villa she found herself surrounded by an extensive collection of painting and sculpture, a colonnaded court, and a mile-long, lushly planted garden, lavish by Roman standards, which to an Egyptian queen was fairly meaningless. By contrast she enjoyed a clear view of the city below. Through the pines and cypresses Cleopatra looked out over the yellowish Tiber to the outlying hills and the red-tile rooftops of Rome, a metropolis that consisted for the most part of a jumble of twisting lanes and densely packed tenements. Rome had recently overtaken Alexandria in population; in 46 it was home to nearly 1 million people. On all other levels it qualified as a provincial backwater. It was still the kind of place where a stray dog might deposit a human hand under the breakfast table, where an ox could burst into the dining room. As displacements went, this one was akin to sailing from the court of Versailles to eighteenth-century Philadelphia. In Alexandria, the glorious past was very much in evidence. Rome's glorious future was from Cleopatra's quarters nowhere visible. It was just still possible to mistake which was the Old World and which the New.

There is every indication that Cleopatra kept a low profile, or as low as she could keep under her unusual circumstances: "For she had come to the city with her husband and settled in Caesar's own house, so that he too derived an ill reputation on account of both of them," chides Dio. As everyone knew, Caesar lived in the center of town, near the Forum, with his wife, Calpurnia. Cleopatra's influence and that of her country were all the same much felt, directly and indirectly. On his return Caesar had begun to institute a number of reforms drawn from his Egyptian stay, during which he had evidently studied innovation as attentively as tradition. Most conspicuously, he went to work on the Roman calendar, which by 46 had crept three months ahead of the season. For some time a Roman year had consisted of 355 days, to which the authorities added an extra month irregularly, when doing so suited their purposes. As Plutarch has it, "Only the priests could say the time, and they, at their pleasure, without giving any notice, slipped in the intercalary month." The result was a thorough mess; at one juncture, Cicero did not know what year he was living in. Caesar adopted the Egyptian calendar of twelve thirty-day months, with an additional five-day period at the end of the year, subsequently deemed "the only intelligent calendar which ever existed in human history." He adopted as well the twelve-hour division between night and day that he had known in Alexandria. Generally speaking, time was a vaguer, more elastic notion in Rome, where it was subject to perpetual debate.* Cleopatra's astronomers and mathematicians assisted in Caesar's planning. The result was a bold correction in 46, "the last year of muddled reckoning" and one of 445 days, the extra weeks inserted between November and December.

The Egyptian episode had exerted a profound influence on Caesar; the only question in the eighteen months to come would be to what degree it had done so. His admiration for Cleopatra's kingdom can be read plainly in his reforms. He laid the foundations for a public library, to make the works of Greek and Latin literature widely available. He engaged an eminent scholar—he counted among those Caesar had spared in battle not once but twice—to assemble that collection. The Alexandrian obsession with accounting proved contagious: Caesar commissioned an official census. (It would reveal that his rivalry with Pompey had ravaged the city. The civil war had substantially thinned Rome's population.) The sophisticated locks and dikes of Egypt left an impression; Caesar proposed draining the unhealthy marshes in central Italy, so as to reclaim prime farmland. Why not engineer a canal from the Adriatic to the Tiber, to facilitate trade? Caesar planned to reengineer the harbor at Ostia, still a minor port, obstructed by rocks and shoals. An Alexandrian-style causeway would open the town to great fleets. He extended citizenship to anyone in Rome who taught the liberal arts or who practiced medicine, "to make them more desirous of living in the city and to induce others to resort to it." He suggested stripping the city of some of its lesser sculpture, which after Alexandria looked decidedly shabby; it was difficult for anyone to come into contact with Ptolemaic Egypt and not contract a case of extravagance. Like Cleopatra herself, not all of Caesar's imports were welcome or entirely logical. Just after her arrival, he recognized the cult of Dionysus, a Greek of even more dubious heritage and questionable habits than the exceedingly rich Egyptian queen. On nearly every front Caesar demonstrated prodigious activity, the maniacal capacity for work that had for years distinguished him from his rivals.

*As Seneca observed: "Easier for two philosophers to agree than two clocks."

Nowhere was the Eastern influence so profoundly felt as in the triumphs Caesar celebrated at the end of September. A Roman general knew no greater glory than those elaborate, self-aggrandizing entertainments. And Caesar had particular reason to take his to new heights. Rome had long been fitful, unsettled by a protracted war and his extended absence. What better way to tame it than with an unprecedented eleven days of public festivities? At such times a general became an impresario; in celebrating his conquests of Gaul, Alexandria, Pontus, Africa, and Spain, Caesar outdid himself, consciously or not vying with the kind of staging he had witnessed in Alexandria. After massive preparations and several disappointing delays, the celebrations began on September 21, 46. They lasted through the first days of October. Rome filled with raucous spectators, only a fraction of whom could be accommodated. Many pitched tents in the city streets and along the roads. In throngs they flocked to the feasts, the parades, and the entertainments; some were trampled to death in the pandemonium. Temples and streets were decorated, temporary stadiums constructed, racecourses expanded. Glory had long been the currency of Rome, but it had never before been a city in which forty elephants bearing lit torches in their trunks escorted a general home at the end of a day's festivities, a parade of revelers and musicians trailing behind. Nor had Rome ever seen banquets of delicacies and fine wines for 66,000 people.

Cleopatra may have already been installed in Caesar's villa by late summer, when he celebrated his Egyptian triumph. Trumpets heralded his approach that morning; in his purple tunic, a wreath of laurels on his bald head, he rode through the city gates in a chariot drawn by four white horses. The crowd greeted him with rose petals and applause. His exultant men marched beside him in metal-plated tunics, chanting both victory odes and obscenities about the romantic conquests abroad. In their raillery Cleopatra's name figured as a punch line, a charge that Caesar in no way denied. By tradition, the procession included the spoils of the campaign and representations of the vanquished; from the Campus Martius in the north to the Via Sacra, through the Circus Maximus and up the

Capitoline Hill, rode effigies of Achillas and Pothinus, along with outsize paintings of the Nile and a model of the lighthouse of Alexandria. The crowds roared with approval. The Egyptian float was itself plated with glossy tortoiseshell, a material new to Rome and one that supported Caesar's boasts about the riches he had acquired abroad. Each of the triumphs included feasts and public performances; athletic contests, stage plays, horse races, musical competitions, displays of wild animals, circus feats, and gladiatorial fights took place all over the city. For three weeks Rome was a thief's paradise, as houses emptied for the spectacle. After the Egyptian triumph came a mock sea battle, for which an artificial lake was engineered. That match featured four thousand rowers and some of the defeated Egyptian ships, which Suetonius would have us believe Caesar towed across the Mediterranean for the occasion.

Certainly Cleopatra did not need to be on hand when Caesar assured the people of the bounties on which Rome might draw abroad, as good an explanation as any for his Egyptian interlude. They exulted in his largesse, which was properly hers. Caesar's soldiers and officers made out handsomely. On every citizen Caesar also bestowed 400 sesterces—the equivalent of more than three months' wages—along with gifts of wheat and olive oil. It is even less likely that Cleopatra would have wished to have been on hand for the Egyptian triumph, a reminder that she was not the only Ptolemaic woman in Rome. Each of the processions ended with a multitude of human captives. (So crucial were they that at an earlier triumph Pompey had appropriated prisoners that did not belong to him. Their number quantified a general's success.) The more exotic the prisoner the better; Caesar's African procession—the last of the performances of 46—included the five-year-old African prince who, in an odd twist of events, was to marry Cleopatra's daughter.* In his Egyptian procession Caesar included another novelty, though one to which the Romans did not

---

*Plutarch deemed the future King Juba "the most fortunate captive ever taken," as fate transported him from his "barbarian" land to Rome, where he was educated. He emerged as an eminent historian who wrote on a variety of subjects, from Roman antiquity to mythology to the behavior of elephants.

thrill as they did to the miniature African prince or the exotic "cameleop-ard." Wrapped in golden shackles, Cleopatra's teenaged sister, Arsinoe, rode through the streets. Behind her followed the spoils and the prisoners of the Egyptian campaign. Intended to impress, this unusual piece of booty instead disturbed the crowd. Arsinoe proved too much for her audi-ence, unaccustomed, Dio tells us, to the sight of "a woman and once con-sidered a queen, in chains—a spectacle which had never yet been seen, at least in Rome." Awe curdled to compassion. Tears sprang to eyes. Arsinoe drove home the human cost of the war, which had affected nearly every family. Even if Cleopatra remained pitiless on her sister's account, even if she preferred to read Caesar's victory as one over a previous administra-tion, she had little to gain from this brutal reminder of Egypt's subjuga-tion. She had narrowly escaped the same disgrace.

As it happened, glamorous guests were as problematic as glamorous prisoners. It is difficult to say which Ptolemy ultimately caused the Romans the greater discomfort: the royal prisoner whom Caesar degraded in the streets, or the foreign queen with whom he consorted at his villa. Soon enough Arsinoe would be banished, dispatched across the Aegean to the Temple of Artemis at Ephesus, a gleaming, white marble wonder of the world. Her older sister spent the winter on the less fash-ionable side of the Tiber. She was without word from Alexandria, as the sailing season was over, to reopen only in March. She would be for some time too without Caesar, who left Rome abruptly, early in November. He was off to Spain, for a final campaign against the Pompeians. Cleopa-tra had known difficult postings before—the desert of the western Sinai comes most readily to mind—but for all the beauty of the Janiculum villa and its panoramic view, this one was less than comfortable. Her welcome was not universally cordial. Rome was chilly, and wet. Latin did not come easily to a Greek speaker; Cleopatra was at a linguistic dis-advantage. And in a city where women enjoyed the same legal rights as infants or chickens, the posting called upon a whole new set of skills. For good reason 46 may have felt to Cleopatra like the longest year in his-tory, as—on account of the attenuated calendar—indeed it was.

CLEOPATRA HAD IN Rome the problem of any celebrity abroad: she knew few people, but everyone knew her. Her presence loomed large, only partly on account of Calpurnia, no stranger to such affronts. Caesar had married his third wife in 59 and spent the intervening years delivering up infidelities, from across town as ably as from abroad. He was himself never above suspicion. He had slept with most of his colleagues' wives, in one case with both a very beautiful mother and her young daughter, whom he had the good taste to seduce sequentially. Between his departure from Alexandria and the return to Rome he had found time even for a dalliance with the wife of the king of Mauretania, an affair to which some—in a swoon of romantic logic—have ascribed Cleopatra's visit. To compete with a wife was one thing. To compete with another Eastern sovereign, even one of lesser import, quite another. (This puts a more emotional spin on the matter than either the era or the evidence allows.) More problematic was Caesar's marked affection for a woman who stood so far outside of, and on many fronts in opposition to, the mores of Rome.

While little about Cleopatra evoked affection abroad, all elicited curiosity. This would have imposed certain restrictions on her movements. It is difficult to believe she appeared often in unmannerly Rome. More likely Caesar visited her in his villa, which he could not have done discreetly. Ptolemies had been Roman houseguests before—Auletes had lodged with Pompey—but the relationship was dissimilar. It was next to impossible for either Caesar or Cleopatra to have done anything secretly; a curtained litter hurtled through the streets by a team of burly Syrians tended to attract attention. (Auletes had traveled about on the shoulders of eight men and with an escort of a hundred swordsmen. There is little reason to believe that his daughter interpreted pomp differently. Certainly she moved about Rome only with bodyguards, advisers, and attendants.) A great man did not travel without his scarlet cloak and retinue; by late 45, Caesar had moreover taken to parading about in red calf-high boots. And by all accounts Rome was a city in which the stones themselves seemed to talk. As Juvenal reminds us, a wealthy Roman deluded himself if he believed in secrets. "Even if his slaves keep quiet, his horses will talk and so will his dog and his doorposts and his marble floors." You could take every possible precaution: "All the same, what the master does at the second cock-crow will be known to the nearest shopkeeper before dawn, along with all the fictions of the pastry cook, the head chefs, and the carvers." Fortunately Cleopatra had little reason to cover her tracks. Nighttime escapades in canvas bags figured nowhere on her agenda.

Caesar made at least one very public attempt to integrate the queen of Egypt into Roman life. In September he dedicated an ornate temple in his Forum to Venus Genetrix, the goddess from whom he claimed descent and to whom he ascribed his victories, as well as the divine mother of the Roman people. Caesar was said to be "absolutely devoted" to Venus, eager to persuade his colleagues "that he had received from her a kind of bloom of youth," no doubt all the more so as his cheeks hollowed, the skin pouched under his eyes, and his hairline vanished entirely. In his favorite temple, at what was essentially his business address, he installed a gold, life-size statue of Cleopatra beside Venus. It was a signal honor, the more so as Caesar had not yet erected a statue of himself. The tribute made some sense; to the Roman mind, Isis and Venus were, in their maternal roles, closely allied. As homages went, it was also excessive and perplexing, an unprecedented step beyond what was required of Caesar if Cleopatra had come, as Dio maintains, for official recognition "among the friends and allies of the Roman people." That diplomatic formula mattered—it had been worth its weight in Auletes' gold—but had not previously entailed costly statues of foreign monarchs at sacred addresses in the heart of Rome. It struck an odd chord in a city where humans did not traditionally mingle among cult images.

Cleopatra may or may not have fully grasped the irregularity of Caesar's tribute; gold statues were not new to her. She would in his villa have acutely felt the oddities of the situation. The very palette of Rome was different. She was accustomed to ocean views, invigorating sea breezes, to sparkling white walls and a cloudless Alexandrian sky. There was no glinting turquoise Mediterranean out her window, no purple light at the end of the day. Nor was there any rapturous architecture. Rome was monochromatic next to the blaze of color to which Cleopatra was accustomed. All was wood and plaster. Music pervaded every aspect of Alexandrian life, where the flutes and lyres, rattles and drums, were everywhere. Only reluctantly did the Romans admit such frivolities to their culture. One apologized for one's ability to dance or play the flute well. "No one dances while he is sober," offered Cicero, the greatest of Roman killjoys, "unless he happens to be a lunatic."*

If she spent any time in the thick of the city, Cleopatra found herself amid a gloomy welter of crooked, congested streets, with no main avenue and no central plan, among muddy pigs and soup vendors and artisans' shops that tumbled out onto footways. By every measure a less salubrious city than Alexandria, Rome was squalid and shapeless, an oriental tangle of narrow, poorly ventilated streets and ceaseless, shutter-creaking commotion, perpetually in shadow, stiflingly hot in summer. Isolated though Cleopatra was on her wooded hill, there were advantages too in Caesar's address. She was at a remove from the incessant hawking and haggling, the pounding of blacksmiths and the hammering of stonemasons, the rattling of chains and squeaking of hoists below. Rome was a city of nonstop construction, as homes collapsed or were torn down regularly. To ease the racket Caesar had curtailed daytime traffic in the streets, with the predictable result: "You have to be a very rich man to get sleep in Rome," asserted Juvenal, who cursed the evening stampede, and felt he risked his life each time he set foot outside. To be trampled by litters or splattered with mud constituted peripheral dangers. Pedestrians routinely crumpled into hidden hollows. Every window represented a potential assault. Given the frequency with which pots propelled themselves from ledges, the smart man, warned Juvenal,

*Some took Cicero's distaste further. If a man was an excellent piper, it followed that he was a worthless man. "Otherwise he wouldn't be so good a piper," notes Plutarch, quoting approvingly. The axiom did not work to the advantage of Cleopatra's father. Despite ample evidence to the contrary, he would be written off as "not a real man, but a pipe-player and a charlatan."

went to dinner only after having made his will. Cleopatra had any number of reasons to yearn for what a Latin poet would later term her "superficially civilized country."

At the time of her visit Rome had only just discovered urban design, another Eastern import. You would search in vain for the famous landmarks; the Coliseum, "the last word in amphitheatres," had not yet been built. Nor were the Pantheon or the Baths of Caracalla. Pompey's theater had been Rome's only structure of distinction; it had inspired Caesar's Forum, which now eclipsed it. Rome remained provincial, but increasingly aware of itself as such. Greece continued to spell culture, elegance, art. If you wanted a secretary, a doctor, an animal trainer, a craftsman, you wanted a Greek. And if you wanted a bookstore, you dearly hoped to find yourself in Alexandria. It was difficult to get a decent copy of anything in Rome, which nursed a healthy inferiority complex as a result. It manifested itself the time-honored way: The Roman waxed superior. His was hardly the first civilization merrily to impugn the one it aspired to be. So the pyramids—marvels of engineering and of ancient exactitude, constructed with primitive tools and equally primitive arithmetic—could be reduced to "idle and foolish ostentations of royal wealth." Gulping down his envy with a bracing chaser of contempt, a Roman in Egypt found himself less awed than offended. He wrote off extravagance as detrimental to body and mind, sounding like no one so much as Mark Twain resisting the siren call of Europe. Staring an advanced civilization straight in the face, the Roman reduced it either to barbarism or decadence. He took refuge in the hard edges and right angles of his own language, even while—sniffing and scorning—he acknowledged it to be inferior to the sinuous, supple, all-accommodating Greek tongue. Latin kept its speaker on the straight and narrow. Regrettably, there was no word in that language for "not possessing." But neither, blessedly, was there a Latin term for "gold-inlay utensils" or "engraved glasses from the warm Nile."

With Caesar's overseas campaigns, with Rome's rising might and fortune, the splendors of the Greek world began to penetrate the Italian peninsula. It would be difficult to overstate the ramifications of those imports for Cleopatra. Pompey had only just introduced ebony to Rome. Myrrh and cinnamon, ginger and pepper, were newly arrived. For the first time, decorative pillars graced the entries of private homes. Only one house in Rome sported marble-paneled walls, although in a few years that home would be rivaled by a hundred others. The culinary arts flourished, as turbot, stork, and peacock found their place on tables. During Cleopatra's stay the relative virtues of mantis prawns versus African snails were vigorously debated. Hers was a Rome in transition; there were both luxurious entertainments and those who stole the fine linen napkins. Latin literature was in its infancy and Greek literature soon to be discounted, written off—the metaphor was apt—as a beautiful vase full of poisonous snakes. The beauty of a toga—that plain, natural wool garment, as uncomfortable as it was impractical—was, like the Latin language itself, in the constraints. At his entertainments Caesar arranged for silk awnings, to shade the spectators along the Via Sacra and up the Capitoline Hill. As Alexandrian imports, those awnings automatically qualified as "a barbarian luxury."

With the nouveau riche embrace of the East came those who parsed each import and read in it the end of civilization, the road to degeneracy. To that end Caesar reenacted the city's long-neglected sumptuary laws, designed to curb private expenditures. He was strict on this count as only a lover of magnificence—as the first host in history to offer his guests a selection of four fine wines—can be. He dispatched agents to confiscate delicacies in the market, to confiscate ornate tableware, mid-meal, in private homes. With few exceptions, he prohibited litters, scarlet garments, pearls. To anyone accustomed to Alexandria, the fashion capital of the world, the idea that Caesar's Rome needed sumptuary laws was laughable. A woman who knew when it was time to downgrade her dinnerware could be trusted to dress appropriately, however; Cleopatra may have toned down the wardrobe. A Roman matron wore white, where the Alexandrian woman relished color. And a woman who could calibrate her humor for different audiences knew better than to scorn a dinner that in no way rivaled her fare at home. As has been observed over the millennia, luxury is more easily denounced than denied; Caesar's edict was more popular with some than others. It won few points from Cicero, who weaned himself with difficulty that winter from peacock, giant oysters, and saltwater eel. (Peacock meat was notoriously tough, but that was not the point.) Oysters and eels, Cicero moaned, had never offended his digestive system as did turnips.

What Cleopatra thought of the puritans—real and purported—among whom she found herself we do not know. We know well what they thought of her. Marriage, and women, were done differently in Rome, where female authority was a meaningless concept. (Similarly, for a man to be called effeminate was the worst insult.) The Roman definition of a good woman was an inconspicuous woman, something that defied Cleopatra's training. In Alexandria she needed to make a spectacle of herself. Here the mandate was reversed. Not only was a Roman woman without political or legal rights, but she was without a personal name; she carried only the one derived from her father. Caesar had two sisters, both named Julia. Roman women cast their eyes down in public, where they were silent and recessive. They did not issue the dinner invitations. They were invisible in intellectual life, represented less often in art than they were in Egypt, where female workers and female pharaohs appear in painting and sculpture, in tomb scenes and on chapel walls, trapping birds, selling goods, or making offerings to the gods.

For a foreign sovereign the rules—like the sumptuary laws—did not entirely apply, but Cleopatra could not have felt at her ease.* As always, what kept women pure was the drudge's life. (Juvenal supplied the traditional formula: "Hard work, short sleep, hands chafed and hardened" from housework.) As a marriage crasher who had somehow hustled

---

*The prevailing ethos is preserved in the literature. In the *Iliad,* women are the most perfect things in creation. They are also, as has been observed, as a general rule "teasing, scolding, thwarting, contradicting, and hoodwinking." In the Greek plays, women have the key parts. There are few outsize female heroines in Roman literature, in which wives come in two varieties: the tyrannical rich and the spendthrift poor. Roman literature is notably short as well on deceived husbands, a comic staple from Aristophanes to Molière.

herself into Venus's exalted company, Cleopatra unsettled Rome on any number of counts: she was female and foreign, an Eastern monarch in what still believed itself to be a king-crushing republic, a stand-in for Isis, whose cult was suspect and subversive and whose temples were notorious spots for assignations. Cleopatra confused the categories and flouted convention. Even by modern standards, she posed problems of protocol. If she was the mistress of a Roman dictator, was she mistress of the Roman world as well? No matter how she comported herself—at all times she seems to have been as deft with her image as her person—she broke every rule in the book. A queen at home, she was a courtesan out of her country. And she was something more dangerous still: a courtesan with means. Cleopatra was not merely economically independent, but richer than any man in Rome.

Her very wealth—the same wealth that had fed Rome during the triumphs—impugned her morals. To wax eloquent on someone's embossed silver, his sumptuous carpets, his marble statuary, was to indict him. The implications were greater for the lesser sex. "There's nothing a woman doesn't allow herself, nothing she considers disgusting, once she has put an emerald choker around her neck and has fastened giant pearls to her elongated ears," went the logic. In that respect the length of her ears would do more to seal Cleopatra's fate than that of her nose.* Even assuming she had left her best jewelry in Alexandria, she was synonymous in Rome with the "reckless extravagance" of that world. It was no less than her birthright. (A proper Roman woman considered her children her jewels.) By Roman standards, even Cleopatra's eunuchs were rich. This meant that every unpardonable evil in the profligacy family attached itself to her. Well before she became the sorceress of legend—a reckless, careless destroyer of men—she was suspect as an extravagant Easterner, a reckless, careless destroyer of wealth. If moral turpitude began with shellfish and metastasized into purple and scarlet robes, it found its ostentatious apogee in pearls, which topped the extravagance scale in Rome. Suetonius invoked

---

*As Blaise Pascal asserted in the seventeenth century: "Had Cleopatra's nose been shorter, the whole face of the world would have been changed."

them to prove Caesar's weakness for luxury. The story of the libertine who sacrificed a pearl to make his point was an oft-told tale, on the books long before 46 and fated to stay there, to indict others, long after. It seemed, however, tailor-made for an audacious Egyptian queen. (There are signs of confabulation as well as conflation here. Within a matter of years, Cleopatra was said to have worn "the two pearls that were the largest in the whole of history." Pliny assigned each a value of 420 talents, which meant Cleopatra dangled the equivalent of a Mediterranean villa from each ear. The sum was the same that she had contributed to the burial of the Memphis bull.) Who else could have been so frivolous, so wanton, so ready to enchant a man that she would pluck a pearl from her lobe, dissolve it in vinegar, and swallow it, to beguile a man with magic and excess?* Such was the story that would circulate later about Cleopatra.

Neither the magic nor the excess was likely to have been much on display over the winter of 46. Cleopatra clearly frequented some fashionable addresses, though it was difficult to believe she was not often at home in Caesar's villa, surrounded solely by her advisers and retainers. Some of those courtiers knew their way around Rome, having lobbied for her father's notorious restoration. She lived these months in Latin; whatever her proficiency in that language, she discovered that certain concepts did not translate. Even the sense of humor was different, broad and salty in Rome where it was ironic and allusive in Alexandria. Literal-minded, the Romans took themselves seriously. Alexandrian irreverence and exuberance were in scant supply.

---

*Many have marveled at the tale, but only one man has sacrificed Tiffany pearls to a laboratory investigation of it. Does a pearl actually disintegrate in vinegar? Yes, if very slowly, reported B. L. Ullman, who in the end resorted to heat to nudge his 1956 experiment along: "When I boiled a pearl for 33 minutes the vinegar boiled off while I was reading a detective story. I can still smell that vinegar. The pearl seemed not to be affected, though I thought it looked a trifle peaked." He got better results with stronger vinegar, the best results with pulverized pearl, which dissolved after three hours and twenty minutes of closely monitored boiling. This is the kind of thing to which Cleopatra has driven scholars. To the question of *why* Cleopatra (or anyone) might have attempted such a display in the first place—surely it made more dramatic sense to swallow the gem whole?—Ullman reminds us that pearls consist primarily of carbonate of lime, the ancient world's bicarbonate of soda. They make an effective, if expensive, antacid.

When spring rolled around and the sea reopened, Cleopatra may have sailed home, to return to Rome later in the year. Two consecutive visits seem more likely than a single extended one; she could hardly have justified an eighteen-month absence, no matter how confident she felt of her authority in Egypt. That would have entailed a grueling amount of travel, though the southbound trip was a less taxing one. Assuming she returned to Alexandria in 45, she set out in late March or early April, by which time the northeasterly squalls had abated, the thunder and lightning off the coast of Egypt with them. One did not brave the gales in winter. One did so only with trepidation in the spring, once "the leaves at the top of the fig tree are as big as the footprint a crow leaves as it goes." If Cleopatra indeed sailed home early in 45, she was again in Rome by the fall. Only an interim return to Alexandria makes sense of Suetonius's account, in which Caesar saw Cleopatra off from Rome. He would not have a second opportunity to do so.

To Suetonius, working from a broad collection of sources if over a century and a half later, the parting was as reluctant as the about-face on the Nile. The Roman commander "did not let her leave until he had laden her with high honours and rich gifts." He acknowledged Caesarion as his son and "allowed her to give his name to the child." There was no reason for him to hesitate to do so. At least in 45, Caesar's plans could only be furthered by an Eastern heir and a living link to Alexander the Great. He was also conceding the obvious. If he had not already begun to do so, two-year-old Caesarion soon enough resembled his father in looks and manner. The acknowledgment may have been the point of the reunion; Caesarion's recognition was easily worth any number of trips across the Mediterranean. As one historian has it—and as many have noted under similar circumstances before and since—their child "was her best card if she aimed at pinning Caesar down to a previous agreement or promise." The nature of that promise eludes us, aside from formal recognition as a friend of Rome, which had cost Cleopatra's father the astounding sum of 6,000 talents.

How else to account for the extended Roman stay or stays? There was

A reconstruction of Alexandria, looking west down the Canopic Way. The colonnade ran the length of the city, offering protection from the sun as well as a highly effective conduit for rumor. Set at the edge of an impossibly blue sea, Cleopatra's Alexandria ranked as "the first city of the civilized world," its fashion capital and seat of learning.

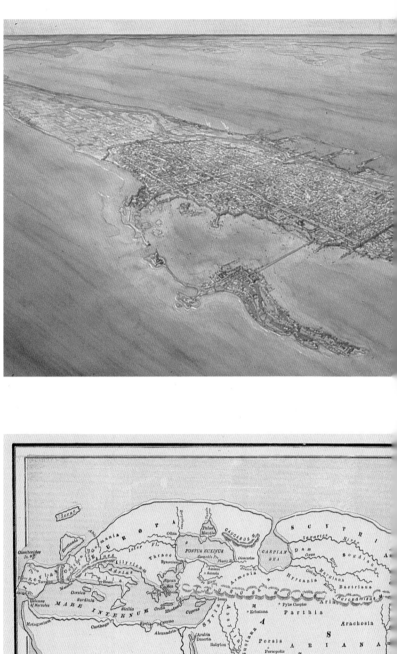

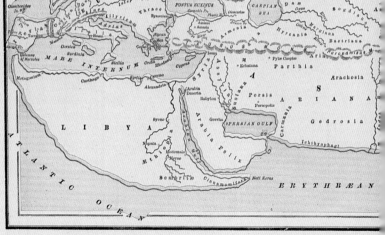

An aerial view of Alexandria, with the double harbor in the foreground and the sprawl of the royal quarters at the left, a sort of city unto itself. Inland lies Lake Mareotis with its vast port, from which Caesar and Cleopatra would have embarked for their Nile cruise. At the end of the man-made causeway before the city stands the famed lighthouse, "like a mountain, almost reaching the clouds," as one Alexandrian described it. So it would have seemed to Julius Caesar, who had never before seen so tall a structure.

The inhabited world as Cleopatra knew it. The concepts of latitude and longitude were already familiar, as was the idea that the world was round.

The usual suspects: four busts of Cleopatra, or of a woman closely resembling her. This one, in expensive Parian marble, greatly resembling the Cleopatra of coin portraits, may be the most likely. Given Pascal's quip — "Had Cleopatra's nose been shorter, the whole face of the world would have been changed" — there is some irony in the missing fragment.

The most flattering of the four busts. Cleopatra was the only Ptolemaic queen to be depicted with her hair in a tight chignon and with curls across the forehead; the arched nose and prominent chin are consistent with her coin portraits. On the other hand, it has been argued that this bust is neither Cleopatra nor even ancient.

A less sensitive rendering, and a Cleopatra without a diadem. The bust may represent a woman from Cleopatra's entourage in Rome, or Cleopatra in Roman guise. All the same the resemblance — with the hooked nose and strong chin, the escaping tendrils of hair on the neck and ears — is striking.

A sterner Cleopatra, with the familiar turned-down mouth, razor-sharp cheekbones, and an air of severity. Again the lack of a diadem suggests that the bust may be of a woman who styled herself upon the Egyptian queen.

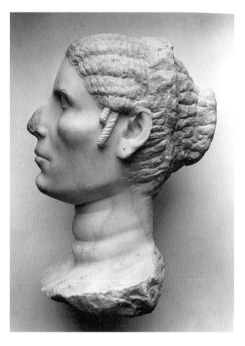

The lives of ordinary women were considered a fair subject for a Hellenistic artist. Here two third-century BC women, once richly painted, play knucklebones, or dice.

A girl holding on her lap a wooden writing tablet composed of multiple wax slates. Alexandrian girls were often literate girls, who would go on to buy houses, lend money, run mills. Herself exquisitely educated, Cleopatra was said by a later chronicler to be "a woman who regarded even the love of letters as a sensuous pleasure."

Ptolemy Auletes, Cleopatra's father, with whom she was close. Representing himself as Dionysus, he wears a garland of ivy wound about his diadem. Auletes would be remembered for his riotous banquets but in Rome distinguished himself as a master negotiator, papering the Senate with flyers and — lavishly and effectively — distributing gifts throughout the city.

An ivory game piece from Alexandria carved with a portrait of one of Cleopatra's younger brother-husbands, probably Ptolemy XIV. The profile is Egyptian, the dress Greek. Cleopatra and her brother married in 48 BC, when he was about eleven. She would have him killed four years later.

A likely Caesarion, in granite, found in eastern Alexandria. He sports a thick Greek head of hair; the piece may originally have been a partner to the Cleopatra below. At the end Cleopatra hoped to leave Egypt to Caesarion and feared particularly for his life; as Seneca observed, mothers are never afraid for themselves, only for their children.

Cleopatra as the goddess Isis, from an Alexandrian temple. She wears the cobra and vulture headdress she would likely have donned when in full Isis regalia, as when presiding over Alexandrian ceremonies at Antony's side. The piece is imposing, both in size (the ears alone are twelve inches long) and in intensity of expression.

too much at stake to subscribe to sentiment over politics. Caesar had summoned Cleopatra once before; his own motives over these eighteen months are among the most probed and least understood in history. It is plausible that the two were planning some kind of future together, as many would conclude, to Caesar's discredit. At the end of her life Cleopatra had in hand a clutch of passionate, admiring letters from Caesar, at least some of which he must have written to her between 48 and 46. Here was the historical version of that beautiful vase of poisonous snakes. It is possible that Cleopatra felt she needed to press her case personally with Caesar's colleagues, to confirm that Egypt was to remain a friend and ally of Rome under her rule. The Senate was a less than cohesive body, invested in private agendas and by no means unanimously inclined toward Caesar's. She knew intimately of its factions; to broaden her base of support abroad was to secure the throne at home. (Cicero's take on official Rome was less flattering: "A more raffish assemblage never sat down in a low-grade music hall," he huffed about a jury of his peers.) Cleopatra's second visit would have coincided with Caesar's autumn return from Spain in 45, by which time he expected to turn to a reorganization of the East. She could not afford to be left out of that conversation, if only for the sake of Cyprus, which formally belonged to her brother, and which had a tendency to resist her authority. If Cleopatra had greater plans still, they are lost to us today. Certainly it was easy to assign her spectacular, designing motives; Rome was accustomed to scheming Ptolemies. What survives instead is the cost of Cleopatra's reunion with Caesar. It was ruinous. While she may have spent her days as quietly as Homer's Penelope, she wound up more like a calamity-causing Helen of Troy. This was to be her illogical adventure.

MAN IS BY NATURE
A POLITICAL CREATURE

"O would that the female sex were nowhere to be found—but in my lap!"
— EURIPIDES

"I DON'T KNOW how a man of any sense *can* be happy at the present time," Cicero had grumbled shortly before Cleopatra first set foot in Rome. After an appalling decade of war, the mood in Rome was sour, that of Cicero— its most prominent citizen, and the most articulate of its discontents— even more so. For some months the city had been in a state of "general perturbation and chaos," as Cleopatra was well aware. Her intelligence would have been detailed. She and her courtiers enjoyed contacts at high levels of society. She could afford to neglect no feature of the political landscape. Throughout town, anxiety about the future was universal. Caesar's civic reforms were promising, but how and when would he put the Republic back together again? Over years of war it had been turned upside down, the constitution trampled, appointments made on whim and against the law. Caesar took few steps toward restoring traditional rights and regulations. Meanwhile his powers expanded. He took charge of most elections and decided most court cases. He spent a great deal of time settling scores, rewarding supporters, auctioning off his oppo- nents' properties. The Senate appeared increasingly irrelevant. Some groused that they lived in a monarchy masquerading as a republic. There were three possibilities for the future, predicted an exasperated Cicero, "endless armed conflict, eventual revival after a peace, and complete annihilation."

When Caesar returned from Spain that fall he had annihilated the surviving Pompeians. The civil war was, Caesar announced, finally over. He settled in Rome for what was to be his longest uninterrupted stay in fourteen years. Whether it was conducted circumspectly or not, he and Cleopatra continued their affair. To many her reasons for being in Rome may have been as opaque as they are to us. She had experience with unpopularity; it would have come in handy now. She lived at a less than desirable address, on a slippery grade between superiority and slight. At the same time, it is impossible to believe that she failed to elicit brisk curiosity, if not starry-eyed admiration. She presumably continued her father's generous gift-giving tradition; he had handed out lavish bribes and incurred great debts, equally fine reasons to seek out his daughter. She was intellectually agile, which always impressed Romans.

Fashion paused to acknowledge her presence; Cleopatra set off a brief vogue for an elaborate hairstyle, in which rows of braids were knotted cornrow-style and caught in a bun behind the head. Rome was moreover a stratified, status-obsessed society. Rank mattered; learning mattered; money mattered. Cleopatra was a member of the elite, to whom the social mores were familiar. So far as the conversation went, a sophisticated Roman dinner was little different from a sophisticated Alexandrian dinner. A subtle and clever guest, Cleopatra would have warmed to the political gossip and to the kind of learned, leisurely discourse prized in Rome, the brand of talk that was said to improve the wine. In the definition of an erudite contemporary, the ideal dinner companion was "neither a chatterbox nor a mute." Over the course of several late afternoon hours, he discoursed fluently on a variety of political, scientific, and artistic subjects, taking aim at the eternal questions: What came first, the chicken or the egg? Why does distance vision improve with age? Why do Jews shun pork? Cleopatra had Caesar's favor; she could not have been friendless. (For his part, Caesar paid no heed to the tongues that wagged over her presence. "He was not at all concerned, however, about this,"

Dio assures us.) At Caesar's villa she was surrounded by distinguished intellectuals and seasoned diplomats. She was refined, generous, charismatic. Some impressions may well have been favorable. We are left, however, with the testimony of a sole witness, at once the most silver- and acid-tongued of Romans, who, it was noted, could always be counted on for "a great deal of barking." "I detest the queen," railed Cicero. History belongs to the eloquent.

The great orator was at the time of Cleopatra's visit a gray and grizzled sixty-year-old monument of a man, still handsome, the even features melting into jowls. In the thick of a furious writing spree, Cicero devoted himself over Cleopatra's time in Rome to the composition of a host of wide-ranging philosophical works. He had the previous year divorced his wife of three decades to marry his wealthy teenaged ward, for which exchange he offered up reasons similar to those that had brought Cleopatra to Rome in the first place: "I knew no security, had no refuge from intrigue, because of the villainy of those to whom my welfare and estate should have been most precious." To his mind the solution was obvious: "Therefore I thought it advisable to fortify myself by the loyalty of new connections against the treachery of old ones." In other words, Cicero—a self-made man from a provincial family, who had risen to prominence on his blazing intellectual gifts and maintained his place there by ceaseless politicking—remarried for money.

It is no more surprising that Cicero called on Cleopatra in the first place than it is that he came to lash her, with a quick and brutal tongue, for the ages. Generally the great Cicero had two modes: fawning and captious. He could apply both equally well to the same individual; he was perfectly capable of maligning a man one day and swearing eternal devotion to him the next. He was a great writer, which is to say self-absorbed, with an outsize ego and a fanatical sensitivity to slights real and imagined. The Roman John Adams, he lived his life with one eye always on posterity. He fully expected that we would be reading him two thousand years later. As accomplished a busybody as he was a master of eloquence, Cicero made it his mission to know precisely which lands every eminent man in Rome possessed, as well as where he lived and what company he frequented. Having stood at the center stage of Roman politics for three decades, he refused to be sidelined. He was irresistibly drawn to power and fame. No celebrity was going to escape his caustic clutches, especially one with an intellectual bent, a glamorous, international reputation, the resources to raise an army, and a habit of entertaining in a style that taxed the Roman vocabulary. The turnips sickened Cicero on several levels. He was a confirmed lover of luxury.

In the misunderstanding that seemed to seal her Roman fate, Cleopatra promised Cicero either a book or a manuscript, possibly one from her library in Alexandria. In any event, she failed to deliver. Plainly she had no regard for his feelings. Those were further frayed when her emissary turned up at Cicero's home. Cleopatra's man wanted not Cicero, but Cicero's highly learned best friend. There is some murkiness here — two thousand years later we are also left parsing the great orator's silences — but from Cicero's deep ellipses and dark hints emerges a man less offended than embarrassed. Suddenly he felt on the defensive, chagrined either that he had asked a service of Cleopatra or that he had socialized with her in the first place. He sounds as if he may have been a little too charmed. To that friend he labored to make clear that his intercourse with the queen was "of a literary kind, not unbecoming to my position — I should not mind telling them to a public meeting." Nothing untoward had transpired; Cleopatra's representative could back him up on this. Cicero's dignity had however been compromised. The result was a blistering rancor. He wanted nothing more to do with the Egyptian. What could she and her representatives have been thinking? Few have paid such a lasting price for a forgotten book; for her oversight, Cleopatra earned Cicero's eternal enmity, though it should be noted that he worked himself up into a lather of indignation only after she had departed from Rome, to which she was unlikely to return. And despite his disaffection, he had clearly frequented the Egyptian queen — in society, if not at Caesar's villa — a statement in itself.

Bibliographic slights aside, there were plenty of reasons why Cicero should have failed to take to Cleopatra. An unreconstructed Pompeian, he had no affection for Caesar, who condescended to Cicero and failed sufficiently to appreciate his wisdoms. Cicero had had harsh words for Cleopatra's father. He had known Auletes and thought him a poor excuse for a king; he dismissed "his Alexandrian majesty" as "royal in neither blood nor spirit." A dyed-in-the-wool republican, Cicero had already devoted more time than he would have liked to Egyptian affairs. They had about them always a whiff of dishonor. He had in Cleopatra's youth hoped to be named envoy to her father's court but worried about how history, and respectable Rome, might view that posting. Cicero had as well a vexed history with women. He had long complained that his first wife had too much taste for public affairs and too little for domestic ones. Having just rid himself of one strong-minded, strong-willed woman, he had no taste for another. By contrast he was passionately, deeply devoted to his daughter, on whom he had lavished a first-rate education. She died suddenly, in childbirth, in February 45. She was not yet thirty. Cicero spent the subsequent months crippled by grief. The pain was nearly physical. He was prone to fits of weeping, which friends gently urged him to restrain.* The loss did nothing to endear to him another cultured and coolheaded young woman of his daughter's generation, her future before her. When his new, teenaged wife proved insufficiently moved by his loss, Cicero got rid of her too, within months of the marriage.

"The arrogance of the Queen herself when she was living on the estate across the Tiber makes my blood boil to recall," Cicero fumed in mid-44. On that count he had met his match. He admitted to "a certain foolish vanity to which I am somewhat prone." Writing later, Plutarch was more explicit on the subject. Brilliant though he was, quotable though he was, Cicero was so keen on extolling himself as to be nauseating. He larded his works with shameless self-advertisements. Dio does not mince words either regarding Cicero: "He was the greatest boaster

---

*He was unapologetic, the more so as he was in the midst of his grief feverishly productive. He defied those "happy souls" who begrudged him his mourning to so much as read half the pages that he, in his misery, had written.

alive." The vanity extended most of all to his library, arguably the real love of Cicero's life. It is difficult to name anything in which he took more pleasure, aside possibly from evasion of the sumptuary laws. Cicero liked to believe himself wealthy. He prided himself on his books. He needed no further reason to dislike Cleopatra: intelligent women who had better libraries than he did offended him on three counts.

Cicero denounced Cleopatra for her insolence, though it should be said that "insolent" was quite possibly his favorite word. Caesar was insolent. Pompey had been insolent. Caesar's trusted associate Mark Antony—for whom Cicero had many far less kind expressions—was insolent. Alexandrians were insolent. Victory in a civil war was insolent. Cicero was accustomed to being the most articulate person in the room. It was annoying that Cleopatra shared his sardonic wit. And was it really necessary for her to act regally? He sniffed that she comported herself like a queen, an offense to his republican sensibilities, no doubt all the more so for his undistinguished birth. Here he had a point. He was not the last to note Cleopatra's high-handedness. Strategy came more naturally to her than did diplomacy. She may have been tactless; megalomania ran in the family. She had no trouble reminding those around her that—as she would assert later—she had for many years governed a vast kingdom by herself. Disdain is a natural condition of the mind in exile; Cleopatra had every reason to believe she hailed from a superior world. No one in Rome had a pedigree to rival hers. It bothered Cicero that she seemed to know as much.

Around the proud queen and the disconsolate philosopher the political situation meanwhile darkened. Caesar was preoccupied by military matters, little focused on the long-neglected issues toward which others urged him. The to-do list staggered. He needed to repair the courts, curtail spending, restore credit, resurrect the work ethic, welcome new citizens, improve public morality, elevate freedom over glory—in short, "rescue almost from the brink of ruin the most famous and powerful of cities." Along with everyone else, Cicero found himself parsing Caesar's motives, as thankless a task in 45 as it has proved ever since. At the end of the year a host of honors was heaped upon Caesar, essentially deifying him in the style of a Hellenistic monarch. Over the next months his statue was erected in temples. An ivory facsimile of his image graced processions, as would a god's. His power swelled to awkward dimensions. (Cicero would be only too happy to catalogue the offenses later. In the meantime, he preened over his visits with the great general.) There was much grumbling about manner. During Cleopatra's stay, Caesar comported himself as the man who had won 302 battles, who had fought the Gauls no fewer than thirty times, who "was impossible to terrify and was victorious at the end of every campaign." On the other hand, he was ill inclined to compromise. He ignored tradition. He behaved too much like a military commander, too little like a politician. The flames of discontent broke out regularly, ably fanned by Cicero and any number of other ex-Pompeians.

In February 44, Caesar was named dictator for life. Further privileges rained down on him. He was to wear triumphal dress and to occupy a raised ivory and gold chair, suspiciously like a throne. His image was to grace Roman coins, a first for a living Roman. Resentment accumulated in equal measure, although it was the Senate itself that "encouraged him and puffed him up, only to find fault with him on this very account and to spread slanderous reports how glad he was to accept them and how he behaved more haughtily as a result of them." Caesar perhaps erred in accepting the tributes but was also in something of a bind: to reject them was to risk offending. It is difficult to say which expanded to meet the other, the superhuman ego or the superhuman honors, under the weight of which Caesar would finally be buried. To complicate matters, Caesar busied himself that winter with a new and supremely ambitious campaign, one that promised to leave Rome again in the lurch. He set his sights on the conquest of Parthia, a nation that stood at Rome's eastern frontier and that had long resisted its hegemony. The prospect was one guaranteed later to make Cleopatra groan, if it did not do so already. Though in disintegrating health and a fatalistic frame of mind, Caesar planned to clear Rome's way to India. He was fifty-five years old, intent on a mission that would consume at least three years. It was the one at which Alexander the Great had nearly succeeded. Cicero doubted that Caesar would return were he actually to head off.

In the spring of 44 he sent sixteen legions and a sizeable cavalry ahead to Parthia, announcing a departure date of March 18. He made arrangements for his absence—presumably Cleopatra did too, and began to pack—but fears and doubts ricocheted around town. When would domestic issues be resolved? How would Rome survive without Caesar? That concern was legitimate, given the mixed performance Mark Antony had turned in during Caesar's time in Egypt. His appointed deputy, Antony had been unreliable and ineffective. He had established a reputation for profligacy. For those who wondered primarily when Caesar would restore the Republic, an oracle of the winter was particularly unwelcome. A prophecy either materialized or was said to, asserting that Parthia could be conquered only by a king. Word had it that the title was to be conferred imminently on Caesar. That may have been little more than a rumor—oracles were nothing if not convenient—but it spoke to the thorny question of why Cleopatra was living in Caesar's villa in the first place. Caesar may have had monarchical ambitions. Or he may not have. Certainly he was carelessly out of touch with Rome, less focused on domestic affairs than was wise, autocratic where he should have been solicitous. If one prefers not to be perceived as a king, one is ill advised, for starters, to spend one's time consorting with a queen.

UNTIL 44 BC, the Ides of March were best known as a springtime frolic, an occasion for serious drinking, like so many others on the Roman calendar. A celebration of the ancient goddess of ends and beginnings, the Ides amounted to a sort of raucous, reeling New Year's. Bands of revelers picnicked into the night along the banks of the Tiber, where they camped in makeshift huts under a full moon. It was a festival often indelibly recalled nine months later. In 44 the day dawned overcast; toward the end of the cloudy morning, Caesar set off by litter for the Senate, to finalize arrangements for his absence. The young and distinguished

Publius Cornelius Dolabella hoped to be named consul in his place, as did Mark Antony, Dolabella's rival in Caesar's affections. The Senate assembled that day in one of the large chambers adjoining Pompey's theater. All rose as Caesar entered, a laurel wreath on his head; at about eleven o'clock, he settled into his new golden chair. He was quickly surrounded by colleagues, many of them devoted friends. One extended a petition, which occasioned a flurry of importuning and kissing of hands. Caesar moved to dismiss the request, at which his petitioner—interrupting him in midsentence—reached out to yank Caesar's toga roughly from his shoulder. It was the predetermined signal. With it the group closed in, baring daggers. Caesar twisted away from the initial knife, which only grazed him, but found himself powerless against the rain of blows that followed. Every conspirator had agreed to participate in the attack and did so, stabbing wildly at Caesar's face, his thighs, his chest, and, occasionally, at one another. Caesar attempted to wrestle away, turning his sinewy neck "from one to another of them with furious cries like a wild beast." He managed finally to emit a single groan and to muffle his face in the fabric of his robe—precisely as Pompey had done off the coast of Egypt—before sinking to the floor.

By the time his assailants rushed to the chamber doors, Caesar lay crumpled on the ground in a soggy purple heap, skewered twenty-three times, his clothing "bloodstained and cut to ribbons." Their togas and senatorial shoes splattered in blood, the murderers fled in different directions, shouting that they had slain a king and tyrant. Terror and confusion swelled in their wake. In the uproar some assumed the entire Senate to be involved. A crowd that had been transfixed by a holiday gladiatorial contest emptied into the street; word flew around that gladiators were slaughtering senators. Others believed an army was at hand, prepared to pillage the city. "Run! Bolt doors! Bolt doors!" went the cries, as shutters slammed shut and Rome retreated behind lock and key, at homes and in workshops. Pandemonium yielded abruptly to paralysis: one minute "the whole place was full of people running and shouting," while the next "the city looked as if it had been occupied by an enemy." In the meeting hall Caesar's body lay alone and untended for several hours, drenched in blood. No one dared touch it. Only late in the afternoon did three slave boys carry it away, amid hysterical weeping and mourning, from doorways and rooftops.

With the possible exception of Calpurnia, to whom the mutilated corpse was delivered, it is unlikely that the news affected anyone as profoundly as Cleopatra. No matter how it registered on a personal level, Caesar's death represented a catastrophic political blow. She had lost her champion. Her situation was now insecure at best. The anxiety was great. Were his friends and relatives also to be murdered? Certainly Mark Antony—by rank the next in command—assumed so. Disguised as a servant, he went into hiding. When he resurfaced it was with a breastplate under his tunic. Those involved in the attack changed their clothes and vanished, as did their defenders. (Cicero approved of the murder but played no part in it. He fled as well.) Given Caesar's anticipated departure, Cleopatra may well have been on the verge of leaving Rome by mid-March. She could by no means have anticipated this finale, however. For years there had been whispers of conspiracies against Caesar, talk that well predated her stay. As for the catalogue of portents, they are impeccable only in retrospect. They might at the time have added up to any number of futures; ancient history is oddly short on incorrect omens. Only later were the unmistakable signs fitted to the occasion, compiled by men who happened to believe Caesar's murder as much justified as preordained.

The explanations similarly piled up later, history being a kind of omen-in-reverse enterprise. As they did so, Cleopatra began to assume a role in the murder. Her presence in Rome demanded an explanation and it got one. She resolved certain mysteries, corralled the stray motives and rogue details of Caesar's story. There was for starters the stubborn problem of the Alexandrian stay. Whether a tribute to Cleopatra's influence or her ambitions, it had to mean something. And what was the significance of her gilded image in the Forum, at Venus's side? Idle tongues and poison pens were in great supply after March 15, when there was much accounting to do, when it became more and more clear that Caesar's assassins had no set plan for the future and that Rome had suffered a terrible loss. Significantly, the person most likely to have incriminated Cleopatra does not: She figures nowhere on Cicero's long list of Caesar's missteps and offenses. In addressing a mournful Rome, Cicero invoked the destruction wrought by Helen of Troy, but he was speaking of Antony rather than Cleopatra.

Caesar had over the previous months evidenced an immoderate taste for extravagant, unprecedented honors. There had been much provocative playacting with diadems, an accessory from which any good Roman recoiled. Whether this was planned by Caesar or inflicted on him is unclear. It seems the first to offer those honors were also the first to condemn, that with each tribute Caesar's colleagues prepared for him a sort of ambush, "because they wished to make him envied and hated as quickly as possible, that he might the sooner perish." Caesar stood supreme; at least in retrospect, it seemed logical that he wanted to be a god in his country as Cleopatra was a goddess in hers. Soon it was bandied about that a law had been in the works "permitting him to have intercourse with as many women as he pleased." (Suetonius cleaned this up, noting that Caesar was to be allowed to marry many wives "for the purpose of begetting children.") He was to be allowed not only to have several wives but to wed his foreign mistress, not then possible under the law, which recognized only marriages between Romans. Caesar was said to have intended as well to transfer the capital of the empire to Alexandria. He was intent on "taking with him the resources of the state, draining Italy by levies, and leaving the charge of the city to his friends." That account made sense not only of Cleopatra, but of the implicit insult that could be read into her lover's architectural ambitions, his manic refashioning of Rome. The two Caesars—before Egypt and after Spain—were incompatible, and incomprehensibly so; Cleopatra supplied a neat dividing line. She could be said to explain his obsession with power and titles in the last five months of his life, the royal trappings and divine cravings, the wayward crowns and the oddly autocratic demeanor. By our century, she had come to have conspired in the diadem-distributing charades. She planted the absolutist ideal in Caesar's mind and was poised to become empress of Rome. She exercised a decisive, corrupting influence on the Roman leader, to the extent that a new Caesar was born in Egypt—and to the extent that Cleopatra properly qualified as the founder of the Roman Empire.

Certainly Cleopatra contributed to Caesar's downfall, although there is no evidence of imperial design on her part or on his, no treachery, or for that matter, any blinding, fatal passion. How much of a role she played is debatable. For all her persuasive talents, she was unlikely to have been much involved in domestic politics in any meaningful way. Were she and Caesar considering a joint monarchy? Possibly, but no evidence remains. Sometimes a business trip is just a business trip. Suetonius recognized the lot of the unadorned historical account, destined to be improved upon by "silly folk, who will try to use the curling-irons on his narrative." The polymathic Nicolaus of Damascus, who tutored Cleopatra's children, was the first to implicate Cleopatra. A century later Lucan was happy to follow that lead, neatly rolling her dual offenses against Caesar into a single line: "She aroused his greed." Those assertions made for a better narrative than did the plain fact that Caesar had plenty of enemies for plenty of reasons, few of which had anything to do with either Egyptian queens or the Roman constitution. Even the reworking of the calendar had earned him enmity, as he had inadvertently curtailed the appointments of men in power. Those who had reason to be grateful to Caesar resented their debts. Others agonized over wartime losses. Some hoped only to upset the system. "And so," conceded one contemporary, "every kind of man combined against him: great and small, friend and foe, military and political, every one of whom put forward his own particular pretext for the matter at hand, and as a result of his own complaints each lent a ready ear to the accusations of the others."

On March 17 Caesar's will was unsealed and read aloud at Mark Antony's home, the large villa that had once been Pompey's, and to which Antony had returned. Although Cleopatra had been in Rome in mid-September when Caesar composed that document, she figured nowhere in it. If she was disappointed she was not alone: It supported none of the nefarious motives attributed to Caesar. Rather the will read as one long rebuke to his assassins. He left the villa and grounds on which Cleopatra lived to the people of Rome. He bequeathed 75 drachmas to every adult Roman male in the city. He could not legally bequeath money to a foreigner and did not; he was hardly as tone-deaf as he had appeared in his last months. He made no provision for or acknowledgment of Caesarion. In a move that startled everyone, he made no provision either for Mark Antony, who had patently expected otherwise. Instead Caesar named Gaius Octavian, his eighteen-year-old grandnephew, as his heir. Formally adopting the boy, he granted him three fourths of his fortune, and—more valuably—his name. Antony was appointed Octavian's guardian, along with several of Caesar's close associates, who happened also to be his assassins.

Some believed business in Rome would simply continue as usual after the Ides. They did not count on Antony's gift for spectacle. Three days later the city erupted in riots when Caesar's funeral turned into a savage hunt for his murderers. Over the body, laid out, with its gaping wounds, on an ivory couch, Antony delivered a stirring oration. He was unshaved, a sign of mourning. On the Senate speakers' platform he hitched up his robes so as to free both hands. A "proud and thunderous expression" fixed on his face, Antony chanted Caesar's praises and catalogued his victories. It was at this time that he defended Caesar from charges of having delayed in Egypt out of voluptuousness. Effectively alternating his tone "from clarion-clear to dirge-like," Antony delivered up a potent cocktail of pity and indignation. Never one to resist a flourish, he went on to display Caesar's bloodied gray head. He then rather unhelpfully stripped the shredded, blood-stiffened clothes from the body and waved them about on a spear. The crowd went wild, indulging in a spur-of-the-moment cremation and destroying the hall in which Caesar had been killed. A frenzied spree of murder and arson followed, during which, as Cicero had it, "almost the whole city was burned down and once more great numbers were slaughtered." Rome was very much unsafe for Cleopatra, or for that matter anyone. All the qualities the Romans attributed to the Alexandrians—those fanatical, intemperate, bloodthirsty barbarians— were on vivid display. In the marketplace a man wrongly understood to be an assassin was torn limb from limb.

Cleopatra was fortunate in one respect. Caesar's assailants had repeatedly stalled, "for they stood in awe of him, for all their hatred of him, and kept putting the matter off." Had they acted when they originally intended, she might have been forced to remain in agitated Rome. She was in town for the furious thunderstorm that followed the funeral, and to see the comet that streaked through the sky every evening that week. From her villa she looked out over a city that was generally pitch-black at night but was now dotted with campfires, stoked until dawn, in the name of public order. And then she was gone, her baggage loaded on wagons and conveyed down the winding road of the Janiculum Hill, by way of a series of switchbacks, to the river and toward the coast. The sailing season was newly open; presumably with the help of Caesar's adherents, she made a hasty departure. Within a month of the Ides she was off, her progress carefully tracked by Cicero, her fate much discussed in Rome. The talk died down only in mid-May. Cicero waited a few more weeks—by which time Cleopatra was certain to be back in Alexandria, and the coast absolutely clear—to vent his disdain. "I detest the queen," he only then exploded, his blood reboiling, without deigning to refer to her by name, a distinction he reserved for enemies and ex-wives. It grated still that he had asked Cleopatra a favor, or that he had compromised himself in doing so, or that he had opened himself to ridicule. Given the turn of events, defaming her suited his purposes as it had not before. Even Cleopatra's representatives felt his wrath, indicted for "general rascality" and impertinence. How had he exposed himself to such rough treatment from that crew? "They must think I have no spirit, or rather that I hardly have a spleen," he raged.

For Cleopatra the departure may have been especially fraught. She had made good on her identification with Venus and Isis; in March she was pregnant again, presumably visibly so, as the secret was out. Cicero had ample reason to follow her closely. A pregnant Cleopatra was the trophy wife who could, at a precarious juncture, complicate Rome's future. Unlike Caesarion, this second child had been conceived on Roman soil. All of Rome knew it to be Caesar's. What if Cleopatra bore a boy, and chose to press her case? Cicero may have worried that she could derail the succession. She was perfectly positioned to do so. It was in any event to be a season of disappointments for Cleopatra, who either miscarried in the course of her flight home or lost the baby shortly thereafter. In Rome Cicero breathed a deep sigh of relief.

On another level Cleopatra was richly rewarded. All parties agreed that none of Caesar's "regulations, favours, and gifts" was to be revoked. Cyprus was secure. Cleopatra would remain a friend and ally of Rome. For its part, that city braced for "an orgy of loot, arson, and massacre," as for a likely reprise of the civil war. After the Ides a lively market opened for defamation and self-justification. There was a run on self-congratulation. Toppling kings was a Roman tradition too, which the conspirators believed they had valiantly upheld that gray spring morning. Even neutral parties happily contributed to the hostilities. As Dio notes, "There is a very large element which is anxious to see all those who have power at variance with one another, an element which consequently takes delight in their enmity and joins in plots against them."

Inculcated from her earliest days with the fear that Rome might dismantle her country, Cleopatra looked on as Rome proceeded instead to demolish itself. It lurched through a dull, damp, dark year, one in which the sun refused to emerge, "never showing its ordinary radiance at its rising, and giving but a weak and feeble heat." (The reason was probably the eruption of Mount Etna in Sicily, though—the contemporary curling irons at work—Rome preferred the political explanation closer to home.) She could only have been pleased to put an ocean between her and the turmoil. Probably she sailed from Puteoli, along the Italian coast, through the rough and inhospitable Strait of Messina, to find herself swept across the open Mediterranean, in April. The wind was at her back. The southbound crossing was an effortless one; an aggressive captain could make the trip in less than two weeks. Within a matter of days Cleopatra traded the persistent gloom and chilly air of Europe for the opulent warmth of Egypt. In sunny Alexandria she returned to the grind of public business and private audiences, to a round of rituals and ceremonies. She would never again set foot in Rome. Nor would she ever let that city out of her sights. She had played the game cannily and correctly, more effectively than any Ptolemy before her, only to find herself back at square one, blindsided by events, sabotaged by a wholesale revision of the rules. As a near contemporary marveled: "Who can adequately express his astonishment at the changes of fortune, and the mysterious vicissitudes in human affairs?" Cleopatra was twenty-six years old.

IN A LIFE of barely salvaged, emotionally overblown scenes, the 44 return to Alexandria is the one that got away, also the most opera-ready. No librettist has touched it, possibly because there is no text. For a woman who was to be celebrated for her masterly manipulation of Rome, Cleopatra's story would be entrusted primarily to that city's historians; she effectively ceases to exist without a Roman in the room. None stood at hand that spring as she sailed toward the red-tiled rooftops of Alexandria, around the flickering lighthouse and the colossal statues of earlier Cleopatras, through the stone breakwaters and into her calm, splendidly engineered harbor. When a foreign sovereign visited, the Egyptian fleet headed out to meet him; it surely did so in full force now. No matter how she had advertised her errand at home, no matter what her actual agenda abroad, Cleopatra could hardly have envisioned this dismal conclusion. She had had a few weeks to come to terms with events and to look ahead; whether she grieved personally or not, she had cause for apprehension. Not only was there no one to intervene on her behalf in Rome, but she had now inserted herself dangerously into the blood sport that was that city's politics. As Caesar's only son, Caesarion was her trump card. He was also a potential liability. She was if anything in greater danger than she had been in 48, when first she had found herself caught between two ambitious foreigners fighting to the death.

If Cleopatra knew the irritating nuisance of self-doubt, all evidence has been lost to history. What Plutarch described as her supreme confidence instead survives her, along with her superlative powers of persuasion. On a later occasion she would pass off a mission entirely botched as one expertly accomplished; it is difficult to believe that, having made her fragrant offerings on deck, she descended the gangplank in Alexandria—again a sovereign, safely returned to her admiring subjects—anything less than triumphantly.* She was free of rustic Rome, delivered from the swells of the waves and the turbulence abroad to a land that recognized her as a living goddess, every bit Venus's equal, returned to a city where monarchy received its proper due, where a queen could hold her head high without being flailed for arrogance, where no one yelped over golden chairs or shuddered at the sight of diadems. She was, in short, back in civilization. That was particularly evident over an Egyptian summer, the season of celebrations. In its festivals too Cleopatra's kingdom inverted the Roman order. With the fields under water, Egypt devoted itself to song, dance, and feasting. "Home is best," went the Greek adage, and so it must have felt to Cleopatra, returning from a land that defined the word differently. "Alexandria," Cicero had railed years earlier, "is home of all deceit and falsehood."

It is unclear who managed Egyptian affairs while Cleopatra was abroad—normally she would have entrusted matters to her minister of finance—but whoever he was he did so expertly. She returned to a kingdom that was prosperous and at peace, no small order given her absence or absences. There are no extant protests concerning tax collection, no evidence of the kind of revolt that had greeted her father's

---

*There was plenty of precedent for this brand of inexactitude. Alexander the Great threw a festival to celebrate his conquest of India, which doubtless surprised the bedraggled, half-starved men who had barely survived that mission, having accomplished no such thing.

return. The temples continued to flourish. Cleopatra slipped smoothly back into her role. The disturbing news came from abroad. In her exile, Arsinoe, Cleopatra's younger sister, persisted in her designs on the throne. Reprising her coup of four years earlier, Arsinoe marshaled enough support in Ephesus to have herself proclaimed queen of Egypt. Her feat speaks both to her tenacity and to the fragility of Cleopatra's position outside her country. The Temple of Artemis was filled with priceless treasure; Arsinoe appears to have had Roman backers as well as a family, or a faux-family, accomplice. At about this time a pretender materialized, claiming to be Ptolemy XIII, miraculously resuscitated after his Nile drowning of three years earlier. Certainly the two sisters despised each other. Arsinoe may have gone so far as to have suborned Cleopatra's commander in Cyprus, whose loyalties wavered. It was an easy trip from Cyprus to Ephesus; the Cyprus commander was traditionally a high-ranking official. To complicate matters, Cleopatra had another brother at her side, the expendable and possibly disloyal Ptolemy XIV. "There's a common proverb scolding people who trip twice over the same stone," Cicero had observed, and Cleopatra—vulnerable again on two fronts—was not prone to clumsiness. At some point over the summer she arranged for the murder of Ptolemy XIV, allegedly by poison.*

Whether the fifteen-year-old had been in league with their exiled sister or not, he was clearly unnecessary, an insult to Cleopatra's autonomy. His murder allowed her to proclaim Caesarion her co-regent, which she did that summer. At some point after July—a newly eponymous month that occurred in 44 for the first time, to much gnashing of teeth at Cicero's address—Caesarion was named pharaoh. With his ascension began the third of Cleopatra's co-regencies. Hers was an original solution, also an ideal one. Caesarion became "King Ptolemy, who is as well Caesar, Father-loving, Mother-loving God." Cleopatra had her obligatory male consort. A Roman, and a doubly divine one, sat on the Egyptian

---

*This happened by necessity in the best of families, Plutarch assures us, monarchy being "so utterly unsociable a thing." The rules for dispensing with fellow royals were, he held, as inflexible as those of geometry.

throne. And a three-year-old was unlikely to meddle in any way with his mother's agenda.

Not only was hers a brilliant strategic calculation—Cleopatra symbolically swathed Egypt in Caesar's mantle, for which she could see a violent contest brewing—it was also a deft iconographical one. If Caesar had returned from Alexandria more royal than before, Cleopatra returned from Rome more godly. She vigorously embraced her role as Isis, with full emphasis on her maternal command, a novel instance of coaxing a promotion from childbearing. At festivals she appeared in her striking Isis attire. Recent events provided a powerful assist; Caesar's assassination may have destroyed Cleopatra's years of meticulous planning but represented a boon to the imagery. In the legend, the enemies of Osiris, Isis's earthly partner and the supreme male divinity, savagely dismember him. Osiris leaves behind a young male heir and a devoted, quick-thinking consort. In Isis's grief, she collects the butchered pieces, to effect his resurrection. The Ides of March handily buttressed the tale; Cleopatra emerged stronger for her loss, the great wife of a martyred deity. It did not hurt that in Rome on the first day of 42 Caesar was—in a solemn religious ceremony—declared a god.

Publicly Cleopatra played up the role of Isis as provider of wisdom and of material and spiritual sustenance, advertising Caesarion's presence, the family trinity, and the spiritual rebirth.* She embarked on an ambitious building program, in much of which she exploited the myth. Caesarion survives in relief on the walls of the Temple of Dendera, a vast project Cleopatra's father had inherited. Possibly to celebrate her son's ascension, Cleopatra had him carved, with the crowns of Upper and Lower Egypt, standing before her, offering incense to Isis, Horus, Osiris.

---

*Florence Nightingale was among those who marveled at the parallels between the Osiris and Christ stories. In Upper Egypt she sat spellbound through a Sunday morning in an Isis temple, one largely decorated by Cleopatra's father. Few places had felt to her so sacred: "I cannot describe to you the feeling at Philae," she wrote her family in 1850. "The myths of Osiris are so typical of our Saviour that it seemed to me as if I were coming to a place where He had lived—like going to Jerusalem; and when I saw a shadow in the moonlight in the temple court, I thought, 'perhaps I shall see him: now he is there.'"

It was an effective conflation of themes; she follows him as both pharaoh and mother, in one depiction shaking an Isis rattle and wearing the goddess's traditional double-crown headdress. Her name takes precedence in the caption below; she likely inaugurated the carvings. She completed work her father had begun at Edfu, in Upper Egypt, to which she probably transferred the teams of Dendera workmen. She established a boat shrine at Koptos, farther north; and built a small sanctuary celebrating the births of divine children behind the main temple at Hermonthis, near Luxor. Caesarion is closely associated there with Horus, who— perhaps not incidentally—is to avenge the death of his father. Cleopatra may already have begun a massive structure dedicated to Caesar and known later as the Caesareum, above the Alexandrian harbor. It would ultimately constitute a precinct unto itself, of porticoes, libraries, chambers, groves, gateways, broadwalks, and courts, fitted with exquisite art. Her largest project was a temple of Isis in Alexandria, entirely lost today.

On other fronts as well she was in the resurrection business. Under Cleopatra, Alexandria enjoyed a robust intellectual revival. Gathering a coterie of thinkers around her, Cleopatra reconstituted a Greek intelligentsia in the city, to which she had no difficulty luring scholars. Among her intimates she counted Philostratus, an orator celebrated for his spellbinding, extemporaneous performances. He may also have been her personal tutor. The only indigenous school of philosophy emerged under Cleopatra; a skeptic, Aenesidemus of Knossos, wrangled with the relativity of human perceptions and the impossibility of knowledge. Scholarly work in grammar and history enjoyed a renaissance, although the revival generated few of the dizzyingly original theoretical leaps of previous centuries. Medicine and pharmacology represented the sole exceptions. Doctors had long been attached to the Ptolemaic court, where they were influential, public-spirited statesmen, and where in Cleopatra's reign the most eminent men in their fields wrote prolifically, on medicine and maladies, on eye and lung ailments, both as scholars and practitioners. In surgery particularly these thinkers made bold strides, producing a new body of specialized skills. The work was otherwise derivative, prone to sterility, given more to classification than to creativity. To it came the first native Alexandrian scholars. Four years Cleopatra's junior and the son of a local saltfish seller, Didymus distinguished himself at court for his lively wit and his prodigious output. He discoursed perceptively on the lexicon, on Homer, on Demosthenes, on history, drama, and poetry. In several volumes he lobbed some satirical shots even at Cicero. It is a wonder he had time for his sovereign; maniacally productive, Didymus turned out more than 3,500 treatises and commentaries, which may explain why he could not remember what he had written and stood regularly accused of contradicting himself. These were the men with whom Cleopatra dined, with whom she lived in close contact and discussed affairs of state. The household thinker served as "intellectual stimulus or as confessor and conscience." He was at once mentor and servant.

Collectively the early 40s are the years that prove Cleopatra to have been far more than the sum of her supposed seductions. She made her first steps toward restoring Ptolemaic glory, again following her father's lead, though with more quantifiable results. She supported and engaged with intellectual endeavors, as befitted her heritage. Hellenistic sovereigns were by definition cultural patrons and scholars; among Cleopatra's forebears were plenty of murderers, also a historian, a zoologist, a playwright. Ptolemy I wrote a much-admired account of Alexander the Great. Reading backward, we are left to gauge Cleopatra's reputation by what was falsely attributed to her. She has received extracurricular credit for a diverse body of literature, which says something of her profile. A decadent abroad, she was an able-bodied intellectual at home. She has been variously cited as an authority on magic and medicine, inseparable still for some time; on hairdressing; on cosmetics; on weights and measures. These were realms Cleopatra may well have explored, at least at the dinner table. As for medicine, she was a great patron of the Temple of Hathor, devoted to female health. She was all the same only slightly more likely to have written about baths of asses' milk than to have invented aspirin.

A curious cure for baldness would be credited to Cleopatra; she was said to counsel a paste of equal parts burnt mice, burnt rag, burnt horses' teeth, bear's grease, deer marrow, and reed bark. Mixed with honey, the salve was to be applied to the scalp, "rubbed until it sprouts." Plutarch holds that she concocted "all sorts of deadly poisons," with which she experimented on prisoners. "When she saw that the speedy poisons enhanced the sharpness of death by the pain they caused," she moved on to a survey of venomous animals. These she studied systematically, daily "watching with her own eyes as they were set one upon another." The Talmud hails her for her "great scientific curiosity" and as "very interested in the experiments of doctors and surgeons." Given the preponderance of medical professionals at court, the progress in the field, and the lively interest demonstrated in the natural sciences by other Eastern kings — many of whom performed experiments and wrote on biology and botany — this was likely true. The rest of the Talmudic passage may be less so. It attributes to Cleopatra a set of experiments on female prisoners, "in order to determine at what point the fetus became an actual embryo." Similarly, the medieval *Gynaecia Cleopatrae* is doubtless apocryphal. It includes instructions for a vaginal suppository "that I always used, and my sister Arsinoe tried." Leaving aside the question as to whether Cleopatra and her usurping younger sister are likely to have traded contraceptive tips over years when they were more likely plotting each other's murder, the text is problematic for having been written in Latin. Cleopatra was rumored to be especially skilled in the occult sciences, though the only alchemy she worked was in turning the fields of Egypt into gold.

Much of Cleopatra's supposed scholarship derives from the Arab world, where Roman propaganda did not penetrate. There she established herself as a philosopher, physician, scientist, scholar. Her name was powerfully resonant, the more so for her association with the pharmacologically inclined, miracle-working Isis. As credible as were some of the imputations, it is difficult to determine how many of the accomplishments were genuine; how many the flattering fallout of Plutarch's account of an intellectually inclined woman, comfortable in the company of philosophers and physicians, living in enlightened times; and how much they constitute the usual assault on the composed, capable woman, suspect for being too good at her craft, whose talents can be attributed only to "magic arts and charms." Dissected or not, the bodies must be buried somewhere, the cauldrons and the books of spells nearby. Cleopatra's abilities were great, but the fertile male fancy incontestably greater.

Her competence would be put to the test in the years following the return, when disaster followed upon disaster. The Nile did not stir over the spring of 43, and that summer failed to rise at all. It proved equally uncooperative the following year. Crops failed to a degree that defied the historical record. Throughout Egypt the misery was acute. Cleopatra eventlessly steered her kingdom through the sustained crisis, doubtless careful about tripping over familiar stones; the previous famine had been a fiasco for her. She may again have declared a state of emergency. Her people were starving. She had little choice but to open the royal granaries and distribute free wheat.* Inflation raged; Cleopatra further devalued the currency. Petitioners from two districts appeared before her for relief from venal tax collectors. Given the "general malaise" and "inspired by a hatred of evil," she granted them exemptions. She posted notices of the amnesty widely. In the midst of the agricultural crisis came reports of odd glandular swellings and nasty black pustules; an epidemic raged either in Egypt or just beyond its borders. The prolific Dioscorides, an expert on medicinal plants, had ample material on which to base a pioneering treatise on bubonic plague.

---

*She would be accused of having withheld distributions from the city's Jews, which is unlikely. Customarily the Jews were loyal supporters of the female Ptolemies. They were river guards, police officers, army commanders, and high-ranking officials. They had fought for Auletes; they numbered among Cleopatra's supporters in the desert in 48. And they had fought for her during the Alexandrian War, at the end of which Caesar had granted them citizenship.

The timing was particularly inauspicious as the Roman civil war returned violently in 43 to Egypt's shores. The Italian peninsula could hardly contain that conflict, a brutal, fitful demonstration that, in Plutarch's words, "No wild beast is more savage than man when his passion is supplemented by power." For Cleopatra the infighting took the form of a sort of perverse fairy tale: She knew that all parties would come calling. (The number of appeals attests to her sustained wealth.) She also knew that to back the wrong party was to invite disaster. While she remained answerable to Rome, it was difficult to do so when she did not know who, precisely, Rome was. And no matter whom she endorsed, the cost was likely to be exorbitant. Already she was well acquainted with the wisdom offered to her father, bluntly apprised in the midst of his negotiations as to "what humiliations and troubles he would run himself into; what bribery he must resort to; and what cupidity he would have to satisfy when he came to the leading men at Rome, whom all Egypt turned into silver would scarcely content."

Cleopatra's best option would have been to do nothing, an option she quickly exhausted. She went finally with her natural sympathies, and at her price. Dolabella had been high in Caesar's favor, his precocious fleet commander, his first choice for consul in 44. He was dissolute and hotheaded, also robust, a fine speaker, and a popular favorite. Still in his twenties, he may have struck Cleopatra as Caesar's natural political heir. When Dolabella applied for assistance, Cleopatra sent him the four legions Caesar had left her, along with a fleet. In exchange she secured a promise that Caesarion would be recognized as king of Egypt, a confirmation crucial to her. Unfortunately, her fleet was intercepted on the high seas. Without a struggle it defected to Cassius, Dolabella's rival and a leader among the assassins. In turn Cassius prevailed upon Cleopatra for assistance. She sent her excuses. Famine and plague ravaged her country. She was utterly without resources. Simultaneously she prepared a second expedition for Dolabella. Foul winds confined that fleet to the harbor. And she met with rebellious subordinates. Her military commander in Cyprus countermanded her order, supplying Cassius with Egyptian ships. Cleopatra would be called upon to answer for his defiance later.

She was playing a dangerous game that only became more so. In July 43 Cassius's army encircled and crushed Dolabella, who committed suicide. If she had not already done so, Cleopatra heard next from Cassius's enemies, Octavian and Antony. The two were in league at the end of 43, intent on revenge against the assassins, primarily led by Brutus and Cassius. For Octavian, Caesar's adopted son and his former counsel, Cleopatra readied a powerful fleet, loaded down with materiel. She intended to deliver it personally to Greece. Meanwhile the assassin Cassius menaced her. She refused to rise to the bait. He threatened again. He had asked only for her cooperation; Cleopatra had instead assisted his enemy. She was by no means proving the obedient female Caesar had advertised. Enraged, Cassius prepared a full-scale Egyptian invasion. The timing was right; Egypt was weak with famine, Cleopatra vulnerable in the absence of her Roman legions. She later insisted that "she had not been terrified of Cassius," but she would have been foolish not to have been. He was a noxious character, composed of equal parts cruelty and greed. Known as "the most aggressive of men," he had been a prime mover among the assassins. He had twelve first-rate legions at his command, as well as an expert force of mounted bowmen. He had been pitiless with those cities into which he had already marched. A skilled general and a former Pompeian admiral, he had fought in the East before. And he was already close at hand, across the Egyptian border, where he had seized control of Syria.

Yet again Cleopatra was spared in the nick of time by competing Roman interests. As he began his march toward Egypt, Cassius was diverted by an urgent summons. Antony and Octavian had crossed the Adriatic. They traveled east to challenge him. Cassius hesitated. Egypt was a rich prize, within easy reach. Sternly, Brutus reminded him that he was not meant to win power for himself, but liberty for his country. The disappointed Cassius reversed direction, to join Brutus in Greece. For Cleopatra the reprieve coincided with unhappy events. She had headed out with her fleet, to join Antony and Octavian. She herself commanded the flagship. Yet again foul weather intervened. In its face a high, square-rigged warship was useless, quickly swamped, easily over-turned. She returned to Alexandria with a battered remnant of a navy. As she explained later, the storm "not only ruined everything but also caused her to fall ill, for which reason she had not put to sea even after-wards." Some have questioned her sincerity, giving Cleopatra's story a suspect I-didn't-want-to-get-my-heels-wet spin. (It is notable that when she is not condemned for being too bold and masculine, Cleopatra is taken to task for being unduly frail and feminine.) She appears to have been true to her word, however. She knew she could not deny assistance to those actively avenging her lover's death. And a Cassius ally who lay in wait to ambush Cleopatra's fleet—with a fleet of sixty decked ships, a legion of Cassius's men, and a stockpile of flaming arrows—both heard of the disaster and came across Egyptian wreckage floating off the coast of southern Greece. Cleopatra limped home in ill health. For her careful and costly efforts she had secured the allegiance of no one.

Having offered the victors no effective assistance, Cleopatra knew she would be held to account soon enough. An emissary arrived in Alex-andria more or less on cue, probably early in 41. He was a suave and tart-tongued negotiator, also a man of acrobatic loyalties. Already Quin-tus Dellius had changed sides three times in the course of the civil war, having leapt from Dolabella's camp to Cassius's, to touch down, tempo-rarily, in Mark Antony's. He had come to Alexandria to exact some answers from the oddly uncooperative queen of Egypt. Why had she collaborated with Cassius? How to explain her tepid support of the Cae-sarians? Where precisely were her loyalties? Presumably Dellius had been briefed on the wonders of Alexandria and its jewel-encrusted pal-ace. Whatever he had heard failed to prepare him adequately for Cleopa-tra. He "had no sooner seen her face, and remarked her adroitness and subtlety in speech" than he realized he would need to reassess his approach. On Cleopatra's disarming effect all sources unanimously, even actively, agree. Plutarch so much falls under her posthumous spell that—

from the moment of Dellius's arrival—he essentially lets her run off with Mark Antony's narrative.

Dellius quickly grasped that he would not be delivering up a sorry, subdued queen for arraignment. The woman before him was not the kind who could be asked to explain herself. Opportunist that he was, he may have seen that something else could be made of the situation. He was himself highly susceptible to beauty. From their lusty escapades together, he knew well the tastes of his commanding officer. Dellius either melted in Cleopatra's hands, realized Antony would, or both. Fortunately the flip side of his inconstancy was a nearly double-jointed agility; he executed an effortless about-face. He flattered and fawned, so much so that it is unclear whose agenda he ultimately advanced. His advice was—Dellius deserves long overdue points for stage management—to engage in a little playacting. Cleopatra was to put on her finest clothes. Her situation was analogous to that of Hera in the *Iliad*, who kneads her skin to a soft glow, anoints herself with enticing oils, braids her bright tresses, wraps herself in ambrosial robes, cinches her waist with tassels, and—gold brooches at her breast and gems dangling from her ears—strides off to meet Zeus. Cleopatra was to come abroad with him posthaste. She had, Dellius assured her, nothing to fear. Mark Antony was "the gentlest and kindest of soldiers."

THREE YEARS EARLIER, as Cleopatra had hurried from Rome under a dull April sky, she crossed paths with another wary traveler. Though he did so as a private citizen, Octavian had made his way to Rome "accompanied by a remarkable crowd which increased every day like a torrent" and borne along by a current of goodwill. Either at the time or in the retelling, he was greeted by the ancient equivalent of special effects. As he neared the Appian Way, the fog lifted and "a great halo with the colours of the rainbow surrounded the whole sun," which had not been seen for weeks. Caesar's heir was as unknown to his followers as they were to him; they flocked to his side—none more enthusiastically than the veterans of Caesar's campaigns—with the expectation that the eighteen-year-old would avenge "the butchery in the Senate." He was noncommittal on that front, proceeding, on his mother's advice, "craftily and patiently," at least until he set foot on Antony's property. The sallow, provincial teenager with the curly blond hair and the eyebrows that joined above his nose had hardly distinguished himself. He had spent little time in Rome. He had neither military experience nor political authority. His constitution was frail, his figure unprepossessing. He had arrived to claim the most coveted inheritance of the age, the name of his granduncle.

Bright and early the next morning Octavian presented himself at the Forum to accept Caesar's adoption. He proceeded to call on Mark Antony, in the garden of his fine estate, to which Octavian was admitted only after a lengthy, humiliating delay. No matter how he announced himself—already his followers called him Caesar—the call would have rankled. If for Cleopatra Octavian's appearance in Rome was uncomfortable, it was for Mark Antony an insult. A strained conversation followed between two men—or in the forty-year-old Antony's opinion, a man and a boy—who felt they had equal right to Caesar's legacy. Octavian was precise and deliberative, later something of a control freak; he no doubt practiced his remarks in advance. (Even when speaking to his wife he preferred to write out his thoughts and read them aloud.) Certainly Octavian delivered those in 44 with chilling confidence and candor. Why had Antony failed to prosecute the assassins? (For the sake of order, everyone had urged an amnesty. Antony had presided over the Senate when it was granted, however.) The prime movers were not only alive, but had been rewarded with provincial governorships and military commands. Octavian entreated his elder "to stand behind me and help me take revenge on the murderers." If he could not, would he please step respectfully aside? After all, Antony might just as well have been Caesar's political heir had he conducted himself more prudently. As for the inheritance, could Antony kindly hand over the gold Caesar had left, for the promised distributions? Octavian added that Antony could keep "the valuables and other finery," less an invitation than an accusation.

Mark Antony was more than twice Octavian's age. He had "all the prestige of his long service with Caesar." Over the previous two years he had exercised great, if not always decorous, authority. He had moreover already liquidated Octavian's inheritance, as he had earlier made a shambles of Pompey's former home, liberally bestowing magnificent tapestries and furniture on friends. He did not need to be reminded that he had narrowly missed out on adoption by the man he too admired above all others. Nor did he need to be lectured by a diminutive, self-righteous upstart. He was much taken aback. In his rich, raspy voice, he reminded the young man before him that political leadership in Rome was not hereditary. Comporting himself as if it were had got Caesar murdered. Antony had run plenty of risks to ensure that Caesar was buried with honors, plenty more for the sake of his memory. It was entirely thanks to him, he testily informed Octavian, "that you in fact possess all the distinctions of Caesar's that you do—family, name, rank and wealth." Antony owed no explanations. He deserved gratitude rather than blame. Unable to resist, as he often was, Antony added a little poison dart to his message, upbraiding the stripling for his disrespect, "and you a young man and I your senior." Octavian was moreover mistaken if he believed Antony coveted political power or resented the newcomer's position. "Descent from Hercules is quite good enough for me," huffed Antony, who—broad-shouldered, bull-necked, ridiculously handsome, with a thick head of curls and aquiline features—entirely looked the part. As for money, there was none in his hands. Octavian's brilliant father had left the treasury quite empty.

Explosive though it was, that interview came as a relief to the Senate, to which there was only one danger greater than a public feud between the two Caesarians. Antony wielded political power. Octavian was respected, and surprisingly popular. Enthusiastic demonstrations greeted him throughout his travels. Far better that the two rivals obstruct each other, went the thinking, than that they join forces. Antony noted as much in his garden that spring morning. Octavian was fresh from his studies. Certainly in the course of them he had learned that the populace

considered it their business to prolong discord, that they built up dema-
gogues for the pleasure of knocking them down, that they encouraged
them to destroy each other. He was of course right. And no one was better at fomenting dissension than Cicero, who could always be counted
on, as a contemporary put it, to malign the prominent, blackmail the
powerful, slander the distinguished. He now gamely obliged.

To Cicero the contest was a baneful one between weakness and
villainy. In truth there were a dizzying number of options. Among
Caesar's assassins, Brutus and Cassius remained very much in the picture. A bold young man with a gift for assembling armies, Pompey's son
was in Spain with the greater part of the Roman navy. Sextus Pompey
had on his side his own father's still-bright reputation; he, too, was looking to avenge a parent and recover an inheritance. (He arguably had a
greater claim on vengeance. As an adolescent, he had witnessed his
father's beheading off the coast of Egypt.) The consul Marcus Aemilius
Lepidus, having succeeded Antony as Caesar's second in command, having dined with Caesar the night before his murder, dreamed too of suc-
ceeding Caesar. He controlled a faction of Caesar's army. Additional
legions reported to additional consuls. Brutus had unexpectedly raised
his army in record time.* It seemed that Octavian alone was without a
command.

The most influential man in Rome after the Ides, Cicero found himself in much the same bind as Cleopatra. Which side to join? He could
see that neutrality would on this occasion—the fifth civil war of his lifetime—not be possible. At the same time, he knew all the parties in question and was enchanted by none. In 44 Octavian struck him as a mere
schoolboy, a nuisance rather than a prospect. "I don't trust his age and I
don't know what he's after," Cicero carped. It was difficult to imagine
Octavian—a pale-faced teenager in a city that preferred its complexions

---

*To complicate matters, there were both assassins and would-be assassins, who—the
French Resistance fighters of their day—enlisted after the fact. Also to complicate mat-
ters, Lepidus and Cassius were brothers-in-law. Both were related by marriage as well to
Brutus.

ruddy—as a commander in chief. He proferred himself as leader, and yet was so naïve as to believe that Rome could keep a secret! (It is interesting that few deigned to take Octavian seriously at eighteen, at which age Cleopatra already ruled Egypt.)

By May 44, when Cicero felt Rome no longer safe for him, he settled on Dolabella, though with a wrinkle. That dashing commander had for four years been his son-in-law. Dolabella and Cicero's daughter had divorced during her pregnancy; Dolabella had subsequently been slow to repay the dowry, as he was obliged to do. Once an ardent Caesarian, Dolabella turned after the Ides against his former benefactor. He pretended even to have been party to the conspiracy, which he publicly approved. Cicero cheered loudly from the sidelines. As of May 1 his former son-in-law was "my wonderful Dolabella." Stocky, long-haired Dolabella delivered a star performance of a speech. Cicero slobbered in admiration. Dolabella had so eloquently defended the assassins that Brutus could practically wear a crown himself! Surely, Cicero assured him, Dolabella knew already of his deep regard? (More likely, Dolabella knew of just the opposite.) Dolabella destroyed a makeshift column, raised to Caesar's memory. He suppressed pro-Caesarian demonstrations. Cicero's esteem only grew. "No affection was ever more ardent," he effused. The Republic rested on Dolabella's shoulders.

A week later Cicero was through with his former son-in-law. "The gall of the man!" he spat, declaring himself a bitter enemy. What had happened in the interim? Despite the fusillade of compliments, Dolabella had neglected to make good on his debt. There was a moment of reprieve; Cicero could not help but repeatedly congratulate Dolabella for a brilliant tirade against Antony, long the way to Cicero's heart. On that count too, personal animosities trumped political issues. Trusted associates of Caesar both, Dolabella and Mark Antony had for several years been at odds following a certain indiscretion on the part of Antony's then wife. (For the same reason, she abruptly became his ex-wife.) Sometimes it indeed seemed as if there were only ten women in Rome. And in Cicero's view, Mark Antony had slept with every one of them.

Politics have long been defined as "the systematic organization of hatreds." Certainly nothing better described Rome in the years following the Ides, when enmity rather than issues divided Caesar's assassins, Caesar's heirs, and the last of the Pompeians, each of whom, it seemed, had an army, an agenda, and ambitions of his own. Among the bumper crop of personal vendettas, none was more savage than that of Cicero and Mark Antony. The bad blood went back decades. Antony's father had died when he was ten, leaving so many debts that Antony had declined his inheritance. His stepfather, a celebrated orator, had been sentenced to death on Cicero's orders. From his father, Mark Antony inherited a joyful, capricious temperament. He was given to sulks and sprees. His mother—by all accounts a force of nature—appeared to have fostered in her reckless son a taste for competent, strong-minded women. Without them Antony arguably would have self-destructed well before March 44. Already his personal life was something of a catastrophe. He cemented the family reputation for insolvency while still in his teens. His sterling military reputation was eclipsed only by his fame as a reveler; he left tutors half-dead in his carousing wake. He was given to good living, great parties, bad women. He was generous to a fault, always easier when the house you are rashly giving away is not yours in the first place. What was said of an earlier tribune was more true of Antony: "He was a spendthrift of money and chastity—his own and other people's." The brilliant cavalry officer had all of Caesar's charm and none of his self-control. In 44 the conspirators had deemed him too inconsistent to be dangerous.

After the Ides Mark Antony was in his glory, entirely the man of the hour—at least until Octavian arrived. Cleopatra was not yet reinstalled in Alexandria when the first tensions were felt. They were entirely public: "All over the city," Appian relates, "Octavian would climb up on to any elevated spot and accuse Antony at the top of his voice." Antony might treat him with as much indignity as he liked, he might condemn him to a life of poverty, thundered Octavian, but would he please "stop plundering his property until the citizens have had their legacy?" He could then take all the rest. Antony hotly bellowed back. He was insulting and obstructionist wherever possible. The Senate did nothing to discourage either man, preferring instead, as Dio has it and as Antony had predicted, "to set them at odds with each other." Antony's men urged reconciliation, all the more crucial as the assassins consolidated their forces. Antony apologized. He promised to control his temper provided that Octavian did the same. One uneasy truce followed another. Antony broke the second with a sensational charge: in October he accused Octavian of bribing Antony's bodyguards to murder him. (In truth Octavian had only tried to bribe them to defect, a practice of which he would make a regular habit. As for Mark Antony's safety, Octavian offered personally to stand guard at his bedside.) Most believed the charge preposterous. Some did not, which left Octavian apoplectic. On one occasion he was reduced to pummeling the locked door of Mark Antony's house in an attempt to clear his name, wildly shouting oath after oath at the servants and at a plank of wood.

Courted assiduously by Octavian, who wrote to him daily, Cicero played for time. It was a delicate business. Were Octavian to come to power, the assassins were lost. Moreover, Octavian was at once alarmingly impressionable and curiously resistant to advice from his elders. Cicero had particular difficulty with the young man's florid encomiums of Caesar. "On the other hand," Cicero reasoned, "if he is beaten, you can see that Antony will be intolerable, so one can't tell which to prefer." Antony was bent on plunder, Octavian blinded by vengeance. Cicero hemmed and hawed, fixing finally on one certainty, which he repeated like a mantra: "The man who crushes Mark Antony will have finished this ghastly and perilous war." By the fall of 44, defending the commonwealth, or what remained of it, became to Cicero synonymous with mauling Antony, against whom he fulminated for the next six months. It was in the course of those harrowing weeks that Cleopatra found herself entangled with Antony and Octavian's real enemies,

collaborating as she was, ingenuously and disingenuously, with Dolabella and Cassius.

In the rabid attacks we know as the Philippics Cicero set out to destroy
Caesar's former lieutenant. Antony was at best "an audacious rascal," at
worst an erratic, drunken, filthy, shameless, depraved, licentious, pillaging madman. "In truth," asserted Cicero, "we ought not to think of him
as a human being, but as a most outrageous beast." Certainly Antony gave
Cicero plenty to work with. He had mismanaged funds. He had indulged
in scandalous affairs. He had appropriated property. He had made a spectacle of himself, at one point allegedly attaching lions to a chariot for a
joyride through Rome. Excess and conviviality were his middle names.
His colorful stunts accounted in large part for his popularity; to his men
he was irresistible. There had been ample carousing, even if "the fume of
debauch" did not attach itself to Antony quite as tenaciously as Cicero
insisted. He was all the same happy to retail and amplify tales of Antony's
indignities. The morning he had opened his mouth to speak in the Senate
and instead vomited the putrid remains of a wedding feast into his lap
was not one Cicero would ever let him forget. Antony was henceforth
"the belching, vomiting brute," prone to "spewing rather than speaking."
He had no ambition beyond providing for Rome's actors, gamblers, pimps.
On this subject Cicero was inexhaustible. As he had admitted long before:
"It is easy to inveigh against profligacy; daylight would soon fail me if I
were to endeavour to expose everything which could be said upon that
topic: seduction, adultery, wantonness, extravagance, the topic is illimit-
able."* So he proved on the subject of Mark Antony.

As the abuse continued, two new themes emerged. Octavian inevita-

---

*A truly eloquent man is the one who can argue both sides of a case with equal finesse.
"And so, if by chance you find anyone who despises the sight of beautiful things," Cicero
noted in the same speech, "whom neither scent nor touch nor taste seduces, whose ears
are deaf to all sweet sounds—such a man I, perhaps, and some few will account heaven's
favorite, but most the object of its wrath." As it happened, Cicero lived in one of the grandest mansions in the grandest quarters of Rome, for which he had paid an astronomical
sum. And while he was pleased that one of his villas had "an air of high thinking that
rebukes the wild extravagance of other country houses," he had to admit that an addition
to it would be awfully nice.

bly went from being "the boy" to "my young friend" to "this extraordinary youngster" to "that heaven-sent young man," on whom Rome's
hopes rested. Also as Cicero ranted, Antony gained a partner in crime.
Summoning every speck of evidence, rumor, and innuendo, Cicero
included Fulvia, Antony's wife of three years, in his rabid denunciations.
Fulvia had participated equally in doling out appointments, auctioning
off provinces, embezzling state funds, asserted Cicero. He indicted her
for her greed, her ambition, her cruelty, her guile. He charged Antony
with the worst crime that could be leveled against Caesar's former lieutenant: Mark Antony, he bellowed, "would prefer to answer to a most
audacious woman than the Senate and Roman people." With his have-
you-no-decency offensive Cicero settled an invaluable inheritance on
Octavian, who would avail himself of each and every line, without once
crediting the best ghostwriter in history.

BY NOVEMBER 43 Octavian and Antony had little choice but to join
forces. It was that winter that Brutus and Cassius united in the eastern
Aegean, Cassius having relinquished his expedition against Cleopatra.
The assassins were well armed and well funded; bowing to necessity,
Antony and Octavian swallowed their mutual disdain and submitted to
a formal alliance. In it they included Lepidus, who commanded a
particularly spirited army. Late in the month the three came together
on a small island in the midst of present-day Bologna, "to exchange
enmity for friendship." They frisked one another for concealed daggers
and sat down to talk, in full view of their armies. There they remained
for two days of dawn-to-dusk discussions, unsurprising given the
conflicting agendas. As the Roman historian Florus put it much later:
"Lepidus was actuated by a desire for wealth, which he might expect
to gain from confusion in the State; Antony desired vengeance upon
those who had declared him an enemy; Caesar [Octavian] was spurred
on by the thought that his father's death was still unpunished and
that the survival of Cassius and Brutus was an insult to his departed
spirit." At the end of two days the three nonetheless hammered out an

agreement, essentially appointing themselves dictators for five years and carving up the empire among them. Each man swore to uphold the terms and joined hands. On the mainland, their exultant armies saluted one another. The agreement—to be known later as the Second Triumvirate—was to take effect as of January 42. Cleopatra could only have been relieved. Together Octavian and Antony had a chance. She was in no position to head off the combined forces of Brutus and Cassius, who would show no mercy to an ally of Caesar's, less so to one who ruled with his child.

The new triumvirs addressed as well the pressing question of finances. The money was all in Asia, where it streamed freely into the assassins' coffers. In Rome the treasury remained empty. That state of affairs led inevitably to the sticky subject of personal enemies. The three men withdrew to compile a list in private. There was some high-level horse trading as they offered up "their staunchest friends in return for their bitterest enemies." In such a way Antony sacrificed a much-loved uncle for Cicero. Lepidus threw over a brother. Your chances of survival were especially poor if you had funds at your disposal. "Extra names were constantly added to the list, some from enmity, others only because they had been a nuisance, or were friends of enemies, or enemies of friends, or were notably wealthy," Appian tells us. Separately the triumvirs hastened with their men to Rome, where they presided over a season of bloodletting. "The whole city," notes Dio, "filled with corpses," often left in the street to be devoured by dogs and birds, or cast into the river. Some of the proscribed descended for safety into wells or filthy sewers. Others took refuge in chimneys.*

Having abandoned various plans for escape, Cicero was at his country villa, south of Rome, on December 7, 43. He had lain down for a rest when a crow flew in the window and began to peck at the bedcovers. His servants read this as a sign of impending danger; they begged Cicero to

---

*One wife hit on a particularly ingenious solution: she secreted her husband off to the coast in a hemp or leather sack, the kind into which Cleopatra had crawled.

allow them to carry him to the sea. He would be well hidden in the dense wood along the way. Reluctantly he climbed into his litter, a copy of Euripides in his hand. Minutes later a centurion broke down the door of his villa. Exacting the information he needed, he ran ahead to intercept the litter on the path. Cicero ordered his terrified servants to set him down among the trees; he wanted to look his murderer in the eye. The great man was unkempt and haggard, "his face wasted with anxiety." Drawing the curtain fully open, he stretched his neck out as far as he could, so that it might be cut properly. He suspected that he was in the hands of an amateur, as indeed he was. With some inexpert sawing, Cicero's head was severed from his body. By Antony's prior command the hands that had penned the Philippics were hacked off as well, to be sent from the seaside for display in the Senate. It was said that Fulvia—a longtime enemy of Cicero's for her own reasons—first spit on the head, forcing open the mouth and piercing the tongue with a hairpin. In the end two thousand prominent Romans lay dead, including nearly a third of the Senate. The triumvirs found themselves unopposed in Rome, at the command of forty-three legions, and broke, the proscriptions having proved less profitable than anticipated.

Ten months later the armies of Cassius and Brutus met those of Antony and Octavian near Philippi, on a broad plain in eastern Macedonia. Two battles ensued, of unprecedented scale and dire import. One side offered to lead Rome toward autocracy. The other fought still for a republic. All was complicated by the fact that the forces were well seasoned and similarly trained; it was difficult for either to achieve supremacy over an enemy that spoke the same language, shared the same tactics, and had submitted to identical training. The two armies of more than 100,000 men met in fierce, face-to-face combat, amid choking clouds of dust, with drawn swords and bare hands, over the crash of shields, shouts of exhaustion and terrible groans, and, ultimately, with horrific casualties on both sides. Only after a second engagement did Octavian and Antony—their men on the brink of starvation—prevail over the

Republicans. Cassius committed suicide, dispatching himself with the same dagger he had sunk into Caesar. Brutus threw himself upon his sword. The victors approached his corpse differently. Antony removed his expensive purple cloak and laid it carefully over the body, to be buried with his brilliant former colleague. Shortly thereafter Octavian arrived on the scene. He ordered Brutus's head severed from the body and displayed in Rome.*

Philippi was still a battle of ideas; in its wake, liberty and democracy could be said to have fallen, Caesar's death to have been avenged. Antony now shaved the beard he had grown in mourning. No issue divided Mark Antony and Octavian, who would have to invent one; they were two men in search of a conflict. Across the Mediterranean, Cleopatra—managing domestic crises of her own—would have been within her rights to wonder why the Romans did not subscribe to the tidier monarchical model, given the bloodshed their personal ambitions had over the previous years cost them. As Dio observed later, democracy sounded very well and good, "but its results are seen not to agree at all with its title. Monarchy, on the contrary, has an unpleasant sound, but is a most practical form of government to live under. For it is easier to find a single excellent man than many of them."

Again in 42 Antony and Octavian divided the Mediterranean world between them, this time shunting Lepidus aside. With signed agreements in hand they parted ways. Antony emerged in his glory, very much the senior member of the partnership. The military victory had been his; he took from Philippi a reputation for invincibility, one that would inspire terror for years to come. He headed east, to restore order and raise funds. Octavian had spent the better part of the month sick, carted about the battle site on a litter. He headed west to regain his health. He was to demobilize the army and distribute lands to the veterans, paid only at the end of a campaign. The world was now in the hands of two men who got on as well as any with diametrically opposed interests and

---

*It was lost en route.

radically different dispositions, one of them ruthless, calculating, patient, the other sentimental, simple, impulsive, which is to say that civil war would rage for the rest of Cleopatra's lifetime. Had it not, we are unlikely ever to have heard of the last queen of Egypt, who stepped into a role that—in part thanks to Cicero—seemed scripted for her in advance.

WE MUST OFTEN SHIFT
THE SAILS WHEN WE WISH
TO ARRIVE IN PORT

"Yet what difference does it make whether the women rule or the rulers are ruled
by women? The result is the same."
— ARISTOTLE

EVEN AFTER DELLIUS'S visit, even after the specific instructions, Cleopatra stalled. She had ample reason to do so. The situation was volatile, the stakes immense. Having adroitly maneuvered her way through years of reckless Roman infighting and backstabbing, she had no intention of making a false step now. Dellius had not pressed for explanations but she owed them all the same. She had remained above the fray when the Caesarians needed her. She had issued no declarations of neutrality. Intentionally or not, she had backed her lover's murderer. She had little choice but to offer an accounting. As a client queen, as a friend and ally of Rome, she also had little choice but to cultivate and mollify Mark Antony. While she may well have preferred to steer clear of him—she had a perfectly good idea what he wanted—Antony controlled the East. Egypt fell under his purview. He was moreover the much-lauded hero of Philippi, where he had seemed uncannily to have been everywhere and accomplished everything at once. As he and his legions had made their way across Asia he was greeted by adoring crowds in Athens, as a god in Ephesus. At forty-two, curly-haired and square-jawed, he was still a chiseled, broad-shouldered paragon of rude health. He installed himself in Tarsus, the flourishing, administrative capital of Cilicia, near the southeastern coast of modern Turkey. To that lush plain, encircled by the steep mountains of southern Asia, he summoned Cleopatra. The requests arrived one after the other. She let them pile up.

Was she temporizing for effect, or engaged in elaborate preparations? She could never be accused of dithering, though at several junctures she did wait purposefully for the air to clear. Presumably this was one of those moments. Plutarch assures us that she entertained no fears, although they would have been warranted; others were punished for their lack of cooperation. Instead he wrote the delay down to strategy. Cleopatra believed Dellius's reassuring reports but had greater faith yet in her own powers. They had now blossomed. Caesar "had known her when she was still a girl and inexperienced in affairs," asserts Plutarch, "but she was going to visit Antony at the very time when women have most brilliant beauty and are at the acme of intellectual power." (As an astute commentator has noted, this "puts the height of beauty encouragingly late and the height of intellectual power depressingly early." Cleopatra was not yet thirty.) With "the greatest confidence in herself, and in the charms and sorceries of her own person," she headed off, not because she was at last ready, or could hesitate no longer, but essentially propelled by scorn. She received many letters from Antony and from his associates, but "she took no account of these orders." Ultimately she sailed, concludes Plutarch, "as if in mockery" of the Roman. It was late summer.

Confident though she may have been, contemptuous though she may have appeared, Cleopatra left nothing in her preparations to chance. It was as if she knew she was playing not only to Mark Antony but far beyond him as well. Certainly she had heard of the elaborate scenes that had greeted Antony elsewhere. Incense and entertainment had followed him across the continent. In Ephesus the women of the town had met him dressed as bacchantes, the men as fauns and satyrs. Singing his Dionysian praises, they had led him into the city, full of ivy-wrapped wands, resonant with pipes and flutes and harps and shouts of acclaim. The invitations poured in; all Asia paid tribute and vied for his favor. From Delius as from others, Cleopatra would have known she was entering a sort of sweepstakes for Antony's attention. She seemed determined to conjure a display so stunning it would propel Plutarch to Shakespearean heights, as it would elicit from Shakespeare his richest poetry. And she succeeded. In the annals of indelible entrances—the wooden horse into Troy; Christ into Jerusalem; Benjamin Franklin into Philadelphia; Henry IV, Charles Lindbergh, Charles de Gaulle, into Paris; Howard Carter into King Tut's tomb; the Beatles onto Ed Sullivan's stage—Cleopatra's alone lifts off the page in iridescent color, amid inexhaustible, expensive clouds of incense, a sensational, simultaneous assault on every sense. She must have made the seven-hundred-mile trip across the Mediterranean by naval galley, pausing for overnight stays, as she had earlier, along the coast of the Levant. At the mouth of the Cydnus sat a lagoon, in which Cleopatra likely transferred her entourage to a local barge, reconfigured and exquisitely decorated for the trip upriver, probably fewer than ten miles in antiquity. A fully manned galley would have traveled with 170 rowers; for her purposes, she may have eliminated as many as a third. An escort of supply ships followed behind. She traveled with an elaborate stage set. Often with Cleopatra there is but a slim convergence between the life and the legend. Tarsus is one of the rare points where the two fully overlap.

The queen of Egypt's presence was always an occasion; Cleopatra saw to it that this was a special one. In a semiliterate world, the imagery mattered. She floated up the bright, crystalline river, through the plains, in a blinding explosion of color, sound, and smell. She had no need for magic arts and charms given her barge with gilded stern and soaring purple sails; this was not the way Romans traveled. As they dipped in and out of the water, silver oars glinted broadly in the sun. Their slap and clatter provided a rhythm section for the orchestra of flutes, pipes, and lyres assembled on deck. Had Cleopatra not already cemented her genius for stage management she did so now: "She herself reclined beneath a gold-spangled canopy, dressed as Venus in a painting, while beautiful young boys, like painted Cupids, stood at her sides and fanned her. Her fairest maids were likewise dressed as sea nymphs and graces, some steering at the rudder, some working at the ropes. Wondrous odors from countless incense-offerings diffused themselves along the river-banks." She outdid even the Homeric inspiration.

Word traveled quickly, more quickly than did the fanciful, fragrant vision, which was surely the point. From the start of the journey a multitude assembled along the bank of the turquoise river to follow Cleopatra's progress. As she floated toward Tarsus proper the city's population ran out to await the remarkable sight. In the end Tarsus emptied entirely, so that Antony, who had been conducting business in the sweltering marketplace, found himself sitting quite alone on his tribune. To him Cleopatra sent word — as much a marvel of diplomatic craft as of cosmic staging — that Venus was arrived "to revel with Bacchus for the good of Asia."

It was a very different approach from that of the girl in the hemp sack, though it yielded comparable results. There is no better proof that Cleopatra had the gift of languages and glided easily among them. As Plutarch notes, she was especially fluent in flattery. She manipulated its dialects like an expert: "Affecting the same pursuits, the same avocations, interests and manner of life, the flatterer gradually gets close to his victim, and rubs up against him so as to take on his coloring, until he gives him some hold and becomes docile and accustomed to his touch." She could not better have calibrated her approach had she known her audience intimately. It is possible that she and Antony had met years earlier, when he had come to Alexandria on the mission that restored her father. (She had been thirteen at the time.) During Caesar's Egyptian stay, Mark Antony had sent an agent to Alexandria on personal business. He was buying a farm from Caesar, a transaction of which Cleopatra may also have known. Very likely she and Antony had crossed paths in Rome, where they had plenty of business in common. His reputation was in any event familiar to her. She knew about his wild youth and his periodically messy adulthood. She knew him to be given to theater, if not melodrama. She knew him to be politically astute only on alternate days of the week, in equal measure ingenious and foolhardy, audacious and reckless. Certainly the spectacle of her arrival confirms that she knew of his tastes. She was among the few in the world who could indulge them. For all the travails of the previous years, she remained the richest person in the Mediterranean.

Antony replied to Cleopatra's greeting with a dinner invitation. What happened next was revealing of both parties and the kind of behavior Cicero had deplored in each. Antony was a little too amenable, Cleopatra decidedly high-handed. It was the mark of status to give the first dinner; she insisted that he come to her, with whatever friends he desired. Such was the prerogative of her rank. From the start she seems to have meant to make a point. She did not answer summonses; she delivered them. "At once, then, wishing to display his complacency and friendly feelings, Antony obeyed, and went," Plutarch manages to tell us, before finding himself so dazzled by the scene before him as to be — even in Greek — at a loss for words. Cleopatra's preparations defied description. Antony thrilled especially to the elaborate constellations of lights she had strung through the tree branches overhead. They cast a gleaming lace of rectangles and circles over the sultry summer night, creating "a spectacle that has seldom been equaled for beauty." It was a scene so stunning that Shakespeare deferred to Plutarch, who had already pulled out all the adjectival stops for him. Surely something curious is afoot when the greatest Elizabethan poet cribs from a straight-backed biographer.

Either that evening or on a subsequent one Cleopatra prepared twelve banquet rooms. She spread thirty-six couches with rich textiles. Behind them hung purple tapestries; embroidered with glimmering threads. She saw to it that her table was set with golden vessels, elaborately crafted and encrusted with gems. Under the circumstances, it seems likely that she, too, rose to the occasion and draped herself in jewels. Pearls aside, Egyptian taste ran to bright semiprecious stones—agate, lapis, amethyst, carnelian, garnet, malachite, topaz—set in gold pendants, sinuous, intricately worked bracelets, long, dangling earrings. On his arrival

Antony gaped at the extraordinary display. Cleopatra smiled modestly. She had been in a hurry. She would do better next time. She then allowed "that all these objects were a gift for him, and invited him to come and dine with her again on the next day along with his friends and commanders." At meal's end she sent her guests off with everything they had admired: the textiles, the gem-studded tableware, and the couches as well.

Just as quietly she raised the bar, enough to make the initial banquet look spartan. Antony returned on his fourth evening to a knee-deep expanse of roses. The florist's bill alone was a talent, or what six doctors earned in a year. In the rippling Cilician heat the perfume must have been intoxicating. At evening's end the trampled roses alone remained behind. Again Cleopatra divided the furnishings among her guests; by the end of the week, Antony's men carted home couches, sideboards, and tapestries, as well as a particularly considerate gift on a searing summer night: "litters and bearers for the men of high rank, and horses decked out with silver-plated trappings for the majority of them." To facilitate their returns, Cleopatra sent each man off as well with a torch-carrying Ethiopian slave. As much as the splendor of her camp "beggared description," the ancients did not stint on their accounts, few of which may actually have done justice to the wonders at hand. In this Cleopatra was by no means alone. "Kings would come often to [Antony's] doors, and the wives of kings, vying with one another in their gifts and their beauty, would yield up their honor for his pleasure." Cleopatra did so only most lavishly and inventively. For this trip, six-year-old Caesarion stayed home.

Plutarch paid tribute to Cleopatra's "irresistible charm" and to the "persuasion of her discourse," but Appian alone attempted to re-create the conversation of the first Tarsan meetings. How did Cleopatra justify her behavior? She had done nothing to avenge Caesar's death. She had assisted Dolabella, a would-be assassin, and a man on whose account Antony had divorced a wife. Her lack of cooperation had been stunning. She sounded no faltering notes of humility and extended no apologies, offering only a bold recitation of fact. Proudly she catalogued all she had done for Antony and Octavian. Indeed she had aided Dolabella. She would have done so more generously yet had the weather complied; she had attempted personally to deliver up a fleet and supplies. Despite repeated threats, she had resisted Cassius's demands. She had not flinched before the ambush she knew lay in wait for her, but had met with the tempest that had shattered her fleet. Only ill health had prevented her from setting out again. By the time she had recovered, Mark Antony was the hero of Philippi. She was unflappable, witty, and—as Antony might have surmised from the masquerade as Venus—entirely blameless.

At some point the two broached the question of money, which to a great extent explained Cleopatra's sumptuous display. It was one way to prove your utility to a man in search of funds. The Roman coffers remained empty. The triumvirs had promised each soldier 500 drachmas, or a twelfth of a talent; they had well above thirty legions in their service. It was more or less incumbent on Caesar's successor—if not on the victor of Philippi—to plan a Parthian campaign, and Antony did so as well. The Parthians had favored the assassins. They were land-hungry and restless. Antony had a humiliating Roman defeat of 53 to avenge; the Roman general who had last ventured beyond the Tigris had not returned. His severed head had wound up as a prop in a Parthian production of Euripides; his eleven legions had been slaughtered. A dazzling military victory would once and for all guarantee Antony's supremacy at home. And whenever a Roman dreamed of Parthia, his thoughts turned inevitably, necessarily, to Cleopatra, the only monarch who could fund such a massive operation.

Eventually Mark Antony reciprocated, inviting Cleopatra to a feast of his own. Unsurprisingly, he "was ambitious to surpass her in splendor and elegance." Also unsurprisingly, he was defeated on both counts. Cleopatra would be credited later with addling Antony's judgment and in one early respect this may have been true; most Romans would have known better than to attempt to beat a Ptolemy at the luxury game. Again Cleopatra proved marvelously supple, more adept than Antony at playing by someone else's rules. As bluff Antony poked fun at himself for his inferior fare, as he disparaged the "meagerness and rusticity" of his feast, Cleopatra joined in. She was entirely irreverent on his account, a made-to-order companion for a man who went out of his way for a good joke and who laughed at himself every bit as heartily as at others. Cleopatra took to Antony's humor with earthy gusto: "Perceiving that his raillery was broad and gross, and savored more of the soldier than the courtier, she rejoined in the same taste, and fell into it at once, without any sort of reluctance or reserve." Having established herself as a sovereign, having flaunted her wealth, she assumed the role of boon companion. It is unlikely that anyone in her entourage had ever seen this particular Cleopatra before.

THE ABILITY TO molt, instantly and as the situation required, to slide effortlessly from one idiom to another, her irresistible charm, were already well established. Cleopatra was additionally fortunate in her circumstances. Whether or not the two enjoyed more than a passing acquaintance, Cleopatra and Mark Antony had a number of things in common. No one else had as much reason to be displeased by Caesar's will or to resent the appearance of his adopted heir. Each held firmly to a shred of the Caesarian mantle. Antony had vouched for Caesarion's divinity in the Senate and begun to conjure with that idiom himself; Cleopatra was not the only one engaging in a cosmic costume drama. Unlike most Romans, Antony had longtime experience with quick-thinking, capable women. His own mother had challenged him to kill her when the two found themselves on opposing sides of a political issue. Antony had no problem entertaining a woman at a political summit or a financial conference, as the meeting in Tarsus plainly was, despite Cleopatra's efforts to transform it into a cult spectacle. Fulvia was wealthy and well connected, as shrewd and courageous as she was beautiful. For her Antony had thrown over his long-term mistress, the most popular actress in Rome. Nor was Fulvia one to stay home and spin wool. Rather "she wished to rule a ruler and command a commander." Over the winter she not only represented Antony's interests in Rome but meddled ferociously in public affairs "so that neither the senate nor the people transacted any business contrary to her pleasure." She had gone from senatorial house to senatorial house door-knocking for her husband. She settled his debts. She would raise eight legions for him. In his absence the previous year she had stood in for him politically and militarily, on one occasion evidently donning a suit of armor.

Nor did Cleopatra's divine pretensions set Antony's teeth on edge. On his way to Tarsus he had been hailed—as Cleopatra knew—as the new Dionysus. That god, too, had made a triumphant tour across Asia. Here Antony not only supplied Cleopatra's cue but recapitulated a Ptolemaic role: Her family claimed descent from the ecstasy-inducing god of wine. They were devotees of his mystical cult. Cleopatra's father had added "The New Dionysus" to his title. Her brother had briefly done so as well. A theater of Dionysus adjoined the palace in Alexandria; Caesar had made it his command post in 48. Mark Antony might all the same have thought harder about the identification. While his cult was wildly popular, while he was the preeminent Greek god of the age, Dionysus was a newcomer to the Olympian pantheon, where he remained the odd man out. He was congenial, mischievous, and high-spirited but—with his lush, perfumed curls—trailed languidly behind him a reputation for effeminacy. He was distinctly foreign. And he was the gentlest of the gods. One of Cleopatra's ancestors had invoked his Dionysian pedigree to justify having absented himself from battle. Worst of all, Dionysus dulled the wits of men and empowered women. Had the East gone after Philippi to Octavian rather than to Antony, Cleopatra would no doubt have adapted, but she would have been at a grave disadvantage. She spoke many languages, some better than others.

She could not have asked for a better stage set. Tarsus was surrounded on all sides by craggy, forested mountains, lush with wildflowers. An administrative center as well as a seat of learning, it was—as its native son Paul the Apostle put it a generation later—"no mean city." Tarsus was celebrated for its schools of philosophy and oratory. It boasted fine fountains and baths, a splendid library. Through the city ran a swift and cold, blue-green river, as crystal clear as the Nile was turbid. On arriving in Tarsus three centuries earlier, Alexander the Great had thrown down his arms and hurled himself, streaked with dust and sweat, into the icy waters. (He was carried, half-conscious, back to his tent. The recovery took three days.) Surrounded by rich farmland, famed for its vineyards, Tarsus worshipped the gods of fertility. It was the kind of place where two deities, one established, the other aspiring, could feel at home, and be set off to advantage. Tarsus was inclined to spectacle and able to facilitate one; it was a city in which you could readily fill a one-talent flower order, which was to say that while its citizens were newly Roman, its culture remained unabashedly Greek. Faced with the same conundrum as Cleopatra, the Tarsans had celebrated Cassius and Dolabella on their arrivals, only to be brutally mistreated by each man in turn. Cassius had overrun the city, exacting vast sums, forcing the Tarsans to melt temple treasures and to sell women and children, even old men, into slavery. Cosmic spectacles and flower budgets aside, its people enthusiastically embraced Cassius's enemies. Antony released the city from its misery.

Cleopatra was in Tarsus only a few weeks but had no need to stay longer. Her effect on Antony was immediate and electrifying.* The first on the scene, Plutarch expounds on her Cilician success and allows her a promotion. While in 48 she was before Caesar a "bold coquette," by 41 she hails from the take-no-prisoners school of seduction. Her conversation is beguiling; her presence sparkling; her voice delicious. She makes quick work of Antony. The cooler-blooded Appian also concedes instant defeat. "The moment he saw her, Antony lost his head to her like a young man, although he was 40 [sic] years old," he marvels. The drama under-

*It takes a hard heart to argue that Antony resisted the irresistible Egyptian queen but it has been done. The great Ronald Syme makes of Cleopatra just another notch on the bedpost, assigning her to a list of more or less interchangeable client queens. In his opinion there was no infatuation at all; Antony "succumbed with good will but did not surrender." And in Syme's view, after the Alexandrian winter of 41 Antony felt for her nothing but indifference.

standably overwhelms the history; it is difficult to trudge soberly through that rustling sea of roses, to strain truth — especially political truth — from the lush, adjectival overload. We hear more of Antony's conquest than of Caesar's for the simple reason that the chroniclers were as eager to discourse on one as they were reluctant to discourse on the other. As Antony must appear the lesser man, Cleopatra becomes a more powerful woman. She played in 41 not only to a different audience, but to a different choir.

Did the confluence of needs add up to a romance? Surely it added up to an easy rapport. As Plutarch noted of another history-making liaison, it was very much a love affair, "and yet it was thought to harmonize well with the matters at hand." Of all the Romans in all the towns in all the empire, Cleopatra had particular reason to cultivate this one. Antony had equal reason to do the same. If it was convenient for Cleopatra to fall in love, or in step, with the man to whom she essentially answered, it was no less so for Antony to fall in with the woman who could single-handedly underwrite his military ambitions. His Parthian obsession was a bold stroke of luck for her.

We know that Antony pined for Cleopatra months later, though she wound up with all the credit for the affair. As one of her sworn enemies asserted, she did not fall in love with Antony but "brought him to fall in love with her." In the ancient world too women schemed while men strategized; there was a great gulf, elemental and eternal, between the adventurer and the adventuress. There was one too between virility and promiscuity: Caesar left Cleopatra in Alexandria to sleep with the wife of the king of Mauretania. Antony arrived in Tarsus fresh from an affair with the queen of Cappadocia. The consort of two men of voracious sexual appetite and innumerable sexual conquests, Cleopatra would go down in history as the snare, the delusion, the seductress. Citing her sexual prowess was evidently less discomfiting than acknowledging her intellectual gifts. In the same way it is easier to ascribe her power to magic than to love. We have evidence of neither, but the first can at least be explained; with magic one forfeits rather than loses the game. So

Cleopatra has Antony under her thumb, poised to obey her every wish, "not only because of his intimacy with her," as Josephus has it, "but also because of being under the influence of drugs." To claim as much is to acknowledge her power, also to insult her intelligence.

Whether or not anyone lost his or her head to the other, it is difficult to believe sex failed to figure in the picture early on. Antony and Cleopatra were at the height of their power, reveling amid heady perfume to sweet music, under kaleidoscopic lights, on steamy summer nights, before groaning tables of the finest food and wine in Asia. And while he was unlikely to have been a slave to his love for Cleopatra, as various chroniclers assert, the truth was that wherever Mark Antony went, sexual charm inevitably followed. His tunic tucked high on his rolling hips, he had slept his way across Asia at least once; he was fresh from his liaison with another client queen. Plutarch assigns him "an ill name for familiarity with other people's wives." He himself later dated the relationship with Cleopatra from the torrid Tarsan summer.

The immediate effects of the meeting were practical: Cleopatra stayed a few weeks and accomplished a great deal. By the time she sailed home, Antony had in hand her list of demands. Given what he had presumably exacted in exchange, they were not outlandish. They reveal that Cleopatra did not feel as secure as she pretended. She was keenly aware that another queen of Egypt waited in the wings. Antony lost no time in simplifying her life. He ordered Arsinoe forcibly removed from the Temple of Artemis. Cleopatra's sister met her end on those marble steps, before the ornate ivory doors that their father had donated to the facade years earlier. She was the last of the four siblings; there would be no further mischief from that quarter. "Now Cleopatra had put to death all her kindred," a Roman chronicler sputters, "till no one near her in blood remained alive." That was true, although it was also true that Arsinoe had left her sister little choice. Caesar had spared her after the public humiliation in Rome. Arsinoe had conspired against Cleopatra ever since. (Isis too is merciful yet just, delivering up the wicked to those against whom they plot.) And Cleopatra was capable of clemency. Antony called in the high priest of the temple, who had proclaimed Arsinoe queen. The Ephesians were beside themselves, and paid a call on Cleopatra to beg for the priest's pardon. She prevailed upon Antony to release him. The priest could recognize no further exiled Ptolemies. He posed no danger now. Antony was not so forgiving with the pretender who had been traveling about Asia passing himself off as Ptolemy XIII, as some have suggested he might well have been. (No body had surfaced at the end of the Alexandrian War after all.) He was executed. The rogue naval commander on Cyprus who had supported Cassius against Cleopatra's orders—he may have been in league with Arsinoe—had fled to Syria, where he sought refuge in a temple. He was dragged out and killed.

This was the kind of behavior that could suggest a man was besotted. "So straight away," concludes Appian, "the attention that Antony had until now devoted to every matter was completely blunted, and whatever Cleopatra commanded was done, without consideration of what was right in the eyes of man or god." It was equally the kind of behavior that suggested that Cleopatra had made some material promises between feasts. Nor did Antony deviate entirely from custom. On leaving Cleopatra in 47, Caesar too had applied himself to settling provincial affairs, "distributing rewards both individually and communally to those who deserved them, and hearing and deciding old disputes." Antony took under his protection those kings that applied to him, making of them firm friends. He established chains of command and raised taxes. The difference lay in what came next. Late in the fall, Antony dispatched his army to various winter quarters. And though provincial affairs remained in disarray, though the Parthians hovered about the Euphrates, aggressively eyeing Syria, Antony headed south, to join Cleopatra in Egypt.

THE TWENTY-EIGHT-YEAR-OLD WHO greeted him in Alexandria may or may not have been at the height of her beauty—a moment a woman knows always to be several years behind her—but she was a manifestly more confident Cleopatra even than the one who had greeted Julius Caesar seven years earlier. She had traveled abroad and given birth. She ruled unchallenged, and unchallenged had weathered severe political and economic storms. She was a living deity with an irreproachable consort, one who relieved her of the obligation to remarry. She had the support of her people and presumably their enthusiastic admiration as well; she had involved herself more closely with native Egyptian religious life than any Ptolemaic predecessor. Not coincidentally we hear her voice for the first time now, in Alexandria, entertaining her patron and partner. She is self-assured, authoritative, saucy.

In light of what came later, Mark Antony's Egyptian visit was assumed to have been Cleopatra's idea and Cleopatra's doing. Ingeniously, seductively, or magically, she spirited him away. "He suffered her to hurry him off to Alexandria," as Plutarch has it. It was of course equally possible that Antony invited himself. He was after all doing what he was meant to do: reshaping the East and raising money. He could advance no further in his Parthian plans without Egyptian funds. He may have felt this was his best chance of securing the monies that a clever queen had promised but not yet delivered. Asia had proved poorer than anyone had realized. Egypt was rich. There was legitimate reason to survey a client kingdom, especially one that would prove an ideal base for an Eastern campaign; Antony would need a powerful fleet, something Cleopatra could provide. The alternative was forever untangling provincial affairs, which played neither to Antony's strengths nor interests. The administrative details had bored even Cicero. The deputations arrived one after another; under the circumstances, Antony could only have been eager to travel to one of the few Mediterranean countries "not ruled by himself." He had been a gifted schoolboy. He was still in many ways a schoolboy. He was also a gifted, straight-thinking strategist. If Cleopatra did not pursue him he had every reason to pursue her, or at least to proceed agreeably and diplomatically, allowing her to feel as if hers were the upper hand, as he had so graciously done in Tarsus. He had already seen

Alexandria, a city that the visitor did not easily forget, one that seemed to have swallowed the whole of Greek culture in one gulp. No one in his right mind would opt to spend the winter elsewhere than in its satiny light, despite its January deluges, especially in the first century BC, especially as the guest of a Ptolemy.

Either out of deference to Cleopatra's authority or to avoid Caesar's mistake, Mark Antony traveled to Egypt without a military escort or the insignia of office, "adopting the dress and way of life of an ordinary person." He lived very little like one. Cleopatra labored to provide him with a magnificent reception. She saw to it that he indulged in "the sports and diversions of a young man of leisure" and that Alexandrian life answered to its reputation. There are cities in which to spend a fortune and cities in which to make one; only in the rare great city can one accomplish both. Such was Cleopatra's Alexandria, a scholarly paradise with a quick business pulse and a languorous resort culture, where the Greek penchant for commerce met the Egyptian mania for hospitality, a city of cool raspberry dawns and pearly late afternoons, with the hustle of heterodoxy and the aroma of opportunity thick in the air. Even the people-watching was best there.

For Antony and Cleopatra euphoric entertainment followed prodigal feast, in observance of a sort of pact the two made, one they termed the Inimitable Livers. "The members," Plutarch explains, "entertained one another daily in turn, with an extravagance of expenditure beyond measure or belief." From an odd, under-the-stairs friendship comes an intimate view of Cleopatra's kitchen that winter. A royal cook promises to secret his friend Philotas into the palace to witness the preparations for one of her suppers; he will be astonished by the goings-on. The kitchen is predictably electric with shouting and swearing, at cooks, waiters, and wine stewards; amid the frezy sit mounds of provisions. Eight wild boars turn on spits. A small army of staff bustles about. Philotas, a young medical student, marvels at the size of the crowd expected for dinner. His friend can only laugh at his naïveté. Quite the opposite, he explains. The operation is at once highly precise and entirely imprecise: "The guests are not many, only about twelve; but everything that is set before them must be at perfection, and if anything was but one minute ill-timed, it was spoiled. And, said he, maybe Antony will dine just now, maybe not this hour, maybe he will call for wine, or begin to talk, and will put it off. So that," he continued, "it is not one, but many dinners must ready, as it is impossible to guess at his hour." Having overcome his surprise and completed his education, the wide-eyed Philotas went on to become a prominent physician, who told his fabulous tale to a friend, who handed it down to his grandson, who happened to be Plutarch.

By all accounts Mark Antony was an exhausting and expensive house-guest. As a younger man he had headed off on military campaigns with a train of musicians, concubines, and actors in tow. He had—according to Cicero, anyway—made of Pompey's former home a pleasure palace, filled with tumblers, dancers, jesters, and drunks. His tastes remained consistent. Cleopatra had her hands full. "It is no easy matter to create harmony where there is an opposition of material interest and almost of nature," Cicero had observed years earlier, and Cleopatra's differences from Antony were marked. She worked overtime to accommodate, despite what must have been a multitude of claims on her time; she already had a full-time job. Antony visited Alexandria's golden temples, frequented gymnasiums, attended scholarly discussions, but evinced lit-tle interest in Egyptian lore, in the architectural, cultural, or scientific underpinnings of a superior civilization. He could not have helped but visit Alexander's tomb, for which there was a Roman mania. He made a trip to the desert, to hunt. Cleopatra may have accompanied him; it was likely that she rode, and either owned or sponsored racehorses. There is otherwise no indication that Antony left Lower Egypt, or traveled to the sites. He was no Julius Caesar. Instead, amid echoing colonnades and a menagerie of glossy sphinxes, along streets named for his lover's illustri-ous forebears, between the closely packed limestone houses, he raised juvenile pranks to high art. Cleopatra made herself at all times available and amenable, contributing "some fresh delight and charm to Antony's hours of seriousness and mirth." If her days were full, her nights were fuller, though her guest needed little instruction. He was a practiced hand at nocturnal rambles, lavish picnics, disguised reunions. He already knew how to crash a wedding. At no time did Cleopatra let him out of her sight. This too was politics of a sort; her kingdom was well worth a prank. "She played at dice with him, drank with him, hunted with him, and watched him as he exercised himself in arms," Plutarch tells us. "And when by night he would station himself at the doors or windows of the common folk and scoff at those within, she would go with him on his round of mad follies, wearing the garb of a serving maiden." Antony disguised himself for those excursions as a servant, usually incurring a round of abuse — often blows — before returning, wholly amused with himself, to the palace.

His capers went over well in Alexandria, a city that conformed in every way to Antony's inclinations and that before him dropped its defenses. It was lighthearted and luxury-loving; Antony was all muscle and mirth. He liked nothing so much as to make a woman laugh. From his youth, when he had studied military exercises and oratory abroad, he was an admirer of all things Greek. He spoke in the florid, Asiatic style, with less bombast than poetry. A later Roman chided the Alexandrians for their buffoonery. A twang of the harp string and they were off and running: "You are forever being frivolous and heedless, and you are practically never at a loss for fun-making and enjoyment and laughter." This was not a problem for Antony, at his ease among low-rent entertainments and roving musicians, in the street or at the racetrack.

He had too an admirable past on which to trade. As a young officer he had urged clemency at the Egyptian frontier, when on his return Cleopatra's father had condemned his disloyal troops to death. Antony had intervened, to secure their pardons. He had arranged for a royal burial for Berenice's husband, also against Auletes' wish. The goodwill was not forgotten. The Alexandrians happily embraced Antony and played along with his disguises, by which they were hardly fooled. Like their queen, they joined in his "coarse wit" and met him on his merry terms.

They declared themselves much obliged to him for donning "the tragic mask with the Romans, but the comic mask with them." Antony effectively tamed a people that only seven years earlier had met Caesar with javelins and slingshots, as much a tribute to Cleopatra's firm grasp of power as to Antony's charm. Certainly it was easier to take to a Roman, who—unlike Westerners before and since—did not play the superiority card. Antony moreover appeared in a square-cut Greek garment rather than a Roman toga. He wore the white leather slippers that could be seen on the feet of every Egyptian priest. He made a very different impression than had his red-cloaked commanding officer, whose influence still hung heavily in the air. It enhanced Cleopatra's allure. If Caesar could feel with Cleopatra as if he were cozying up to Alexander the Great—and no Roman ever marched east without the image of Alexander before him— Antony could feel as if he were communing with Caesar as well.

Appian has Antony exclusively in the company of Cleopatra, "to whom his sojourn in Alexandria was wholly devoted." He sees in her a poor influence. Antony "was often disarmed by Cleopatra, subdued by her spells, and persuaded to drop from his hands great undertakings and necessary campaigns, only to roam about and play with her on the seashores." More likely the opposite was true. And while Cleopatra focused exclusively and intently on her guest, she did so without sacrificing her competitive spirit, her sense of humor, or her agenda. Here are the two on an Alexandrian afternoon, relaxing on the river or on Lake Mareotis in a fishing boat, surrounded by attendants. Mark Antony is frustrated. He commands whole armies but on this occasion somehow cannot coax a single fish from the teeming, famously fertile Egyptian waters. He is all the more mortified as Cleopatra stands beside him. Romance or no, to prove so incompetent in her presence is a torture. Antony does what any self-respecting angler would: Secretly he orders his servants to dive into the water and fasten a series of precaught fish to his hook. One after another he reels these catches in, a little too triumphantly, a little too regularly; he is an impulsive man with something to prove, never particularly good at limits. Cleopatra rarely misses a trick and does not miss this one. She feigns admiration. Her lover is a most dexterous man! Later that afternoon she sings his praises to her friends, whom she invites to witness his prowess for themselves.

A great fleet accordingly heads out the following day. At its outset Cleopatra issues a few furtive orders of her own. Antony puts out his line, to instantaneous results. He senses a great weight and reels in his catch, to peals of laughter: From the Nile he extracts a salted, imported Black Sea herring. Cleopatra profits from the ruse to prove her superior wit — Antony was not the only one who felt compelled to impress — but also to remind her lover deftly, firmly, sweetly, of his greater responsibilities. She is no scold, having instead mastered that formula for which every parent, coach, and chief executive searches: She has ambition, and no trouble encouraging the same in others. "Leave the fishing rod, General, to us," Cleopatra admonishes, before the assembled company. "Your prey," she reminds Antony, "are cities, kingdoms, and continents." An expertly mixed cocktail of flattery, one that answered perfectly to Plutarch's definition: "For such a rebuke as this is just like the bites of a lecherous woman; it tickles and provokes, and pleases even while it pains you."

If Cleopatra treated Antony like a schoolboy on holiday, that was precisely how he appeared in Rome, to which he turned his back over these convivial months. He celebrated his forty-third birthday in Alexandria and yet distinguished himself mostly for his capers and caprices, ironic given that his original charge against Octavian was that he was a mere boy. (Few accusations stung a Roman more deeply. This one so riled Octavian that he would pass a law prohibiting anyone from referring to him as such.) Where Cleopatra failed to urge Antony toward his public responsibilities, dire dispatches that arrived at the end of the winter did. From the east came word that the Parthians were causing a commotion. They had invaded Syria, where they had murdered Antony's newly installed governor. From the west came equally disturbing word. Fulvia had created a dangerous diversion. With Antony's brother, she had incited a war against Octavian, in part to lure her husband away from Cleopatra. Having met with defeat, she had fled to Greece.

In or just before April Antony sprang into action, marching overland to meet the Parthians. He got no farther than northern Syria when he received a miserable letter from Fulvia. It left him with little choice but to renounce his offensive and — with a fleet of two hundred newly built ships — change course for Greece. Antony had not been unaware of his wife's activities, about which both sides had written him repeatedly. A winter delegation had further expanded on the details. He had evidenced little interest; he was as ill inclined to reproach his wife as to break with Octavian. Fulvia's disturbances may well have kept her husband in Alexandria every bit as much as did Cleopatra's diversions. Certainly Antony was slow to bestir himself, for which he would be taken to task later. As Appian acidly notes of the repeated and increasingly urgent communiqués: "Although I have made enquiries, I have failed to find out with any certainty what Antony's replies were." Fulvia felt herself to be in danger. She feared even for their children, not unreasonably. A century later she was largely forgotten. It was tidier to indict the Alexandrian Antony for being "so under the sway of his passion and of his drunkenness that he gave not a thought either to his allies or to his enemies."

THE REUNION IN Greece was stormy. Antony was severe with his wife. She had overstepped her bounds and overplayed his hand. Plutarch thought Cleopatra much in Fulvia's debt, "for teaching Antony to endure a woman's sway, since she took him over quite tamed, and schooled at the outset to obey women." Fulvia may well have taught her husband to obey a woman but could not persuade him either to challenge Octavian or to aspire to more than half an empire. Repeatedly she exhorted him to ally with Pompey's son, Sextus. Together the two could handily eliminate Octavian. Antony would not hear of it. He had signed an accord. He did not violate his agreements. (Weeks later, on the high seas, Antony confronted one of Caesar's assassins. He had been proscribed, had opposed Antony at Philippi, and now approached swiftly, with a full fleet. A terrified aide suggested that Antony turn aside. He would consider no such thing, swearing "that he would rather die as a result of a breach of treaty than be recognized as a coward and live." He sailed on.) To repair the damage with Octavian, Antony left without saying goodbye. Fulvia was ill when he did so. Many of the charges against her may have been invented; impugning independent-minded women was a subspecialty of the Roman historian. And Fulvia had had plenty of accomplices. Antony's procurer had encouraged her, having repeatedly and maliciously pointed out "that if Italy remained at peace, Antony would stay with Cleopatra, but if there were a war, he would come back without delay."

With his new fleet Antony headed to the Adriatic. In his absence Fulvia became seriously depressed and died. The cause is unclear. Appian supposes she may have taken her own life out of spite "because she was angry with Antony for leaving her when she was sick." She may simply have been exhausted from the incessant meddling. She could not have been much mourned in Alexandria. Antony on the other hand was deeply affected by the death, for which he berated himself. He had not even returned to see his wife in her illness. Others held him responsible too, writing the neglect down — as Dio chides — to "his passion for Cleopatra and her wantonness." Fulvia had been handsome and serious-minded and devoted. She had come to the marriage with money, influential friends, and shrewd political instincts. She had borne Antony two sons. If in truth she was a virago, she was, as has been pointed out, "at least an infinitely loyal virago." Antony had thrived at her side.

Fulvia's death was arguably her most pacific act. It opened the way for a reconciliation between Octavian and Antony, "now rid of an interfering woman whose jealousy of Cleopatra had made her fan the flames of such a serious war." As it was easy to write an absurd and costly war down to a woman's machinations, so it was easy to write off an accord to her demise, the more so as no one was inclined to fight in the first place. Sextus Pompey remained active at sea. He had vigorously blocked the grain routes to Rome. Incessant war had destroyed Italian agriculture. Rome was a starving, unruly city, at the limits of its endurance. The countryside was in revolt. Soldiers lobbied for the funds Antony was to have obtained abroad and had yet to distribute. Friends stepped in as go-betweens, again reconciling the two men, who again divided the world between them, with Octavian making out more handsomely than he had two years earlier.

This was the Treaty of Brundisium, of early October 40. By its terms, Antony was to battle the Parthians, while Octavian was to fend off or reach an agreement with Sextus Pompey. Some eight months later, the three men would accordingly sign a new agreement in Misenum, across the bay from Naples, the summit of Pompeii in the background. No sooner had those pacts been drafted, no sooner had the men embraced, than "a great and mighty shout arose from the mainland and from the ships at the same moment." Even the mountains resounded with joy. In the ensuing harborfront chaos many were trampled, suffocated, or drowned, as "they embraced one another while swimming and threw their arms around one another's necks as they dived." Armed conflict had again been averted, although the all-night Brundisium celebrations spoke as loudly as did the agreements themselves. In tents along the coast both camps feted each other through a day and a night. (Octavian did so in the Roman fashion, Antony in the Asiatic and Egyptian style, which passed without comment.) All the same, when they did so at Misenum "their ships were moored close by, guards were stationed around, and those actually attending the dinner carried daggers concealed beneath their clothing." Conspiracies brewed and plots were extinguished throughout the cordial banqueting.

To join the two men personally after Brundisium, Octavian offered up his adored half sister to Antony. Here was the one realm in which a Roman woman commanded a premium: She made for an invaluable personal guarantee, especially when it came to closing a political deal. Circumspect and sober, Octavia had at twenty-nine all the makings of the long-suffering political wife. She was intelligent but not independent, a mediator rather than a manipulator. While she had studied philosophy, she harbored no political ambitions. "A wonder of a woman," she was an acknowledged beauty, graceful, fine-featured, with a glossy mane of magnificent hair. Conveniently, she had been widowed months earlier. She was precisely what the situation required, an eminently qualified counterweight to Cleopatra, from whom she was intended to divert Antony. By his own admission he remained under that faraway spell. "His reason was still battling with his love," as Plutarch has it, and as Antony's men well knew. They ribbed him mercilessly about the affair. By law a widow was to wait ten months before remarrying, to allow for the birth of any progeny. All parties counted so fervently on Octavia to "restore harmony and be their complete salvation" that the Senate hurriedly passed an exemption. At the end of December 40 the Brundisium festivities continued in Rome, where Antony and Octavia celebrated their marriage.

Rome was hardly in a festive mood—it was famished, plundered, exhausted—but the news must especially have rankled in Alexandria. The pacts of 40 and 39 could not have surprised but may have alarmed Cleopatra. Antony's marriage was one thing, his commitment to his brother-in-law another. It was not in Cleopatra's best interest for Antony and Octavian to join forces. Octavian was her mortal enemy, a walking, plotting insult to her son. On the other hand, she knew her man. Antony would be back. She did not need to make any advances, as the Parthians could be counted on to do so. She may well have come to feel perversely grateful to the Parthians, who distracted the Romans from Egypt. They accentuated her importance; Antony could hardly effect his part of the Brundisium bargain without her. Cleopatra had fair reason to believe that reconciliation fragile if not hollow. Antony and Octavian could reconcile as many times as they liked. The enmity—as Fulvia had forcefully argued months earlier—would not vanish. Cleopatra could have guessed at the daggers and did not need to. She had informers in Antony's camp, who conveyed news of every detail—of the plots and counter-plots, the skirmishing and banqueting—to Alexandria.

She was in contact at least indirectly with Mark Antony, to whom she sent a caller that winter. The Parthians swept through Phoenicia, Palestine, and Syria, to plunder Jerusalem at the end of the year. Herod, the thirty-two-year-old Judaean tetrarch, or prince—Rome would crown him king only the following year—managed a harrowing escape. Having settled his family at the fortress of Masada, he cast about for asylum. It was not immediately forthcoming; his neighbors were unwilling to displease the invaders. Herod made his way finally to Alexandria, where Cleopatra received him in style. She knew him primarily as an excitable friend of Antony's and as a fellow Roman client but had additional reason to be favorably disposed toward him: Herod's father had twice assisted in Ptolemaic restorations, both hers and that of her father. In 47 he had personally launched a vigorous, artful assault on the eastern frontier and rallied Egypt's Jews to Caesar's cause. Like their fathers, Cleopatra and Herod were former Pompeians, late converts to Caesar. They had a common enemy in the Parthians.

Herod was moreover an entertaining companion, glib and keen, fanatical in his loyalties, expert in his displays of deference. Evidently Cleopatra attempted to enlist the dashing prince in an expedition, either of her own, into Ethiopia, or with Antony, in Parthia. It was unsurprising that she should offer him a command. Jewish officers had long served in the Ptolemaic forces, and Herod was particularly distinguished. An expert horseman, he could throw a javelin with unerring precision. He declined the offer. In the end Cleopatra supplied him with a galley—she seemed forever to be handing out ships—in which to make a risky winter crossing to Rome, an unusual kind of hospitality, and one that involved Herod in a shipwreck off the coast of Cyprus. (He washed up in Rome only weeks later, to be welcomed warmly by Octavian and Antony.) In the worst light, Cleopatra's was a diversionary tactic. Grateful though she may have felt toward Herod's family, she had no great interest in encouraging her neighbor's friendship with Antony.

We have no idea how or if Cleopatra delivered another piece of news, which likely preceded Herod across the Mediterranean. At the end of the year she gave birth to twins. Their father was absent—he was at about this time either marrying Octavia or on the verge of doing so—but the children did not want for glorious antecedents. In naming them Cleopatra made no concessions to their paternal heritage. She went Rome one better: she named Antony's children Alexander Helios and Cleopatra Selene, at once summoning the sun; the moon; her great-aunt, the remarkable second-century Ptolemaic queen; and the greatest commander of the age, the one who had tamed even the Parthians, and to whom she alone among reigning sovereigns maintained a link. Given the way she was stockpiling successors, Cleopatra was arguably doing more to unite East and West than had anyone since Alexander the Great. The sun and the moon figured in the Parthian king's title; Cleopatra may have been sending him a message. Surely there was no better way to inaugurate a golden age than with a sun god. We know nothing of Antony's reaction to the news but Octavian's would have been yet more interesting. In some roundabout way, Cleopatra had seen to it that the two men were, by way of her children, again related.

She did not have to broadcast word of the sensational births. News that the enterprising queen of Egypt had borne a son named Alexander—whose father was Mark Antony and whose half brother was a child of Caesar—constituted a banner headline in 39 BC. It was enough to make Cleopatra, to borrow a much later phrase, an object of gossip for the whole world.

FROM 40 TO 37, Cleopatra lived as in a Greek drama; all the violence occurred offstage. Reports were conveyed to her from a distance. She parsed them carefully. With the Treaty of Brundisium, the Mediterranean world breathed a sigh of relief, if one that felt cold on the back of the Egyptian neck. Antony's marriage was a thrilling solution for a worn and depleted Roman people. Throughout Italy Antony and Octavian were "immediately praised to the skies for bringing peace: men were rid of war in their own country and of the conscription of their sons, rid of the violence of military outposts and of the desertion of their slaves, rid of the plundering of farmland and of the interruption to agriculture, and rid above all of the famine which had brought them to the limits of their endurance." In the countryside people sacrificed, "as if to savior gods," a role both Antony and Octavian embraced. Statues were erected to the peace and coins minted. With the celebrations came misty-eyed dreams and colorful prophecies. Suddenly a rosy age of brotherhood and prosperity dawned. Virgil wrote his much palpated Fourth Eclogue at this time, possibly to celebrate the marriage of Antony and Octavia, certainly to summon a golden age. The poet pinned messianic hopes on a child who was yet to be born, a savior who would usher in a new dawn and reign over a world of piety, peace, and plenty.

For those breathless prophecies to be realized the world had to wait a little longer. In the spring of 38 Octavia dutifully produced a child. It was a daughter, however, rather than the much-heralded son. And the Parthians continued their westward advance, delighted to exploit Rome's internal distractions. Cleopatra too kept a careful eye on the invaders as they neared her border. They were intent on expansion; the empire of their Persian predecessors had included Egypt. Antony dispatched a trusted general to engage the Parthians. Much to Antony's annoyance, he did so beautifully, soaking up the glory for which his commander thirsted. And hungry Rome exploded again in riots. The unrest had been so great earlier that Octavian had found himself surrounded in the Forum by a seething mob, which castigated him for having exhausted the public funds. Paving stones met his attempts to explain himself. The bombardment continued even as the blood began to flow. Antony had swooped in to effect a spectacular rescue, snatching Octavian, with some difficulty and amid shouts and screams, from his assailants. He escorted his fellow triumvir to his house, for what was a very different visit from their initial interview there.

Otherwise Antony's brother-in-law was not proving a cooperative partner, as Fulvia earlier had warned him, and—from thousands of miles away—as Cleopatra managed still to do. A friendly spirit prevailed between the two men, on congenial terms and best behavior. All the same Mark Antony—the war hero, the senior statesman, the popular favorite—seemed continually to be bested by his stubborn and sickly brother-in-law. Certainly he had reason to be astounded by Octavian's very ability to continue on the scene. Octavian had already been several times on his deathbed. Continually coughing and sneezing, susceptible to sunstroke, a reluctant warrior, he hardly seemed a worthy match for the barrel-chested, mighty-thighed Mark Antony. Octavian was morose, paranoid, fastidious. He wore lifts in his shoes. And yet at every juncture he continued to surprise Antony. A victim of his own easygoing confidence, acting from what he perceived to be his superior position, Antony regularly found himself manipulated. He engaged in a rivalry he had not even considered one, with a "rash boy" who had come from nowhere. Antony was without guile, of which he was often oblivious. Octavian was without charm, equally lost on him. He was the kind of man who would later brag about the number of triumphs he had been offered but had not celebrated, which amounted to boasting about his humility. Antony would never for a minute have turned down such honors and cheerfully admitted as much.

Somehow Octavian managed to best his elder even in casual games of skill and chance. Whether the two bet on a cockfight or played cards, when they cast lots to decide political matters, if they tossed a ball between them, Mark Antony inevitably, improbably, wound up diminished. (It is easy to see why: Octavian could spin any outcome to his advantage. If he lost excessive amounts at the gaming table, it was, he explained, only because he "behaved with excessive sportsmanship.") At Antony's side Cleopatra had installed a soothsayer; many in Rome believed that an astrologer could predict a human career with as much accuracy as a solar eclipse. Antony spoke of his frustation to the seer, who cast his horoscope. Speaking either the truth or for his employer, he offered up a frank analysis. Antony's prospects were splendid, but fated to be eclipsed by Octavian's. The problem, explained the seer, was that Antony's "guardian genius" lived in fear of his colleague's, "and though it has a spirited and lofty mien when it is by itself, when his comes near, yours is cowed and humbled by it." He was to steer clear of his colleague. The explanation made sense to Antony, who held the astrologer in new esteem and approached his brother-in-law with new wariness. In what was perhaps a veiled invitation to Alexandria, the seer "advised Antony to put as much distance as possible between himself and that young man."

He got only as far as Athens, where he settled for the winter, and which he made his headquarters for the next two years. He passed the winter of 39 much as he had passed the previous one, in a comfortable, cultivated city of superb architecture and fine statuary. He left lieutenants in the field but did no more than look over their reports. He dismissed his entourage. He made the rounds of lectures and festivals, with a few friends and attendants or with Octavia, with whom he appeared deeply happy. Again he exchanged the purple cloak of a commander for Eastern dress. Again he exultantly passed himself off as Dionysus, his preferred form of address. He allowed Octavia — who quickly bore him a second daughter — to be hailed as Athena. We know how those tributes registered in Alexandria as Cleopatra collected every detail of them. They were particularly galling as they verged on the sacred and the imperial. What a difference an address — or a change of consort — makes: there would be no Roman hand-wringing in 39 over Antony's winter of dissipation. In Athens he dressed like a Greek and reveled like a Greek, but he did so under the watchful eye of the virtuous Octavia. It was moreover difficult to attack his divine pretensions when Octavian affected the same. He threw a costume party for which he dressed as Apollo. Only Antony, however, conspicuously built a hut of branches, decorated it with drums, tambourines, greenery, animal skins, and other Dionysian props, and "lay inside with his friends, beginning at dawn, and got drunk." He summoned musicians from Italy to entertain at his hillside den. At times he moved his installation up to the Acropolis, "and the entire city of Athens was illuminated by the lamps that hung from the ceilings."

He continued to be perplexed by his brother-in-law's ability to control the conversation. While commanding a reputation for stolid probity, Octavian managed in 38 to slip out of his marriage on the day his wife gave birth, to wed Livia, six months' pregnant with her previous husband's child. It was a marriage that delivered Octavian to the upper ranks of Roman society, making him Antony's equal. (Despite the connection to Caesar, Octavian's lineage was not noble.) Repeatedly he managed to cripple and confound his brother-in-law: If he promised one thing he delivered another. If Antony headed east Octavian summoned him west—then neglected to appear. He allowed Antony to recruit soldiers on Italian soil, next to impossible, as Octavian governed that territory. It made for a tenuous balancing act, but one that Antony was determined to maintain. He swallowed his pride and masked his irritation, even as his patience was rubbed raw.

Matters came finally to a head late in the spring of 37, when the two met alongside a river, in the south of the Italian peninsula, to air several seasons of grievances. Octavia helped to broker a peace, delivering an impassioned Helen of Troy speech. She had no desire to watch her husband and brother destroy each other. The result was the Pact of Tarentum, a renewal of the expired triumvirate. Antony would be recognized as dictator in the East through December 33. He emerged satisfied: "Nearly everything," notes Dio, "was going as he wished." He prepared at last for his campaign and headed east, to Syria. Octavia and their two daughters accompanied him as far as western Greece, where he sent them back. Octavia was pregnant again. Further travel, Antony protested, would be detrimental to her health. Already she had six children—including those from prior marriages—in her care. He was eager that, as he put it, "she might not share his danger while he was warring against the Parthians." This was all perfectly true.

If Octavian was a flinty master of indirection, capable of appearing to cooperate while doing no such thing, Antony was a quick-change artist, given to dramatic about-faces. In Athens he was one day the layabout, languidly attending festivals in Octavia's company and neglecting public business, the next, having rethought his wardrobe and snapped to attention, the sharp-minded military man, a tornado of activity, all diplomatic business, at the magnetic center of an entourage. Something gave way in the last months of 37. Possibly the long list of insults, disillusionments, and dodges suddenly added up. Possibly he burst with pent-up frustration. He was a soldier, whose glorious campaign had been postponed and postponed. His lieutenant reaped a series of victories in the East, victories that were rightfully his. Perhaps Antony realized that between them his wife and brother-in-law were holding him in check, that he was being played for the fool, that collaboration seemed less and less possible. Certainly the obvious way to secure the upper hand at home was with a blazing military victory abroad. To crush the Parthians was to eliminate Octavian, a strange sort of assymetrical accounting, not entirely unlike Auletes' Roman calculation of two decades earlier.

Plutarch offers a different explanation for the reversal of 37. He acknowledges the Parthian fixation but cites as well "a dire evil which had been slumbering for a long time." Antony's friends assumed that over the course of three and a half years that hankering had released its hold, charmed away by Octavia, or at least "lulled to rest by better considerations." In Plutarch's account the desire suddenly smoldered, to grow more and more combustible as Antony traveled east, where ultimately it reignited and burst into flames. Plutarch meant to get his history right but it should be remembered that he was making of Antony's life a cautionary tale. His Antony is a talented man brought to ruin by his own passion; the moral may have been more important than the details. Whatever the circumstances, safely arrived in Syria, Antony defied both his better instincts and cool counsel. He sent a messenger to Alexandria. Cleopatra was to meet him in Antioch, the third great city of the Mediterranean world. This time she set sail posthaste. Not long after the couple's arrival in the Syrian capital, coins circulated bearing joint portraits of Antony and Cleopatra. It is unclear who is meant to be on the obverse and who on the reverse, which was, in brief, the intermittent riddle of the next seven tumultuous years. Antony never saw Octavia again.

AN OBJECT OF GOSSIP
FOR THE WHOLE WORLD

"The greatest achievement for a woman is to be as seldom as possible spoken of."
— THUCYDIDES

SHE HAD NO need to indulge in costume drama this time around. Cleopatra knew before she sailed that fall that Mark Antony was heading east, finally to settle the Roman score with Parthia, a campaign he had delayed now for four years. She knew of his preoccupation from their riotous winter together. From Caesar she would have heard details of the original plans for that expedition. As he made his way toward Antioch, Antony reorganized Asia Minor, carving out kingdoms for those he trusted and those who supported him. He established a stable frontier; it was essential that he shore up his rear before proceeding east. To the same end Antony and Octavian had together arranged a kingship for Herod when he had finally washed up in Rome that winter. Of Idumaean and Arab descent, Herod was by no means the obvious candidate for the Judaean throne. His tenacity rather than his heritage secured him the crown. No dynast more eloquently explained away his misguided loyalty to Cassius; it would fairly be said of Herod that he had "slinked into" power. Antony had known his father, also a friend to Rome. And he had met Herod as a teenager. The personal rapport counted for a good deal.

A rough-edged opportunist, Herod was endearingly reckless, a master of the miraculous escape. The evidence suggests a fascination with him in Rome, on Octavian's part as much as on Antony's. Not coincidentally, Herod was as much a swashbuckler when it came to raising funds as throwing a javelin; he had an astonishing talent for plucking gold from thin air. (His subjects had some insight into his methods.) The Senate unanimously confirmed the kingship after which Octavian and Antony escorted Herod between them to the Capitol, a signal honor. Consuls and magistrates led the way. Antony argued that the appointment would be advantageous to the Eastern campaign; he afterward threw a banquet in the new king's honor. By some accounts Herod owed his throne equally to Cleopatra. The Senate was as much motivated by fear of her as by admiration of him. They distinctly preferred two monarchs in the region to one. There was ample reason to be wary of a client queen at the head of a rich kingdom, with her finger on Rome's grain supply.

That logic worked as well to Cleopatra's advantage. Antony could risk no upheavals in Egypt. She alone could rule that kingdom with authority. Clearly few could run the country better. As ever, she left Alexandria secure in the knowledge that no Roman could succeed against Parthia — a rich, immense, and well-defended empire — without her financial support. In other words, as she made her way north that fall, along the rocky coast of the eastern Mediterranean, she knew that the balance of power had subtly shifted. For all of Antony's bravado, despite his superb army, she was very much in possession of the upper hand. Vanity having changed little in two millennia, it seems fair to assume that she and her attendants took scrupulous pains with her appearance. She had not seen Mark Antony in three and a half years, years any woman would want to render invisible. She had heard about Octavia, the round-faced, gleaming-haired beauty. There was no call for ambrosial robes, gem-encrusted party favors, wall-to-wall roses this time around, however. Cleopatra had something better. On this trip she took the children.

In Antioch, a miniature, less profligate version of Alexandria, Alexander Helios and Cleopatra Selene met their father for the first time. He

acknowledged the twins as his own. It could only have been a joyous
meeting. Antony had Hellenistic pretensions. He had insinuated himself
into the Ptolemaic dynasty; his children were now in line for the Egyptian throne. Moreover, he had a new son, something Octavia, a paragon
on every other front, had not produced. (Antony had two older sons, by
Fulvia.) Some have gone so far as to suggest that it was precisely her failure to provide a male heir—one who would fulfill Virgil's prophecy and
usher in the much-awaited golden age—that drove Antony into the
arms of Cleopatra. Generally Antony liked children and did not believe
it possible to have too many. He was fond of saying that "noble families
were extended by the successive begettings of many kings." He was
hardly the kind of man who could have resisted a Greek-speaking minor
deity of a three-year-old who dressed as a royal, who addressed Antony
as Father, and who—if sculpture can be trusted—in his fleshy face and
mop of bouncing curls resembled him as well. Establishing a divine
claim had been at the top of Antony's agenda for years. He had been edg-
ing that way since Philippi, following the example of his illustrious mentor. With his illegitimate children, Antony legitimately stepped—as a
modern historian has put it—"into his predecessor's bedroom slippers."
It was especially appropriate that he do so in Antioch, a scenic, well-
provisioned river city at the foot of a majestic mountain, with a colonnaded downtown grid and an ample supply of stadiums and gardens,
monumental fountains and natural springs. Bathed in westerly breezes
from May to October, Antioch was sunny and windless in winter, with
delightful baths and a lively market. Well inclined toward Caesar, who
had commissioned a statue of himself there after leaving Cleopatra in 47,
the Syrian capital warmly welcomed his celebrated protégé.

Cleopatra had every personal reason to delight in the long-delayed
family reunion, but the political satisfactions were greater still. Antony
had taken her fishing advice. He was doing what she felt—or for her
own reasons led him to believe—he did best. Devoting himself to a worthy sport, he was reeling in "cities, provinces, and kingdoms." It is not
inaccurate to say that "realms and islands were as plates dropped from

his pocket," as would be suggested later; for the most part there was a compelling logic to Antony's dispositions. He engaged in a long-needed, often-attempted ordering of the restive East. In a multiethnic, multicultural region of shifting alliances—one that had resisted thirty years of Roman efforts at reorganization—he recognized talent, rewarded competence and loyalty. As Antony liked to say, "The greatness of the Roman empire was made manifest not by what the Romans received, but by what they bestowed." Consolidating kingdoms, he ably merged territories and assigned lands. He redrew geography.

He was in his element, and manifestly invincible. No one doubted his imminent triumph over the dreaded Parthians. Rarely had anyone assembled "an army more conspicuous for prowess, endurance, or youthful vigor." Antony's "made all Asia quiver." It was the greatest force he would command, its men uniquely devoted to their largehearted, freewheeling general. Each preferred his good opinion to their very lives, a devotion born, Plutarch effuses, of "the nobility of his family, his eloquence, his frank and open manners, his liberal and magnificent habits, his familiarity in talking with everybody." Antony's mood was contagious; there were high spirits all around. Handing out gifts is always uplifting, and munificence was something he did especially well. It was a corollary to his embrace of large families. In sunny Antioch—the two likely stayed at the island palace, nestled in the bend of the placid river—Cleopatra had reason to congratulate herself, and to believe that, emerging from five years of chaos and confusion, she had backed the right horse.

Upon her September arrival Antony moreover made her an extraordinary present. Not only did he acknowledge his three-year-old twins, but he showered a vast collection of territories on their mother. He confirmed her authority over the island of Cyprus, which even Caesar had not officially granted her. The memory of its loss, and the effects of that monumental loss, could only have burned bright. To Cleopatra's lands he added as well wooded Coele-Syria (part of which is today Lebanon); lush, far-off Cyrene (in modern Libya); a generous swath of cedar-heavy Cilicia (the eastern coast of Turkey); portions of Crete; and all but two cities of the thriving Phoenician coast. In several cases Antony eliminated sovereigns—if an offense could not be found, one could always be fabricated—so that Cleopatra might assume their territories. As of 37 Cleopatra ruled over nearly the entire eastern Mediterranean coast, from what is today eastern Libya, in Africa, north through Israel, Lebanon, and Syria, to southern Turkey, excepting only slivers of Judaea.

Antony's military needs and Roman score-settling largely determined the size and shape of the grant. So did his opinion of Cleopatra; she was proficient, reliable, resourceful. This was what Rome looked for in its client rulers, who had several advantages over Roman appointees, one of which was that they did not need to be paid. More to the point, Antony needed a navy. By the time of the Tarentum treaty he had delivered one hundred bronze-beaked galleys and ten triremes to Octavian. Cleopatra knew how to build ships. For good reason Antony assigned timber-rich provinces to a monarch who had the tradesmen and the resources to transform them into a worthy fleet; in that regard no one in the Mediterranean world was as valuable to Antony as was Cleopatra. As Plutarch acknowledged, her gifts were but some among many distributed to Eastern rulers. At the same time, she was one of the rare sovereigns who remained in place; Antony regularly circumvented established dynasties in making appointments. And Cleopatra received a far more generous gift than that bestowed on any other ruler. By September 37, she had nearly reconstituted the Ptolemaic Empire in its third-century glory.

For good reason she declared a new era for Egypt. Cleopatra's sixteenth regnal year was henceforth to be known as the year one, a double dating she continued throughout her reign. And at thirty-two she redefined herself, assuming an original title. Among the many unconventional privileges Cleopatra enjoyed, naming herself surely figured among the most significant, on par with choosing her consort or managing her own income. She was henceforth "Queen Cleopatra, the Goddess, the Younger, Father-Loving and Fatherland-Loving." She was as astute a manipulator of nomenclature as of much else, and a good deal has been read into that title. With it Cleopatra announced not only a new age but a full-scale political reorientation. She may have appended the final term to discourage murmurs that she was selling out to the Romans; with it Cleopatra signaled to her subjects that she was first and foremost their pharaoh.* Certainly the imagery on her coins is reassuringly consistent with that of previous Ptolemies. By any name she was as powerful a figure as existed on the non-Roman stage. When Antony had vanquished the Parthians, she would be empress of the East. Various coastal cities acknowledged as much, issuing coins in Antony and Cleopatra's honor. She had every reason to be ecstatic. There was not a smudge on the horizon.

Cleopatra could only have looked forward to celebrating the new dawn in Alexandria. Having sacrificed all after the Ides of March, she had not only regained a foothold but fared better this time around. Their pride in the newly established empire aside, how did her subjects take to her close collaboration with a second Roman? There is no trace of scandal. Her people remained focused on the practical implications of Cleopatra's diplomacy. "It seems to me," an eminent scholar has suggested, "that the loves and births of a female pharaoh struck them as divine matters, and that they questioned their queen only when her tax collectors pressed too stringently." She had cleverly solved a political puzzle. The lack of resistance at home may indicate as well that she was not unduly generous with Mark Antony. She may have agreed to pay for his legions, but that Cleopatra could afford without oppressive levies on her people. Nor was there reason to believe Antony's territorial dispositions set off alarms in Rome. They were part of a consistent foreign policy. They enriched the coffers and secured the frontiers. In Egypt, Cleopatra's popularity could only have been at an all-time high.

In light of the gift, many have concluded that Mark Antony and Cleo-

---

*Some have read into her grandiloquence an alignment instead with her Greek heritage. Genuine or not, a revival was unfailingly welcome in a world that measured itself against the past. Hers may have been an expansive, inclusionary gesture; Macedonia had produced not only the Ptolemies but the rival Seleucid dynasty as well. And the once-powerful Seleucids had controlled much of the territory now in Cleopatra's hands.

patra married in Antioch that fall, an awkward proposition as Antony already had a wife. And given his munificence, many have assumed that Cleopatra specified what she would like on the occasion, to which request Antony acceded. There is no evidence of either in Plutarch, the sole source for the reunion, and not a chronicler inclined to omit such a transaction. He allows only that Antony acknowledged their mutual children, by no means tantamount to marriage. Certainly Antony had as much if not more to be gained as did Cleopatra: Even Plutarch could not call it a mistake for the Roman triumvir to ally himself with the richest woman in his world. His immediate, practical needs dovetailed neatly with her long-range imperial ambitions. There is less evidence of a wedding than of Cleopatra's thirst for territory, which manifested itself for the first time now. Either in 37 or the following year, she is said to have pestered Antony for the bulk of Judaea. He apparently refused. (His tenacity on that front has been held up as evidence that he was not putty in her strong hands. He withheld the grant, hence he was not out of his mind with love. Just as possibly, Cleopatra knew her limits and never asked for Judaea, which leaves open the question of Antony's emotional state.) It is unlikely that she had to haggle for territory, though she was well positioned to do so. Antony needed to finance a campaign, pay an army, supplement a navy. Cleopatra needed nothing. Hers was the better negotiating position.

Whatever transpired between the two, the perception among the other client kings in the region was that Antony was deeply, resolutely attached to Cleopatra. It is more difficult to read what was in her heart, at least in 37. We have a few hints, however. Before or after Egypt expanded to its third-century proportions, before or after she reset the calendar, Antony and Cleopatra resumed their sexual relationship, picking up where they had left off in Tarsus. And evidently Antony's presence meant as much to Cleopatra as did his patronage. In March or April 36, she accompanied him along the broad, flat road from Antioch to the edge of the Roman empire, an overland trip that took her hundreds of miles out of her way. It was unnecessary for her and less comfortable than it might otherwise have been, as she was again pregnant. Antony and Cleopatra said their good-byes on the banks of the Euphrates, where the river narrowed into a deep channel, in what is today eastern Turkey. He crossed the wooden bridge into Parthian territory, to march north with his resplendent army, through the vast obstacle course of steppes and rugged mountains that stretch beyond the Euphrates. Cleopatra headed south.

SHE TOOK THE long way home, making a kind of triumphal, overland tour of her new possessions. Many were happy to receive her; some of the despots Antony eliminated on her behalf had been nefarious. Around Damascus, for example, Cleopatra now ruled a territory previously controlled by a tribe of predatory, archery-obsessed bandits. With her entourage she wound her way over the rolling hills and rugged cliffs of modern-day Syria and Lebanon, through twisting passes and deep ravines, to wind up on the crest of a mountain chain, between two lofty hills, in Jerusalem. Surrounded by turreted walls and a series of square, thirty-foot towers, Jerusalem was an eminent commercial center, rich in the arts. Cleopatra had business with Herod, who—though an untiring negotiator—could not have been in any great hurry to discuss it.

When last they had met, Herod had been a fugitive and a suppliant. He now sat uneasily on the Judaean throne, king of a people he had had to conquer in order to rule.* Presumably Cleopatra and her retinue stayed with the newly established sovereign, a collector of homes and a man with a Ptolemaic taste for luxury, though his legendarily opulent palace south of the city had yet to be built. Probably Cleopatra was Herod's guest at his home in the Upper City of Jerusalem, by her definition more of a fortress than a palace. In the course of the visit she met Herod's fractious extended family, with whom she was about to enter into a subversive correspondence. Herod had the misfortune to share an address with several implacable enemies, first among them his con-

*Herod too is a sovereign without a face. Possibly because of the biblical commandment against graven images, we have no likeness of him.

temptuous, highborn mother-in-law, Alexandra. She represented but one aggravation in Herod's largely female household. He lived as well with his insinuating mother; a grievance-loving, overly loyal sister; and Mariamme, the cool, exceptionally beautiful wife who had married him as a teenager, and who, to his frustration, somehow could never get past the fact that Herod had murdered half of her family. Though Cleopatra had assisted him three years earlier, though they shared a patron and were together navigating the same roiling Roman waters—each was doing his best to sustain a skittish, peculiar country in the shadow of a rising superpower—he had no need for yet another domineering woman. Unlike the others, this one moreover had designs on his treasury.

For Cleopatra's visit we have only one source, hostile to his native East, much taken with Rome, working at least partially from Herod's account. The Jewish historian Josephus obscures but cannot entirely camouflage what transpired: Herod and Cleopatra spent some intensive time in each other's company, part of it hammering out the details of his obligations. Antony had granted Cleopatra the exclusive right to the Dead Sea bitumen, or asphalt, glutinous lumps of which floated to the surface of the lake. Bitumen was essential to mortar, incense, and insecticide, to embalming and caulking. A reed basket, smeared with asphalt, could hold water. Plastered with it, a boat is waterproof. The concession was a lucrative one. Also Cleopatra's were the proceeds of Jericho, the popular winter resort, lush with date-palm groves and balsam gardens. Very likely she rode out across a searing desert to inspect those two hundred acres in the Jordan River valley, where Herod had a secondary palace. All other scents paled in comparison to sweet balsam, which grew exclusively in Judaea. The fragrant shrub's oil, seed, and bark were precious. They constituted the region's most valuable export. As for Jericho's dates, they were the finest in the ancient world, the source of its most potent wine. In modern terms, it was as if Cleopatra had been granted no part of Kuwait, only the proceeds of its oil fields.

Herod found the transaction particularly painful as Judaea was a poor country, parched and stony, with few fertile areas, no port, and a rapidly expanding population. His revenues were a risible fraction of Cleopatra's. At the same time his ambitions exceeded his territory; he had no desire to be "King of a wilderness." There appears to have been some bickering over terms, in a negotiation that proved Cleopatra more intently focused on bitumen deliveries than seductions. She was relentless and unsparing; the result was highly favorable to her. Herod agreed to lease the Jericho lands for 200 talents annually. He consented as well to guarantee and collect the rent on the bitumen monopoly from his neighbor, the Nabatean king. By agreeing to do so Herod spared himself the company of any of Cleopatra's agents or soldiers. Otherwise the arrangement worked entirely to her benefit, all the more so as it made both men miserable. It left Herod to extract funds from a sovereign who had denied him refuge during the Parthian invasion, and who made his payments only under duress. Purposely and effectively, Cleopatra set two men who disliked her, a Jew and an Arab, against each other. (Malchus, the Nabatean sovereign, would have his revenge later.) Herod nonetheless upheld his end of the agreement with Cleopatra. He felt that "it would be unsafe to give her any reason to hate him."

The visit was by all other measures an unsuccessful one. The two inveterate charmers failed entirely to endear themselves to each other. Cleopatra may have patronized her fellow sovereign. As his royal mother-in-law tirelessly reminded him, Herod was a commoner. Nor was he exactly Jewish, given his mother's religion; in the eyes of the Jews Herod was a gentile, while in all other eyes he was a Jew. He was as a consequence perennially insecure about his throne, a situation not unfamiliar to Cleopatra, who may have exacerbated it. Her Aramaic may have been better than his Greek; several years her senior, Herod was little educated, sorely deficient in history and culture, sensitive on both counts. (It says a good deal that when he decided to remedy the situation years later he hired the finest tutor in the business, one who—in addition to his own literary and musical accomplishments—had the best credential possible: he had been tutor to Cleopatra's children.) It could not have helped that Herod would have appeared graceless in Cleopatra's silken presence.

Where passions run high, the reverse of the great foreign policy axiom can also prove true: the friend of one's friend is one's enemy. Perhaps Herod felt about Cleopatra the way you inevitably do about someone whose palace puts yours to shame. She may have been too flush with her Antioch success to conciliate; she may well have hinted that she coveted Herod's land. Debts are difficult to acknowledge, and each owed the other. Cleopatra had underwritten Herod's flight to Rome. His father had rushed to Caesar's aid in Alexandria. In any event the famously entertaining Herod had a violent reaction to his visitor. He doubtless arranged a series of royal banquets for Cleopatra. And arguing that he would be providing a community service, he recommended to his council of state that they arrange as well for her murder. It could easily be done, while she was in Jerusalem and at their mercy. He would eliminate a covetous, conniving neighbor, but everyone stood to benefit, Antony most of all. Heatedly Herod explained himself: "In this way, he said, he would rid of many evils all those to whom she had already been vicious or was likely to be in future. At the same time, he argued, this would be a boon to Antony, for not even to him would she show loyalty if some occasion or need should compel him to ask for it."

Herod buttressed his case in the usual way; as ever, the diabolical woman was the sexual one. In addition to all else, he explained to his advisers, the Egyptian hussy had "laid a treacherous snare for him"! Declaring herself overcome with love, she had attempted to force herself upon him, "for she was by nature used to enjoying this kind of pleasure without disguise." Herod had as much reason as anyone to observe that Cleopatra was a tough negotiator. And if you are being taken advantage of by a woman, it is convenient to turn that woman into a sexual predator, capable of unspeakable depravity, "a slave to her lusts." (It was not such a great leap. "Cupidity" and "concupiscence" have the same Latin root.) Having managed to evade her unblushing proposals, Herod took his offended sensibilities to his council. The woman's lewdness was an outrage.

Herod's advisers begged him to reconsider. He was being rash. The risks were too great, as Cleopatra herself—closely guarded, well surrounded, and surely more astute about the political ramifications—surely knew. His council offered Herod a little lesson in the perverse dynamics of affection, one that might have come in handy later. In the first place, Antony would fail to appreciate Cleopatra's murder even were its advantages pointed out to him. Second, "his love would flame up the more fiercely if he thought that she had been taken from him by violence and treachery." He would emerge a man obsessed. Herod would be roundly condemned. He was, Herod's advisers emphasized, out of his league with this woman, the most influential of the day. Could he not bring himself to take the high road?

Cleopatra was of course far too smart to seduce—or attempt to seduce—a small-time sovereign. She had nothing to gain by trapping Herod in such a way. It was unlikely that she would seduce a subordinate of her patron, especially improbable that she would fling herself into Herod's arms at a time when she was—by now quite visibly; it was nearly summer—pregnant with Antony's child. A Roman legion was stationed in Jerusalem to secure Herod's throne. Those men were unlikely to remain silent. Artful though he was, Herod had, as later events would reveal, a limited understanding of the human heart. With difficulty, his council dissuaded him from any assassination attempts. He would have no defense, the plot "being against such a woman as was of the highest dignity of any of her sex at that time in the world." Herod could afford neither to offend Cleopatra nor allow her any reason whatever to hate him. Surely he could bring himself to shrug off the dishonor her brazen advances had caused him?*

*The charge was a familiar one. In inciting a coup, Herod's son later condemned his aunt for having "one night even forced her way into his chamber and, against his will, had immoral relations with him."

Assuming these deliberations reached Cleopatra's ears, it is difficult not to hear her cackling with delight. She had and knew she had Antony's loyalty. She had better reason to consider disposing of Herod, who alone stood between her and full possession of the eastern coastline. As she well knew, his land had at several junctures belonged to the Ptolemies. In the end Herod's council calmed him. Respectfully and politely, he escorted his visitor through the blazing heat of the Sinai to the Egyptian border. If Cleopatra knew of the discussions—and it is difficult to believe that she did not—theirs must have been a charged, tedious trip over molten sand. Surely it was so for the resentful Judaean king. At Pelusium he sent Cleopatra off, heavily pregnant and laden with gifts, a very different return than the furtive one she had made from that outpost in 48.

Early in the fall, one blessed with a copious flood, she gave birth to her fourth child. In the ancient world perhaps more than in any other there was a good deal in a name; she called her new son Ptolemy Philadelphus, baldly evoking the glory days of the third century, the last time her family had reigned over as great an empire as did Cleopatra, the Goddess, the Younger, Father-Loving and Fatherland-Loving, in 36.

TO HEROD'S CHAGRIN, he was not so easily rid of this grasping, business-minded woman. During her stay at the Judaean court Cleopatra had made a few friends, to whom she was about to prove devilishly helpful. Shortly after the return to Egypt, she received word from Alexandra, Herod's mother-in-law. The Hasmonean princess had found in the Egyptian queen a sympathetic spirit, reason enough for Herod to have resented his royal visitor. He would condemn Cleopatra for having coolly eliminated most of her family—it was a rich accusation, coming from someone who had murdered his way to the throne and would continue his bloody spree for decades—but he had equal reason to envy her for having done so. For the most part, class and religious differences accounted for Herod and Alexandra's mutual antipathy. Not only was Herod Jewish on the wrong side, but the Idumeans were new converts to

Judaism. The Jews had little use for them. Herod's wife and her family were by contrast noble-born descendants of generations of Jewish high priests, an office said to have originated with Moses's brother. In 37 Herod ventured outside that family to appoint a new high priest. He did so although there was an obvious and immensely appealing candidate at hand: Mariamme's sixteen-year-old brother, the tall, disarmingly attractive Aristobulus. Herod preferred an undistinguished official in the lucrative, commanding office; its trappings alone conferred a kind of otherworldly power. Fitted with a gold-embroidered diadem, the high priest ministered to his people in a floor-length, tasseled blue robe, set with precious stones and hung with tinkling golden bells. Two brooches fixed a purple, scarlet, and blue cape, also studded with gems, upon his shoulders. Even on a lesser individual, the accessories were enough "to make one feel that one had come into the presence of a man who belonged to a different world."

In bypassing his young brother-in-law Herod set off a maelstrom in his household. To Alexandra—daughter of a priest and widow of a prince—the appointment was an "unendurable insult." With the help of a traveling musician she smuggled word of the indignity to Cleopatra, on whom she felt she could count for female solidarity, especially royal female solidarity. She knew Cleopatra had little patience with Herod and that she had Antony's ear. Could she not intercede with him, implored Alexandra, to obtain the high priesthood for her son? If Cleopatra did so, Antony appears to have had greater matters on his mind than the domestic affairs in Herod's household. He made no effort to intervene, although at some later date in 36 the double-jointed Dellius turned up in Jerusalem on unrelated business. Dellius had been the one to lure Cleopatra to Tarsus; the match of the conspiring mother-in-law and the contortionist adviser was almost too perfect. Alexandra's children were uncommonly handsome, to Dellius's eye more "the offspring of some god rather than of human beings." As ever, pulchritude sent his lively mind whirring. He persuaded Alexandra to have portraits painted of Mariamme and Aristobulus and to submit them straightaway to Antony. Were the Roman triumvir to set eyes upon them, promised Dellius, "She would not be denied anything she might ask."

Alexandra did as Dellius asked, which suggests either naïveté on her part or something more toxic. She could be trusted to detect a plot from one hundred paces away and to supply one, should none be brewing. If Josephus can be taken at his word, Dellius intended to recruit sexual partners of both genders for Antony. In receipt of the portraits Antony hesitated, at least so far as Mariamme was concerned. He knew Cleopatra would be furious. Josephus leaves unclear whether Cleopatra was likely to object on moral grounds or out of jealousy. She would in any event be slow to forgive. Evidently Antony did not hesitate to send for Mariamme's brother. Here Herod changed his mind. For his part, he deemed it unwise to send the most powerful Roman of his time a striking sixteen-year-old boy, "to use him for erotic purposes." Instead Herod assembled his council and his family, to complain of Alexandra's incessant complots. She colluded with Cleopatra to usurp his throne. She schemed to replace him with her son. He would do the right thing and appoint her son to the priesthood. Dellius's proposition may obliquely have prompted the concession; Aristobulus's appointment would keep him in Judaea, out of Antony's clutches and far from Cleopatra's schemes. Alexandra responded with a flood of tears. She begged her son-in-law for forgiveness. She regretted her "usual outspokenness," her heavy-handedness, doubtless an unhappy consequence of her rank. She was overcome with gratitude. Henceforth she would be obedient in all ways.

Aristobulus had barely donned the brilliant robes of the priesthood when Alexandra found herself under house arrest, with round-the-clock surveillance. Herod continued to suspect his mother-in-law of treachery. Alexandra exploded with rage. She had no intention of living out her life "in slavery and fear" and turned to the obvious address. To Cleopatra went "a long sustained lament about the state in which she found herself, and urging her to give her as much help as she possibly could." Again taking a page from Euripides—"it is right for women to stand by a woman's cause"—Cleopatra contrived an ingenious escape. She sent a ship to convey Alexandra and Aristobulus to safety. She would provide asylum for them both. It was now that—either on Cleopatra's counsel or her own initiative—Alexandra arranged for two coffins to be built. With her servants' assistance, she and Aristobulus climbed inside, to be carried from Jerusalem to the coast, where Cleopatra's ship waited. Unfortunately, one of the servants betrayed Alexandra; as the fugitives were conveyed from the palace, Herod stepped from the darkness to surprise them. Though he yearned to do so he did not dare punish Alexandra, for fear of inciting Cleopatra. Instead he made a great show of forgiveness, while quietly vowing revenge.

By October 35 Herod was at his wits' end with his wife and her family. His mother-in-law was in league with his greatest rival. With a far more legitimate claim to the throne, his brother-in-law commanded a dangerous degree of popular devotion. For Herod, the sight of the young man, with his noble bearing and his impeccable good looks, in his majestic robes and golden headdress, presiding at the altar over the Sukkoth festivities, was unbearable. In his subjects' affection for the high priest he read a rebuke to his kingship. Meanwhile Herod was undone in the intimacy of his home by his wife, whose "hatred of him was as great as was his love of her." She manifested little of the lewdness Herod condemned in Cleopatra and had taken to groaning aloud at his embrace. He could not retaliate, even indirectly, against his mother-in-law, too closely bound to Cleopatra. He could neutralize his overly promising brother-in-law, however. In the course of the unseasonably hot fall, Herod invited Aristobulus to join him at Jericho for a swim in the palace pool, nestled amid formal gardens. With friends and servants, the two roughhoused in the cool water at dusk. By nightfall, the seventeen-year-old Aristobulus had—amid the merrymaking—been held underwater a little too long. The high priest was dead.

Grand shows of counterfeit emotion followed on both sides. Herod arranged for an expensive, incense-heavy funeral, shed abundant tears, and mourned loudly. Alexandra bore up bravely and quietly, the better to avenge her son's murder later. (Only Mariamme was candid. She denounced both her husband and his uncouth mother and sister.) In no way deceived by Herod's account of the accident, Alexandra wrote again to Cleopatra, who commiserated with her. The loss was tragic and unnecessary. Alexandra could entrust the unseemly matter to her; she would take it up with Antony. On his return from Parthia Cleopatra urged him to punish Aristobulus's murderer. Surely it was not right, she contended hotly, "that Herod, who had been appointed by him as king of a country which he had no claim to rule, should have exhibited such lawlessness toward those who were the real kings." Hers was a petition in favor of proper convention, of knowing one's station, for the rights of sovereigns. Antony agreed she had a point.

Herod's fears of Cleopatra's influence were well founded. A summons arrived in due course from the Syrian coast; he was to explain himself to Antony. Having proceeded thus far by bribery and bravado, Herod was not generally cowed by authority. He tended rather to merry displays of presumption. And though he was said to have headed off timidly, he proved as adept at defusing the situation as had Cleopatra, six years earlier, in Tarsus, which was another way of saying either that Mark Antony had no great gift for calling client kings to account, or that he was powerless in the presence of a master sycophant. The visit does reveal Antony to have been in no way putty in Cleopatra's hands. Herod arrived with lavish gifts and equally lavish explanations. He handily neutralized Cleopatra's arguments. Surely, Antony assured him, "it was improper to demand an accounting of his reign from a king, since in that case he would not be a king at all, and those who had given a man this office and conferred authority upon him should permit him to exercise it." He purportedly said the same to Cleopatra, who would do well to concern herself less with Herod's affairs — or so Herod claimed, while boasting of the many honors Antony had shown him. The two dined together daily. Antony invited Herod to accompany him as he transacted business. And all this "in spite of Cleopatra's bitter charges." There was nothing but goodwill between the two men; the Judaean king reported that he was safe from that "wicked woman" and her insatiable greed.

He was on that count slightly mistaken, although Herod did manage more or less to extricate himself from the feminine machinations at home. Within months of his return, his maniacally vindictive sister convinced him that her husband and Mariamme had had an affair in his absence. It was a surefire way of dispensing both with a malignant sister-in-law and an unwanted husband. The claim was perfectly calibrated to fluster an unloved, besotted man; it worked the desired effect. (As Euripides observed in a Hellenistic favorite among his plays, "There seems to be some pleasure for women in sick talk of one another.") Without so much as a hearing, Herod ordered his brother-in-law to be put to death. And for good measure, he threw Alexandra into prison, on the grounds that she must at least in some part be responsible for his troubles. Herod was someone whose loyalties could be bought and who assumed the same of others. He was forever revising his will.

Even without Alexandra's assistance, Cleopatra would continue to cause Herod headaches—or attempt to—for a few years longer. He was said to have fortified Masada out of fear of her, stockpiling grain, oil, dates, and wine in the fortress. He could not rest easy with the Egyptian queen in the neighborhood.* And Herod's female relations continued to seethe with hatred for his wife. They easily convinced him that Mariamme had in the end secretly sent her portrait to Antony. Herod had "a ready ear only for slander" and inclined always toward those who

---

*Another intrigue followed, involving Costobar, the governor of a neighboring region, south of Judaea. He owed his position to Herod, whom he disdained. Nor had Costobar any affection for the Jews; he preferred to restore polytheism to his people. And he knew precisely where he might appeal for relief: He wrote to Cleopatra, a clearinghouse for Antonian questions. His land had long belonged to her ancestors. Why did she not ask Antony for it? He himself, he swore, stood ready to transfer his loyalty to her. Costobar did so not out of affection for Cleopatra but distaste for Herod. He got nowhere, as Antony refused Cleopatra's request. Herod hesitated to take revenge on Costobar, again for fear of Cleopatra. To forestall any future plots, Herod instead arranged for Costobar to marry his newly widowed sister, a death sentence of a kind. She would ultimately betray her second husband as she had the first.

indulged it; he liked to be proved right in his dire delusions. The accusation "struck him like a thunderbolt" and caused him to obsess anew about Cleopatra's deadly schemes.* Surely this was her doing: "He was menaced, he reckoned, with the loss not merely of his consort but of his life." He sentenced his wife to death. As she was led to her execution her mother leapt out at her, to scream and pull at her hair. She was, Alexandra berated her daughter, an evil, insolent woman, insufficiently grateful to Herod, and entirely deserving of her fate. Mariamme walked serenely past, without acknowledging her mother. She was twenty-eight. In an additional proto-Shakespearean twist, Herod was undone by her death. His desire for Mariamme only increased; he convinced himself that she was still alive; he was physically incapacitated. He suffered precisely as his advisers had predicted Antony would if deprived of Cleopatra. Ultimately Herod left Jerusalem on an extended, recuperative hunting trip. Alexandra hatched a few new conspiracies in his absence. He ordered her execution on his return.

THROUGHOUT 36 MARK ANTONY reported on his dazzling success in Parthia to Rome; the city held festivals, and performed sacrifices, in his honor. Cleopatra's intelligence may have been better. She was well over a thousand miles from the snowy theater of action but closer than was the Italian peninsula. She was every bit as invested in Antony's victory; she had the resources to arrange for regular emissaries. Nonetheless she may have been surprised by the messenger who arrived in Alexandria late in the year. He had an urgent summons, unlike any she had previously received. Probably a month in coming, it brought a season of exhilarations to an end. Antony and his army had returned from their Parthian adventure. It had taken them nearly to the Caspian Sea, in what is today northern Iran. Theirs had been a mere jaunt compared to Alexander the Great's, but they had made an eighteen-hundred-mile trek all the same. They camped now in a small village south of modern-day Beirut, with an excellent harbor, in

*His sister would not be happy until she had wrought vengeance as well on Herod and Mariamme's sons, whom Herod later murdered. They were buried alongside Aristobulus.

which Cleopatra could land without difficulty. Antony implored her to join him posthaste, and to bring with her substantial gold, provisions, and clothing for his men. She had by no means expected to see him so soon. Parthia could hardly have been conquered in a matter of months. Caesar had anticipated a campaign of at least three years.

Plutarch reports that Cleopatra was slow in coming, but it is unclear whether she actually delayed or if it only seemed as if she did to Mark Antony, for whom she could not arrive quickly enough. It was winter; heavy rains and gale winds lashed the Mediterranean. She had supplies to assemble and a fleet to prepare. She needed either to collect or mint silver denarii. She had given birth months earlier. She knew she was heading toward disturbing news. For his part, Antony was restless and agitated, though Plutarch may have erred in imputing cause and effect, alleging that Antony was beside himself because Cleopatra was dilatory. The purported delay had little to do with the authentic distress. Antony attempted to distract himself by drinking heavily—already it was acknowledged that "there is no other medicine for misery"—but was without the patience to sit through a meal. He interrupted each one to run to shore, where he scanned the horizon again and again for Egyptian sails, irregular behavior in a precise and precisely disciplined Roman camp, where everyone dined together. Plutarch accuses Cleopatra of having dawdled but the point is that she came, in a season of short days and long nights, with the requested items, probably arriving soon after Antony's forty-eighth birthday. She delivered "an abundance of clothing and money." Both Plutarch and Dio retail a disgruntled rumor: Some claimed that she brought clothing and supplies but that Antony settled his own gold on his men, passing the monies off as a gift from Cleopatra, who had little patience for his Parthian obsession. Either way he was buying goodwill toward Egypt, clearly a priority for him, and at a time when he could ill afford to do so.

Slow-moving Egyptian queens aside, Antony had every reason for despair. There had been no dazzling success in Parthia, only a demoralizing campaign followed by a disastrous retreat. From the start he had made strategic mistakes. Given the size of his army and the length of their march, he had left his siege equipment behind. He could not always find the Parthians but they could always find him: swarms of talented archers and pikemen repeatedly ambushed the regular Roman rows. Antony had relied on the Armenians—Parthia's western neighbor—for military aid. They had not proved the faithful allies he anticipated. Not for the first time, they lured the Romans into "a yawning and abysmal desert" only to abandon them. No battle had been as costly as the retreat. Having marched for thirty miles in darkness, Antony's exhausted men threw themselves upon brackish water. Starving, they feasted on poisonous plants that made them stagger and vomit. Convulsions, dysentery, and delusions followed. What stagnant water and poisonous plants failed to claim, the heat in Armenia and the unending snows of Cappadocia did. Ice congealed on beards. Toes and fingers froze.

By the time he reached the Syrian coast, by the time he had begun obsessively to scan the horizon for Cleopatra, Antony had lost nearly a third of his splendid army and half his cavalry. In eighteen modest battles he had secured few substantial victories; in his catastrophic retreat, he lost some 24,000 men. In something of a backhanded compliment, Cleopatra would be assigned blame for his Parthian missteps. "For so eager was he to spend the winter with her that he began the war before the proper time, and managed everything confusedly. He was not master of his own faculties, but, as if he were under the influence of certain drugs or of magic rites, was ever looking eagerly towards her, and thinking more of his speedy return than of conquering the enemy," Plutarch explains. Yet again, Cleopatra was said to have thrown off Antony's timing. Or yet again Antony fumbled, and Cleopatra wound up with the blame.

The campaign proved as revealing as it was disastrous. Repeatedly Antony found himself outwitted by a cunning enemy, deceived by friends. The Parthian months were less about loving the wrong woman than trusting the wrong men. Antony was a compassionate general, so much "sharing in the toils and distresses of the unfortunate and bestowing upon them whatever they wanted" as to elicit more loyalty from the wounded than the able. He seemed sorely deficient in the vengeance department. The Armenian king, Artavasdes, had encouraged Antony to invade neighboring Media (modern Azerbaijan, a land of fierce tribes and towering mountain ranges), then double-crossed him. His men encouraged him to call Artavasdes to account, which Antony refused to do. He "neither reproached him with his treachery nor abated the friendliness and respect usually shown to him." He knew how to play on the heartstrings; when he needed to rally his men against dismal odds, he "called for a dark robe, that he might be more pitiful in their eyes." (Friends dissuaded him. Antony made the appeal to his troops in the purple robe of a Roman general.) The greatest casualty of the expedition was arguably his peace of mind. At least once he was on the brink of suicide. He was badly shaken, as only a commander who in the past had proved resourceful, valorous, omnipresent, could be. Worse yet, after the wretched expedition—having lost tens of thousands of his men, distributed what remained of his treasure, and begged to be put to death—he convinced himself in Syria "by an extraordinary perversion of mind," that, by escaping as he had, he had actually won the day.

Such was the exhausted, distraught man Cleopatra found on the Syrian coast. Despite the charges that she had shortchanged him, her arrival brought relief to his hungry troops, demoralized and in tatters. She very much played the bountiful, beneficent Isis. Of how she handled delusional Antony we have no clue. She must have been taken aback by what nine months had done to a well-drilled, superbly supplied army. From the start there were irritations and tense differences of opinion in the Syrian camp. It was at this time that Cleopatra urged Antony to punish Herod for his mistreatment of Alexandra and that Antony instructed Cleopatra not to meddle, a message she was unaccustomed to hearing. Under the circumstances, it would have struck her as particularly undeserved. She remained with Antony for several weeks, at the center of the regularly spaced tents, the improvised Roman city, as he pondered his next steps. Word had reached him that the Median and Parthian kings had quarreled in the wake of his retreat, and that the Median king—whose lands abutted Parthia—now proposed to join forces with Antony. Revived by the news, he began to prepare a fresh campaign.

Cleopatra was not the only woman to come to Antony's rescue. He had too a very loyal wife. She applied for permission to fly to her husband's aid, permission her brother cheerfully granted. Octavian could well afford to send supplies. His own campaigns had gone well. And Octavia's trip was essentially an ambush. In 37 Octavian had promised Antony 20,000 men for Parthia, which he had not delivered. With his sister, he now sent an elite corps of 2,000 handpicked, sumptuously armored bodyguards. For Antony to accept them was to forfeit 18,000 men, at a time when he desperately needed to replenish the ranks. To decline was to insult his rival's sister. For Octavian, eager for a plausible excuse for a breach, it was an irresistible opportunity; Antony could not do the right thing. Octavia hastened to Athens, sending word ahead to her husband. Dio has Antony in Alexandria at this time, while Plutarch implies that he and Cleopatra remained on the Syrian coast. Two things are certain: Antony and Cleopatra were at this juncture very much together. And Antony held Octavia off. She was to come no farther. He was set to depart again for Parthia. In no way fooled by his message, Octavia sent a personal friend of Antony's to pursue the matter—and to remind Antony of his wife's many virtues. What, asked that envoy, loyal to both husband and wife, was Octavia to do with the goods she had with her? Here she came close to showing up Cleopatra, which may have been the point. Octavia had in hand not only the richly equipped praetorian guards, but a vast quantity of clothing, horses and pack animals, money of her own, and gifts for Antony and his officers. Where was she to send them?

She was throwing down the gauntlet, to which Cleopatra responded, though not in kind. In Octavia she recognized a serious rival, alarmingly close at hand. Her loyal representative was on Cleopatra's territory. Cleopatra had heard reports of Octavia's beauty. Roman men could be catty, too; those who had set eyes on her would later wonder aloud about Antony's preference for the Egyptian queen. "Neither in youthfulness nor beauty," they concluded, "was she superior to Octavia." (The two women were in fact the same age.) Cleopatra worried that Octavia's authority, her brother's influence, "her pleasurable society and her assiduous attentions to Antony," would make Octavia irresistible. The sovereign who had proceeded by bold maneuver and steely calculation here attempted — or was said to attempt — a different tack, resorting to loud, choking sobs, depending on the occasion the first or last weapon in a woman's arsenal. Plutarch sniffs that Cleopatra pretended to be desperately in love with Antony; in a Roman account, she cannot even secure credit for an authentic emotional attachment. If his report can be believed — it reads a little like a cartoon frame spliced into a nuanced narrative — she was as effective a woman as she was a sovereign. She could have offered Fulvia a very valuable tutorial. Cleopatra neither begged nor bargained. She did not raise her voice. Instead she swore off food. She appeared languid with love, undone by her passion for Antony. (Already the hunger strike was the oldest trick in the book. Euripides' Medea too waged one, to win back a wayward husband.) Cleopatra affected "a look of rapture when Antony drew near, and one of faintness and melancholy when he went away." She dragged herself about, dissolved in tears, which she made a great show of drying whenever Antony turned up. She meant of course to spare him any distress.

Cleopatra rarely did anything alone, and for her wail-and-whimper act recruited a supporting cast. Her courtiers worked overtime on her behalf. Mostly they upbraided Antony. How could he be so heartless as to destroy "a mistress who was devoted to him and him alone"? Did he not grasp the difference between the two women? "For Octavia, they said, had married him as a matter of public policy and for the sake of her brother, and enjoyed the name of wedded wife." She hardly bore comparison to Cleopatra, who, although a sovereign, the queen of millions, "was called Antony's mistress, and she did not shun this name nor disdain it, as long as she could see him and live with him." Hers was the noblest of sacrifices. She was neglecting a great kingdom and her many responsibilities, "wearing her life away, as she follows with you on your marches, in the guise of a concubine." How could he remain indifferent? There was no contest between the two women. Cleopatra would forsake all, "as long as she could see him and live with him; but if she were driven away from him she would not survive it," a conclusion she effectively supported with her shuddering gasps and inanition. Even Mark Antony's closest friends chimed in, enthralled by Cleopatra, and doubtless well aware of Antony's leanings.

As campaigns went, this one involved skirmishes if not outright battles; the atmosphere around Antony and Cleopatra was highly charged. The tactics also proved highly effective. Cleopatra's theatrics melted Antony. The reproofs of his friends flattered him. A man of disorderly passions, Antony seemed to count on chiding, to which he gamely responded. He was a happy subordinate, arguably at his best in that role. Plutarch has him taking more pleasure in the rebukes than he did in any commendations: Scolded for his hard-heartedness, he "failed to see that by this seeming admonition he was being perversely drawn towards her." He convinced himself that she would kill herself were he to leave her. It was particularly difficult for him to be angry under the circumstances; he had already the death of one loyal, intelligent woman on his conscience. Whatever else could be said of Antony he was compassionate, as any of his men could attest. He rebuffed Octavia. She returned to Rome a woman scorned in all eyes but her own. She refused to dwell on the insult; when her brother ordered her to leave the marital home, she refused to do so. Again she renounced the Helen of Troy role, claiming that "it was an infamous thing even to have it said that the two greatest commanders in the world plunged the Romans into civil war, the one out of passion for, and the other out of resentment in behalf of, a woman."

Cleopatra showed no such disinclination. With Antony's affections went the throne of Egypt. To lose him to Octavia was to lose everything. Hers was a virtuoso performance that yielded enduring results. From this point on the two were inseparable, for which Dio credits "the passion and witchery of Cleopatra" and Plutarch "certain drugs or magic rites." Antony's men—and Octavia—instead acknowledge a very real affection. Geography suggests as much as well. Antony remained with Cleopatra in Alexandria for the winter. He had a sliver of a practical reason to do so, as he intended to march east again come spring. As of the winter of 35 it is impossible to deny a full-blooded romance, if by romance we mean a congenial, intimate past, a shared family, a shared bed, and a shared vision of the future.

CLEOPATRA'S BLUE-RIBBON RENDITION of the lovesick female distracted Antony from a second Parthian offensive, which he postponed, to be at her side. She was thin and pale. Her state of mind worried him. In 35 she did, very intentionally, throw off his timing. An Eastern triumph remained as critical for Antony as ever, if not more so; while he licked his Parthian wounds, Octavian had been piling up successes. He had crushed Sextus Pompey and sidelined Lepidus. (With bribes, Octavian also lured Lepidus's eighteen legions out from under him.) Only Antony and Octavian remained. And only an Eastern victory could once and for all secure Caesar's glorious mantle. Antony had unfinished business as well with the Armenian king, who he belatedly decided should be held accountable for the catastrophic outing. Cleopatra has been assumed not to have smiled on Antony's military ambitions and to have preferred his attentions directed elsewhere. Certainly Parthia was of less concern to her than were Roman politics; Egypt was for the most part insulated against an Eastern invasion. At the same time that kingdom was entirely vulnerable to Rome. Military glory was by no means the coin of her realm; a Parthian expedition would have struck her as futile on many counts. It is easy to hear how the argument might have gone, important to remember it a matter of speculation. What would have made eminent good sense for Antony was a return to Rome, from which he had been absent for five years. That outing Cleopatra must have resisted with every fiber of her theatrical being. An Eastern expedition was expensive, but by her calculation a trip to Rome—a return to Octavia and Octavian—would have been infinitely more costly.

Antony remained sorely in need of a victory. He was also eager to settle a score. "In his endeavor to take vengeance on the Armenian king with the least trouble to himself," he sent the ever-inventive Dellius east, to Armenia. As usual, Dellius had a proposition. It this time amounted to the traditional diplomatic bandage. Would Artavasdes, the Armenian monarch, not like to promise his daughter to Cleopatra and Antony's six-year-old son, Alexander Helios? Cleopatra presumably signed off on this appeal, which would have established a Ptolemy on the Armenian throne. It would also have secured a peaceful alliance with a mountain kingdom crucial to a Parthian invasion and divided in its loyalties. Several times a Roman ally, Armenia was in both sympathy and civilization Parthian. The offer evidently made less sense to Artavasdes, a supple and unflinching statesman. He resisted Dellius's blandishments and his bribes. Antony countered in the spring by invading Armenia. In little time he subdued the country, declaring it a Roman province. This was vengeance more than victory; Armenia was a strategically located buffer state but by no means a great power. And Antony knew the conquest satisfied his men, who had for months howled that Artavasdes had cost them Parthia. In anticipation of a larger campaign, Antony left the bulk of his army in the East for the winter. He returned to Alexandria in triumph, taking with him not only the collected treasure of Armenia, but its king, his wife, their children, and the provincial governors. Out of deference to their rank, he bound the royal family in chains of gold.

This time Cleopatra received a jubilant message from her lover. She issued orders for an extravagant ceremony to mark his return. She likely took her cues from Antony: her immediate family were not conquerors. Processions were, however, a Ptolemaic specialty. The sphinx-lined avenues of Alexandria were designed for them, and the Roman triumph derived from them. That of autumn 34 was sensational. Antony sent his captives ahead of him into the city, which he entered in his purple cloak, aboard a chariot. Presumably they paraded past the marble colonnades and the awnings of shuttered shops, along the Canopic Way, lined with vibrant banners and cheering spectators. Here was the kind of show at which Ptolemies excelled. To this one Antony and Cleopatra added a new twist. As he marched his booty and captives into the heart of the city Antony presented them to the queen of Egypt, in ceremonial attire on a lofty, golden throne, atop a silver-plated platform, amid her adoring subjects.

Antony had long been good at paying homage to his mistresses; Cleopatra received not only the spoils of his campaign, the royal treasury and its officials, but the proud Armenian king and his family, in their golden fetters. A discordant note was struck when the fresh-faced Artavasdes arrived before her. The Armenian king was neither a fool nor a philistine; he wrote histories and intricate speeches. For years he had shrewdly played Parthia and Rome off against each other. True to tenacious form, he approached but would neither sink to his knees before her nor acknowledge her rank. Instead he addressed her by name. All coercion was futile; though treated harshly, no member of the Armenian royal family would prostate himself before the queen of Egypt. (It is notable that despite the misbehavior, Artavasdes survived the display. In Rome a captive king was rarely so lucky, no matter how well he behaved.) It was Cleopatra's first experience of a royal humiliation and a monarch's proud resistance. There was every reason why they should have made an impression. A lavish banquet for the people of Alexandria followed, with celebrations at the palace and with public entertainments. She distributed coins and food freely.

The military-themed procession was an oddity to the Alexandrians, though it had at least Ptolemaic roots. There was no precedent for the splendid ceremony that followed. Several days later a throng filled Alexandria's colonnaded gymnasium, west of the city's main crossroads, minutes from the palace. Six hundred feet long, the city's largest structure, the gymnasium stood at the center of Alexandria as at the center of its intellectual and recreational life. It was the opera hall of its day; a gymnasium's presence was what made a town a city. In the open court of the complex that fall day the Alexandrians discovered another silver platform, on which stood two massive golden thrones. Mark Antony occupied one. Addressing her as the "New Isis," he invited Cleopatra to join him on the other. She appeared in the full regalia of that goddess, a pleated, lustrously striped chiton, its fringed edge reaching to her ankles. On her head she may have worn a traditional tripartite crown or one of cobras with a vulture cap. By one account Antony dressed as Dionysus, in a gold-embroidered gown and high Greek boots. In his hand he held the god's fennel stalk. An ivy wreath circled his head. It seemed a second act of the exultant play begun in Tarsus, when—as Cleopatra made her way upriver—word preceded her that Venus had arrived to revel with Dionysus for the happiness of Asia.

Cleopatra's children occupied four smaller thrones at the couple's feet. In his husky voice Antony addressed the assembled multitude. By his command Cleopatra was henceforth to be known as "Queen of Kings." (On coins, she was "Queen of Kings, whose sons are Kings." The titles would change with the territory, so that an Upper Egypt stela of four years later has her as "Mother of Kings, Queen of Kings, the Youngest Goddess.") As for her consort, thirteen-year-old Caesarion, Antony promoted him to King of Kings, a pointed recycling of an Armenian and Parthian title. Antony conferred these honorifics in the name of Julius Caesar, Cleopatra's husband and Caesarion's father, an unusual case of flaunting a lover's prior sexual history. Also on Caesar's behalf, Antony proceeded to name his sons with Cleopatra as King of Kings. Producing the boys in turn, he assigned vast territories to each; the Eastern-inflected names came in handy now. At his cue, little Alexander Helios stepped forward, in the loose leggings and caped tunic of a Persian monarch. On his head he wore an upright, pointed turban topped with a peacock feather. His territories stretched to India; he was to rule over Armenia, Media, and—once his father had conquered it—Parthia. (He was again promised in marriage, this time to the daughter of the Median king, Artavasdes' traditional enemy.) Two-year-old Ptolemy Philadelphus, the fruit of Antony and Cleopatra's Antioch reunion, was an Alexander the Great in miniature. He wore the high boots, the short purple cloak, and the brimmed woolen hat—in this case wrapped with a diadem—of a

Macedonian. To him went Phoenicia, Syria, and Cilicia, the lands west of the Euphrates. Cleopatra Selene was to preside over Cyrene, the Greek settlement in what is today eastern Libya, hundreds of miles across the desert. The distributions made, each of the two younger boys rose to kiss his parents. They were then surrounded by a colorful phalanx of bodyguards, Armenians in Alexander's case, Macedonians in Ptolemy's.

In such a way Antony parceled out the East, including lands not yet in his possession. For the young woman who fourteen years earlier had smuggled herself into Alexandria to plead for her diminished kingdom, it was a sensational reversal. Cleopatra stood divine and indomitable, less queen than empress, the supreme Roman commander at her side. Her rule extended over a vast swath of Asia, its frontiers established and now at peace. She was protected by Roman legions; with her children, she now reigned, at least nominally, over more land than had any Ptolemy in centuries. On coins minted for the occasion — with them she became the first foreigner to appear on a Roman coin — she appears majestic, authoritative. She has also aged. Her mouth is fuller, and she is noticeably fleshier, especially around the neck.

It is impossible to say whose ambition had brought about the sparkling ceremony, to be known later as the Donations of Alexandria. It is especially difficult to locate Cleopatra's fingerprints; the truth is smudged forever by Roman manhandling. At least in part the message of the day was clear. On their golden thrones sat what even a coolheaded modern historian has reasonably called "the two most magnificent people in the world." Together they seemed to resurrect if not expand upon the dream of Alexander the Great, promoting a universal empire, one that transcended national boundaries and embraced a common culture, that reconciled Europe and Asia. They announced a new order. Cleopatra presided over the ceremony and the citywide banqueting that followed not only as a sovereign but as a deity after all, with the divine Caesar's son on one side, Dionysian Antony on the other. Old prophecies evidently resurfaced now. The Jews linked Cleopatra's rule with a golden age and with the coming of the Messiah. The queen of Egypt answered the call for an Eastern savior. She would rise above Rome for a better world. In conflating the political and the religious, the imagery was all on Cleopatra's side.

Mark Antony had a habit of jumping to conclusions, and in many ways the Donations were an exercise in wishful thinking. Certainly they made no difference to the administration of the lands in question, many of them governed by Roman proconsuls. The Armenian king was still very much alive. Parthia was not Antony's to distribute. A two-year-old child was in no position to rule. As much as the ceremony was a stunning act of assimilation and appropriation, entirely Ptolemaic in its gigantism, it was probably not intended solely for the Alexandrians. Pageantry was never lost on them, but by 34 Cleopatra's subjects needed no confirmation of her steady rule, of her divinity, her supremacy, or even of Antony's role in her court. They knew him already more as Dionysus than as Roman magistrate. The two may have intended to formalize arrangements for a subdued but still messy East; Antony may have meant only to rebuke those monarchs who had defied him in Parthia. Or Antony and Cleopatra may have been delivering a powerful, unsubtle message to Octavian. His power derived solely from Julius Caesar. He might well be Caesar's adopted son, but Caesar's natural son was, Antony and Cleopatra emphasized, very much alive, nearly adult, and suddenly sovereign over a vast expanse of territory. That message was particularly crucial at a time when Octavian was said to be busy behind the scenes undermining Antony's efforts in Armenia, where he attempted to suborn Artavasdes.

Even if Antony and Cleopatra were not broadcasting to Rome, it is from Rome that our accounts derive. It is impossible to disentangle what the two may have meant to convey; what Rome actually heard; and what the propagandists turned out, magnified and distorted. The language of the display was Eastern. Especially in 34, it translated poorly. Antony should have known better than to emphasize Caesarion's paternity. (He may well have known better. Plutarch does not mention the inflammatory remarks.) Octavian had reason to play up the insult, as he did the un-Roman magnificence. It was incumbent on him to blunt the potent symbolism, to turn a military triumph and royal pageant into a drunken revel and a specious, silly costume drama. One did not pay tribute to Julius Caesar in Alexandria, after all. Nor did one celebrate a triumph outside Rome, far from the Roman gods. And why this riotous celebration of an Armenian victory when Parthia remained to be punished?

Whatever his message, Antony meant the Donations as an official act. He sent reports of the triumph and the ceremony back to Rome, for Senate ratification. Devoted friends intervened, aware that his dispatches would be read in an unflattering light. Antony appeared "theatrical and arrogant," precisely the crimes that had cost Caesar his life. If he intended to dazzle his compatriots with the gorgeous display, the laws of optics worked differently from what he had remembered. Rome had to shield her eyes from the glare of golden thrones. Definitions were less fluid in that city, where Antony's dual role as commander in the West and monarch in the East taxed the orderly Roman mind. He dangerously mixed his metaphors. If Cleopatra were the queen of those territories, what role was the Roman commander to play? Antony had after all claimed no territories for himself. Cleopatra's title was preposterously, objectionably large, an insult not only to Rome, but to her fellow sovereigns. She had long occupied an exceptional position in the Roman constellation of client kings. She now outranked them in both wealth and influence. And Antony and Cleopatra's relationship was problematic. What was a foreign woman doing on a Roman coin? It did not help that Antony shared denarii with a woman not his wife. He appeared to be distributing Roman lands to a foreigner.

Only one man wanted Antony's dispatches published. Octavian did not succeed, although he did manage to suppress reports of the Armenian victory. He had no intention of allowing Antony a Roman triumph, which would have counted for a very great deal. The Donations may have been at the time little more than an exercise in Alexandrian grandiosity, in Ptolemaic boasting, a provocative display of symbols, Antony's version of erecting a golden statue of Cleopatra in the Forum. At best the celebrations were simply tone-deaf. At worst they were an insult to Octavian, a brazen power play. The intention hardly mattered given how the exercise looked in Rome, which was how Octavian wanted it to: as an empty gesture, a farcical overreaching by two slightly demented, power-drunk dissolutes, "a Dionysiac revel led by an eastern harlot." With the Donations a munificent Antony handed out plenty of gifts, none more generous than that he settled on Octavian.

ILLICIT AFFAIRS AND BASTARD CHILDREN

"For talk is evil: It is light to raise up quite easily, but it is difficult to bear, and hard to put down. No talk is ever entirely gotten rid of, once many people talk it up: It too is some god."

— HESIOD

CLEOPATRA TURNED THIRTY-FIVE without a change in her considerable and accumulating good fortune; the year ahead promised to be among the happiest and most auspicious of her reign. With her hybrid family, she had ingeniously solved the Roman problem, the consort problem, the shrinking-empire problem. She no longer needed to be propped up by foreign troops. Nor could any Alexandrian critic conceivably object to her friendship with a Roman. She had tamed that power, and augmented Egypt through its largesse. With the Donations she experienced a surge of popularity; her shipyards were busy, as she doubled the size of Antony's navy. The revenues flowed in. From Damascus and Beirut in the east to Tripoli in the west, cities minted coins in her honor. She had made good on a third-century poet's promise, by which a Ptolemy — simultaneously safeguarding and supplementing his inheritance — outweighs all other monarchs in wealth, given "the abundance that flowed hourly to his sumptuous palace from every quarter."

Antony obliged her in her greatest desire: After the celebrations, he did not return to Rome, where he might have fleshed out his army with new recruits and neutralized Octavian's influence. Nor did he even journey to Antioch, a logical base for an Eastern operation. Instead he settled down for a third festive winter in Alexandria, an imperial city that felt increasingly like the home of a new empire. In vivid illustration of the point, Cleopatra either put the finishing touches on or began to enjoy the newly constructed Caesareum, her vast harborside complex, which she may have modeled on the Forum of Rome. Fusing Egyptian and Greek styles, the Alexandrian version was slathered with gold and silver, stuffed with paintings and statuary, embellished with "galleries, libraries, porches, courts, halls, walks, and consecrated groves, as glorious as expense and art could make them." Cleopatra stood at the helm of the mighty power that a nervous Roman had a century earlier predicted Egypt might one day be, "if ever that kingdom found capable leaders."

Around her assembled loyal, long-serving advisers, dedicated Romans, and an extended family, which by year's end included the teen-aged Marcus Antonius Antyllus, the elder of Antony's two sons by Fulvia. Cleopatra took the children's schooling seriously. In the wake of the Donations she entrusted their education in part to Nicolaus of Damascus, a lanky diplomat's son several years her junior, with a ruddy face, an affable temperament, and a taste for Aristotle. Handy with an anecdote, Nicolaus was a gifted logician, the kind of man you could rely on to finish your speech, persuasively and eloquently, if you happened to dissolve into tears before you reached its end. He moved into the palace. Under his guidance Cleopatra's children read philosophy and rhetoric but especially history, which their new tutor deemed "the proper study of kings." Genial though Nicolaus may have been, he was sharp-tongued when necessary and a relentless taskmaster. His idea of leisure would be to add 25 volumes to his comprehensive history of the ancient world, already 140 volumes long, and a project its author compared to the labors of Hercules. Around the children the festivities and frivolities continued. Many threw themselves into court life with enthusiasm. Lucius Munatius Plancus, one of Antony's closest advisers and a former provincial governor, appeared at a dinner naked and painted blue. He entertained Cleopatra's banqueters with his best sea nymph imitation, wriggling across the floor on his knees, attired only in a fish tail and a crown of reeds.

The taste for indulgence was contagious, or possibly inherited. At dinner one night a physician from young Antyllus's retinue began to pontificate, boorishly and interminably. When a second court physician stopped him in his windy tracks—it was the former medical student who had toured Cleopatra's kitchen—Antyllus whooped with delight. With a wave of his arm, he gestured to the sideboard. "All of this I bestow upon thee, Philotas," he exclaimed, forcing a collection of gold beakers on the quicker-witted of his guests. Philotas hardly took the teenager at his word but nonetheless found himself presented with a bulging sack of elaborately worked, antique vessels. (He headed off with its cash equivalent instead.) Throughout the city the music, mimes, and stage productions continued. As one clever stonemason saw it, the merry pact that joined Antony and Cleopatra merited an alternate interpretation. From December 28, 34, survives a basalt inscription, presumably from a statue of Antony. Whatever Cleopatra made of his ardent affections, the Alexandrians wholly reciprocated. The sporting Antony is hailed in stone not as an "Inimitable Liver" but—the pun requires more of a stretch in Greek than in English—the "Inimitable Lover."

Official business was by no means neglected among the revelries. Cleopatra continued to receive petitions and envoys, to participate in religious rites, to mete out justice. She supervised economic discussions, met with advisers, and presided over the innumerable Alexandrian festivals. Increasingly state business included Egypto-Roman business. Legionnaires had been posted in Egypt for half of Cleopatra's lifetime; in one account, her Roman bodyguards now inscribed her name on their shields. And in a mutually beneficial arrangement, Roman futures were decided in Alexandria rather than the other way around. In 33 Cleopatra dictated an ordinance to a scribe, in which she awarded a substantial tax exemption to one of Antony's top generals. Publius Canidius had served in Parthia and distinguished himself in Armenia. For his services, Cleopatra accorded him a waiver of export duties on 10,000 sacks of wheat and import duties on 5,000 amphorae of wine. He was exempted from land taxes in perpetuity, a privilege Cleopatra extended equally to his tenants. Even Canidius's farm animals were to be above taxes, requisition, seizure.* It was an agile way to keep Antony's men both loyal and local, in the unlikely event that the enchantments of Alexandria proved insufficient. It was also a more effective way of courting an ambitious Roman than paying bribes, which, it has been noted, "only made them come back for more." Much of their business the Roman triumvir and the Egyptian queen transacted together. Cleopatra frequented the marketplace with Antony, "joined him in the management of festivals and in the hearing of lawsuits." At her urging, Antony took charge of the city's gymnasium, as he had done in Athens. As de facto leader of the Greek community, he directed its finances, teachers, lectures, athletic contests. With Cleopatra he posed for painters and sculptors; he was Osiris or Dionysus to her Isis or Aphrodite. In mid-33 Antony marched again to Armenia, where he arranged a peace with the Median king. They would henceforth serve each other as allies, against the Parthians and, if need be, against Octavian. Asia was now quiet. Antony returned to Alexandria with the Median princess Iotape, Alexander Helios's intended.

WITH THE DONATIONS Antony and Cleopatra had sent Octavian one unmistakable message. Whatever they intended for the East, their plans did not include him. The two men were still in touch, closely and more or less cordially. Envoys and informers frequently sailed between them. They continued to correspond with mutual friends. They were joined in the triumvirate through the end of 33. (They were free now of both Lepidus and the intractable Sextus Pompey, with whom they had dispensed. Defeated by Octavian, Sextus was executed, most likely on Antony's orders.) Antony had reason to feel invulnerable, and sent another message to Octavian at about this time. He would relinquish his powers and restore a republic

---

*There was some irony in Canidius's good fortune. As a young man, he had been charged with transporting to Rome the treasure of Cleopatra's deposed uncle, the king of Cyprus. There had been some concern over whether Canidius could be trusted to acquit himself honestly of that lucrative task.

in Rome if Octavian would agree to do the same. Antony may have been bluffing. He may have been expending cheap political capital; Roman titles, and the composition of the Roman government, were of little concern to him in the East, where he seemed inclined to remain. He got a straightforward reply, which may even have been the one he expected. For some time it had been clear where the long Alexandrian sojourn, the repudiation of Octavia, the recognition of Caesarion, were leading; friends had surely kept Antony and Cleopatra apprised of the mood in Rome. Early in the year, Octavian rose in the Senate to deliver a virulent, direct assault on his colleague. From that point on it is impossible to say which was greater: Alexandria's royal extravagances, or Rome's version of them; Cleopatra's ambition, or Rome's version of it; Antony's affections for Cleopatra, or Rome's version of his affection. Cleopatra's palace was certainly the most luxurious building in the Mediterranean world in 33, but it never looked as magnificent as it did from Rome that winter.

Antony and Octavian had years of bad blood on which to trade. When finally the floodgates opened, they unleashed a torrent. Each accused the other of misappropriating lands. Octavian demanded his share of the Armenian spoils. Antony sputtered that his men had received no part of Octavian's distributions in Italy. (Octavian replied that if Antony wanted land he was free to carve up Parthia, an accusation that must have stung.) Octavian condemned Antony for the murder of Sextus Pompey, a murder that Octavian had himself celebrated in Rome, and that had followed Sextus's defeat at Octavian's hands.* Antony denounced Octavian for

---

*Sextus Pompey complicated the picture from many angles. He enjoyed warm relations with several monarchs considered to be deadly enemies of Rome and Cleopatra was well disposed toward him, given their fathers' relationship. (He in fact made overtures to Cleopatra, which Antony discouraged. He was wise enough to see he should not be in league both with a foreign queen and a swaggering compatriot who—despite popular support at home—behaved like a pirate. Antony's instincts were correct; ever the adventurer, Sextus had simultaneously offered up his services to the Parthians, behind Antony's back.) According to Appian, Antony refused to sign the order for Sextus's execution. He was ashamed to do so personally, as he knew the death would displease Cleopatra and did not want her to hold him responsible. Appian likewise suggests that sentence was desirable; better to eliminate Sextus, lest that talented naval commander and Cleopatra league together to "disturb the auspicious respect which Antony and Octavian had for each other."

having unlawfully forced aside Lepidus. And what had happened to his right to raise troops in Italy? Octavian had long obstructed those efforts, to which he had agreed by treaty. He left Antony to assemble an army of Greeks and Asiatics. For that matter, where was the remainder of the fleet Antony had lent Octavian four years earlier? And the 18,000 men Octavian had promised in exchange? Antony had been scrupulously faithful to their agreements. Octavian had not, repeatedly summoning Antony to meetings at which Octavian failed to appear. As ever, nothing worked as effectively as personal invective, the more scurrilous the better. Antony taunted Octavian with accounts of his humble origins. He was descended on his father's side from rope makers and money changers, on his mother's from bakers and keepers of perfume shops. For good measure Antony threw in an African grandfather. Worse, Octavian the parvenu harbored divine pretensions. When grain shortages plagued Rome, he and his wife, Livia, had thrown a lavish banquet. Their guests arrived in costume, as gods and goddesses. They ate obscenely well, with Octavian presiding over the table in the guise of Apollo. Octavian was moreover a coward. He had disappeared for days on end at Philippi. His gifted lieutenant, Marcus Agrippa, fought his battles for him. Possibly to deflect attention from Cleopatra and certainly overlooking his Median arrangements, Antony ridiculed Octavian for attempting to marry off his daughter to a barbarian, for the sake of a political alliance. Not all of the accusations were false or even vaguely fresh. Some were neatly repackaged from 44, when Cicero's account of Antony's misdeeds had been so extensive that, it was conceded, no one man could ever suffer adequate punishment for them all.

Where Antony alleged that Octavian was disabled by fear, Octavian asserted that Antony was undone by drink. On that front Octavian had several advantages: He was a modest drinker, or at least advertised himself as one. Alexandria threw a better party than did Rome. And Octavian had history on his side. It was fairly easy to claim that Antony had disappeared into a bacchanal, the more so as Octavian was in Rome while Antony was not. In his defense Antony countered with a satiric pamphlet, "On His Drunkenness." Generally 33 was a heyday for poets, lampoonists, apologists, graffitists, as for all lovers of idle talk and outlandish fictions. Intrigue came more naturally to Octavian than to Antony, but both men displayed a pitiless talent for defamation. Octavian resorted to indecent verse. Antony distributed slanderous handbills. Each man engaged propagandists. Many practices once acceptable were suddenly objectionable. Antony took charge of the gymnasium in Alexandria, which was unspeakable—whereas his having done so five years earlier, with Octavia, in Athens, had elicited no comment. Similarly, Antony's affair with Cleopatra had once afforded an endless source of ribald dinner jokes. Such had been the case over the summer of 39, in the celebration near Naples; Cleopatra was where the conversation wound up as the evening reached full tilt, when the lusty "good fellowship was at its height." She was a laughing matter no longer.

The pummeling continued both above and below the belt. Between them Antony and Octavian covered the usual schoolyard litany: effeminacy, sodomy, cowardice, unrefined—or overly refined—practices of personal hygiene. Octavian was "a veritable weakling." Antony had passed his prime. He could no longer win any contest save those in exotic dancing or the erotic arts. Antony sneered that Octavian had slept with his illustrious granduncle. How else to account for his unexpected adoption? Octavian countered with something sturdier and more pertinent, if equally untrue: Cleopatra had *not* slept with his granduncle. Caesarion was hardly the divine Caesar's son, news Octavian enlisted a pamphleteer to disseminate. Antony condemned Octavian's hasty marriage to Livia, hugely pregnant with another man's child on her wedding day. He decried Octavian's habit of making off with the wives of his banquet guests and returning them, disheveled, to the table. He advertised Octavian's well-known (and in all probability invented) habit of procuring and deflowering virgins. (According to Suetonius, Octavian seduced scientifically. He targeted the wives of his enemies, to learn what the husbands were saying and doing.) In the depravity department Octavian had no need to resort to fictions. He had his weapon close at hand. In defiance of Roman custom and his impeccable Roman wife, Octavian's fellow triumvir disported himself in a foreign capital with a rapacious queen, on whose account he had lost his head, forsaken his illustrious country, and shed all remnant of his manly Roman virtues. What self-respecting Roman would, as Cicero had put it, foolishly prefer "invidious wealth, the lust for despotism" to "stable and solid glory"? In many ways the contest boiled down to one of magnificence versus machismo.

At some point in the year Antony replied to Octavian privately, with a letter of which one scrap survives. He does not sound like a man spoiling for a fight. Nor does he sound out of his mind with love, in the throes of a transporting passion. The seven surviving lines dedicated to Cleopatra have been translated in countless ways, from the indecorous to the risqué to the raunchy. The last is the most precise. Antony's tone was unsurprising for Rome, where political and financial considerations determined upper-class marriages. Sex could be had anywhere. What, demanded Antony in 33, had come over Octavian? Why the fuss exactly? Could it really matter so much that he was "screwing the queen"? Octavian was no model husband himself, as they both knew.* Nor was he an innocent. He had amply enjoyed what Antony termed their "amorous adventures and youthful pranks." It was only sex after all, and hardly qualified as news; as Octavian well knew, Antony's relationship with Cleopatra had been going on for nine years. (He dated it from Tarsus.) It is not entirely clear whether he meant to legitimize the affair or to diminish it. The line that follows "screwing the queen" can be rendered as "she is my wife" or "is she my wife?" Given the rapid-fire rhythm of his queries, Antony seems intent on downplaying the liaison. He was after all writing to his brother-in-law. His implication appears to be: "She isn't my wife, is she?" The answer was in any event immaterial. "Does it really matter," Antony concluded, "where and in whom you get it up?" No matter how his final phrase is rendered, its verb belongs to the animal kingdom. It is

---

*Antony named names, five in all. Elsewhere he noted that Octavian had divorced his previous wife on the grounds of "moral perversity"; she had been a poor sport about his mistress.

unclear how closely those seven vulgar lines hewed to reality; what has come down to us may well be a paraphrase, more salacious than the original. Octavia aside, Antony and Cleopatra were not married by Roman standards, as Cleopatra well knew. In any event she here stepped into—or was fitted into—her greatest role. Octavian needed nothing further with which to bludgeon his rival. Judging from the fragments that remain, it was Octavian who turned the Alexandrian idyll into a sultry love affair.

As the clock ticked toward the end of the triumvirate, unlikely to be renewed, Antony and Cleopatra decamped for Ephesus. Ephesus had been the first city to recognize Antony as Dionysus incarnate and to have welcomed him at the city gates with loud cheers and a musical medley. After Philippi he had offered up splendid sacrifices and generous pardons there, to a people brutalized by Caesar's assassins. The city of 250,000 remained kindly disposed toward him. He arranged now for the Ephesians to greet Cleopatra as his royal mistress. A rich banking center of narrow streets and shady, marble colonnades, Ephesus enjoyed a magnificent location. Built in a steep-sided valley, it gave onto rugged mountains on one side, the sea on the other. Ephesus boasted several remarkable temples, of which the most celebrated was that of Artemis, where both Cleopatra's father and sister had sought asylum, and before the slender Ionic capitals of which her sister had met her end.

Strategically located across the Aegean from Athens, at the edge of a fine harbor, Ephesus was also the ideal address at which to establish a military base. From the coast of Asia Minor Antony set about assembling a navy, dispatching word to every client king in the region. They answered with fleets and submitted to oaths of loyalty. Cleopatra was the greatest single supplier of materiel, furnishing 200 of Antony's 500 warships, fully manned, along with 20,000 talents and all the supplies required to sustain a vast army—in this case, 75,000 legionnaires, 25,000 infantry, 12,000 cavalry—for the duration of a war. She was unlikely to have hesitated before doing so. Improbably, Octavian's star had ascended in Rome. He had piled up victories as Antony bogged down in the East.

For the two triumvirs to coexist peacefully was difficult. For an implacable, ambitious Octavian and Caesarion to coexist was impossible. Unlike Parthia, this campaign was as vital to Cleopatra as to Antony. She had every reason to throw herself, and Egypt, into it. On the last day of 33, the triumvirate officially expired.

EARLY IN JANUARY 32 a new consul spoke out forcefully in the Roman Senate in praise of Antony. He went on to savage Octavian. On hearing of the denunciation, Octavian paid the Senate a visit, with a bodyguard of soldiers and supporters. They made no effort to conceal the daggers beneath their togas. In 44 Cicero had wondered if Caesar's adopted son intended to stage a coup; he did so now. Offering his own scalding stream of accusations, he terrified the opposition into silence. "By certain documents," Octavian promised to demonstrate that Antony constituted a threat to Rome. He fixed a date on which he would present his evidence. The opposing consuls had seen the daggers; they knew better than to await that session, and secretly fled the city. Nearly four hundred senators followed, sailing to Ephesus, where they reported on the political climate in Rome. Surely Antony underestimated Octavian's strength and position. And he allied himself with Cleopatra at great risk. She seriously compromised the cause.

Many of Antony's colleagues—at least a third of the Senate was with him—argued for her removal. Yet again Antony bowed to reason and agreed to dismiss Cleopatra. He ordered her "to sail to Egypt, and there await the result of the war." She refused, possibly, as Plutarch asserts, because she feared that Octavia would again intervene, to prevent a war that Cleopatra knew for her own sake to be essential; possibly because she mistrusted Antony's judgment; possibly because it would have been irresponsible to do otherwise. She was no warrior queen; recent Ptolemies had not evidenced a great taste for warfare. They did not die on the battlefield, as did other Eastern monarchs. They subscribed to the belief that an empire could be acquired with money, rather than money with an empire. She was, however, her men's commander in chief, responsible for their preparations and operations. She was as well Antony's paymaster. A sober struggle of wills ensued. This time Cleopatra refrained from swooning hunger strikes. She took the opposite approach, assisted by Canidius, Antony's gifted general, whom she allegedly bribed to argue her case. He may just as easily have been impressed with her. Surely, Canidius protested, it was not fair to banish an ally so instrumental to their campaign? She fed the troops. She provided the fleet. She was as capable as any man. Did Antony not understand that the Egyptian crews would be demoralized by her departure? Those men formed the backbone of his navy. They would fight for their queen, not necessarily for a Roman general. Were Antony to refute his Egyptian affections he would moreover offend his Eastern allies. Cleopatra challenged Antony to explain how she "was inferior in intelligence to any one of the princes who took part in the expedition, she who for a long time had governed so large a kingdom by herself, and"—she appended a compliment—"by long association with Antony had learned to manage large affairs." Either her arguments made sense or her war chest did. She got her way.

In April 32 Antony and Cleopatra sailed with Antony's staff to the island of Samos, off the coast of modern-day Turkey. Samos was a stepping-stone to Greece, where the struggle for control of the Roman world would most likely take place. While the couple settled in on the mountainous island their troops were ferried west, across the Aegean, an operation that would have required a good month. Antony's veterans had returned from Armenia; along with the Eastern recruits, he had assembled some nineteen legions. Whatever the military or political preoccupations of the summer, they are lost to us, obliterated by Plutarch's descriptions of the merrymaking on Samos. The lush resort island was the ideal place to throw a party, and Antony was well positioned to do so. He had time on his hands. Octavian made much of the extravagance, which has come down to us as another Dionysian revel. Just as every king and prince east of Athens contributed forces, so every dramatic artist reported to Samos. They arrived in throngs. For days on end the lute players and flutists, actors and dancers, acrobats and mimes, harpists and female impersonators—"a rabble of Asiatic performers"—delivered a resplendent, multilingual festival of music and theater. "And while almost all the world around was filled with groans and lamentations," Plutarch relates through pursed lips, "a single island for many days resounded with flutes and stringed instruments; theatres there were filled, and choral bands were competing with one another." Every city also sent animals for sacrifice; the client kings "vied with one another in their mutual entertainments and gifts." The question on all minds was how Antony and Cleopatra would stage a triumph that could conceivably surpass the prodigal prewar festivities.

In May Antony and Cleopatra made the short trip west, to hilly Athens. The revels continued in the theaters and the vast, marble-seated stadium of that city, which had welcomed Antony as Dionysus nine years earlier, and where he may now have embraced the role most closely. It seemed that no one who could afford to had passed through Athens without contributing a sculpture, a theater, a gymnasium of creamy marble; when they did not, the Athenians erected the statue for them. (Cleopatra's forebears had bestowed a gymnasium, east of the marketplace.) While sports and drama distracted Antony, two matters clarified themselves, in quick succession. Cleopatra spent her summer in the storied city where Antony had spent the bulk of his years with Octavia. Antony's wife had attended lectures in his company. They had conceived a second child there. She remained a vivid presence; her statues adorned the venerable city, as did inscriptions in her honor. The Athenians embraced her as a goddess. The annual religious festival paid her tribute. This was unacceptable to Cleopatra, for whom much had changed in the fourteen years since she had lived quietly across town from Caesar's wife. She had heard enough of what Lucan would term "illicit affairs and bastard children." Cleopatra was moreover the first Ptolemaic queen to set foot in Athens, a city that had reason to warm to her: At various junctures it had relied on her family—for grain, for military assistance, for political refuge—since the beginning of the third century. Athens had erected statues to earlier Ptolemies, including Cleopatra's great-aunt. Cleopatra focused, however, an another woman; she had kept careful account of the tributes accorded Octavia. She was jealous. She went on the offensive, attempting "by many splendid gifts to win the favor of the people," in other words to blot out her predecessor's traces. Realistic and reasonable, the Athenians obliged, to Antony's delight. They voted his lover multiple honors. They planted statues of Cleopatra and Antony in the Acropolis, at the center of the city. On one occasion Antony appeared amid a delegation to pay Cleopatra tribute, delivering up a speech on the city's behalf.

From the summer of 32 dates too a remarkable gift: Antony bestowed on Cleopatra the library of Pergamum, the only collection that rivaled Alexandria's. The four rooms of that scenic hilltop library housed some 200,000 scrolls; for centuries, busts of Homer and Herodotus had kept them company. History has made of Antony's gift a wedding present, or recompense for the volumes Caesar inadvertently destroyed in the Alexandrian War. In context, the largesse required no explanation. Pergamum was not far from Ephesus. It is likely that Antony and Cleopatra paid a visit to that city, a few days' ride away. For years too the way to assemble a collection had been to plunder someone else's. Already there was some tradition of this in Rome, where libraries were still in their infancy.

For the most part the reports of Antony's disorienting, degrading passion for Cleopatra date from the Athenian summer. If in Alexandria he had distracted her from state business, the tables now turned. He attended principally to her. "Many times, while he was seated on his tribunal and dispensing justice to tetrarchs and kings, he would receive love-billets from her in tablets of onyx or crystal, and read them," Plutarch tells us. (Antony was not the first to receive love letters on state occasions. Caesar too had received "wanton bits" during Senate sessions. That mistress did not write on onyx tablets, however.) At one juncture Cleopatra happened to ride conspicuously past the courts on the shoulders of her servants as Antony presided over a legal case. A distinguished Roman orator held the floor, or did until Antony caught sight of Cleopatra. He then "sprang up from his tribunal and forsook the trial, and hanging on to Cleopatra's litter escorted her on her way." It was ignoble behavior; a Roman could indulge in as diversified, as lurid, a sexual life as he pleased, but he was meant to be discreet and unsentimental in his affections. Pompey had made himself a laughingstock for his indecent habit of falling in love with his own wife. In the second century a senator was expelled from that assembly for kissing his wife in public, in full view of their daughter. Antony had been reprimanded years earlier for having openly nuzzled his wife. He was said these days to rise during banquets, before his assembled guests, to massage Cleopatra's feet "in compliance with some agreement and compact they had made." (The relationship proceeded by pacts, wagers, and competitions, something Cleopatra evidently brought to the table. Antony was little inclined to formalities.) The gesture was in itself offensive; one had servants for such indulgences. And the stories—of what another age might term gallantry or devotion, of what the East deemed proper obeisance, of what were in Rome indecencies and indignities—piled up. Antony fawned over Cleopatra, which was what eunuchs did. He trailed her litter through the streets, among her attendants. And this, sniffed the Romans, heaping upon the Egyptian queen the usual abuse of the other woman, when she was not even beautiful!

From Octavian's point of view, the Athenian reports were too good to be true, as they may well have been. For all of the martial preparations, for all of the governmental irregularities in Rome, despite the gathering sense of inevitability, there was no real cause for a rupture; Antony and Octavian remained two men in search of a conflict. They found one in 32. Antony evidently felt some degree of attachment to Cleopatra or felt with her invincible: In May, he divorced Octavia. From Athens, he instructed her to leave their comfortable home. We cannot know how much that gesture was directed at Octavia and how much at her brother. Coming as it did after years of disingenuous reconciliations and flimsy agreements, after a season of slanders, it may only have preempted a salvo from the other direction. Octavia could have elected to end the marriage herself. The divorce itself was simple, an informal procedure for which there was no paperwork. Its ramifications were more complex. As Plutarch remarks on the death of Pompey's wife and Caesar's daughter, the family alliance "which had hitherto veiled rather than restrained the ambition of the two men was now at an end." Cleopatra could only have been thrilled; already she had enlisted a friend of Antony to distract him from all thoughts of his wife. Octavian was overjoyed. Octavia was bereft. Tearfully she packed her bags. With her she took her children by Antony, as well as his second son by Fulvia. There were no recriminations. Octavia worried only that she would be said to have precipitated a war.

Insofar as a propaganda-free chronology can be established, relations were strained in Antony's camp well before the divorce. For all of the later assertions that highborn Romans lay powerless and enchanted at her feet, in 32 we hear no chime, no caress of Cleopatra's silvery voice. There were as many opinions on the looming conflict as there were advisers to Antony. For a variety of reasons, many of them legitimate, some continued to see Cleopatra as a liability. A military camp was no place for a woman. Cleopatra distracted Antony. She should not take part in a council of war; she was no general. Antony could not enter Italy in the presence of a foreigner and was unwise to wait to do so. He frittered away his advantage, on the Egyptian queen's account. The criticism did not bring out the best in her. At one point Antony's associates in Rome dispatched his friend Geminius to Athens, to plead their case. Antony must defend himself at home, where he was badly battered by Octavian. Why allow himself to be portrayed as a public enemy, in thrall to a foreigner? Geminius was an inspired choice for the delicate mission, having had some experience himself with what it is to fall unwisely and unreasonably in love. Cleopatra assumed that Octavia had dispatched him and treated Geminius accordingly. She kept him as far as possible from Antony. At dinner she seated him among the least significant guests. She pelted him with sarcasm. Geminius endured the insults in silence, patiently holding out for an audience with Mark Antony. Before it was accorded, Cleopatra challenged Geminius, in the midst of a raucous dinner, to explain his errand. He replied that its details "required a sober head, but one thing he knew, whether he was drunk or sober, and that was that all would be well if Cleopatra was sent off to Egypt." Antony erupted in fury. Cleopatra was more brutal. She commended Geminius for his honesty. He had spared her from having to torture him. Several days later he fled to Rome, to join Octavian.

Cleopatra's courtiers failed equally to recommend themselves to the Romans, dismayed by the "drunken tricks and scurrilities" of the Egyptians. For reasons that are unclear, Plancus, the dancing fish of the Alexandrian revel, deserted as well, to return to Rome. He was disgusted. The defection may have had nothing to do either with Cleopatra or her advisers. A born courtier, Plancus inclined to the path of least resistance. He betrayed every bit as well as he bowed and scraped. "Treachery," it would be said, "was a disease with him." He was, however, a man of impeccable political instincts. Something had clearly transpired to make him doubt that Antony—despite his outsize power and prestige, his years of experience—could prevail over Octavian. Plancus counted among Antony's closest advisers. For some time he had been in charge of Antony's correspondence. He knew his secrets. He fled to Octavian with fulsome reports of foot massages, prodigal banquets, and high-handed queens, as well as with information concerning Antony's will, to which Plancus had been a witness. Octavian at once pried that document from the Vestal Virgins, with whom it should have been safe. In it he found, or claimed to find, a number of scandalous passages. These he helpfully annotated so that he might read them aloud to the Senate. Most members of that body had no desire to participate in his transgression. A man's will was to be opened after his death, which was why it happened to be illegal to unseal such a document before the event. Those qualms vanished as Octavian neared the end of his presentation, to reveal a heinous provision. Even if he should die in Rome, Antony had directed that his body "should be borne in state through the Forum and then sent away to Cleopatra in Egypt."*

Genuine or not, the clause ignited a brilliant bonfire, for which Octavian had relentlessly stockpiled kindling. In his January coup he had promised the Senate documentary evidence against Antony. He now richly delivered. Suddenly reports of Athenian excess, of Antony's subservience to Cleopatra, the sensational, salacious details of which had been widely understood to be falsehoods, appeared credible. In a world entranced by rhetoric—addicted to "honeyballs of phrases, every word and act besprinkled with poppy-seed and sesame"—the plausible reliably trumped the actual. Octavian had at his disposal plenty of generous veins to mine. The depredations of the East alone—that intoxicating, intemperate, irrational realm—supplied a mother lode of material. Like its queen, Egypt was beguiling and voluptuous; the modern association between the Orient and sex was hoary already in the first century. Already Africa was the address of moral decay. From there it was no great leap to transform the Antony of the Donations into a power-crazed, dissolute, Eastern despot: "In his hand was a golden scepter, at his side a scimitar; he wore a purple robe studded with huge gems; a crown only was lacking to make him a king dallying with a queen." It was the diadem and golden statues business all over again; the accessories of kingship unnerved Romans even more than did autocracy itself, which they had tolerated in a more subtle version for at least a decade. In Octavian's account, Antony was irredeemably contaminated by the Oriental languor and the un-Roman luxuries of the East as, arguably, Caesar and

---

*No one saw the will other than Octavian, who may have fabricated it himself. Plancus may equally well have forged it; in urgent cases, he had authority to sign Antony's name and affix his seal. The document evidently included a confirmation of the gifts Antony had bestowed on Cleopatra's children, as well as of Caesarion's paternity. So far as we know, Antony never refuted the terms. Nor, for that matter, did Octavian refute the claim regarding Caesarion, which at this point he was wiser to ignore. It is all the same difficult to imagine any circumstances under which Antony might actually have committed to paper the provisions Octavian read aloud.

Alexander the Great had been before him. In turn Octavian would soon enough discover that Egypt conferred on its conqueror a mixed blessing, a literal embarrassment of riches. Like a prodigious trust fund, it convinced men they were gods.

Octavian wrung the most mileage from Antony's affair with Cleopatra. She allowed him to recycle the oldest trope: the allergy to the powerful woman was sturdier even than that to monarchy, or to the depraved East. Whether or not Cleopatra controlled Antony, she unequivocally permitted Octavian to control the narrative. He had at his disposal a whole grab bag of Cicero's rantings against Fulvia, that avaricious, licentious virago. Diligent as ever, Octavian improved upon them. In his expert hands the Egyptian affair blossomed into a tale of blind, irresponsible passion. Antony was under the influence of some powerful narcotic, "bewitched by that accursed woman." Writing closest to events, Velleius Paterculus provided the official version, distilled to pure cause and effect: "Then as his love for Cleopatra became more ardent," explains Velleius, acknowledging Antony's embrace of Eastern vices, "he resolved to make war upon his country." Cleopatra does not so much corrupt Antony as she "melts and unmans him." In Octavian's version, she is masterful and Antony servile, a radically different account of the relationship than that which the sporting Mark Antony had supplied months earlier. Even while conceding that the charges were questionable, every chronicler subscribes to the party line. Antony became "a slave to his love for Cleopatra," "he gave not a thought to honour but became the Egyptian woman's slave," he surrendered his authority to a woman to the extent that "he was not even a master of himself." The construct was old enough to have a mythical equivalent, to which Octavian eagerly appealed. Antony claimed descent from Hercules. Octavian let no one forget that Hercules spent three years, disarmed and humiliated, as the slave of the rich Asian queen Omphale. She removes from him his lion skin and his club, and— donning his lion skin herself—stands over him as he weaves.

To the charges Octavian fixed an imaginative twist. He needed after all to rally an exhausted, hungry country, depleted after nearly two decades of civil war. To the hot baths and the mosquito nets, the golden accessories and jeweled scimitars, the illicit affair and bastard children, he added a rousing fillip. "The Egyptian woman demanded the Roman Empire from the drunken general as the price of her favors; and this Antony promised her, as though the Romans were more easily conquered than the Parthians," relates Florus. Dio arrived at the same conclusion, by way of more tenuous logic: "For she so charmed and enthralled not only him but all the rest who had any influence with him that she conceived the hope of ruling even the Romans." Cleopatra already had the Pergamum library. She had Herod's balsam gardens. Reports circulated that Antony pillaged the best art from the temples of Asia—including famed colossi of Heracles, Athena, and Zeus that had stood in Samos for centuries—to gratify the Egyptian queen. If Antony was to send his body to her, what would he conceivably deny her? And for what would she hesitate to ask?

Octavian seems to have been the one who decided that Cleopatra plotted to make Rome a province of Egypt, an idea very unlikely to have crossed her quick mind. He had on his side the familiar type, the scheming, spendthrift wife, for whom no diamond is large enough, no house spacious enough. As Eutropius put it centuries later, Antony began a war at the urging of the queen of Egypt, who "longed with womanly desire to reign in the city as well."* Already it was acknowledged "that the greatest wars have taken place on account of women." Whole families had been ruined on their account. And already—the fault as ever of the sultry, sinuous, overtly subversive East—Egyptian women had caused their share of trouble. They were endowed with insatiable ardor and phenomenal sexual energy. One husband was not enough for them. They attracted and ruined men. Octavian only corralled the evidence.

He had found a cunning disguise for a civil war, which four years

---

*That was an acknowledged weakness. As Plautus, Rome's most popular playwright, had growled: "I don't much like these highly connected women, their airs, their huge dowries, their loud demands, their arrogance, their ivory carriages, their dresses, their purple, who reduce their husbands to slavery with their expenses."

earlier he had declared officially over, and into which he had promised never again to lead his men. How much more palatable, how much more credible, that Antony should be destroyed by an illicit love than by his countrymen! It was by no means difficult to rally legions—or tax the populace, or set fathers against sons—with the claim that Cleopatra was poised to conquer them as she had conquered Antony. As Lucan formulated the battle cry a century later, "Would a woman—not even Roman—rule the world?" The logic was simple. The Egyptian queen had subdued Antony. Rome, Octavian warned, was next. At the end of October he declared war—on Cleopatra.

THE DECLARATION COULD not have been unexpected. It may even have come as a relief. Cleopatra must all the same have been surprised by its terms. She had engaged in no hostilities toward Rome. She had comported herself like the ideal vassal—if a vassal with privileges. She had maintained order in her kingdom, supplied Rome when called upon to do so, materialized when summoned, aggressed upon no neighbors. She had done everything in her power to uphold and nothing to diminish the surpassing greatness of Rome. Traditionally, a three-step process preceded a Roman declaration of war: The Senate submitted a demand for restitution, followed after a month by a solemn reminder that satisfaction was still wanting. Three days later, a messenger traveled to enemy territory, formally to open hostilities. Octavian summoned Cleopatra neither for an accounting nor an airing of charges. He made no overtures through diplomatic channels. Instead, deft as ever with the mise-en-scène, he dusted off the ceremonial portion of the process. In a military cloak he personally launched a spear drenched in pig blood toward the East, from a ritual patch of "hostile soil" in Rome. (There is speculation that he invented this ancient rite for the occasion, that Octavian was making up the history as he went along. He was very good at restoring traditions, including those that had never existed.) There were no official charges for the simple reason that none could be leveled. Insofar as Cleopatra stood accused of any hostile intent, she was condemned "for her

Ptolemy Philadelphus, Cleopatra's youngest child by Mark Antony. He appears with a Macedonian cap, to which an Egyptian cobra has been affixed. Probably sculpted to celebrate the Donations of Alexandria, between 34 and 30 BC, when Ptolemy was between the ages of two and six.

A basalt Cleopatra, featured with a conventional wig and diadem and in transparent, clinging drapery. She has filled out a little and carries a traditional bar in her hand. In similar depictions she holds a cornucopia; a Ptolemaic queen went in for public displays of munificence. She took caring for her subjects seriously.

An Alexandrian statute of a child in regal pose, very likely Alexander Helios, Cleopatra and Mark Antony's elder son. The costume is eastern, the tiara Armenian, the child five or six, all of which arguably adds up to Alexander Helios at the time of the Donations, when he was appointed to rule over Armenia, Media, and Parthia. Cleopatra may have commissioned the statue to celebrate the occasion. Half cherub, half child, the figure shares Antony's head of bouncing curls.

Cleopatra in male dress, at right, offering to the goddess Isis, nursing a baby. Inscribed during her first months in power, the stela is the oldest evidence of Cleopatra's reign. She shared the throne at the time with her brother, whose name is notably absent; Cleopatra's can be read in the second line. Very likely the limestone stela was their father's, which Cleopatra arranged to have recarved. Given the turbulent times, re-working was a Ptolemaic stonecutter's specialty. Note the two serpents hanging above.

A stela commemorating the death of the Buchis bull — an earthly incarnation of the war god — in February 180 BC. Cleopatra's great-great-grandfather stands before the bull, at his eye level, with an offering; the king's wife, Cleopatra I, is named in the heiroglyphs but not depicted. The bull had lived for nearly fifteen years, although the scribe did his math wrong, inadvertently abbreviating the sacred animal's life. The stela would have been in place when Cleopatra traveled south to install the new Buchis bull in 51.

Caesar with a garland of flowers, an Alexandrian specialty, ordered by the hundreds for that city's banquets. He wears as well a Greek robe, pinned at the shoulder, and a laurel crown. Everything about the portrait — including the sunken cheeks — supports the thesis that it dates from the celebrations following the Alexandrian War and the spring of the Nile cruise.

An exceptionally expressive Caesar, made after his death, and returning to him the head of hair he had lost by the time Cleopatra knew him. Lines have etched themselves across the broad forehead, the cheeks hollowed and begun to fold around the mouth. Suetonius applauded Caesar's memoirs as "naked in their simplicity, straightforward yet graceful." They are also perfectly self-serving. In them he mentions the queen of Egypt, the mother of his only son, precisely once.

Mark Antony, whose virile features confirmed his purported descent from Hercules. Audacious and foolhardy, joyful and artless, he made for a compelling commander. His men were devoted to him, Plutarch tells us, for "the nobility of his family, his eloquence, his frank and open manners, his liberal and magnificent habits, his familiarity in talking with everybody."

A particularly fine portrait of Antony, in red jasper, from his years with Cleopatra. The powerful neck, mane of hair, and boxer's nose are much in evidence. A similar portrait survives in amethyst.

Our most accurate depictions of Cleopatra come from coins. Roundly admired, much examined, they qualified as propaganda pieces; here was how she presented herself to her people.

A bronze coin from Cleopatra's mint in Cyprus, from 47 or early 46 BC, to commemorate the birth of Caesarion. The imagery works equally well with Cleopatra as Aphrodite or Isis. She wears a broad diadem and holds Caesarion in her arms; her scepter protrudes awkwardly from her back.

An 80-drachma bronze coin minted in Alexandria. Cleopatra reintroduced the metal, long out of production and to which she added denominational marks for the first time. Regardless of its weight, the coin was worth what she said it was worth, a profitable arrangement for her.

A silver tetradrachm of 36 BC, minted in Antioch, announcing Antony and Cleopatra's political alliance. In a nod to Isis, she is identified as "Queen Kleopatra, the New Goddess." She wears a magnificent pearl necklace and — in a challenge to the engraver — pearls in her hair as well. She also bears a striking resemblance to Mark Antony — or, as has been suggested, he to her.

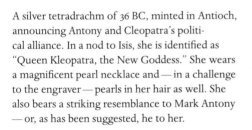

A silver coin from Ascalon, in Judaea, a city never subject to Cleopatra. Possibly minted to assist in her restoration, the tetradrachm may date from 50 or 49 BC, the years the teenaged Cleopatra spent in exile. Otherwise it qualifies as a tribute to her power; many cities outside her realm issued coins in her honor. A faint smile plays on her lips.

A Ptolemaic queen with the traditional headdress of cobras, sun disk, and cow's horns, wearing several necklaces and a simple sheath. She is presumably Cleopatra costumed as Isis, which would explain the frontally displayed right breast. Reproduced on busts and jewelry, Cleopatra's features were well known to her people.

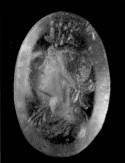

A woman in Greek dress, with a wide, knotted diadem and an Egyptian cobra crown. Even without the familiar features it would be difficult to believe her anyone but Cleopatra. The image is carved into blue glass; the cobras sport sun disks.

Cleopatra and (before her) Caesarion offering to the gods, from the south wall of the Temple of Hathor at Dendera. Caesarion is thought to be between eight and eleven in this depiction; Cleopatra cannily takes second place to Caesar's son. The pair offer to Hathor, appropriately, as has been noted: Hathor too is married to a nonresident god, whose realm lies elsewhere. An effective propaganda piece, the massive carving occupies the entire lower section of the temple's rear wall.

Cicero, the great orator, at the age Cleopatra would have known him. "I detest the queen," he sputtered, once she had left town. He did not take well to a woman who could "make others laugh in spite of themselves" every bit as well as he. He choked especially on her arrogance, but then Cicero was said to be "the greatest boaster alive."

A bronze statute of the young Octavian, Cleopatra's steely, single-minded opponent, six years her junior. After defeating Cleopatra he would see to it that his statues replaced hers throughout Egypt.

Octavia, Octavian's half sister and Antony's fourth wife. "A wonder of a woman," she raised Cleopatra's three surviving children after her suicide.

A second- or early first-century mosaic, excavated from a site not far from Cleopatra's palace. The apologetic family dog (he wears a collar) looked no different for having upset the bronze and wooden jug two thousand years ago than he might today.

Pendant earrings, from the third or second century BC, in the shape of Egyptian crowns, sun disks sprouting black and white feathers. Cleopatra's jewelry would have been opulent, elaborately worked in gold, with insets of coral and carnelian, lapis, amethyst, and pearl. A Ptolemy aimed to outweigh all other monarchs in wealth, a feat easily accomplished given the abundance that "flowed hourly to his rich palace from every quarter."

A coin issued to commemorate the Roman annexation of Egypt. Octavian appears on the obverse. The caption reads: "Egypt captured."

acts," conveniently left unspecified. Octavian gambled that Antony would remain true to Cleopatra, a loyalty that—under the circumstances—allowed Octavian to charge that his compatriot "had voluntarily taken up war on the side of the Egyptian woman against his native country." At the end of 32 the Senate deprived Antony of his consulship and relieved him of all authority.*

Antony and Cleopatra did their best to spin the underhanded provocation. They were obligatory allies now. Under the circumstances, they cried, how could anyone trust a blackguard like Octavian? "What in the world does he mean, then, by threatening us all alike with arms, but in the decree declaring that he is at war with some and not with others?" Antony implored his men. His double-dealing colleague schemed only to sow dissension, the better to rule as king over them all. (In that he was no doubt correct. Octavian would have found a way to initiate a war with Antony even if Antony had thrown over Cleopatra.) Why would anyone associate with a man who unceremoniously disenfranchised a colleague, who illegally seized the will of a friend, companion, kinsman? Octavian was without the courage to declare himself openly, Antony thundered, although he "is at war with me and is already acting in every way like one who has not only conquered me but also murdered me." The experience, the popularity, the numbers, were all on Antony's side; he was the skilled commander behind whom stood the most powerful dynasts in Asia. Five hundred warships, a land army of nineteen legions, more than 10,000 cavalry, answered to his orders. It made no difference that he had no authority in Rome. A third of the Senate was at his side.

For twelve years Antony had contended that Octavian plotted to destroy him. Realistically and opportunistically, Cleopatra could only have agreed. The couple were finally right. Antony was equally correct that in a contest of disingenuousness he could not rival his former

---

*Stripped of his powers, Antony was now formally without the right to call upon assistance from client states or to distribute Roman territories. By some contorted logic it could be argued that Cleopatra therefore abetted a private citizen hostile to Rome, and that she stood in possession of lands that should not have been hers. To do so was, however, to include Antony in the indictment, in which he nowhere figured.

brother-in-law. (Cleopatra might have, but she was obliged to let Antony do the talking.) It was most unfortunate that Antony had made himself a traitor to Rome, clucked Octavian. He was heartsick about the state of affairs. He had felt so affectionately toward him that he had entrusted him with a share in the command and with a much-loved sister. Octavian had not declared war even after Antony had humiliated that sister, neglected their children, and bestowed upon another woman's children the possessions of the Roman people. Surely Antony would see the light. (Octavian had no such hopes for Cleopatra. "For I adjudged her," he scoffed, "if only on account of her foreign birth, to be an enemy by reason of her very conduct.") He insisted that Antony would "if not voluntarily, at least reluctantly, change his course as a result of the decrees passed against her." Octavian knew full well that Antony would do no such thing. He and Cleopatra were well beyond that point. Matters of the heart aside, he was the most faithful of men. The situation with Octavian was moreover untenable. It would be difficult to say to whom Cleopatra was more vital in 32: the man to whom she was the partner, or the man to whom she was the pretext. Antony could not win a war without her. Octavian could not wage one.

Philippi had bought Antony a decade of goodwill; it abruptly came to an end now. In the fall he and Cleopatra moved west to Patras, an undistinguished town at the entrance of the Gulf of Corinth. From that point they established a defensive line up and down the west coast of Greece, distributing men from Actium in the north to Methoni in the south. The intention seems to have been to protect the supply lines to Alexandria, along with Egypt itself, on which Octavian had after all declared war. Cleopatra profited from the pause to issue coins, on which she appears as Isis. Antony sent considerable quantities of gold back to Rome, distributing bribes left and right. He had the greater force but labored all the same to undermine the loyalty of Octavian's men. The bulk of those funds were presumably Cleopatra's. Octavian's war levies meanwhile set off riots in Rome. Also back and forth over the winter went various spies and senators, their loyalties fragile and mercurial. Many had faced this quandary at least once before: whom to flee, and whom to follow? It was a test of personalities rather than principles. Elsewhere it seemed as if a magnet had passed over the Mediterranean world, drawing the skittering sides into a taut alignment that "as a whole far surpassed in size anything that had ever been before." The sovereigns Antony had installed in 36 turned out in full force. Among others, the Libyan, Thracian, Pontic, and Cappadocian kings joined him, with their fleets.

The winter passed in a fever pitch of inertia. For the second time the usually rash Antony appeared slow to open a campaign, one for which Cleopatra could only have been impatient. With every month she was running up considerable expenses. (The rule of thumb was 40 to 50 talents per legion per year, which put Cleopatra's summer outlay for the infantry alone in the vicinity of 210 talents.) It was difficult to escape the impression that Antony, the most famous soldier alive, had no desire for an epic battle. Of an earlier occasion it would be said of Caesar that "he sought a reputation rather than a province," an assertion that was arguably more true of his protégé. Octavian invited Antony to an absurd staged encounter. Antony challenged Octavian to a duel. Neither materialized. Mostly the two sides confined themselves to insults and idle threats, to "spying upon and annoying each other." The air pulsed with rumor, much of it generated by Octavian. In 33 he expelled the multitude of astrologers and soothsayers from Rome, ostensibly to purge the growing Eastern influence, actually better to control the story line. In their absence it was easier to elicit the kinds of omens Octavian preferred; he wanted to be the only one in the prophecy business. So it was that Antony and Cleopatra's statues in the Acropolis were said to have been struck by lightning and to lie in sorry ruins. Eighty-five-foot-long two-headed serpents appeared. A marble statue of Antony oozed blood. When the children of Rome divided themselves into Antonians and Octavians for a fierce two-day-long street battle, the miniature Octavians prevailed. The truth was closer to that suggested by two talking ravens. Their equitable trainer had taught the first to squawk, "Hail Caesar, our victorious commander." The other learned: "Hail Antony, our victorious commander." A smart Roman had every reason to hedge his bets—and to believe that with their hotheaded rhetoric, their personal agendas, Antony and Octavian were perfectly interchangeable. Even those on intimate terms with both conceded that each "desired to be the ruler, not only of the city of Rome, but of the whole world."

While the funds and experience were largely on Antony and Cleopatra's side, so too were the ambiguities, beginning with the matter—not necessarily more transparent in 32 than it is today—of their marriage. As a foreigner, Cleopatra could not under Roman law become Antony's wife, even after his divorce. Only by the more supple, accommodating logic of the Greek East could the two have been said to have married. From the Egyptian point of view the question was irrelevant. Cleopatra had no need to be married to Antony, who was without any official status in Egypt, which she ruled with Caesarion. Antony was there a queen's consort and patron, not a king. That was unproblematic in Egypt. It was a muddle to Rome. Was Cleopatra meant to play a role in the West? Again there was no category for her, or rather there was: If she was not a wife, she was by definition a concubine. In which case why did Antony stamp her image on Roman coins? Antony and Cleopatra's joint intentions too were murky. Did they mean to realize the dream of Alexander the Great, to unite men across national boundaries and under one divine law, as the prophecy had it? Or did Antony intend to set himself up as an Oriental monarch, with Cleopatra as empress? (He made it easy for Octavian: a Roman surrendered his citizenship if he formally attached himself to another state.) Their agenda may have been better defined—probably they meant to establish two capitals—but generally they taxed the category-loving Roman mind. And they turned the client king arrangement on its head. A foreigner was meant to be subservient, not equal, to a Roman. As such, it was easy for Octavian to make a case for the transgressive, insatiable woman, intent on conquest. He did so convincingly and enduringly. One of the greatest twentieth-century classicists has Cleopatra working through Antony, like a parasite, to realize ambitions she may never have considered. The military intentions were opaque as well. For what precisely was Antony fighting? He might well mean to restore the Republic, as he claimed, but what then to make of the mother of his three half-Roman children?

For Octavian, by contrast, all was crystalline and categorical, or at least it was once he had passed off a personal vendetta as a foreign war. His argument had cleaner lines and better visuals. He made a splendid, splashy appeal to xenophobia. Surely his men—"we who are Romans and lords of the greatest and best portion of the world"—were not going to be rattled by these primitives? Not for the last time, the world divided into a masculine, rational West and a feminine, indefinite East, on which Octavian declared a sort of crusade. He fought against something but for something as well: for Roman probity, piety, and self-control, precisely those qualities his former brother-in-law had shrugged off in his embrace of Cleopatra. Antony was no longer a Roman but an Egyptian, a mere cymbal player, effeminate, inconsequential, and impotent, "for it is impossible for one who leads a life of royal luxury, and coddles himself like a woman, to have a manly thought or do a manly deed."* Octavian savaged even Antony's literary style. And incidentally, had anyone noticed that Antony drank? Octavian stressed his role as Caesar's heir less often. Instead he went in for tales of his own divinity, which he broadcast widely. Few in Rome failed to hear of his descent from Apollo, to whom he was dedicating a fine new temple.

In reducing Antony to a cymbal player Octavian accomplished an especially difficult feat. He publicly acknowledged what many men who have faced a woman across a tennis net have since noted: in such a contest, there is greater pride to be lost than glory to be gained. By the Roman definition, a woman hardly qualified as a worthy opponent. Coaxing a tinny accusation into a series of resonant chords, later scored for a full orchestra, Octavian rhapsodized about Cleopatra. He endowed

---

*Nicolaus of Damascus was quick to assert that even as a teenager, even at the age when youth "are most wanton," Octavian had abstained from sexual gratification for an entire year. And in the face of all evidence to the contrary, it was inevitably asserted that he lived simply and austerely. In truth Octavian was as fond of costly furniture and Corinthian bronzes as the next man, more fond yet of the gaming table.

her with every kind of power, to create an enduring grotesque. This brutal, bloodthirsty Egyptian queen was no latter-day Fulvia. She was a vicious enemy, with designs on all Roman possessions. Surely the great and glorious people who had subdued the Germans, trampled the Gauls, and invaded the Britons, who had conquered Hannibal and burned Carthage, were not going to tremble before "this pestilence of a woman"? What would their glorious forefathers say if they learned that a people of singular exploits and vast conquests, to whom every region of the world had now submitted, had been trodden underfoot by an Egyptian harlot, her eunuchs, and her hairdressers? Indeed they faced a formidable array of forces, Octavian assured his men, but to win great prizes, one waged great contests. In this one the honor of Rome was at stake. It was the obligation of those destined "to conquer and rule all mankind" to uphold their illustrious history, to avenge those who insulted them, and "to allow no woman to make herself equal to a man."*

EARLY IN 31 Octavian's superb admiral, Agrippa, made a swift, surprise crossing to Greece. A longtime friend and mentor to Octavian, he supplied the military acumen his commander lacked. Agrippa disrupted Antony's supply lines and captured his southern base. In his wake, Octavian transferred 80,000 men from the Adriatic coast across the Ionian Sea. The move forced Antony north. His infantry was not yet in place; he was wholly taken aback. Cleopatra attempted to calm him by making light of the enemy's sudden presence in a fine natural port (it was probably modern Parga) on a spoon-shaped promontory. "What is there dreadful in Caesar's sitting at a ladle?" she scoffed. Straightaway, Octavian offered battle, which Antony could not yet manage. His crews were incomplete. By an early morning feint he forced Octavian to withdraw. Weeks of taunts and skirmishes followed, as Octavian roamed freely among the harbors of western Greece, and as Antony settled his legions on a sandy spit of land at the southern entrance to the Ambracian Gulf.

*As the poet Propertius asked later: What does our history mean if it leads to the rule of a woman?

Actium offered an excellent harbor, if in a damp, desolate area; Antony and Cleopatra could not have been long in realizing that the swampy lowland, thick with ferns and grasses, was infinitely more suitable as a battle site than as a campsite. The weeks passed in attempted engagements and attenuated decisions. Octavian could not lure Antony out to sea. Antony could not coax Octavian out on land. He remained more intent on cutting Antony's supply lines, at which, over the spring and early summer, he proved highly proficient. Cleopatra may have affected perfect insouciance about his landing but the truth was that in the wake of a series of inexplicable, slow-motion decisions—they may not have made sense even before Octavian's eulogists got hold of them—Antony and Cleopatra began to cede the advantage. Meanwhile the question of strategy hung heavily over Antony's head: to meet Octavian on land or at sea? For the most part the two armies glared at each other across the narrow strait, from one grassy promontory to the other.

From the distance Antony's camp must have offered a splendid sight, with its vast and variegated armies, the flashes of gold-spangled purple-red robes. Towering Thracians in black tunics and bright armor mingled with Macedonians in fresh scarlet cloaks, Medians in richly colored vests. A Ptolemaic military cloak, woven with gold, might feature a royal portrait or a mythological scene. The scruffy Greek lowland blazed with costly equipment, with gleaming helmets and gilded breastplates, jeweled bridles, dyed plumes, decorated spears.* The bulk of the soldiers were Eastern, as were an increasing number of rowers, many of them raw recruits. With them assembled an ecumenical collection of arms: Thracian wicker shields and quivers joined Roman javelins and Cretan bows and long Macedonian pikes.

Cleopatra footed much of the bill but contributed something else too; unlike Antony, she could communicate with the assembled dignitaries

---

*In this realm alone ostentation met with Roman approval. As Plutarch explains: "For extravagance in other objects of display induces luxury and implants effeminacy in those who use them, since something like a pricking and tickling of the senses breaks down serious purpose; but when it is seen in the trappings of war it strengthens and exalts the spirit."

of the East. She spoke the language of the Armenian cavalry, the Ethiopian infantry, the Median detachments, as well as that of royalty. There was a code of behavior among Hellenistic sovereigns. Most had experience of powerful queens. And Canidius had not misspoken. By her presence, Cleopatra reminded her fellow dynasts that they were battling for something other than a Roman republic, in which they had no interest. They had little sympathy for either Antony or Octavian, against either of whom they might just as easily have aligned, as they had aligned against Rome in 89, with Mithradates. Had she not launched herself directly into the heart of Roman affairs with her call on Caesar in 48, Cleopatra would have been in precisely their position. She and Antony turned away only one sovereign, naturally the most enthusiastic of the bunch. Herod arrived with money, a well-trained army, equipment, and a shipment of grain. He delivered as well some familiar advice. Were Antony only to murder Cleopatra and annex Egypt, his troubles would be over. Herod's army and provisions remained but his stay in camp was brief. For his priceless counsel he was packed off to fight Malchus, the Nabatean king, said to be delinquent with his bitumen payments. Simultaneously Cleopatra ordered her general in that stony region to frustrate both monarchs' efforts. She preferred that they destroy each other.

Closer up all was not quite so rosy. The wait—in a vast, multiethnic military camp, under less than salubrious conditions—took its toll. As the temperature rose, conditions deteriorated. Cleopatra's presence did little for morale. No doubt accurately, Herod wrote his dismissal down to her. That she occupied a vital position in camp and did little to apologize for that position is clear; as Egypt's commander in chief, she believed war preparations and operations to be her duty. She seems to have assumed that Antony was the only friend she needed. She was unwilling to be silenced, ironic given how little of her voice survives; there would be none of Queen Isabella of Spain's deferential "May your Lordship pardon me for speaking of things which I do not understand." It is impossible to say what came first, the Roman humiliation at Cleopatra's presence, or Cleopatra's superciliousness with the Romans. Antony's officers were said to be ashamed of her and of her status as equal partner. His closest companions objected to her authority. She had backed herself into a corner: To relax her guard was to be sent home. To maintain it was to offend. She may have been rattled too. There were stormy scenes with Antony.

Cleopatra failed in particular to endear herself to Gnaeus Domitius Ahenobarbus, arguably Antony's most distinguished supporter. A proud Republican, Ahenobarbus had led the consuls who had fled to Ephesus the previous spring. He was resolute and incorruptible. From the start he and Cleopatra had trouble. He refused to address her by her title; to him she remained simply "Cleopatra." She attempted to buy him off, only to discover that Ahenobarbus was as straight-spined as Plancus was invertebrate. True to his reputation, Ahenobarbus was vocal, too. He made no secret of his opinion that she was a liability. And he believed a war could be avoided. Implicated in and condemned for Caesar's murder, later proscribed, Ahenobarbus had fought at Philippi against Antony. The two reconciled afterward, since which time Ahenobarbus had occupied every high office and counted among Antony's most devoted adherents. He had been instrumental in opposing Octavian. He had fought to suppress the damaging news of the Donations. Already Ahenobarbus's son was promised to one of Antony's daughters. Together the two men had survived all kinds of adversity: They had been through Parthia together, where Ahenobarbus proved himself stalwart and a leader. When Antony had been too despondent to do so himself, Ahenobarbus had addressed the troops on their commander's behalf. As morale deteriorated in Actium the senior statesman this time took a different route. In a small boat, he defected to Octavian. Antony was devastated. True to form, he sent his former colleague's baggage, friends, and servants to join him. Cleopatra disapproved of his magnanimity.

She could not have been unaware of the discomfort her presence caused in the sweltering, mosquito-infested camp, where her retinue and tents made for a discordant sight, and where her immense flagship, the *Antonia,* with its ten banks of oars and carved and decorated bow, presumably evoked little pride. Rations were curtailed. The men were hungry, the mood sour. Cleopatra sat on a pile of closely guarded treasure. A Roman soldier liked to see his general eating stale bread and sleeping on a simple pallet. Cleopatra disturbed that equation. From all sides Antony—his tent positioned squarely at the center of the vast camp—heard that Cleopatra should be sent away, to which pleas he remained deaf. Even the trusted Canidius, who had earlier argued on her behalf, wanted her gone. She knew of the ridicule Fulvia had inspired. Even in Egypt, female commanders were not popular, as Cleopatra understood from her sister's short career during the Alexandrian War. She had no experience of armed conflict on this scale. Herod's theory was that Antony would not send her away as "his ears, it seems, were stopped by his infatuation." Why, then, did she not step aside, as she had with Caesar?

Octavian had declared war on her alone. She had every reason to demand vengeance. She had been shunted aside by military advisers before, to wind up in the Sinai desert, homeless and disenfranchised. She had been ill served by intermediaries; she may have been unwilling to entrust Egypt's fate to Antony alone. All was at stake: The future of the Ptolemaic dynasty hung in the balance. Were Octavian and Antony to come to terms now, she would be the price of that accord. The real mystery of 31 is less why Cleopatra remained than why—having expertly neutralized cultural collisions in Egypt, having artfully assuaged Roman egos—she neglected to work her charm on Antony's officers. In camp she seems to have been an infuriating and exhausting presence. Many were treated to the scorn she had heaped on the straight-talking Geminius. Friends of Antony and Roman consuls alike suffered at her hands, universally reported to have been "abused by Cleopatra." She was vindictive, peremptory, brittle. Experience had not made her any more tractable than she had been as a teenager, with her brothers' advisers. She was after all accustomed to exercising supreme authority, poor at taking orders. Meanwhile morale plunged as Octavian's blockade tightened around the gulf, as swarms of mosquitoes descended upon the camp, and as an epidemic—it was likely malaria—set in. Conditions were deplorable. Relief came only toward midday, when with a rustle the wind picked up from the west. For a few hours a fresh, brisk breeze swept in, growing stronger as it pivoted from west to north, to subside as the sun set.

Months passed in readiness and inactivity, and with them a gradual reordering of the odds. While the idea had presumably been to trap Octavian in the Ambracian Gulf, Antony and Cleopatra found themselves bottled up in the bright blue bay, a shifting of realities to which they were slow to adjust. Notes Plutarch: "The chief task of a good general is to force his enemies to give battle when he is superior to them, but not to be forced himself to do this when his forces are inferior." Antony had long relinquished that advantage. By August he had no choice but to enlist whole towns to carry supplies overland to camp. Plutarch's great-grandfather was among those miserably pressed into service, to make the trek over mountain paths to the gulf, sacks of wheat on their shoulders, whips at their backs.

What the blockade, the disease, the debilitating inactivity, the heat, did not affect, the desertions did. Slaves and client kings alike abandoned the cause. Antony made an example of two near-deserters, a senator and a Syrian king, tortured and executed to discourage imitators. Antony was himself rattled, enough so to attempt a solitary stroll along the fortifications, toward the sea, in the course of which Octavian's men nearly succeeded in kidnapping him. Ahenobarbus's defection affected him deeply; he was afterward fiercely paranoid. By one account, he distrusted even Cleopatra, whom he suspected of attempting to poison him. To prove her innocence she was said to have prepared a lethal drink, only to intercept the goblet as Antony raised it to his lips. Had she intended to kill him she would not have done so, would she? She then sent for a prisoner, to whom she handed the potion. It had the advertised effect. (The story is suspect, as Cleopatra could hardly proceed without Antony. He was unlikely to have forgotten as much, even in an agitated state.) Cleopatra quarreled as well with Dellius, who had spent his summer recruiting mercenaries. The two came to blows at dinner one night, when Dellius complained of the wine. It was sour, he scoffed, while in Rome Octavian's staff downed the finest vintages. Dellius emerged from the tussle convinced that Cleopatra meant to murder him. One of her physicians, he claimed, confirmed as much. It was a perfectly legitimate excuse for his third and final defection. He fled to Octavian, depriving Antony of what Caesar had termed the mightiest of weapons: surprise. With Dellius went Antony's battle plans.

Toward the end of August Antony called a war council. Sixteen weeks of blockade had taken a toll. The situation was bleak. Supplies were short; the night air was crisp. Winter would soon be upon them. Antony needed finally to resolve the question that had plagued him through the scorching summer. Tactics came more easily to him than did strategy; he could be indecisive. If she had not already done so, Cleopatra now fell out even with Canidius. He preferred to march north and to decide the contest on land. They were Romans after all; to wage battle atop scudding waves was in his opinion folly. Antony had never before commanded a fleet. He could yield the sea to Octavian without shame. There were moreover recruits to be had in Macedonia and Thrace. Of course Canidius knew well that to fight on land was to sacrifice Cleopatra's fleet and with it her usefulness. Cleopatra knew that to sacrifice the fleet was to imperil Egypt. Her chests of silver denarii could not be carted across mountains. She argued vigorously for a naval engagement. Her reasons were perfectly sound: Antony was seriously outnumbered on land. He could not ultimately cross to Italy without a fleet. Nor was it easy to move an army over mountains; five years had not erased the memory of Parthia. There was another consideration as well, an analogue that no one involved in the Actium deliberations could have ignored. For his showdown with Caesar, Pompey too had marshaled a massive, noisy, polyglot force of Asiatic kings and princes in Greece. Cleopatra had contributed sixty ships to that fleet. Ahenobarbus had been present, as had his father, who had perished in the battle. Antony had commanded with distinction on the opposite side. In August 48 Pompey had elected to ignore his navy, far superior to Caesar's. Hardly was the day out when he realized that he had blundered grievously in opting for a land battle. The result was utter carnage, a speechless, senseless commander, robbed of his army, his wits, and his pride, and—days later—decapitated off the coast of Egypt.

ANTONY OPTED FOR a naval campaign. Plutarch has him swayed by emotion. More likely the most experienced general of his day meant neither to accommodate Cleopatra nor to showcase her navy but bowed in the end to necessity. Octavian had not only a more coherent narrative but a more cohesive force, an army of Latin-speaking, well-drilled Romans. The land advantage was his. At sea the two sides were more evenly matched. Antony explained as much to his restless men, few of whom could swim. He did not care to open a campaign with a defeat. "I have chosen to begin with the ships, where we are strongest and have a vast superiority over our antagonists, in order that after a victory with these we may scorn their infantry also." (Elaborating on the same theme, Octavian proved himself more psychologically astute: "For in general it is a natural characteristic of human nature everywhere, that whenever a man fails in his first contests he becomes disheartened with respect to what is to come.") Despite the explanations, a battle-worn veteran threw himself upon Antony with an emotional appeal. He displayed an astonishing collection of scars. How could Antony insult those wounds, to invest his hopes "in miserable logs of wood"? The soldier pleaded with his commander: "Let Egyptians and Phoenicians do their fighting at sea, but give us land, on which we are accustomed to stand and either conquer our enemies or die." Antony—"better endowed by nature than any man of his time for leading an army by force of eloquence"—looked upon him kindly but could not manage a reply.

Over the last days of August a familiar smell greeted Cleopatra. The afternoon breeze lifted the acrid odor of flaming cedar and resin throughout camp. It was a smell she knew from the Alexandrian harbor seventeen years earlier; in what must have seemed to be a regular Roman tradition, Antony dragged some eighty of her ships to the beach and set fire to them. He no longer had the crew to man the fleet and could not risk its falling into Octavian's hands. That was no secret; the blaze was bright and pungent. A storm soon extinguished the lingering wisps of smoke; for four days, gale winds and drenching rains lashed the coast. By the time the weather cleared only warped fittings and scorched rams remained. Under cover of darkness on the evening of September 1 Cleopatra's officers secretly loaded her chests of treasure onto the massive *Antonia*. Several transport ships took on additional monies, as well as a hoard of royal tableware. Masts and bulky sails went aboard both Cleopatra's ships and Antony's. By sunrise Antony had embarked 20,000 soldiers and with them thousands of archers and slingers, wedging a colossal number of men into slivers of space. The sky was crystal clear and the sea a glassy sheet as they rowed out, with a crash and clatter of oars, to the mouth of the gulf. There Antony's three squadrons stationed themselves in close, crescent formation. Cleopatra and her remaining sixty ships took up the rear, as much to head off deserters as for protection. She was not meant to take part in the fighting.

Outside the strait Antony's men discovered Octavian's fleet assembled in a similar formation, about a mile off. The gulf resounded with the high-pitched blasts of trumpets; criers and officers urged the men on. And Antony's 240 ships, oars poised, prows pointed, facing Octavian's 400, sat through the morning, prepared to fight, hulls crammed together, creaking and motionless, as the land armies watched from shore. Finally at midday Octavian ordered his northernmost squadron to row backward, in an attempt to draw Antony out. His ships advanced into open water. Instantly the air was thick with shouts, onshore and on the water. From the lofty towers of Antony's fleet a dense hail of stones and arrows and metal shards rained down. On Octavian's side oars shattered and rudders snapped. Despite the sea churning beneath her, it was from Cleopatra's perspective an odd floating land battle, with Octavian's men playing the cavalry and Antony's men repelling the assault from their floating fortresses, the largest of which loomed ten feet above the waterline. The fierce ramming and grappling continued inconclusively until late in the afternoon. At about three o'clock Octavian's left wing shifted, to outflank Antony's; Antony's in turn edged north. The center of the line dissolved. Suddenly Cleopatra's squadron hoisted sail and—expertly plying the wind—broke coolly through the middle of the battle, past the flying slings and missiles, beyond the spears and axes of the enemy line, sowing confusion on all sides. Octavian's men looked on in amazement as Cleopatra sped south in her majestic flagship, its purple sails billowing. For the most part the enemy was powerless to overtake her. Their shock only increased when, moments later, Antony transferred from his flagship to a swift galley and followed behind, with forty ships of his personal squadron.

Octavian's men were arguably less bewildered, as Plutarch has it, than impressed. Antony and Cleopatra had slipped away with a third of the remaining fleet and all of her treasure. Clearly the flight had been prearranged; there would have been neither valuables nor sails stowed on Cleopatra's ships otherwise. She timed her move perfectly to take advantage of the brisk and favorable rise in the wind. And from Dellius, Octavian had known of the blockade-breaking plan. Antony and Cleopatra had had no intention of prolonging a battle. Earlier in the month they had already once attempted to force their way through the blockade. If they could nudge Octavian out to sea they could escape to Egypt; they made this sally only in order to do so. In the prebattle speech Dio supplies him, Octavian alerts his men to precisely this course of events: "Since, then, they admit that they are weaker than we are, and since they carry the prizes of victory in their ships, let us not allow them to sail anywhere else, but let us conquer them here on the spot and take all these treasures away from them." On September 2 a few of Octavian's swift ships—light, highly maneuverable galleys, with streamlined prows—indeed headed off in pursuit.

On the high seas Cleopatra signaled to Antony. With two companions he climbed over the whitecaps to board the *Antonia*. The reunion was not a happy one; Antony neither saw nor spoke to Cleopatra, on account of what sounds more like shame than anger. Something had gone very wrong. Probably Antony's men were not meant to have remained behind. Cleopatra had earlier argued that the bulk of the army return with her to Egypt. The fleet had either been unable to escape or had elected not to do so. They may have preferred to fight a Roman rather than follow a foreigner; certainly there were mutinous murmurs in camp. Antony and Cleopatra may have planned the maneuver only in case of necessity, and alone or together acted peremptorily. Or Cleopatra may have made her exit prematurely. She must have been longing to sail off to Alexandria, a city that—were she vanquished off the coast of Greece—she knew she would never see again. Dio suggests that Antony fled because he (erroneously) read a concession of defeat in Cleopatra's departure. Or all went precisely according to plan, and its repercussions emerged only after the fact; we are left to square unintelligible decisions with obscure accounts. In any event Antony could not have bowed his head in defeat, as the engagement—less a skirmish than a melee—continued inconclusively for some time. Even Octavian would not know by day's end who had prevailed. Whether the plan had been misconceived or had miscarried, the I-told-you-so's hang palpably in the salty breeze. If Plutarch can be believed, Antony choked on his helplessness. Ignoring Cleopatra, "he went forward alone to the prow and sat down by himself in silence, holding his head in both hands." He stirred only at dusk, when two of Octavian's galleys materialized in the distance. Antony commanded the flagship to be swung around so that he might stand and face the enemy head on. A skirmish ensued, from which the *Antonia* escaped, but to which Cleopatra sacrificed a command ship and a second vessel, packed with a quantity of rich plate and furniture.

Having fended off the assailants, Antony returned to the prow. Head bowed, he stared listlessly out to sea, the hero of Philippi, the new Dionysus, reduced to a great brooding hulk, the powerful arms and shoulders startlingly still. The cruise south was a bitter one, infected by mutual anxieties and private losses. It was also quiet. Antony spent three days alone, "either in anger with Cleopatra, or wishing not to upbraid her." While it may have been forged of desperation, the plan had at one time seemed a sensible one. Antony could not now escape the impression that he had deserted his men. They had remained steadfast while kings, senators, officers, had abandoned him. He had left them in the lurch, to find himself in an untenable position with Cleopatra. The outcome of the battle of Actium remained unclear, as it would for several days, but he understood the implications of what he had done and how it appeared. A Roman commander was meant to stare down defeat, to persist regardless of all debilitating odds. And history was entirely palpable to Mark Antony; in Rome he lived grandly in a house decorated by ninety bronze rams captured at sea. (They were Pompey's.) He understood what glory had just slipped, forever, through his fingers.

After three days Cleopatra put in for water and supplies at Taenarum, the southernmost point of the Peloponnesian peninsula. (Fittingly, it was the cape where Hercules was believed to have searched for the entrance to the underworld.) There two of her servants, Iras the hairdresser and Charmion the lady-in-waiting, urged a reconciliation. With some coaxing, the two women persuaded Antony and Cleopatra to speak, eventually even "to eat and sleep together." Several transport ships joined them, with news of what had transpired after their Actium departure. The battle had intensified and continued on for hours. Antony's fleet had held out but was ultimately destroyed. For some time the surf delivered up bodies and timber, flecked—if a particularly colorful account can be believed—with the purple and gold spangles of the East. Antony's land forces held firm. At the end of the meeting Antony attempted to distribute gifts to his men. From one of the transport ships, he handed around gold and silver treasures from Cleopatra's palace. In tears, his men refused the prizes. Their commander showered them instead with affection. He would, he promised, arrange for them to be hidden away safely until they could agree on terms with Octavian. With Cleopatra he continued on across the Mediterranean, to the flat coast of Egypt. They made landfall in a desolate outpost in the northwestern corner of the country, where they separated, along an expanse of sandy beach.

Antony headed to Libya, where he had posted four legions. He planned to regroup. Cleopatra, her fleet lost, her treasure partly dispersed, her ally ruined, hurried to Alexandria. She had left Actium before anyone else, and in a powerful, well-equipped ship. If she moved rapidly she could outsail news of the fiasco. She knew what it was to return to Egypt under catastrophic conditions and took precautions: she ordered some quick floral arranging. When she glided past the lighthouse of Alexandria the following day she did so serenely, her ships garlanded with wreaths of flowers. Accompanied by flute players, an on-deck chorus chanted victory songs. To those who rowed out to meet her Cleopatra imparted the news of her extraordinary triumph, presumably without a trace of dryness in her throat. Nearly simultaneously, Antony's nineteen legions and 12,000 cavalry—having finally given up hope that their commander would return to them, and after a week of stubborn negotiation—surrendered to Octavian, who was only just beginning to grasp the scale of his victory.

THE WICKEDEST WOMAN
IN HISTORY

"I was equal to gods, except for the mortal part."
— EURIPIDES

MISFORTUNE, WENT THE saying, has few friends; Cleopatra did not wait to discover if the adage was true. If her ruse had not already been discovered it was confirmed quickly enough now, in blood. The Alexandrian elite had disapproved of her before. She feared their reaction on learning of the Actium debacle; they could now fairly accuse her of having delivered Egypt to Rome. She did not care to watch them exult in her defeat. Nor did she care to be replaced on the throne. She no sooner returned than she embarked on an unbridled killing spree, ordering her most prominent detractors arrested and assassinated. From their estates she confiscated great sums. She appropriated additional monies wherever she could find them, seizing temple treasures. For whatever came next a fortune was required. It would be expensive to buy off the inevitable; in one form or another, Octavian would come calling. She equipped new forces and cast about for allies, whom she courted baldly. Artavasdes, the defiant Armenian king, had remained a prisoner in Alexandria, where his three years of captivity now came to an end. Cleopatra sent his severed head some 1,200 miles east, to his Median rival. She calculated that he would need no further encouragement to rise to her assistance. He demurred.

As in the past, she reached out to the East, where she had trade contacts and longtime partisans, where Octavian was without traction, and where royalty was royalty. When Antony returned to Alexandria he found her consumed by "a most bold and wonderful enterprise." An isthmus separated the Mediterranean from the Gulf of Suez, at the eastern frontier of Egypt. With a large force Cleopatra attempted to lift her ships out of the Mediterranean and haul them forty miles overland, to be relaunched via the gulf into the Red Sea. With her men and money she proposed to make a new home for herself, well beyond the borders of Egypt, possibly even in India, "far away from war and slavery." In a blind alley it seemed Cleopatra's nature to envision broad, unbounded horizons; the grandiosity and bravado were staggering, practically enough to suggest that she truly had contemplated an assault on the Roman world.

Cleopatra's Red Sea venture was not impossible in a country that had for centuries hauled immense stone blocks across vast distances. A monstrosity of a two-prowed Ptolemaic vessel—it was said to have been nearly four hundred feet long and to sit sixty feet above the water—had centuries earlier been launched along wooden rollers, set at even intervals along a harborside ditch. Greased hides occasionally served the same purpose. Ships could be broken as well into sections. The enterprise was less feasible for a sovereign who had antagonized the tribe on the far side of the isthmus. Those happened to be the Nabateans, the shrewd, well-organized traders who had spent a year fighting Herod, thanks in part to Cleopatra's sabotage. They did not need Herod—who had finally just defeated them—to remind them that Cleopatra was their common enemy. The Nabateans set fire to each of the Egyptian ships as it was drawn ashore. For Cleopatra the failure was particularly bitter. This was the corner of the world from which she had successfully relaunched herself in 48.

Herod was of course the obvious ally; in the desert, Octavian would be no match for their combined forces. To no one, however, was Cleopatra's misfortune so profoundly satisfying. Cleopatra had dealt Herod a get-out-of-jail-free card in dismissing him from Actium; he lost no time in making his peace with Octavian. Probably in Rhodes that fall the

Judaean king made a great show of contrition. Dressed as a commoner, he removed his diadem as he set foot on shore. Before the new master of the Roman world he was frank and forthright. Indeed he had been loyal to Antony. Such, alas, was his nature. Integrity was his stock-in-trade. In his book, explained Herod, a friend ought to risk "every bit of his soul and body and substance." Had he not been off assailing the Nabateans he would, he assured Octavian, be at Antony's side even at that very moment. He abandoned his good friend of over two decades now only on account of that Egyptian woman, he admitted, proceeding to cough up the official version of Octavian's war on Cleopatra. He had *told* Antony to do away with her. There is no indication of how Herod got through this speech with a straight face. At its end Octavian professed himself grateful to Cleopatra. She had, he reassured his caller, bequeathed him a fine ally. (Herod had reason to be doubly grateful to Cleopatra. He owed his crown to Roman fears of her in the first place.) Graciously, Octavian replaced the diadem on Herod's head. He sent him off with Roman reinforcements. Meanwhile Cleopatra continued tirelessly to court neighboring tribes and friendly kings. She was able to mobilize only a troop of gladiators, highly skilled fighters who had been training for what were presumed to be Antony and Cleopatra's victory celebrations. Answering her call, they headed south from what is today modern Turkey. Herod saw to it that they got no farther than Syria.

Failing the East, Cleopatra could look in the opposite direction. Rome had not fully conquered Spain, a restive region, hugely fertile and rich in silver mines. Even if the Mediterranean were closed to her, even if she were unable to continue the war against Octavian, she might sail west via the Indian Ocean, circumnavigating Africa. With her vast resources she and Antony might stir up Spain's native tribes and found a new kingdom. It was not such a far-fetched idea; Cleopatra had before her the example of another linguistically gifted, charismatic leader. In 83 a rogue Roman proconsul had seized control of Spain, to the horror of his countrymen. Hailed by his native recruits as "the new Hannibal," Sertorius had incited a revolt. He had very nearly gone on to establish an independent Roman state.* Cleopatra considered the prospect seriously; Octavian worried that she would manage to repeat Sertorius's coup. A military operation at home was after all unlikely; with the defections of Herod and of Antony's Cyrenean troops, Egypt was all that remained. It was firmly behind Cleopatra—in Upper Egypt her partisans offered to rise up on her behalf, an effort she discouraged—but unlikely to hold out long against Octavian. She had at best four hundred fiercely loyal Gaulish bodyguards, a modest number of troops, and a remnant of a fleet.

Nothing about the battle of Actium had been as brilliant as the blaze of invective that preceded it; most of the drama, and many of the casualties, came after the unspectacular fact. It was anticlimactic in the extreme, which could not be said of the months that followed in Alexandria. Yet again Cleopatra's plans had miscarried. Yet again she cast about vigorously to ensure that all was not lost. All was a whirl of feverish activity at the palace; Plutarch has her not only looking to Spain and India but experimenting daily with deadly poisons. To one end or another she made a collection of these, testing them on prisoners and on venomous animals to determine which toxin yielded the most expeditious, least painful results. She was neither humbled nor panic-stricken but every bit as inventive as she had been when the first reverse of her life had landed her in the desert. The word "formidable" sooner or later attaches itself to Cleopatra and here it comes: she was formidable—spirited, disciplined, resourceful—in her retreat. There were no hints of despair. Two thousand years after the fact, you can still hear the fertile mind pulsing with ideas.

The same could not be said for Antony. He roamed restlessly about North Africa, mostly with two friends, a rhetorician and an especially clever, steadfast officer. Antony dismissed the rest of his entourage. The

*Nor was Cleopatra the first savvy Easterner to team up with a Roman general. Sertorius had joined forces with Mithradates, the Pontic king who in 69 so eloquently warned of Rome's rise. Mithradates too had envisioned precisely the sort of amalgamated empire Cleopatra and Antony represented. He put decades toward its realization, to be vanquished by Pompey. Pompey ultimately defeated Sertorius as well, after a vicious four-year campaign.

relative solitude comforted him. He counted on marshaling reinforcements but in Cyrene discovered that his four legions had defected.
Crushed, he attempted suicide. The two friends intervened, to deliver
him to Alexandria. He arrived at the palace without the expected reinforcements, and, concedes Dio, "without having accomplished anything." It was probably late in the fall, toward the end of the sowing
season. Cleopatra was in the midst of her ill-fated Red Sea venture. She
settled for fortifying the approaches to Egypt. She may also have contemplated Octavian's assassination. For his part, Antony withdrew from
the city and from society. He ordered a long causeway built into the
Alexandrian harbor, at the end of which he fixed a modest hut, near the
foot of the lighthouse. He declared himself an exile, a latter-day Timon
of Athens, "for he himself also had been wronged and treated with
ingratitude by his friends, and therefore hated and distrusted all mankind." Dio slips in a bitter note of sympathy; he cannot help but marvel at
the great number of people who—having received lavish honors and
favors from Antony and Cleopatra—left them now in the lurch. Cleopatra appeared not to stumble over the injustice. Her understanding of
gratitude may have been more realistic than Antony's. She accepted the
rude truths more easily than did he.

Antony did not last long as a hermit and turned up at the palace soon
enough. Cleopatra purportedly coaxed him out, to the lush groves and
the colorful royal lodges on which he had turned his back. If indeed she
did so, it was one of the less difficult assignments of her life. The news
continued to be bleak: Canidius appeared in Alexandria to report that
Antony's land forces had in the end surrendered to Octavian. Many of
them joined that army; Octavian had now more men than he could use.
He burned what remained of the captured warships. Antony and Cleopatra learned next of Herod's defection, especially painful as they had sent
their most persuasive messenger to plead for his continued loyalty. (It
was the friend whom Cleopatra had enlisted to clear Antony's head of
Octavia.) Not only did he fail with Herod, but he took advantage of his

trip to defect. The Roman governor of Syria also went over to Octavian, as would Nicolaus of Damascus.

The recriminations were kept to a minimum. Cleopatra appears to have looked to the future rather than to the past, to have calculated that Antony was well beyond the tickle and tease of admonition, the love bites. She subscribed to Plutarch's counsel on rebuke: better in time of calamity to opt for sympathy over blame, for "at such a time there is no use for a friend's frankness or for words charged with grave and stinging reproof." Antony was, however, a different man, the storied audacity and "irresistible courage" wrung from him by Actium. Cleopatra was left with two projects, to minister to her distressed lover and to plot their escape. Somehow she comforted Antony, or numbed him, so that the dire reports seemed to agitate him less. She addressed his frustrations and calmed his suspicions. She did the thinking for them both.

By relinquishing hope Antony discovered that he could relinquish anxiety as well; he returned to the palace and—never in need of an occasion—"set the whole city into a course of feasting, drinking, and presents." Together Antony and Cleopatra staged too an elaborate coming-of-age party for their sons by their previous marriages, fifteen-year-old Antyllus and sixteen-year-old Caesarion. By the Greek reckoning, Caesarion was now of military age.* For his part Antyllus was ready to shed the purple-edged toga of a Roman child. In a mingling of traditions, Antony and Cleopatra ushered the boys into adulthood. Both enlisted in the military to boost Egyptian morale. For days banquets and revels and feasts distracted the city. Dio asserts that Antony and Cleopatra staged the celebrations to stoke a new spirit of resistance; to her subjects Cleopatra conveyed the message that they were "to continue the struggle with these boys as their leaders, in case anything should happen to the parents." Come what may, the Ptolemaic dynasty would survive, and with a male sovereign to boot. Indeed Caesarion was hailed as pha-

---

*In the normal course of events he would have been preparing to depose his mother about now.

raoh in inscriptions that autumn. Antony and Cleopatra might just as well have desperately been throwing sand in Octavian's face. They had sons, by which the future was calibrated. He had none.

Over the fall a flurry of envoys traveled back and forth, with bribes and proposals from one side, threats and promises from the other. Initially Cleopatra pleaded for the only thing that mattered to her: Could she pass down her kingdom to her children? To lose her life was one thing; to sacrifice her children—and with them her country—was unthinkable. They were now between the ages of seven and seventeen; she pinned her hopes on Caesarion, whom she had already promoted to rule in her absence. Later she sent Octavian a golden scepter, crown, and throne. She would abdicate in exchange for clemency, suggests Dio, "for she hoped that even if he did hate Antony, he would yet take pity on her at least." Antony hoped to be allowed to live as a private citizen in Egypt or—if that was asking too much—in Athens. Octavian had no time for Antony's proposal but he answered Cleopatra. Publicly he threatened her. Privately he replied that he would be perfectly reasonable with her on one condition: she was to arrange for Antony's execution, or at the very least his exile. (Octavian kept the gifts.) Antony tried again, defending his relationship with Cleopatra, reminding Octavian of their family ties, their "amorous adventures," their shared pranks. To prove his sincerity he delivered up a remaining assassin of Caesar's, then living with Antony. He proposed something else as well. He would kill himself "if in that way Cleopatra might be saved." Again he elicited only an icy silence. The assassin was put to death.

The sad truth was that Antony had nothing to offer. Cleopatra had a stronger hand, with the greatest treasure still outside Roman control. Octavian could not succeed without her famed gold and pearls and ivory. They had long motivated his men; more than anything else, Cleopatra's hoard held his rank and file in check. So much were Antony and Cleopatra alone, so regular were the desertions, that they had no emissary to entrust with these messages. They were left to press one of the children's tutors into service. With his third overture Antony dispatched fifteen-year-old Antyllus and a vast quantity of gold. Octavian kept the gold and dismissed the boy. It is unclear how sincere the proposals were; Dio suggests that Antony and Cleopatra were simply biding their time while plotting revenge. The overtures were in any event no less genuine than the replies. Octavian could not truly expect Cleopatra to murder Antony. Her brother had won no points for eliminating the distressed and defeated Pompey seventeen years earlier. Nor had she any guarantee that Octavian would honor his end of the bargain. Was he likely to pardon a woman on whom he had so theatrically declared war? Cleopatra might well agree to disassociate herself from Antony, but she hardly had reason to go further. She knew an ambush when she saw one. Octavian would have to figure out how to dispense with his former brother-in-law himself.

With Cleopatra's last messenger Octavian sent to Alexandria an especially clever emissary of his own. (It is notable, though usually forgotten, that Octavian by this arrangement tried his wiles on Cleopatra.) Thyrsus was handsome, persuasive, and more than adequately qualified to negotiate with "a woman who was haughty and astonishingly proud in the matter of beauty," as Plutarch has it, or who "thought it her due to be loved by all mankind," as Dio concludes. Dio finds Cleopatra vain to the point of delusion, so taken with her own charms as to allow an emissary to convince her that Octavian, a young general who had never set eyes upon her, was infatuated with her, simply because she wished him to be, and because in the past she had had that effect on Roman commanders. Cleopatra spent a great deal of time closeted with the superbly intelligent Thyrsus, on whom she lavished special honors. She had every reason to win his favor; the two conferred privately and at length. We have no account of his response but we do of another. Antony exploded with jealousy. He had Thyrsus seized, whipped, and returned to Octavian with a letter. Octavian's man had provoked him, and at a time when he was already irritable. He had enough on his mind. If Octavian objected to what he had done he could easily settle the score. Mark Antony's man was with Octavian in Asia. (He had defected early on.) Octavian had only "to hang him up and give him a flogging," suggested Antony, "and we shall be quits."

Cleopatra too had plenty on her mind but before all else humored Antony. It was difficult to say what value he added to the equation at this juncture, which makes her solicitude all the more remarkable. She calmed him with every imaginable attention. At the end of the year she celebrated her thirty-eighth birthday modestly, in a style "suited to her fallen fortunes." She spared no expense when it came time for Antony's in January. He continued to count on a future in which he might live, retired from public affairs, either in Athens or Alexandria, rather unrealistic prospects under the circumstances. Cleopatra saw to it that he rang in his fifty-third year with the greatest of splendor and every kind of magnificence, among friends who had little reason to question their loyalty, as "many of those who were bidden to the supper came poor and went away rich."

Otherwise Alexandrian affairs took on a melancholy complexion. Octavian continued to threaten Cleopatra publicly while privately he maintained that if she killed Antony she would have her pardon. Silver-tongued messengers aside, she had no intention of accepting the offer. She continued with her poison experiments, though probably not with a cobra, as Plutarch asserts. She was in search of a toxin that subtly, painlessly overwhelmed the senses. Its victim should submit to what appeared to be a profound natural sleep. Much of this was common knowledge to a Hellenistic sovereign, reliably familiar with her toxins and antidotes, and well aware that a cobra bite did not answer to that description. In all such matters Cleopatra's personal physician, Olympus, at her side over these weeks, would also have been eminently well versed; if you wanted an excellent poison, you procured it in Egypt, from an Alexandrian doctor. The suppers and drinking bouts continued, with as much profligacy as ever but under a different name. Cleopatra and Antony dissolved the Society of the Inimitable Livers to found another, every bit that association's equal in "splendor, luxury, and sumptuosity." Out of black humor or bleak despair, they called this new society the Companions to the Death. Those who reclined on the plush palace couches vowed to die with their hosts. And Cleopatra oversaw the hurried construction of an elaborate, two-story building, adjacent to an Isis temple, with a commanding view of the Mediterranean, probably on a sandy strip of palace ground, her "surpassingly lofty and beautiful" mausoleum.

THERE WAS A reprieve of sorts over the winter, when it became clear that Octavian would make no expedition until the weather warmed. Urgent matters intervened. From Samos he returned to Rome, where there were demonstrations and disturbances of all kinds. Discharging an army was always complicated, and—short on funds—Octavian had thousands of mutinous veterans on his hands. Only early in the spring did he make a lightning trip east. The sailing season had not yet opened; he moved so quickly "that Antony and Cleopatra learned at one and the same time both of his departure and of his return." His cordial new friend greeted him in Syria; no sooner had Octavian and his men disembarked on the Phoenician coast than Herod was on hand with gifts and provisions. He installed the weary travelers in magnificently appointed apartments. And he saw to it that they lacked nothing for the desert march before them, sending Octavian off precisely as he had sent off Cleopatra six years earlier, though this time tossing goodwill and funds into the bargain. To Octavian's cause Herod contributed monies equal to four years of Cleopatra's Jericho revenue. (The logic was transparent. Herod meant to make it blindingly obvious to the Romans that his "realm was far too restricted in comparison with the services which he had rendered them.") Without any touristic detours Octavian headed to Pelusium, where Herod left him, early in the summer. The idea was to assault Egypt simultaneously from two sides, through Syria and Libya, mobilizing Antony's former legions in the West.

In Alexandria Cleopatra continued the "strange, wild life" with Antony, without which she could not have reconstituted the Ptolemaic Empire, and on account of which she now found herself in dire straits. There may have been another covert set of negotiations that winter; although their accounts differ wildly elsewhere, both Plutarch and Dio assert that Octavian crossed easily into Egypt, without any resistance at the Eastern frontier, because Cleopatra secretly arranged for him to do so. The accounts may derive from the same inimical report; Cleopatra's treachery was a fertile subject, on which a Roman could, for a few hundred years, dilate inexhaustibly. She may well have been double-dealing, bowing to the inevitable, bargaining for leniency. She had been ruthlessly pragmatic before. At this point her interests substantially diverged from Antony's. He could hope for little more than a brilliant last stand. She fought to preserve a dynasty, if not a country. (By one account she both bribed the general at Pelusium to surrender and allowed Antony to murder the general's family for his cowardice. And, naturally, the accusations of her collusion did not prevent Octavian from asserting later that he took Pelusium by storm.)

Cleopatra knew that she could not hold out militarily against Octavian; certainly there was acquiescence, if not treachery. As she had discouraged the partisans of Upper Egypt from rising up in her defense (she claimed she did not care to see them needlessly massacred; she may have been banking still on a negotiation), she discouraged the Alexandrians in their resistance. Dio assigns her a second, infinitely less plausible motive as well. He asserts that she believed Thyrsus when he said that Octavian was smitten with her. Why should Octavian be any different from Caesar and Antony? So obsessed is Dio with Cleopatra's vanity that he forgets she was also a skilled politician. She yields Pelusium, he asserts, as "she expected to gain not only forgiveness and the sovereignty over the Egyptians, but the empire of the Romans as well." Cleopatra could generally be counted on to do the intelligent thing. Dio has her engaged with the nonsensical. She was fighting for her life, her throne, and her children. She had ruled for two decades, and was without illusions. She knew Octavian was deeply enamored not with her but with her wealth. Into the mausoleum she heaped gems, jewelry, works of art, coffers of gold, royal robes, stores of cinnamon and frankincense, necessities to her, luxuries to the rest of the world. With those riches went as well a vast quantity of kindling. Were she to disappear, the treasure of Egypt would disappear with her. The thought was a torture to Octavian.

As Octavian advanced on Alexandria Antony experienced a sudden surge of energy. Rallying a modest force, he rode out to meet the enemy's advance guard in the outskirts of the city, several miles east of the Canopic Gate. Octavian's army was depleted from the march; Antony's cavalry won the day, routing Octavian's, and pursuing them all the way back to camp. At breakneck speed Antony galloped to Alexandria to share the brilliant news: "Then, exalted by his victory, he went into the palace, kissed Cleopatra, all armed as he was, and presented to her one of the soldiers who had fought most spiritedly." For his courage Cleopatra rewarded the dusty young man with a golden breastplate and helmet. With respect and gratitude, he accepted both. He defected in the night to Octavian. Undeterred, Antony attempted yet again to suborn Octavian's men, some of whom had after all been his. He sent as well an invitation to his former brother-in-law, challenging him to single combat. This time he got a response. Octavian observed frostily that there were many ways in which Antony might die.

He determined to wage another assault, simultaneously on land and sea. A morbid dinner preceded that sortie, on the evening of July 31. Octavian camped outside Alexandria's east gates, near the city's hippodrome. His fleet rode at anchor just beyond the harbor. An eerie calm descended over the hyperkinetic city. Surrounded by friends at the palace, Antony urged his servants to drink copiously. They would have no such opportunity the next day, when they might well have a new master, and he would be, at best, "a mummy and a nothing." Again his friends wept at his words. Antony consoled them. He would involve them in no useless battles. He aspired only to an honorable death. At dawn on August 1 he marched the remainder of his infantry out of the city gates, stationing them at a vantage point from which they might follow the engagement at sea. Around them the city was hushed. Antony stood motionless in the silvery morning air, tense with the anticipation of victory. His fleet rowed directly for Octavian's — and saluted the enemy with their oars. Octavian's ships returned the gesture. From shore Antony watched the fleets return peacefully to the harbor, now united as one. No sooner had their prows aligned than his cavalry deserted as well. His infantry put up a desultory fight. Incensed, Antony flew toward the palace, raving "that Cleopatra had betrayed him to the enemies he had made for her sake." The charge tallies with his addled state of mind. Dio takes it at face value, again impugning Cleopatra. Obviously she had double-crossed Antony and caused the ships to desert. She was in league with Octavian. It is not impossible; she may well have preferred her own last-ditch efforts—she still had a negotiating position, as Antony had not—to his. On this count the spotty record is less problematic than are the personalities of our two chroniclers, which Cleopatra neatly draws out. Dio is excited by treachery, Plutarch undone by emotion. Now in a panic, the city was Octavian's.

Whether or not she had betrayed him, Cleopatra did not wait for Antony's return. She had heard his rants before. She had no desire to hear them again. She knew now that her lover was finally, irrevocably, inconsolably ruined. Fleeing Antony, she rushed to the mausoleum with her maidservants and staff. Behind them they lowered the massive doors, evidently a sort of portcullis. Once in place the panels would not again budge. Cleopatra secured the entry as well with bolts and bars. For Dio, the flight to the mausoleum was all playacting; Octavian had kept up his regular stream of comforting messages. Clearly Cleopatra had agreed to his demand that she sacrifice her lover in exchange for Egypt. She made the dramatic move only to encourage Antony to kill himself. Antony suspected a ruse, "yet in his infatuation he could not believe it, but actually pitied her more, one might say, than himself." There was no shortage of causes for pity. Dio allows Cleopatra at least a nod to Antony's affection—she may be duplicitous, but she is not coldhearted—though again he mangles her motives. Were Antony to believe her dead he would surely not care to go on living. Having barricaded herself in the mausoleum, Cleopatra sent a messenger to Antony, with a report of her death.

Did she deliberately deceive him? She stands accused of so many betrayals that it is difficult to know what to do with this one, arguably the most humane and least surprising. The two were after all partners in death; Antony had already offered to kill himself to save her. Octavian had no further use for Antony, an impediment to Cleopatra at this point as well. Someone had to put him out of his misery, a task defeated Roman generals traditionally handled themselves. The message may have been bungled in transmission, well before it was mauled by historians. In any event Antony lost no time; in Cleopatra's absence he was without a reason to live. Nor was he particularly eager to be shown up by a woman. He received the news in his room, among his staff. Plutarch has him instantly unfastening his breastplate and crying out, "O Cleopatra, I am not distressed to have lost you, for I shall straightaway join you; but I am grieved that a commander as great as I should be found to be inferior to a woman in courage." By prearrangement, his servant Eros was designated to kill him should the need arise. Antony now requested he do so. Eros drew his sword and—turning from his master—slew himself. He collapsed at Antony's feet. Antony could only applaud his courage and his example. Brandishing his own sword—the blade would have been about two and a half feet long, with an extended steel point—he ran it straight into his ribs, missing his heart, puncturing his abdomen. Bloodied and faint, he dropped to the couch. He had not succeeded in his task, however, and shortly regained consciousness. It was somehow typical of Antony to leave the job half-done. He begged those around him to deliver the coup de grâce but again and for the last time found himself deserted. To a man, his retinue fled the room.

An outcry followed, which brought Cleopatra to the upper story of the mausoleum. She peered either through the second-floor windows or the unfinished roof; she had built quickly, but not quickly enough. The sight of her caused a commotion—so she was not dead after all!—though if Dio is correct, no one could have been more surprised than Antony. Again Plutarch and Dio's accounts are incompatible. It is unclear whether Antony first learns that Cleopatra is still alive, or if Cleopatra first learns that Antony is half-dead. Antony then either orders his servants to take him to her (Dio), or Cleopatra sends her servants for him (Plutarch). Already Antony had lost a great deal of blood. Cleopatra's secretary found him on the floor, writhing and crying out.

In their arms, Antony's servants carried him, bleeding to death and in agony, to the mausoleum. From the windows above Cleopatra let down the ropes and cords that had been used to hoist stone blocks atop the structure. To these the servants fastened the limp body. Cleopatra drew her lover up herself, with the aid of Iras and Charmion, long familiar with Antony. It is impossible to improve upon Plutarch's version of the ordeal; even Shakespeare could not do so. "Never," Plutarch writes, working from an eyewitness account, "was there a more piteous sight. Smeared with blood and struggling with death he was drawn up, stretching out his hands to her even as he dangled in the air. For the task was not an easy one for women, and scarcely could Cleopatra, with clinging hands and strained face, pull up the rope, while those below called out encouragement to her and shared her agony." No sooner had she hauled Antony up and laid him out on a couch than Cleopatra began to rip and tear at her robes. It is one of only two recorded moments in which she loses her colossal self-possession. She yields to raw emotion; "she almost forgot her own ills in her pity for his." The two had been together for the better part of a decade; Cleopatra wiped the blood from his body and smeared it across her face. She beat and scratched at her breasts. She called Antony master, commander, husband; she always knew how to talk to a man. He silenced her cries and demanded a sip of wine, "either because he was thirsty, or in the hope of a speedier release." Once served, he encouraged Cleopatra to attend to her own safety and to cooperate with Octavian so far as her honor allowed, advice that suggests some doubt on Antony's part as to her intentions. Among Octavian's men he recommended that she entrust herself in particular to Gaius Proculeius. He had been a friend as well to Antony. She was not to pity him his fate, but to rejoice for the happiness and honors that had been his. He had been the most illustrious and powerful of men, and he now died a noble death, vanquished in the end only by a fellow Roman. The waves murmured outside. Antony died in Cleopatra's arms.

AS ANTONY MADE his excruciating trip to the mausoleum, one of his bodyguards sped—with Antony's sword secreted under his cloak—to Octavian's camp, outside the city. There he produced the heavy blade, still smeared with blood, and an early account of the botched suicide. Octavian retired immediately to his tent, to weep the same brand of crocodile tears that Caesar had wept for Pompey, "a man who had been his relation by marriage, his colleague in office and command, and his partner in many undertakings and struggles." The relief must have been great; dispensing with Antony had been a problem. While Antony lay dying in Cleopatra's arms Octavian indulged in a little ceremony of self-justification, producing copies of the letters that he and his former brother-in-law had exchanged over the previous years. These he read aloud to his assembled friends. Was it not remarkable "how reasonably and justly he had written, and how rude and overbearing Antony had always been in his replies"? (He took care later to burn Antony's side of the correspondence.) After the dramatic reading Proculeius set off. He was on Cleopatra's doorstep within minutes of Antony's death.

To the end Antony proved overly trusting. Proculeius had two commissions. He was to do all in his power to extract Cleopatra from the mausoleum. And he was to see to it that the treasure Octavian so urgently needed to settle his affairs did not go up in flames. Herod had supplied him with a taste of the East; Octavian could not afford to sacrifice the fabulous hoard of Egypt, the subject of dreams and exaggerations since the time of Homer, to a funeral pyre. His debts were his only remaining obstacle in Rome. He also needed a live Egyptian queen, which he calculated would "add greatly to the glory of his triumph." Dio devotes a great deal of attention to Cleopatra's wiles and feints over the next days but knew he was writing of two slippery characters, both deeply invested in the duplicity business. Octavian wanted to seize Cleopatra alive, Dio allows, "yet he was unwilling to appear to have tricked her himself." Mild-mannered Proculeius was to keep her hopes up and her hand from the fire.

Despite Antony's assurances, Cleopatra refused to grant Proculeius an interview in the mausoleum. If he wanted to speak to her, he would have to do so through the well-bolted door. Octavian had made her certain promises. She wanted guarantees. She threatened to burn her treasure without them. Repeatedly she pleaded that her children—three of them were under respectful guard, with their attendants—might inherit the kingdom. Repeatedly Proculeius circumvented the request. He assured her that she had no worries. She could trust Octavian entirely. She was unconvinced on that front and had taken various precautions. She wore a small dagger at her hip, inserted into her belt; it could not have been the first time she did so. And she had long before dispatched Caesarion up the Nile. She knew she could ask no favors on her eldest child's count. With his tutor, Rhodon, and a small fortune, he was to make his way overland to the coast and to sail for India, the established source of Ptolemaic ivory and dyes, spices and tortoiseshell. Proculeius made little progress, though he did have ample opportunity to survey the mausoleum, to which he returned with Gaius Cornelius Gallus—who had entered Egypt from the west, at the head of Antony's legions—for a second interview. Gallus outranked Proculeius. A poet and an intellectual, he enjoyed a facility with language; he was a pioneer of the love elegy. (Ironically, he addressed his work to the actress who had been Antony's mistress.) Again he faced one of Antony's women. Perhaps he could negotiate a surrender. Gallus met Cleopatra outside the door for a prolonged conversation, presumably little different from the one she had had with Proculeius. She remained intransigent.

Meanwhile Proculeius fixed a ladder to the side of the building and climbed in the upper-story window through which Antony had been carried. Two servants scurried up the wall behind him. Once inside the three descended to the ground floor, where they stole up on Cleopatra, at the mausoleum door. Charmion or Iras noticed the intruders first and cried out: "Wretched Cleopatra, you are taken alive!" At the sight of the Romans, Cleopatra reached for the dagger to stab herself, but Proculeius was quicker. Throwing himself upon her, he enveloped Cleopatra in both arms. He wrested away the dagger and searched the folds of her clothing for poisons, all the while affably reassuring her, as he had been instructed. She should not act rashly. She did herself a disservice, and Octavian too. Why rob him of the opportunity to prove his kindness and integrity? He was after all—she had heard the claim before, from a messenger who had defected, about a man whose lifeless body lay upstairs in a pool of blood—"the gentlest of commanders."

Octavian installed a freedman named Epaphroditus at Cleopatra's side. He had firm instructions. He was to keep the queen of Egypt alive "by the strictest vigilance, but otherwise to make any concession that would promote her ease and pleasure." All instruments by which she might again attempt to kill herself were confiscated. Presumably the pile of treasure was at this juncture carted away as well. Cleopatra was, however, supplied with all she requested—incense, and oils of cedar and cinnamon—with which to prepare Antony for burial. She spent two days purifying the body, a courtesy Octavian was no doubt happy to grant. He could win points for honoring an unwritten code of warfare while at the same time delivering the scandalous burial that he claimed Antony had requested. Octavian's men removed none of Cleopatra's retinue or attendants, "in order that she should entertain more hope than ever of accomplishing all she desired, and so should do no harm to herself." The three children were treated sympathetically and as befit their rank, for which she had reason to be grateful. Octavian's men tracked down Antyllus, betrayed by his tutor, entranced by the priceless gem he knew the sixteen-year-old to be wearing under his toga. Antony's son had sought refuge in a shrine, probably within the massive walls of the Caesareum. He begged for his life. Octavian's men dragged him out and beheaded him. The tutor lost no time in snatching the jewel from the corpse, for which he was later crucified.

Cleopatra asked for and obtained permission to bury Antony herself. Accompanied by Iras and Charmion, she did so "in sumptuous and royal fashion." A first-century woman grieved with much ritual screaming and thrashing and clawing at the skin, and Cleopatra was no exception: her display was so extreme that her chest was inflamed and ulcerated by the end of the funeral on what was probably August 3. Infection set in, accompanied by a fever. She was pleased; if she now swore off food, she could, she reasoned, manage a quiet, Roman-free death. She confided as much in Olympus, who counseled her and promised his assistance. Her method was hardly subtle, however; Octavian learned quickly enough of her compromised state. He had a trump card as great as Cleopatra's treasure. He "plied her with threats and fears regarding her children"—another kind of warfare, concedes Plutarch, and a most effective one. Cleopatra surrendered to food and treatment.

Octavian had by now bought some goodwill, which may have partly reassured Cleopatra. He called for a public assembly; late on the afternoon of August 1, the day of Antony's death, he rode into the city with a prepared scroll. He always wrote out what he meant to say in Latin; this speech was afterward translated into Greek. In the gymnasium where Antony and Cleopatra had crowned their children Octavian ascended a specially built platform. The terrified Alexandrians prostrated themselves at his feet. Octavian bade them stand. He meant no harm. He had resolved to pardon their city for three reasons: In honor of Alexander the Great; because of Octavian's great admiration for their home, "by far the richest and greatest of all cities"; and to gratify Areius, the Greek philosopher at his side. The truth of the matter, concedes Dio, is that Octavian did not dare "inflict any irreparable injury upon a people so numerous, who might prove very useful to the Romans in many ways."

Events, Cleopatra would have noticed, were moving quickly. Urgently she requested an interview with Octavian, granted on August 8. While in broad outline Plutarch and Dio's accounts of that meeting are similar, the mise-en-scène differs radically. Plutarch is writing for Puccini, Dio for Wagner. There may be more art than truth in both versions; either way, it was quite a performance. (It made too for a revealing contrast to Herod's interview.) Plutarch sends up the curtain with Cleopatra lying frail and disheveled on a simple mattress, clad only in a tunic, without any kind of cloak. Octavian has elected to surprise her. At the sight of her caller she springs up and throws herself at his feet. The wretched week has taken its toll: "Her hair and face were in terrible disarray, her voice trembled, and her eyes were sunken. There were also visible many marks of the cruel blows upon her bosom; in a word, her body seemed to be no better off than her spirit." Dio prefers Cleopatra in her regal splendor and at her histrionic best. She has prepared a luxurious apartment and an ornate couch for her visitor. She is groomed to perfection, superbly turned out in mourning clothes that "wonderfully became her." As Octavian enters she leaps girlishly to her feet, to find herself face to face with her mortal enemy, for what was almost certainly the first time. Octavian had come into his looks, or into his panegyrists; he was highly attractive to women, "for he was well worth beholding," as Nicolaus of Damascus put it later. Cleopatra must have experienced a certain relief. "To be so long prey to fear is surely worse than the actuality we are afraid of," Cicero had observed. Before Cleopatra stood after all only a man, about five feet seven, with tousled blond hair, benign in his expression, more comfortable in Latin than in Greek, six years her junior, sallow, stiff, and ill at ease.

Someone embroidered on the sources, and it is difficult to believe that was not Dio. His account is so cinematic as to be suspect, too purple even for a Hellenistic queen. On the other hand, had Cleopatra lacked a flair for drama, she would not have come this far. On the couch beside her she has laid out various busts and portraits of Caesar. At her breast she carries his loving letters. She greets Octavian as her master but at the same time wishes him to understand her earlier distinction. He should know in what esteem the divine Caesar, his father, her lover, held her. To that end she proceeds to read selections from the correspondence, limiting herself to the most ardent passages; Octavian was not the only one who knew how to excerpt a document. She is shy, sweet, subtle. They are related! Surely Octavian had heard of the many honors he had accorded her? She is a friend and ally of Rome; Caesar had crowned her himself! Throughout this performance "she would lament and kiss the letters, and again she would fall before his images and do them reverence."

As she does so, she repeatedly turns her eyes on Octavian, offering up melting looks, subtly attempting to swap one Caesar for another. She is seductive, eloquent, audacious—though naturally no match for Octavian's Roman rectitude, which may have been Dio's point. Octavian betrays no glimmer of emotion. He is immune to tender glances. He prided himself on the burning intensity of his gaze but on this occasion refuses to so much as make eye contact, preferring instead to study the floor. Nor will he make any commitment. He will speak—he was laconic to the point of awkwardness, and here probably did not dare wander far from his prepared remarks—neither of love nor of Egypt's future nor of Cleopatra's children. Dio focuses on Octavian's dispassion but something else is noticeably absent from the interview: Cleopatra demands no credit for having yielded Pelusium, for having delivered up Antony's fleet, or for having induced Antony to kill himself, presumably because there was none to be had. If she had held up her end of a prior bargain, she would surely have demanded her reward now. Finally she bursts into tears and throws herself at Octavian's feet. She had, she sobbed, no wish to live. Nor could she continue to do so. In memory of his father, would Octavian not grant her a single favor? Could she not join Antony in death? "Grudge me not burial with him," she begs, "in order that, as it is because of him I die, so I may dwell with him even in Hades." Again she failed to move Octavian either to pity or a hint of a promise. He could only exhort her to be of good cheer, resolving all over again to sustain her hopes. He wanted her alive. She would brilliantly ornament his triumph.

Cleopatra is physically more disheveled, mentally more dignified in Plutarch's version, not necessarily more accurate for having derived from Cleopatra's doctor; everyone was a propagandist now. Gracefully, Octavian bids her to return to her pallet. He seats himself nearby. Cleopatra unfurls a ribbon of justifications similar to that she had unfurled in Tarsus, ascribing her actions "to necessity and fear of Antony." When Octavian refutes her argument point by point, she changes tack, resorting to pity and prayers. Ultimately she begs for her life. She is desperate and magnificent, where in Dio she is only desperate. She sounds no seductive notes, which indeed appear to have been added later, when all kinds of chroniclers had Cleopatra throwing herself vigorously at all kinds of feet. Certainly she flings herself around more in the literature than she did in life. Downright fictions and convenient distortions aside, Dio and Plutarch agree in substance. Disheveled or not, Cleopatra remains a wonder to look upon: "The charm for which she was famous and the boldness of her beauty" shone forth despite her plight, "and made themselves manifest in the play of her features." She remains supple and shrewd, modulating the "musical accents" and the "melting tones" as the situation required, her arguments along with them. Half-starved and partly incapacitated, she is as feisty as ever. In both scenarios she leaves Octavian in a puddle of embarrassment.

When her prayers fail to move him, Cleopatra resorts to her trump card. She had drawn up an inventory of her treasures, which she hands to Octavian, surrender of a kind. As Octavian examines the list, one of Cleopatra's stewards steps foward; the situation brought out the best in no one. Seleucus cannot help but observe that Cleopatra has omitted several exceptionally valuable items. Before Octavian he accuses his queen of "stealing away and hiding some of them." At this Cleopatra flew from her mattress, "seized him by the hair and showered blows upon his face." Unable to suppress a smile, Octavian rose to stop her. The adroit response was vintage Cleopatra, pure sinuous subtlety: "But is it not a monstrous thing, Caesar, that when you have deigned to honor me with a visit in my wretched condition, one of my slaves should denounce me for reserving some women's adornments—not for myself, indeed, unhappy woman that I am—but that I may make some trifling gifts to Octavia and to your Livia, and through their intercession hope to find you more merciful and more gentle?" Dio too has Cleopatra circling back to Octavian's wife and sister, though not by way of comic opera. Invoking female solidarity, Cleopatra promises to set aside a few especially striking jewels for Livia. She places great hope in her. Both interviews are composed of feint and farce, of counterfeit claims and artificial emotions. Divergent details aside, they are all bluff and pantomine. Octavian fully intends for Cleopatra to walk through the streets of Rome as his captive but pretends otherwise. Cleopatra suspects as much but purports to steel herself to live. She has no intention of returning to a city, in chains, where she had once lived as Caesar's honored guest. To her mind that humiliation is "worse than a thousand deaths." She knew well what Rome meant for captive sovereigns. If they survived they did so in Roman dungeons. Hellenistic sovereigns had killed themselves — and gone mad — there. Much pleased with the overture to Livia, Octavian left Cleopatra reassured, and did some reassuring, promising her "more splendid treatment than she could possibly expect." At which he went off, well satisfied, "supposing that he had deceived her, but rather deceived by her."

CLEOPATRA MADE ONE last conquest, but it was not to be Octavian. His staff included a young aristocrat named Cornelius Dolabella. Plutarch tells us Dolabella harbored "a certain tenderness" for Cleopatra; the emotion may have been nearer to pity. She had urged him to keep her abreast of all developments. Dolabella had agreed to do so. On August 9 he sent word to her privately. Octavian planned to depart within three days. Cleopatra and her children were to go with him. Instantly Cleopatra dispatched a messenger to Octavian. Might she be permitted to make offerings to Antony? The request was granted. The following morning a litter carried her to his tomb, along with Iras and Charmion. At the graveside Plutarch offers a wrenching sob of a speech, a rhetorical exercise more likely to derive from Greek tragedy than from Hellenistic history; he is already ten chapters beyond Antony, his ostensible subject, and more than a little taken with his accidental one. Falling on and wrapping her arms around the tomb, Plutarch's Cleopatra explains to her dead lover that she is a prisoner. Tears well in her eyes. She is "so carefully guarded that I cannot either with blows or tears disfigure this body of mine, which is a slave's body, and closely watched that it may grace the triumph over you." Nothing in life had been able to part them, but death is about to. Antony had breathed his last in her country, and she, "hapless woman," was to meet her end in his. The gods of the world above have forsaken them. If the gods of the afterlife have any power she entreats Antony to appeal to them. Could they spare her from marching in any victory procession over him? She begged that they hide and bury her in Egypt with him, "since out of all my innumerable afflictions not one is so great and dreadful as this short time that I have lived apart from you." The scene is short on vengeance and long on affection; Plutarch's Cleopatra is to die of love rather than enmity. Wreathing and kissing his tomb, amid a cloud of myrrh, she tenderly informs Antony that these are the last libations she will be able to offer him.

On the return to the mausoleum that afternoon she ordered a bath to be prepared. Afterward she reclined at table, where she enjoyed a sumptuous meal. Toward day's end a servant appeared outside her doors with a basket of figs, direct from the countryside. The guards examined its contents carefully. The figs of Egypt were especially sweet; the Romans marveled at the succulent fruit. With a smile the traveler offered samples all around, after which he was waved into the monument. Some time later Cleopatra set her seal to a letter she had prepared in advance. She then called for Epaphroditus. Could he relax his guard long enough to carry a communication to Octavian? It concerned a minor matter; there was no fuss. Epaphroditus headed out, across the sand outside. Cleopatra then dismissed her retinue save for Iras and Charmion. The three women closed the mausoleum doors behind them; the bars and bolts had presumably been removed along with the treasure. If they had not done so already, her maidservants fitted Cleopatra in her formal robes, to which they added the ornaments of her office, the pharaonic crook and flail. Around her forehead they tied her diadem, its ribbons dangling down her neck.

Octavian opened the letter—he could not have been far away, and was most likely in the palace—to read Cleopatra's fervent request that she be buried at Antony's side. Instantly he guessed what had happened. He was astounded. In haste he began to head off and then, changing his mind—he was flustered—dispatched messengers to investigate for him.

They rushed to the mausoleum, where Octavian's guards stood sentry, unperturbed and unsuspecting. Together they burst through the doors. They were too late. "The mischief," Plutarch tells us, "had been swift." Cleopatra lay on a golden couch, probably an Egyptian-style bed with lion paws for legs and lion heads at its corners. Majestically and meticulously arrayed in "her most beautiful apparel," she gripped in her hands the crook and flail. She was perfectly composed and completely dead, Iras very nearly so at her feet. Lurching and heavy-headed, almost unable to stand, Charmion was clumsily attempting to right the diadem around Cleopatra's forehead. Angrily one of Octavian's men exploded: "A fine deed this, Charmion!" She had just the energy to offer a parting shot. With a tartness that would have made her mistress proud, she managed, "It is indeed most fine, and befitting the descendant of so many kings," before collapsing in a heap, at her queen's side.

Charmion's was an epitaph no one could dispute. (Nor could it be improved upon. Shakespeare used it verbatim.) "Valor in the unfortunate obtains great reverence even among their enemies," notes Plutarch, and in Octavian's camp there was admiration and pity all around. Cleopatra had demonstrated tremendous courage. How she accomplished her final feat is less evident. Octavian was under the impression—or meant to convey the impression—that she had enlisted an asp. Arriving on the scene after his messengers, he attempted to resuscitate Cleopatra. He called in the psylli, Libyans believed to enjoy a magical immunity to snake venom. By taste they were said to be able to determine what kind of snake had bitten; by murmuring spells and sucking at the wound they were said to be able to extract death from an icy corpse. The psylli who knelt over Cleopatra worked no miracles. The Egyptian queen could not be revived. That was not altogether surprising. Neither Dio nor Plutarch was at all sure of the asp, who surely crept into the story later rather than arriving in Cleopatra's lifetime, amid a basket of figs. Even Strabo, who landed in Egypt shortly after her death, was unconvinced.

For any number of reasons Cleopatra was unlikely to have recruited an asp, or an Egyptian cobra, for the job. A woman known for her crisp decisions and meticulous planning would surely have hesitated to entrust her fate to a wild animal. She had plenty of quicker, less painful options. It was as well a little too convenient to be killed by the royal emblem of Egypt; the snake made more symbolic than practical sense. Even the most reliable of cobras cannot kill three women in quick succession, and the asp is a famously sluggish snake. An Egyptian cobra, bristling and hissing and puffing itself up to its six-foot splendor, could hardly have hidden in a fig basket or remained hidden in one for long. The job was too great and the basket too small. Poison was a more likely alternative, as Plutarch seems to imply with his survey of Cleopatra's experiments. Most likely she swallowed a lethal drink—the hemlock and opium of Socrates would have done the trick—or applied a toxic ointment. Hannibal had resorted to poison when backed into a corner 150 years earlier; Mithradates had attempted the same. Cleopatra's uncle, the king of Cyprus, had known precisely what to have on hand when Rome had come calling in 58. Assuming she died of the same cause as Charmion, assuming she died in the state in which she was discovered, Cleopatra suffered little. There were no shuddering paroxysms, which cobra venom would ultimately have induced. This toxin's effect was more narcotic than convulsive, the death peaceful, swift, and essentially painless. "The truth of the matter," Plutarch announces, to centuries of deaf ears, "no one knows."

Dismissed for nearly two hundred years, the snake clings tenaciously to the story. Cleopatra's asp is the cherry tree of ancient history, a convenience, a shorthand, most of all a gift to painters and sculptors through the centuries. It made poetic sense and good art. (So did the naked breast, also not part of the original tale.) And the snake multiplied immediately: Horace wrote "sharp-toothed serpents" into an ode. Virgil, Propertius, and Martial would follow suit. The beast or beasts figure in every early account. Octavian would further clinch the deal by displaying a model of Cleopatra with an asp in his triumph. Not only was the snake a potent symbol of Egypt, where coiled cobras had adorned pharaonic brows for

millennia, but snakes crawled all over Isis statues as well. They had insinuated themselves in the Dionysian cult. Iconography aside, it is easy to
see what someone is trying to communicate when he pairs a lady with a
snake. Alexander the Great's mother—as murderous and maniacal a
Macedonian princess who ever lived—kept serpents as pets. She used
them to terrify men. Before her came Eve, Medusa, Electra, and the
Erinyes; when a woman teams up with a snake, a moral storm threatens
somewhere. Octavian may have confused the issue for all time with his
call to the psylli. He controlled the historical record every bit as firmly as
he was said to have controlled his adolescent sexual urges. Very likely he
sent us off, for thousands of years, in the wrong direction.

He may have done so intentionally. There is an alternate version of
the death; it has long been clear that we may be missing something here,
that one farce of August 10 could well conceal another, that the greatest
deathbed scene in history is perhaps not what it seems. In the earliest
prose account, "Cleopatra cheated the vigilance of her guards" to pro-
cure an asp and stage her death. Octavian is vexed, furious that she has
slipped through his fingers. He had, however, an immense, dedicated
staff. By August few in Alexandria would have hesitated to cooperate
with him, as Cleopatra's steward demonstrated. Octavian was as careless
as Cleopatra was naïve; the kind of man who marked both the date and
the time on his letters was not the kind of man to let a prize captive slip
through his fingers. When Octavian left her on August 8 he may well
have deceived Cleopatra into believing he was deceived, and essentially
orchestrated her death. He would not have cared to have been outwitted
by a woman—unless of course the alternative were more damaging.
And Cleopatra was as problematic a captive as she had been an enemy.
Octavian had attended the triumphs of 46. He had even ridden in one of
them. He knew of the sympathy Cleopatra's sister had elicited on that
occasion. He had publicly condemned Mark Antony for having paraded
Artavasdes in chains. That kind of behavior, Octavian had scolded, dis-
honored Rome. There was too an additional wrinkle in Cleopatra's case:
This particular prisoner had been the divine Caesar's mistress. She was

the mother of his son. In some eyes, she was a goddess in her own right. She could be trusted to live out her days quietly in some Asian outpost about as much as could her younger sister. Twice Cleopatra had tried to kill herself. It was clear that unless guarded carefully she would sooner or later succeed.

Octavian would have been left to calculate which embarrassment was greater: to be outwitted by a woman, or to return to Rome without the villain of the piece. It could be difficult to gauge the occasionally tender sensibilities of his countrymen. Sometimes they met the children of defeated kings with jeers and ridicule. Sometimes those innocents marred the exercise, eliciting tears and discomfort. Cleopatra had been declared a public enemy, but an effigy would serve perfectly well in a triumph, as had effigies of Roman adversaries in the past. While her death reduced the glory a little, it also eliminated a host of complications. Octavian may have preferred to shuffle Cleopatra off the stage in Alexandria than to make a misstep in Rome. He was genuinely terrified that she might destroy her treasure, by no means terrified that she would destroy herself, in which act he may essentially have colluded. Young Dolabella was then but a tool in Octavian's game. It was after all unlikely that one of his staff officers would risk a friendship with Cleopatra. And Octavian did not in fact leave Alexandria on August 12, as Dolabella had heatedly warned. He may have delivered the message — possibly even a more ominous one — to hasten the course of events. Both Dio and Plutarch point to Octavian's repeated injunctions that Cleopatra be kept alive rather than to any complicity in her death. That does not mean there was none. A fourth casualty on August 10, 30, may well have been the truth.

(The counterarguments go something like this: Cleopatra had attempted both to starve and skewer herself. Why had Octavian foiled those attempts, to torture her with threats about her children? Nine days passed between Antony's death and Cleopatra's. Surely it would have been preferable to have eliminated her at once? She had already sworn to die with Antony after all. And she would have known of Octavian's predicament; she was as aware as he of the sensation her sister had caused.

She might have gambled that Octavian would not risk parading her and her half-Roman children through the streets of Rome. Octavian seems truly and uncharacteristically unnerved by the news of Cleopatra's death. He did not make a great deal of the mercy he had shown her, as he might have been expected to have done and as he usually did. Instead he boasted in his memoirs that various kings — and nine children of kings — had marched, in the course of three triumphs, before his chariot. No future historian, even those antipathetic to Octavian, ventures an assertion of complicity, although it could be argued that by then the case was closed, the truth known only to a few in the first place. We are ultimately left chasing our tails. The best that can be said of her last act is that Cleopatra acted heroically in a great set piece that may be on several counts ahistorical and is certainly in some part her opponent's invention. The sole consolation is a perverse one: The death of Alexander the Great is well documented and no less a perfect riddle.)

Plutarch has Octavian torn between two emotions on the evening of August 10. He is both "vexed at the death of the woman" and in awe of "her lofty spirit." In Dio too Octavian is admiring and sympathetic, if "excessively grieved" on his own account. His triumph will be less magnificent. While it is unclear who had done so, someone had produced a heroine. Cleopatra's was an honorable death, a dignified death, an exemplary death. She had presided over it herself, proud and unbroken to the end. By the Roman definition she had at last done something right; finally it was to her credit that she had defied the expectations of her sex. Women inevitably win points in Roman histories for swallowing hot coals or hanging themselves by their hair or hurling themselves from rooftops or handing bloody daggers along to their husbands with three quiet words of encouragement: "It isn't painful." (Plenty of female corpses litter the Greek stage as well, the difference being that in Greek drama the women also get the last word.) The panegyrics were immediate. In an ode written shortly after her suicide, Horace set out to condemn Cleopatra for her folly and ambition but wound up eulogizing her. "No craven woman, she," he concludes, marveling at the clear mind, the calm countenance, the courage. Cleopatra's final act was arguably her finest one. That was a price Octavian was perfectly happy to pay. Her glory was his glory. The exalted opponent was the worthy opponent.

Octavian arranged for Cleopatra to be buried "with royal splendor and magnificence." To do otherwise was to risk inciting the Alexandrians, who no doubt mourned their queen publicly, despite the Roman presence. According to Plutarch, Octavian honored also her request to be laid to rest at Antony's side. Iras and the eloquent Charmion received similarly fine burials, with their queen. It is unclear if the three were mummified. Their splendid joint monument would have been lavishly and colorfully decorated, as were the royal tombs of Cleopatra's ancestors, with Roman twists in the iconography. By one account, statues of Iras and Charmion stood sentry outside. Plutarch implies that the burial place was in the center of Alexandria, along with those of previous Ptolemies. Octavian ordered the mausoleum to be finished as well, work presumably completed in a subdued city, numb with uncertainty; the Alexandrians were now Roman subjects. That Cleopatra's monument was adjacent to a temple of Isis essentially means it could have been anywhere. The most recent theory is that Antony and Cleopatra's final resting place is twenty miles west of Alexandria, on a sun-bleached hillside in Taposiris Magna, overlooking the Mediterranean. Neither the tomb nor the mausoleum (they were almost certainly separate structures) has been found.

Cleopatra was thirty-nine years old and had ruled for nearly twenty-two years, about a decade longer than had Alexander the Great, from whom she had inherited the baton that she inadvertently passed on to the Roman Empire. With her death, the Ptolemaic dynasty came to an end. Octavian formally annexed Egypt on August 31. His first year was Cleopatra's last; he started the clock again with August 1, the date on which he had entered Alexandria. Cleopatra is said to have brought down the curtain on an age, although of course from the Egyptian perspective Antony too could be said to have done so. It is easy to forget he was Cleopatra's undoing every bit as much as she was his.

———

TO THE END Ptolemaic tutors proved fickle. Caesarion got as far as a port on the Red Sea when Rhodon convinced him to return to Alexandria, possibly to negotiate with Octavian in his mother's stead. The ancient world was at times an uncomfortably small place; Octavian could afford neither to let his cousin live nor to exhibit a son of the divine Caesar in a triumph. The name "Caesarion" alone posed a problem. The much publicized coming-of-age ceremony did not help. Octavian's men returned the seventeen-year-old to Alexandria, where they murdered him, possibly having tortured him first. As they posed no real danger, Alexander Helios, Cleopatra Selene, and Ptolemy Philadelphus returned to Rome with Octavian, to be raised by his always amenable sister. They grew up in her large, comfortable household, with Antony and Octavia's daughters, and with Antony's surviving children by his previous marriages. (Iotape, Alexander Helios's intended, returned to her family in Media.) A year after the death of their mother, Cleopatra's surviving children walked in Octavian's triumph, surely an awkward event for three youngsters said to be raised as attentively as if they were his own. He later married Cleopatra Selene off to Juba II, who at the age of five had walked in Caesar's African triumph and was thereafter educated in Rome, where he developed a passion for history. Husband and wife had known similar formations and similar humiliations; the Roman civil wars made orphans of them both. A man of culture, something of a poet, a favorite of Octavian's, Juba was sent with his bride to rule Mauretania. (It is today Algeria.) Cleopatra's daughter was probably fifteen at the time, Juba twenty-two. As a favor to the young royals, Octavian spared Cleopatra Selene's brothers, who may have traveled to western Africa as well. After the triumph we lose sight of the two boys forever.

On the Mauretanian throne Cleopatra Selene continued her mother's legacy; her coins bear her likeness and are inscribed in Greek. (Juba's are in Latin.) Together the couple transformed their capital into a cultural and artistic center, complete with a splendid library. Plenty of Egyptian sculpture—including a piece from July 31, 30, the day before Octavian entered Alexandria—has turned up in the area, where Cleopatra Selene evidently assembled a gallery of Ptolemaic busts. She continued the Isis association, and named her son Ptolemy. She kept sacred crocodiles. Cleopatra's only known grandson, Ptolemy of Mauretania, succeeded Juba in AD 23. Seventeen years into his reign he visited Rome at the invitation of Caligula. Both men descended from Mark Antony; they were half cousins. The Roman emperor greeted the African king with honors, until Ptolemy one day swept into a gladiatorial show in a particularly splendid purple cloak. Heads turned, to Caligula's displeasure. He ordered Ptolemy's murder, an appropriate end to dynasty steeped, from the start, in blazing, supersaturated color.*

Octavian obliterated all traces of Antony in both Rome and Alexandria. January 14, his birthday, was deemed an unlucky day, on which no public business could be transacted. By Senate decree, the names "Mark" and "Antony" were never again to be conjoined. Otherwise he was discarded, a historical inconvenience. Octavian would mention neither Antony nor Cleopatra by name in his account of Actium. He sentenced several of Antony's close associates to death, Canidius and the Roman senator who supervised Cleopatra's textile mills chief among them. Those who had sworn to perish with Antony and Cleopatra were presumably relieved of the need to see to the job themselves. Other partisans disappeared. The influential high priest at Memphis—who was born the same year as Caesarion, and who had remained personally bound to Cleopatra—died mysteriously several days before her. It was imperative that no one survive who might exercise authority, rally the people, reassemble Cleopatra's kingdom. Octavian's men collected the pile of Ptolemaic treasure from the palace and exacted fines throughout the city, inventing misdemeanors as they went. Where imagination failed, they simply confiscated two thirds of a victims' property. It was a polite kind of plunder; the Romans made out handsomely. Octavian removed from Alexandria the fine statuary and precious art that

---

*Caligula descended from both Mark Antony (his paternal great-grandfather) and Octavian (his maternal great-grandfather). He posed alternately as a descendant of each, depending on his agenda. It was easy to trip up under his reign, when sacrifices to celebrate Antony's overthrow might be objectionable one day, the reluctance to offer sacrifices to Augustus's victory the next.

Antony and Cleopatra had pillaged throughout Asia, restoring it, for the most part, to the cities to which it belonged. A few of the finest pieces wound up in Rome, where the best art had long come from the second-century sack of Corinth. Seventeen years after Cleopatra's death, Octavian finished the Caesareum, that pharaonic and Greek marvel, in his honor.

Cleopatra had plenty of partisans, as faithful as had been her ladies-in-waiting, whose devotion was the talk of Alexandria. A servant did not normally die for her mistress. Those who had offered to rise up for their queen remained loyal. Cleopatra had her country's favor; there had been no revolts under her reign. Alexandria must have given itself over to mourning. There were processions and hymns and offerings, the city would have been loud with keening and wails as the women of Alexandria shredded their garments and beat their breasts. On behalf of the native priests, a cleric offered Octavian 2,000 talents to preserve Cleopatra's many statues. She might remain noble, but she was also dead; the offer was too attractive to refuse. It saved Octavian as well from the thorny business of tangling with Isis, who continued to be worshipped for some time. Cleopatra was often indistinguishable from that goddess; Octavian could not very well go around volatile Alexandria toppling religious statuary. Cleopatra's statues, and her cult, lived on actively for hundreds of years, no doubt reinforced by her steely last stand against the Romans.

Octavian did not tarry in Egypt, henceforth a Roman province, to which no prominent Roman traveled without express permission. One of the few imperialists in history who did not care to be Alexander the Great—all would have worked out very differently for Cleopatra if he had—he was more invested in raw power than its glorious accessories. He evidenced little interest in Egyptian history, to the dismay of Cleopatra's former subjects, eager to display the remains of her ancestors. Octavian made it known that he had little patience for dead Ptolemies. He paid his respects only to Alexander the Great, removed from his sarcophagus for the visit. The story goes that Octavian accidentally brushed against the body—he may have been strewing flowers—detaching a piece of mummified nose in the process.

Susceptible as Octavian was to sunstroke—he went nowhere without his broad-brimmed hat—he could not have much enjoyed the liquid heat of an Alexandrian August. In the fall he withdrew to Asia. No one profited more from Cleopatra's death than Herod, who hosted the Romans again on their northbound trip. Octavian returned to him his precious palm and balsam groves and the coastal cities that Antony had appropriated for Cleopatra, supplementing them with additional territories. Herod's kingdom swelled finally to dimensions commensurate with his kindnesses. Rome's new favorite among non-Romans, he inherited as well the four hundred strapping Gauls who had served as Cleopatra's bodyguard. Nicolaus of Damascus stepped in as his tutor, to become his close confidant. He produced a court history for Herod, from which Josephus—a major source for the life of Cleopatra, and himself a midcareer convert to the Roman cause—would work. Octavian left Gallus in charge of Egypt, as prefect. He too would discover that the province was difficult to rule—in 29 he subdued the people around Thebes, "the common terror of all kings"—and that its riches went to one's head. He exceeded his command, commissioned too many statues of himself, inscribed his great deeds on the pyramids, and, indicted by the Senate, wound up a suicide.

Almost precisely a year after Cleopatra's death, she paraded in effigy down the streets of Rome, in the last and most sumptuous of Octavian's three days of triumph. With her a veritable river of gold, silver, and ivory flowed down the Via Sacra and through the Forum. Dio tells us that the Egyptian procession surpassed all others "in costliness and magnificence." After the coffers of gold and silver; the wagons of jewelry, weapons, and art; the colorful placards and pennants; the defeated soldiers, marched the prized prisoners, the ten-year-old twins and six-year-old Ptolemy Philadelphus, in chains. Cleopatra was featured on her deathbed, in plaster or paint, along with the asp who may have started it all. Surrounded by his officers, the purple-cloaked Octavian followed behind. Cleopatra had been wrong in one assessment: Antony was conspicuously missing from the occasion. She was right in another: The only sovereign who did walk in that triumph, an ally of Antony's, was executed soon afterward. The city glimmered with the spoils of Egypt; tons of Ptolemaic gold and silver, breastplates and tableware, crowns and shields, gem-studded furniture, paintings and statuary, had sailed with Octavian, as had several crocodiles. Some have placed a lumbering hippopotamus and a rhinoceros at the triumph as well. Octavian could well afford to be generous, and there were substantial gifts all around. The Egyptian victory was celebrated with particular élan, not only because it could afford to be. There was a civil war to camouflage.

Cleopatra's statue remained in the Forum. It was the least Octavian could do for the woman whose golden couches and jeweled pitchers financed his career. Cleopatra allowed him to discharge every one of his obligations. She guaranteed Roman prosperity. So vast were the funds Octavian injected into the economy that prices soared. Interest rates tripled. As Dio summed up the transfer of wealth, Cleopatra saw to it that "the Roman empire was enriched and its temples adorned." Her art and obelisks decorated its streets. Soundly defeated, she was nonetheless celebrated, in the beauty of a foreign city. With the riches came a rush of Egyptomania. Sphinxes, rearing cobras, sun disks, acanthus leaves, hieroglyphs, proliferated throughout Rome. Lotus blossoms and griffins decorated even Octavian's personal study. Cleopatra earned a second backhanded tribute: In her wake, a golden age of women dawned in Rome. High-born wives and sisters suddenly enjoyed a role in public life. They interceded with ambassadors, counseled husbands, traveled abroad, commissioned temples and sculptures. They become more visible in art and in society. They joined Cleopatra in the Forum. No Roman woman would ever attain the exalted status or enjoy the unprecedented privileges granted Livia and Octavia, which they owed to a foreigner, to whom they served as counterweight. Livia compiled a fat portfolio of properties, one that would include lands in Egypt and palm groves in Judaea. Octavia would go down in history as the un-Cleopatra, supremely modest, prudent, and pious.

Cleopatra got a promotion as well, from pretext to punctuation point. If you were looking for a date for the beginning of the modern world, her death would be the best to fix upon. With her she took both the four-hundred-year-old Roman Republic and the Hellenistic Age. Octavian would go on to effect one of the greatest bait and switches in history; he restored the Republic in all its glory and—as would be apparent within a decade or so—as a monarchy. Having learned from Caesar's example, he did so subtly. Octavian was never a "king," always a "princeps," or "first citizen." For a title that was at once sufficiently grand and free of all monarchical odor, he turned to Cleopatra's former friend Plancus, the painted sea nymph. Plancus coined the name "Augustus," to signify that the man formerly known as Gaius Julius Caesar was more than human, that he was precious and revered.

There was some irony in fact that the West quickly began to resemble Cleopatra's East, the more so as Octavian had advertised Cleopatra as a threat to the Republic, something she had never intended. Around Octavian formed a kind of court. He fell out with nearly every member of his immediate family. The Roman emperors became gods. They had their pictures painted as Serapis, following Antony's Dionysian lead. And professions of austerity aside, the mantle of magnificence passed easily. While Octavian was said to have melted down Cleopatra's fabulous gold tableware, Hellenistic grandeur prevailed. "For it is fitting that we who rule over many people," reasoned one of Octavian's advisers, "should surpass all men in all things, and brilliance of this sort, also, tends in a way to inspire our allies with respect for us and our enemies with terror." He counseled Octavian to spare no expense. Rome represented the new luxury market. The artisans and industries followed. Livia had a personal staff of more than a thousand. So impressed was Octavian by Cleopatra's lofty mausoleum that he built a similar one in Rome; Alexandria deserves much credit for Rome's transformation from brick to marble. Octavian died at age seventy-six, at home in his bed, one of the few Roman emperors not murdered by close kin, another Hellenistic legacy. Having ruled for forty-four years—twice as long as Cleopatra—he had plenty of time in which to refashion the events that had brought him to power.* He had

---

*As ever, a capable woman was suspect. It would be whispered that Livia killed him. Curiously, she was said to have done so with poisoned figs.

too cause to note "that no high position is ever free from envy or treachery, and least of all a monarchy." The enemies were bad but the friends arguably worse. The office, he concluded, was utterly dreadful.

THE REWRITING OF history began almost immediately. Not only did Mark Antony disappear from the record, but Actium wondrously transformed itself into a major engagement, a resounding victory, a historical turning point. It went from an end to a beginning. Augustus had rescued the country from great peril. He had resolved the civil war and restored world peace after a century of unrest. Time began anew. To read the official historians, it is as if with his return the Italian peninsula burst— after a crippling, ashen century of violence—into Technicolor, as if the crops sat suddenly upright, plump and golden, in the fields. "Validity was restored to the laws, authority to the courts, and dignity to the senate," proclaims Velleius, very nearly cataloguing the duties with which Caesar had been meant to contend in 46. Augustus's ego is embedded in the calendar, where it remains to this day, commemorating the fall of Alexandria and Rome's reprieve from a foreign menace.* Calendars of the time acknowledge the date as one on which he freed Rome "from a most grievous danger."

Cleopatra was particularly ill served; the turncoats wrote the history, Dellius, Plancus, and Nicolaus of Damascus first among them. The years after Actium were a time of extravagant praise and lavish mythmaking. Her career also coincided with the birth of Latin literature; it was Cleopatra's curse to inspire its great poets, happy to expound on her shame, in a language inhospitable to her and all she represented. Horace wrote exuberantly of Actium. The first to celebrate Octavian's splendid victory, he did so while Cleopatra was still frantically fortifying Alexandria. He celebrates her defeat before it has occurred. Virgil and Propertius were on hand for the Egyptian triumph, by which time both the asp

---

*The practice of renaming months ended with Tiberius, who—urged to appropriate November—scoffed that all would become highly problematic if there turned out to be thirteen Caesars.

and Cleopatra's pernicious influence were already set in stone. In every reckoning Antony is made to flee Actium on Cleopatra's account. She helpfully illuminated one of Propertius's favorite points: a man in love is a helpless man, shamefully subservient to his mistress. It is as if Octavian delivers Rome from that ill as well. He has restored the natural order of things: men ruled women, and Rome ruled the world. On both counts, Cleopatra was crucial to the story. Virgil composed the *Aeneid* in the decade after Cleopatra's death; he put snakes in her wake even at Actium. She had no hope of faring well in a work read aloud both to Augustus and Octavia, as were portions of that epic poem. For the rest, her story would be shaped by a Roman she met once, in the last week of her life, who elevated her to a perilous adversary, at which altitude thick mists and obscuring myths settled comfortably around her. She counts among the losers whom history remembers, but for the wrong reasons.* The mythmakers all aligned on one side. For the next century, the Oriental influence and the emancipation of women would keep the satirists in business.

Since Cleopatra's death her fortunes have waxed and waned as dramatically as they did in her lifetime. Her power has been made to derive from her sexuality, for obvious reason; as one of Caesar's murderers had noted, "How much more attention people pay to their fears than to their memories!" It has always been preferable to attribute a woman's success to her beauty rather than to her brains, to reduce her to the sum of her sex life. Against a powerful enchantress there is no contest. Against a woman who ensnares a man in the coils of her serpentine intelligence — in her ropes of pearls — there should, at least, be some kind of antidote. Cleopatra unsettles more as sage than as seductress; it is less threatening to believe her fatally attractive than fatally intelligent. (Menander's fourth-century adage — "A man who teaches a woman to write should recognize that he is providing poison to an asp" — was still being copied

*She may well have known Aesop's fable: As the Lion said to the Man, "There are many statues of men slaying lions, but if only the lions were sculptors there might be quite a different set of statues."

out by schoolchildren hundreds of years after her death.) It also makes a better story. Propertius sets the tone. Cleopatra was for him a wanton seductress, "the whore queen," later "a woman of insatiable sexuality and insatiable avarice" (Dio), a carnal sinner (Dante), "the whore of the eastern kings" (Boccaccio), a poster child for unlawful love (Dryden).* Propertius has her fornicating with her slaves. A first-century Roman would assert (falsely) that "ancient writers repeatedly speak of Cleopatra's insatiable libido." In one ancient account she is so insatiable that "she often played the prostitute." (She is also both so beautiful and toxic that "many men bought nights with her at the price of their lives.") In the estimation of one nineteenth-century woman, she was "a dazzling piece of witchcraft." Florence Nightingale referred to her as "that disgusting Cleopatra." Offering her the movie role, Cecil B. DeMille is said to have asked Claudette Colbert, "How would you like to be the wickedest woman in history?" Cleopatra stars even in a 1928 book called *Sinners Down the Centuries*. In the match between the lady and the legend there is no contest.

The personal inevitably trumps the political, and the erotic trumps all: We will remember that Cleopatra slept with Julius Caesar and Mark Antony long after we have forgotten what she accomplished in doing so, that she sustained a vast, rich, densely populated empire in its troubled twilight, in the name of a proud and cultivated dynasty. She remains on the map for having seduced two of the greatest men of her time, while her crime was to have entered into those same "wily and suspicious" marital partnerships that every man in power enjoyed. She did so in reverse and in her own name; this made her a deviant, socially disruptive, an unnatural woman. To these she added a few other offenses. She made Rome feel uncouth, insecure, and poor, sufficient cause for anxiety without adding sexuality to the mix. For some time she haunted the ancient imagination, primarily as a cautionary tale. Under Augustus the institution of marriage took on a new luster, a development that

---

*Dante at least places her seven circles above her brother in hell. Her sin (lust) was against herself. Her younger brother's (betrayal) was against another.

boded poorly for Cleopatra, the destabilizing, domineering home wrecker.

She elicited scorn and envy in equal and equally distorting measure; her story is constructed as much of male fear as fantasy. From Plutarch descends history's greatest love story, though Cleopatra's life was neither as lurid nor as romantic as has been made out. And she became a femme fatale twice over. For Actium to be the battle to beat all battles, she had to be the "wild queen" plotting Rome's destruction. For Antony to have succumbed to something other than a fellow Roman, Cleopatra had to be a disarming seductress "who had already ruined him and would make his ruin still more complete." It can be difficult to say where vengeance ends and homage begins. Her power was immediately enhanced because—for one man's historical purposes—she needed to have reduced another to abject slavery. It is true that she was a dutiful, father-loving daughter, a patriot and protector, an early nationalist, a symbol of courage, a wise ruler with nerves of steel, a master at self-presentation. It is not true that she built the lighthouse of Alexandria, could manufacture gold, was the ideal woman (Gautier), a martyr to love (Chaucer), "a silly little girl" (Shaw), the mother of Christ. A seventh-century Coptic bishop termed her "the most illustrious and wise of women," greater than the kings who preceded her. On a good day Cleopatra is said to have died for love, which is not exactly true either. Ultimately everyone from Michelangelo to Gérôme, from Corneille to Brecht, got a crack at her. The Renaissance was obsessed with her, the Romantics yet more so. She sent even Shakespeare over the top, eliciting from him his greatest female role, his richest poetry, a full, Antony-less last act, and, in the estimation of one critic, a rollicking tribute to guilt-free middle-aged adultery. Shakespeare may be as much to blame for our having lost sight of Cleopatra VII as the Alexandrian humidity, Roman propaganda, and Elizabeth Taylor's limpid lilac eyes.

A center of intellectual jousting and philosophical marathons, Alexandria did not immediately surrender its vitality. It continued as the brain of the Mediterranean world for another century or so. Then it began to dematerialize. With it went legal autonomy for women; the days of suing your father-in-law for the return of your dowry when your (insolvent) husband ran off and had a baby with another woman were over. After a fifth-century earthquake, Cleopatra's palace slid into the Mediterranean. The lighthouse, the library, the museum, have all vanished. The Alexandrian harbor bears no relation to its Hellenistic proportions. The Nile itself has changed course. The city has sunk more than twenty feet. Even the coast of Actium—which Cleopatra must practically have memorized—has changed. Her Alexandria has long been almost entirely invisible, either underwater or buried beneath a teeming city that has largely forgotten its Hellenistic chapter. Ptolemaic culture evaporated as well. A great deal that Cleopatra knew would be forgotten for fifteen hundred years. A very different kind of woman, the Virgin Mary, would subsume Isis as entirely as Elizabeth Taylor has subsumed Cleopatra.

Our fascination with Cleopatra has only increased as a result; she is all the more mythic for her disappearance. The holes in the story keep us under her spell. And she continues to unsettle. All the issues that disrupt the dinner table, that go to our heads like snake venom, combine in her person. Two thousand years after she taunted Octavian with a very costly bonfire, nothing enthralls so much as excessive good fortune and devastating catastrophe. We still fight the battle of East and West, still lurch as uneasily as did Cicero between indulgence and restraint. Sex and power continue to combust in spectacular ways. Female ambition, accomplishment, authority, trouble us as they did the Romans, for whom Cleopatra was more a monster than a marvel, but undeniably a little of both.

Two thousand years of bad press and overheated prose, of film and opera, cannot conceal the fact that Cleopatra was a remarkably capable queen, canny and opportunistic in the extreme, a strategist of the first rank. Her career began with one brazen act of defiance and ended with another. "What woman, what ancient succession of men, was so great?" demands the anonymous author of a fragmentary Latin poem, which positions her as the principal player of the age. Boldly and bodily, she inserted herself into world politics, with wide-reaching consequences. She convinced her people that a twilight was a dawn and—with all her might—struggled to make it so. In a desperate situation, she improvised wildly, then improvised afresh, for some a definition of genius. There was a glamour and a grandeur to her story well before either Octavian or Shakespeare got his hands on it. Hers was an exhilarating presence; before she sent Plutarch many pages out of his way she had the same effect on his countrymen. From our first glimpse of her to the last, she dazzles for her ability to set the scene. To the end she was mistress of herself, astute, spirited, inconceivably rich, pampered yet ambitious.

In her adult life Cleopatra would have met few people she considered her equal. To the Romans she was a stubborn, supreme exception to every rule. She remains largely incomparable: She had plenty of predecessors, few successors. With her, the age of empresses essentially came to an end. In two thousand years only one or two other women could be said to have wielded unrestricted authority over so vast a realm. Cleopatra remains nearly alone at the all-male table, in possession of a hand both flush and flawed. She got a very good deal right, and one crucial thing wrong. It is impossible to fathom how she could have felt at the end of the summer of 30, as Octavian closed in, as it became more and more clear that there were to be no further reversals of fortune, no more brilliantly salvaged futures, that she and Egypt were this time plainly lost. "What is it to lose your country—a great suffering?" a queen asks her son in Euripides. "The greatest, even worse than people say," he replies. The fear and fury must have shattered Cleopatra as she realized she was to become the woman "who destroyed the Egyptian monarchy," as a third-century AD chronicler has it. For her monumental loss there were no consolations, including—assuming she believed in one—a brilliant afterlife.

Acknowledgments

"I HAVE THUS endeavored to sum up the evidence upon the case, as fairly as I can, and the result seems to be that the world must vibrate in a state of uncertainty as to what was the truth," Boswell concludes of Richard Savage, proffering hope to generations of biographers. A number of scholars substantially reduced the Hellenistic vibrations, fielding questions that ranged from the elementary to the outlandish to the unanswerable. For their time, wisdom, and patient good humor I am grateful to Roger S. Bagnall, Mary Beard, Larissa Bonfante, the late Lionel Casson, Mostafa El-Abbadi, Bruce W. Frier, Norma Goldman, Mona Haggag, O. E. Kaper, Andrew Meadows, William M. Murray, David O'Connor, Sarah B. Pomeroy, John Swanson, Dorothy J. Thompson, and Branko van Oppen. I owe Roger Bagnall additional thanks for his close reading of the manuscript; any remaining inaccuracies are my own.

For help with and in Alexandria I am indebted to: Terry Garcia, Jean-Claude Golvin, Nimet Habachy, Walla Hafez, Mona Haggag, Zahi Hawass, Kate Hughes, Hisham Hussein, William La Riche, Mohamed Abdel Maksoud, Magda Saleh, and Marion Wood. Jack A. Josephson, Shelby White, and the American Numismatic Society's Rick Witschonke kindly helped to locate or identify images.

It is a pleasure finally to acknowledge my admiration for the matchless Michael Pietsch, publisher extraordinaire, and for his colleagues at Little, Brown. At every stage they have set the gold standard. In particular I owe thanks to Mario Pulice, Vanessa Kehren, Liz Garriga, Tracy

Williams, Heather Fain, Heather Rizzo, and Betsy Uhrig. Jayne Yaffe Kemp read these pages sensitively and copyedited ruthlessly. It has been a privilege to work with Eric Simonoff, whose enthusiasm for this project has at times exceeded even my own. At William Morris I am grateful as well to Jessica Almon for shepherding book and author along.

For research and translation assistance I owe debts to Karina Attar, Matthew J. Boylan, Raffaella Cribiore, Kate Daloz, Sebastian Heath, Inger Kuin, the indefatigable Tom Puchniak, and Claudia Rader. At the New York Society Library Brandi Tambasco worked her customary interlibrary loan magic. I am grateful as well to the staff of the University of Alberta's Rutherford Library and to the New York Public Library, as much a monument to civilization as was the ancient library of Alexandria.

For sound advice, kind words, and caffeine I have leaned on many indulgent friends but most heavily upon Wendy Belzberg, Lis Bensley, Alex Mayes Birnbaum, Judy Casson, Byron Dobell, Anne Eisenberg, Benita and Colin Eisler, Ellen Feldman, Patti Foster, Harry Frankfurt, Azza Kararah, Mitch Katz, Souad Kriska, Carmen Marino, Mameve and Howard Medwed, Helen Rosenthal, Andrea Versenyi, Meg Wolitzer, and Strauss Zelnick. Elinor Lipman remains the most discerning, generous, and articulate of first readers. On every level she has enhanced these pages and their author's life. I would be lost without her.

For miracle-working—a category that includes producing a pencil out of thin air, comparing two-thousand-year-old currencies, scuba diving in the Alexandrian harbor, and equably sharing an address with a writer—I owe an incalculable debt to Marc de La Bruyère. He makes the last line easiest, as none of the preceding ones would have been written without him.

Notes

THE DEAD ENDS and missing pieces in Cleopatra's story have worked a paradoxical effect; they have kept us relentlessly coming back for more. To centuries of literature on the last queen of Egypt add a recent surge in fine Hellenistic scholarship; a catalogue of the secondary sources would easily amount to a fat volume of its own. I have opted not to write it. Where much material has been distilled into little, chapter headnotes indicate central texts. Volumes that have shaped the narrative as a whole—the ones I have pulled most frequently from the shelf—appear in the selected bibliography. Those texts are cited here by author's last name and publication date. Primary sources and periodicals appear exclusively below. Footnotes offer an occasional elaboration on a theme.

Translations of the Greek or Latin are from the Loeb Classical Library unless noted and with three general exceptions: For Appian and for Caesar's *Civil War* I have used John Carter's fluid translations (Penguin, 1996, and Oxford, 1998, respectively). For Lucan I have drawn from Susan H. Braund's 2008 Oxford University Press edition. Where translations differ markedly from published texts I am grateful to Inger Kuin, who untangled awkward phrasings and reconciled contradictory ones. Cleopatra VII, Julius Caesar, and Mark Antony are abbreviated as C, CR, and A. Names of principal sources are rendered as follows:

Appian	Appian, *The Civil Wars*
Athenaeus	Athenaeus, *The Learned Banqueters*
AA	Augustus, *Res Gestae Divi Augustus (The Acts of Augustus)*
AW	Caesar, *Alexandrian War*
CW	Caesar, *The Civil War*
Cicero	Cicero's letters
Dio	Dio Cassius, *Roman History*
Diodorus	Diodorus of Sicily, *Library of History*
Florus	Florus, *Epitome of Roman History*
JA	Josephus, *Jewish Antiquities*
JW	Josephus, *The Jewish War*

366

Lucan	Lucan, *Civil War*
ND	Nicolaus of Damascus, *Life of Augustus*
Pausanias	Pausanias, *Description of Greece*
NH	Pliny, *Natural History*
Flatterer	Plutarch, "How to Tell a Flatterer from a Friend," *Moralia*
MA	Plutarch, *Lives*, "Antony"
JC	Plutarch, *Lives*, "Caesar"
Pompey	Plutarch, *Lives*, "Pompey"
Quintilian	Quintilian, *The Orator's Education*
Strabo	Strabo, *Geography*
DA	Suetonius, *The Deified Augustus* (*Lives of the Caesars*)
DJ	Suetonius, *The Deified Julius* (*Lives of the Caesars*)
Valerius	Valerius Maximus, *Memorable Doings and Sayings*
VP	Velleius Paterculus, *Compendium of Roman History*

CHAPTER I: THAT EGYPTIAN WOMAN

1 "That Egyptian woman": Florus, II.xxi.11. Translation from Ashton, 2008, 2.
1 "Man's most valuable": From Euripides' "Helen," in *Euripides II: The Cyclops, Heracles, Iphigenia in Tauris, Helen*, David Grene and Richmond Lattimore, eds.; Richmond Lattimore, tr. (Chicago: University of Chicago Press, 1959), 1615.
2 greater prestige: JA, XV.lol.
3 "either destroy everything": Sallust, "Letter of Mithradates," 21.
4 A Roman historian: JA, XIII.408 vs. XIII.430.
4 marriage contract: Rowlandson, 1998, 322.
4 "by being scrupulously chaste": Dio, LVIII.ii.5.
4 "natural talent for deception": Cicero to Quintus, 2 (I.2), c. November 59. Cicero had no taste for the "whole tribe" of easterners: "On the contrary I am sick and tired of their fribbling, fawning ways and their minds always fixed on present advantage, never on the right thing to do."
5 "a loose girl of sixteen": James Anthony Froude, *Caesar: A Sketch* (New York: Scribner's, 1879), 446.
5 "odious extravagance": Pompey, 24.
7 The historical methods: Writing a good 130 years after C, Josephus attacked the veracity and the methods of his contemporaries: "We have actually had so-called histories even of our recent war published by persons who never visited the sites nor were anywhere near the actions described, but, having put together a few hearsay reports, have, with the gross impudence of drunken revelers, miscalled their productions by the name of history" (*Against Apion*, I.46). He simultaneously maligned the ancient Greeks for offering contradictory accounts of the same events—after which he proceeded to do so himself.

306

7 The reliance on memory: The point is K. R. Bradley's, introduction to Suetonius, *Lives of the Caesars I*, 14.

7 no plain, unvarnished stories: Andrew Wallace-Hadrill, *Suetonius* (London: Bristol Classical Press, 2004), 19. See also Fergus Millar, *A Study of Cassius Dio* (Oxford: Oxford University Press, 1999), 28. On the practice of extracting brilliant history from "next to nothing," T. P. Wiseman, *Clio's Cosmetics: Three Studies in Greco-Roman Literature* (Bristol: Bristol Phoenix Press, 1979), 23–53. See also Josephus, *Against Apion*, I.24–5. All illuminate Quintilian's first-century AD point: "History is very near to poetry, and may be considered in some sense as poetry in prose."

8 "the most unfortunate of fathers": JW, I.556.

8 Hellenistic Age defined: "The Greek world with the Greeks taken out," Daniel Ogden, *The Hellenistic World: New Perspectives* (London: Duckworth, 2002), x.

9 "And the endeavor": Thucydides, *History of the Peloponnesian War*, I, XXII.4–XXIII.3.

CHAPTER II: DEAD MEN DON'T BITE

On the "strange madness" (Cicero to Tiro, 146 [XVI.12], January 27, 49) of the Roman civil wars: Appian, JC, Dio, Florus, Plutarch. Suetonius provides the portrait of CR. For a different view of C's removal from power, Cecilia M. Peek, "The Expulsion of Cleopatra VII," *Ancient Society* 38 (2008): 103–35. Peek argues that C was removed only in the spring of 48.

Among the classical sources on Alexandria, I have leaned most heavily on Achilles Tatius, Ammianus Marcellinus, Arrian, Diodorus, Pliny, Plutarch, Polybius, Strabo, Theocritus, and Philo, especially "On the Contemplative Life," "On Dreams, Book 2," "On the Embassy to Gaius." Josephus provides descriptions of Herod's temple and palace in JW, V.173–225; C's could only have been more opulent. Athenaeus, V. 195–7 offers details on the fittings. I have taken Lucan and Aristeas's palatial descriptions with a grain of salt. Among modern reconstructions: Inge Nielsen, *Hellenistic Palaces: Tradition and Renewal* (Aarhus, Denmark: Aarhus University Press, 1999); and Maria Nowicka, *La maison privée dans l'Egypte ptolémaïque* (Wroclaw, Poland: Wydawnictwo Polskiej Akademii Nauk, 1969).

For modern accounts of Alexandria: Pascale Ballet's very good *La vie quotidienne à Alexandrie* (Paris: Hachette, 1999); Diana Delia, "The Population of Roman Alexandria," *Transactions of the American Philological Association* 118 (1988): 275–292; Jean-Yves Empereur, *Alexandria: Jewel of Egypt* (New York: Abrams, 2002); E. M. Forster, *Alexandria: A History and a Guide* (London: André Deutsch, 2004); Franck Goddio, *Alexandria: The Submerged Royal Quarters* (London: Periplus, 1998); William LaRiche, *Alexandria: The Sunken City* (London: Weidenfeld, 1996); John Marlowe's exquisite *The Golden Age of Alexandria* (London: Gollancz, 1971); *Alexandria and Alexandrianism*, papers delivered at J. Paul Getty, April 22–5, 1993, Symposium (Malibu: The J. Paul Getty Museum, 1996); Justin Pollard and Howard Reid, *The Rise and Fall of Alexandria: Birthplace of the Modern Mind* (New York: Viking, 2006); J. Pollitt,

Art in the Hellenistic Age (Cambridge: Cambridge University Press, 1986); Paul Edmund Stanwick, *Portraits of the Ptolemies: Greek Kings as Egyptian Pharaohs* (Austin: University of Texas Press, 2002); Theodore Vrettos, *Alexandria: City of the Western Mind* (New York: Free Press, 2001). On the city plan itself, W. A. Daszweski, "Notes on Topography of Ptolemaic Alexandria," Mieczysław Rodziewicz, "Ptolemaic Street Directions in Basilea (Alexandria)," and Richard Tomlinson, "The Town Plan of Hellenistic Alexandria," in *Alessandria e il Mondo Ellenistico-Romano* (Rome: L'Erma di Bretschneider, 1995); and Barbara Tkaczow's illuminating *The Topography of Ancient Alexandria* (Warsaw: Travaux du Centre d'Archéologie Méditerranéenne, 1993).

On education, to Aristotle "an ornament in prosperity and a refuge in adversity": Cicero, in particular *Brutus* and *On the Orator;* Seneca, *Epistulae Morales, II;* Suetonius, "On Grammarians" and "On Rhetoricians"; Quintilian, "Exercises"; Lucian, "Salaried Posts in Great Houses." On the subjects for composition, Quintilian, III.8.48–70 and Seneca, *Epistulae Morales,* LXXXVIII.6–9. Among modern sources: Stanley F. Bonner, *Education in Ancient Rome* (Berkeley: University of California Press, 1977); Alan K. Bowman and Greg Woolf, eds., *Literacy and Power in the Ancient World* (Cambridge: Cambridge University Press, 1994); M. L. Clarke, who is especially good on the rhetorical assignments, *Higher Education in the Ancient World* (London: Routledge, 1971); Raffaella Cribiore's excellent work, in particular *Gymnastics of the Mind* (Princeton: Princeton University Press, 2001); Bernard Legras, "L'enseignement de l'histoire dans les écoles grecques d'Egypte," in *Akten des 21. Internationalen Papyrologenkongresses, Berlin 1995* (Stuttgart: Teubner, 1997), 586–600; H. I. Marrou's superb *A History of Education in Antiquity* (Madison: University of Wisconsin Press, 1956); Teresa Morgan, *Literate Education in the Hellenistic and Roman Worlds* (Cambridge: Cambridge University Press, 1998); Rawson, 1985.

On the Ptolemaic marriages and intermarriages: Chris Bennett, "Cleopatra V Tryphaena and the Genealogy of the Later Ptolemies," *Ancient Society* 28 (1997): 39–66; Elizabeth Carney, "The Reappearance of Royal Sibling Marriage in Ptolemaic Egypt," *La Parola del Passato* XLII (1987): 420–39; Keith Hopkins's fine "Brother-Sister Marriage in Roman Egypt," *Comparative Studies in Society and History* 22, no. 3 (1980): 303–354; Daniel Ogden, *Polygamy, Prostitutes and Death: The Hellenistic Dynasties* (London: Duckworth, 1999); Brent D. Shaw, "Explaining Incest: Brother-Sister Marriage in Graeco-Roman Egypt, *Man* 27, no. 2 (1992): 267–99.

Relatedly, on women in Ptolemaic Egypt: Roger S. Bagnall, "Women's Petitions in Late Antique Egypt," in *Hellenistic and Roman Egypt: Sources and Approaches* (Burlington, VT: Ashgate Publishing, 2006); Bagnall and Cribiore, 2006; J. P. V. D. Balsdon, *Roman Women: Their History and Habits* (London: Bodley Head, 1962); Joan B. Burton, *Theocritus's Urban Mimes: Mobility, Gender, and Patronage* (Berkeley: University of California Press, 1995), 147–55. Elaine Fantham and others, *Women in the Classical World* (New York: Oxford University Press, 1994); Mary R. Lefkowitz and Maureen B. Fant, *Women's Life in Greece and Rome* (London: Duckworth, 1992); Nori-Lyn Estelle Moffat, *The Institutionalization of Power for Royal Ptolemaic Women*

(MA thesis, Clemson University, 2005); Kyra L. Nourse, *Women and the Early Development of Royal Power in the Hellenistic East* (PhD dissertation, University of Pennsylvania, 2002); Pomeroy, 1990; Claire Préaux, "Le statut de la femme à l'époque hellénistique, principalement en Egypte," *Receuils de la Société Jean Bodin* III (1959): 127–75; Rowlandson, 1998. On marrying later, Donald Herring, "The Age of Egyptian Women at Marriage in the Ptolemaic Period," *American Philological Association Abstracts* (1988): 85.

11 Dead men don't bite: Pompey, LXXVII; Plutarch, "Brutus," XXXIII. (Here and elsewhere I have opted for the Dryden translation, revised by Arthur Hugh Clough [New York: Modern Library, 1992]; henceforth "ML translation.")

11 "It's a godsend": Menander, "The Doorkeeper," *Menander: The Plays and Fragments* (New York: Oxford University Press, 2001), 264.

13 "wretched little boat": Appian, II.84. On Pompey's end, Appian, II.83–6; Dio, LXII. iii–iv; CW, 103; Plutarch, "Pompey," LXXVII.

13 The plague, flood, fire comparison: Florus, II.xiii.5.

13 CR's arrival in Egypt: Appian, II.89; Dio, XLII.vi–viii; CW, 106; AW, 1; JC, XLVIII; Plutarch, "Pompey," LXXX.5–6.

14 "to put an end to": CW, III.10.

15 "she was at a loss": JC, XLIX (ML translation); Plutarch, JC, XLIX. For the best discussion of C's arrival, John Whitehorne, "Cleopatra's Carpet," *Atti del XXII Congresso Internazionale di Papirologia* II (1998): 1287–93. On the coastal road geography, Alan H. Gardiner, "The Ancient Military Road between Egypt and Palestine," *Journal of Egyptian Archeology* 6, no. 2 (April 1920): 99–116. Achilles Tatius describes the trip from Pelusium to Alexandria via the Nile, III.9; see also Polybius, V.80.3. Interviews with Lionel Casson, April 18, 2009; John Swanson, September 10, 2008; Dorothy Thompson, April 22, 2008. Roger Bagnall points out that C might also have crossed the delta below the coastal area, where she would have had the advantage of a road, Bagnall to author, June 8, 2010.

15 "malevolent cunning": Diodorus, I.30.7. Similarly MA, III.

16 "majestic": Dio, XLII.xxxiv. 6.

16 "knowledge of how to make": Dio, XLII.xxxiv.5.

16 impossible to converse with her: MA, XXVII; Dio, XLII.xxxiv.5.

17 "by his rapidity": Dio, XLII.lvi.1.

17 "love-sated man": Ibid., XLII.xxxiv.5.

17 "every woman's man": Suetonius, citing Curio, DJ, LII.3.

18 "a mere boy": Dio, XLII.iii.3.

18 The depraved and wanton C: C is far from alone in having developed a retroactive sexual history. As Margaret Atwood notes of Jezebel, "The amount of sexual baggage that has accumulated around this figure is astounding, since she doesn't do anything remotely sexual in the original story, except put on makeup." "Spotty-Handed Villainesses: Problems of Female Bad Behavior in the Creation of Literature," http://gos.sbc.edu/a/atwood.html.

18 "all men work more": Dio, XXXVII.lv.2.

18 As one chronicler pointed out: "To the king I could have given back what he deserves, and in return for such a present to your brother, Cleopatra, could have sent your head." Lucan puts words in CR's mouth, 1069–71.

18 "Nothing was dearer": AW, 70.

19 On Alexander the Great's resting place: For an artful reconstruction of the tomb and its location, see Andrew Chugg, "The Tomb of Alexander the Great in Alexandria," *American Journal of Ancient History* 1.2 (2002): 75–108.

20 household statues of Alexander: Robert Wyman Hartle, "The Search for Alexander's Portrait," in W. Lindsay Adams and Eugene N. Borza, eds., *Philip II, Alexander the Great and the Macedonian Heritage* (Washington, DC: University Press of America, 1982), 164.

21 Ptolemaic history: On the troublesome Ptolemaic genealogy, Bennett, 1997. Strabo is also eloquent on the subject. For the shaky argument that C was the daughter of a priestly Egyptian family, see Werner Huss, "Die Herkunft der Kleopatra Philopater," *Aegyptus* 70 (1990): 191–203. And on the wobbly Ptolemaic grasp of power, Brian C. McGing, "Revolt Egyptian Style: Internal Opposition to Ptolemaic Rule," *Archiv für Papyrusforschung* 43.2 (1997): 273–314; Leon Mooren, "The Ptolemaic Court System, *Chronique d'Egypte* LX (1985): 214–22. Anna Swiderek offers a nearly humorous overview of the family violence in "Le rôle politique d'Alexandrie au temps des Ptolémées," *Prace Historyczne* 63 (1980): 105–15.

22 "an orgy of pillage": François Chamoux, *Hellenistic Civilization* (Oxford: Blackwell, 2003), 135.

23 On Auletes the piper: The name may as well have been fitted to Ptolemy XII on account of his Dionysian devotion, Bianchi, 1988, 156.

24 house of her choice: Cited in Hopkins, 1980, 337.

24 On women and business: See especially Pomeroy, 1990, 125–73. The one-third estimate is Bowman's, 1986, 98, and in part the result of inheritance and dowries.

25 "the women urinate" to "defy description": Herodotus, *The Histories*, George Rawlinson, tr. (New York: Knopf, 1997), II.xxxv. On paradoxical Egypt, Diodorus, I.27.1–2; Strabo, 1.2.22, 17.2.5; the upside-down conviction dates back to Sophocles. Generally for the Greek view of Egypt, Phiroze Vasunia, *The Gift of the Nile: Hellenizing Egypt from Aeschylus to Alexander* (Berkeley: University of California Press, 2001).

25 "Built in the finest": Philo, "On the Embassy to Gaius," XLIII.338. C. D. Yonge translation, *The Works of Philo* (Peabody, MA: Hendrickson Publishers, 1993).

26 the contested kingship: In some interpretations the petitioner, Cleopatra Selene, was in fact Auletes' own mother. Either way, a Ptolemaic woman did not hesitate to make her opinion known—and was willing to cross an ocean to do so.

26 C's mother: In Chris Bennett's reconstruction, Cleopatra VI Tryphaena was Auletes' cousin rather than his sister, 1997, 39–66.

27 giraffes, rhinoceroses, bears: Athenaeus, cited in Tarn and Griffith, 1959, 307.

27 death has been said: The point is Thompson's, 1988, 78.

28 She did not have to venture far: The point is E. M. Forster's, Forster, 2004, 34.

28–29 "The ears of a youth" to "be educated": Cited in Cribiore, 2001, 69.

29 "prince of literature": NH, II.iv.13.

29 "nursed in their learning": Heraclitus, *Homeric Problems,* 1.5.

31 "for ... as reason is the glory": Cicero, *Brutus,* XV.59. As Elizabeth Rawson put it, "The end of rhetoric tended to be persuasion rather than truth, while the extravagant subjects set for the budding orator to prove his skill on often stimulated ingenuity rather than serious thought about important problems" (*Cicero: A Portrait* [London: Bristol Classical Press, 2001], 9).

31–32 On Pompey's murder as exercise: Quintilian, 7.2.6 and 3.8.55–8.

32 "The art of speaking": Ibid., 2.13.16. The lunatic ravings, Ibid., 2.10.8.

32 "Some women are younger": George Bernard Shaw, "Notes to Caesar and Cleopatra," in *Three Plays for Puritans* (New York: Penguin, 2000), 249.

33 "sparkling eyes": Boccaccio, *Famous Women* (Cambridge: Harvard University Press, 2001), 363. Boccaccio gives C the best of both worlds: As she "could captivate almost anyone she wished with her sparkling eyes and her powers of conversation, C had little trouble bringing the lusty prince [CR] to her bed."

33 On hieroglyphs: John Baines, "Literacy and Ancient Egyptian Society," *Man* 18, no. 3 (1983): 572–99.

33 On the population: Estimates range from 3 million (Thompson, 1988) to 6 million (Walter Schiedel, *Death on the Nile* [Leiden: Brill, 2001]) to 10 million (Grant, 2004); the Loeb editors (Diodorus, I) and Fraser (1972, II, 171–2) prefer 7 million. In the first century AD Josephus estimated the population of Egypt *excluding* Alexandria to be 7.5 million. Diodorus gives Alexandria a population of some 500,000, which seems plausible; Fraser prefers 1 million. See Roger S. Bagnall and Bruce W. Frier, *The Demography of Roman Egypt* (New York: Cambridge University Press, 1994).

33 seven nationalities: Mostafa El-Abbadi, *The Life and Fate of the Ancient Library of Alexandria* (Paris: Unesco, 1990), 45.

34 "unlike that of": Herodotus, 1997, IV.clxxxii.

34 "It was a pleasure": MA, XXVII (ML translation).

34 a very similar Greek: On the koine of C and CR, interview with Dorothy Thompson, April 22, 2008; Geoffrey C. Horrocks, *Greek: A History of the Language and Its Speakers* (New York: Longman, 1997), 33–108.

34 "The better one gets": Cicero, quoting his grandfather, *On the Orator,* 2:17–18, translation from Gruen, 1984, I, 262.

34 sex manuals: Andrew Dalby, *Empire of Pleasures: Luxury and Indulgence in the Roman World* (London: Routledge, 2000), 123.

34 "with fingers of its own": Juvenal, Satire 6, 200.

34 "including some I should not care": Quintilian, 1.8.6. He was referring in particular to Horace.

35 "extremely learned": Cited in Lionel Casson, *Libraries in the Ancient World* (New Haven: Yale University Press, 2001), 78.

35 "She loved her husband": Cited in M. I. Finley, *Aspects of Antiquity* (London: Chatto, 1968), 142.

35 "highly educated": Pompey, LV.1–2 (ML translation).

35–36 "she was a woman": Sallust, *War with Catiline*, XXV. Notes Cicero approvingly of a good Roman matron: "'There was never a topic she thought she knew well enough.'" Clement of Alexandria inventories female intellectuals in *The Stromata*, 4.19, citing especially the cake bakers among them.

36–37 On the library and museum: Roger S. Bagnall, "Alexandria: Library of Dreams," *Proceedings of the American Philosophical Society* 146, no. 4 (December 2002): 348–62; Casson, 2001; El-Abbadi, 1990; Andrew Erskine, "Culture and Power in Ptolemaic Egypt: The Museum and Library of Alexandria," *Greece & Rome* 42, no. 1 (April 1995): 38–48. Fraser I, 1972, 452; Roy MacLeod, *The Library of Alexandria* (London: Tauris, 2000). Frederic C. Kenyon offers a fine guide to the scrolls themselves, *Books and Readers in Ancient Greece and Rome* (Oxford: Clarendon Press, 1932). A volume of Plato's *Symposium*, notes Kenyon, might be twenty-three feet long.

36 "he's either dead": Cited in Marrou, 1956, 145.

38 CR's fondness for pearls: DJ, XLVII.

38 "braver than all the men": Manetho, *The History of Egypt*, Fr. 21b (Armenian version of Eusebius).

38 only one Latin poet: Lucan, X.60–1.

38 "was not in itself" to "bewitching": MA, XXVII.2–3 (ML translation).

39 "striking," exquisite: Dio, XLII.xxxiv.4. The sixth-century AD Byzantine writer John Malalas also extols her beauty.

39 "famous for nothing": Boccaccio, cited in Walker and Higgs, 2001, 147.

CHAPTER III: CLEOPATRA CAPTURES THE OLD MAN BY MAGIC

For the Alexandrian War, Appian, Dio, CR, Lucan, and Plutarch, with caution. The finest modern source remains Paul Graindor, *La guerre d'Alexandrie* (Le Caire: Société Anonyme Egyptienne, 1931). It should be noted that CR and his ghostwriter offer the sole contemporary accounts of the war.

No one is better on Auletes and his travails than Mary Siani-Davies, especially her "Ptolemy XII Auletes and the Romans," *Historia* 46 (1997): 306–40; reprinted, in slightly different form, in *Cicero's Speech: Pro Rabirio Postumo* (Oxford: Clarendon Press, 2001), 1–38. See also Dio, XXXIX.xiii–xv and liv–lix; Herwig Maehler, "Egypt under the Last Ptolemies," *Bulletin of the Institute of Classical Studies* 30 (1983): 1–19. On the restoration, Dio, Plutarch, and most pointedly Cicero; Israel Shatzman's fine "The Egyptian Question in Roman Politics," *Latomus* 30 (1971): 363–9; Richard S. Williams, "*Rei Publicae Causa*: Gabinius's Defense of His Restoration of Auletes," *Classical Journal* 81, no. 1 (1985): 25–38.

For CR's Egyptian stay and the Nile cruise: Appian, Dio, Diodorus, Pliny, Strabo, Suetonius, Tacitus. I have relied a great deal on Victoria Ann Foertmeyer's especially fine "Tourism in Graeco-Roman Egypt" (Ph.D. dissertation, Princeton University, 1989). Also: Abdullatif A. Aly, "Cleopatra and Caesar at Alexandria and Rome," *Roma e l'Egitto nell'antichita classica*, Atti del I Congresso Internazionale Italo-Egiziano

(1989): 47–61; Lionel Casson, 1974, 256–91; Casson, *Ships and Seamanship in the Ancient World* (Baltimore: Johns Hopkins University Press, 1971); T. W. Hillard, "The Nile Cruise of Cleopatra and Caesar," *Classical Quarterly* 52, no. 2 (2002): 549–54; Louis E. Lord, "The Date of Julius Caesar's Departure from Alexandria," *Journal of Roman Studies* 28 (1930): 19–40; J. Grafton Milne, "Greek and Roman Tourists in Egypt," *Journal of Egyptian Archeology* 3, 2/3 (1916): 76–80; Neal, 1975, 19–33; Thompson, "Hellenistic Royal Barges," unpublished talk, Athens, 2009. The point of the trip: Willy Clarysse, "The Ptolemies Visiting the Egyptian Chora," in *Politics, Administration and Society in the Hellenistic and Roman World*, Leon Mooren, ed., Bertinoro Colloquium (Leuven, Belgium: Peeters, 2000), 33–40. For winds, weather, wildlife: Sophia Poole's vivid *The Englishwoman in Egypt* (Cairo: The American University in Cairo Press, 2003). For the second-century account of Lucius Memmius's visit: George Milligan, ed., *Selections from the Greek Papyri* (Cambridge: Cambridge University Press, 1910), 29–31.

41 Cleopatra captures the old man: A variation on Lucan, 360.

41 "A woman who is generous": Quintilian, V.11.27.

41 "captivated" to "overcome": Plutarch, XLIX (ML translation).

41–42 "to such an extent" to "assumed to be": Dio, XLII.xxxiv.ii–xxv–ii.

42 "on the condition": JC, XLIX (ML translation).

42 They assumed that they had signed: Florus, II.xiii.55–6.

42 a blundering sixth-century AD account: *Chronicle of John Malalas*, Books VIII–XVIII (Chicago: University of Chicago Press, 1940), 25.

43 depleted legions: A. B. Bosworth supplies an idea of their exhaustion, "Alexander the Great and the Decline of Macedon," *The Journal of Hellenic Studies* 106 (1986): 1–12.

43 "promised to do": Dio, XLII, xxxv.4.

43 "ability to inflame": Cicero, *Brutus*, LXXX.279.

43 "particularly anxious": CW, III.109.

44 "had given the kingdom": Dio, XLII.xxxvi.3.

44–45 "busy, listening fellow" to "embarrassing war": JC, XLIX (ML translation).

45 "a man of remarkable nerve": CW, III.104.

45 "that the royal name": CW, III.109.

46 Arsinoe burned with ambition: By one account (Strabo, 17.1.11) the two sisters had escaped together to Syria during the earlier uprising.

46 "One loyal friend": Euripides, "Orestes," in *Euripides IV: Rhesus, The Suppliant Women, Orestes, Iphigenia in Aulis*, David Grene and Richmond Lattimore, eds.; William Arrowsmith, tr. (Chicago: University of Chicago Press, 1958), 805.

46 "She would not have been": Graindor, 1931, 79. *"Elle n'eut pas été femme — et une femme de la race des Lâgides — si elle n'avait été à la fois jalouse et humiliée de la séduction qu'exerçait Cléopatre sur César."*

46 Epic struggle: For Mithradates' epic battle against Rome, Philip Matyszak, *Mithridates the Great: Rome's Indomitable Enemy* (Barnsley: Pen & Sword Military, 2008); and Adrienne Mayor, *The Poison King: The Life and Legend of Mithradates* (Princeton: Princeton University Press, 2010).

46–47 "no laws, human or divine" to "payment of money": Sallust, "Letter of Mithradates," 12, 17.

47 "fence of client states": Polybius, V.34.

47 "a loss if destroyed": Ronald Syme, *The Roman Revolution* (New York: Oxford University Press, 2002), 260.

48 consistent foreign policy: On Rome and the client kings, see Richard D. Sullivan's superb *Near Eastern Royalty and Rome* (Toronto: University of Toronto Press, 1990). Also David Braund, *Rome and the Friendly King* (New York: St. Martin's, 1984); Anssi Lampela, *Rome and the Ptolemies of Egypt: The Development of Their Political Relations, 273–80 BC* (Helsinki: Societas Scientiarum Fennica, 1998); Mayor, 2010, on Mithradates's parallel struggle; Willy Peremans and Edmond Van 't Dack, "Sur les rapports de Rome avec les Lagides," *Aufstieg und Niedergang der römischen Welt* (1972): 660–7; Shatzman, 1971. The housing project, Holbl, 2001, 224–25.

48 "just one continuous revel": Dio Chrysostom, "The 32nd Discourse," 69.

49 "These men habitually": CW, III.110.

49 "They may be irrational animals": Clement of Alexandria, "The Exhortation to the Greeks," II.33p. The cat incident, Diodorus I.83. Evidently cats were a rarity on the northern side of the Mediterranean at the time. The animal worship invited ridicule from all quarters. See among others Juvenal, Satire 15.1; Philo, "On the Decalogue," XVI.78–80, and "On the Contemplative Life," 8; Josephus, *Against Apion*, II.81.

50 "bedeviled by certain individuals": Cicero to Lentulus, 13 (I.2), January 15, 56.

50 "gained a highly invidious" to "royal largesse": Ibid. 12 (I.1), January 13, 56.

51 "in his rage and spite": MA, III (ML translation).

52 On the succession: J. C. Yardley, tr., *Justin: Epitome of the Philippic History of Pompeius Trogus* (Atlanta: Scholars Press, 1994), 16.iiff; Jean Bingen, "La politique dynastique de Cléopâtre VII," *Comptes Rendus: Académie des Inscriptions et Belles-Lettres* 1 (1999): 49–66; Lucia Criscuolo, "La successione a Tolemeo Aulete ed i pretesi matrimoni di Cléopâtre VII con i fratelli," in *Egitto e storia antica dall'ellenismo all'età araba* (1989): 325–39. Working from several double-dated papyri, Ricketts, "A Chronological Problem in the Reign of Cleopatra VIII," *Bulletin of the American Society of Papyrologists* 16:3 (1979): 213–17, advanced the theory that C attempted to eliminate Ptolemy XIII by installing their younger brother as her consort in the spring of 50. Certainly relations had already soured with their older brother. See also Ricketts, "A Dual Queenship in the Reign of Berenice IV," *Bulletin of the American Society of Papyrologists* 27 (1990): 49–60; T. C. Skeat (who argues against a joint Auletes-Cleopatra rule), "Notes on Ptolemaic Chronology," *Journal of Egyptian Archeology* 46 (Dec. 1960): 91–4; and (for Berenice's murky reign) John Whitehorne, "The Supposed Co-Regency of Cleopatra Tryphaeana and Berenice IV," in *Akten des* 21. *Internationalen Papyrologenkongresses* (Stuttgart: B. G. Teubner, 1997), II, 1009–13.

52 "habituated to the ill-disciplined ways": CW, III.110.

53 On C's ascension: There is another possible explanation for Auletes' choice of the two siblings. Heinen, 2009, speculates that C's father early on recognized the

powerful personality and dangerous ambitions of his second daughter and invited Roman backing expressly to neutralize them, 35–6.

54 On Memphis: See especially El-Abbadi, 1990, 58; Lewis, 1986, 69ff; Thompson, 1988.

54 "boasting made permanent": John D. Ray, "The Emergence of Writing in Egypt," *World Archaeology* 17, no. 3 (1986): 311.

57 The burning of the Alexandrian library: Seneca is the first to mention the book burning, citing a figure of 40,000 volumes, a number that swells in subsequent accounts, to become 700,000 by the fourth century AD. Both Dio and Plutarch believed the library to have burned. Centuries of scholarship have been devoted to the vexed question; see Fraser, 1972, I, 334–5, 476; Edward Alexander Parsons, *The Alexandrian Library: Glory of the Hellenic World* (New York: Elsevier, 1967). Will, 2003, 533, believes that the destruction was less than legend has implied. For a roundup of the sources, http//www.bede.org.uk/library.htm. By that estimate, 500,000 scrolls would require 24.5 miles of shelving, or a two-story building measuring 100 feet by 100 feet.

57 "And there was not a soul": AW, 15.

57 It has been suggested that he broke off: John Carter, introduction to CW (New York: Oxford University Press, 2008), xxix. See also John H. Collins, "On the Date and Interpretation of the Bellum Civile," *American Journal of Philology* 80, no. 2 (1959): 113–32.

58 "put into effect": AW, 3.

59 "most ready to assume": Dio, XXXIX.lviii.1–2.

60 "in order, as they claimed": Ibid., XLII.xlii.2.

60 "against a king": AW, XXIV. Heinen, 2009, reads CR's release of Ptolemy as an act of desperation, 106–113. Unaware that reinforcements were on their way, CR had not yet begun to feel the tide turning; he was frantically buying time. On the constitution of the Egyptian army, Polybius, V.35.13 and V.36.3; G. T. Griffith, *The Mercenaries of the Hellenistic World* (Cambridge: Cambridge University Press, 1935); Marcel Launey, *Recherches sur les armées hellénistiques*, 2 vols. (Paris: Boccard, 1949); Raphael Marrinan, "The Ptolemaic Army: Its Organisation, Development and Settlement," (PhD dissertation, University College, London, 1998). Marrinan places a barracks of elite guards on or near the palace grounds.

60–61 "to think of his ancestral" to "tears of joy": AW, 24.

61–62 "The entire population": AW, 32.

62 "a prodigy of activity": Gaston Boissier, *Cicero and His Friends* (New York: Cooper Square Publishers, 1970), 185.

62 CR acquitted himself: Volkmann, 1958, 75.

62 "which blew absolutely": CW, III.107.

63 "had remained loyal": AW, 33.

63 "out of voluptuousness": Dio, XLIV.46.2. See also Cicero to Atticus, 226 (XI.15), May 14, 47, and 230 (XI.18), June 19, 47. In the fourth century AD Eusebius returned to the theme, charging that CR returned C to the throne "in return for sexual favors" (Eusebius, 183.2).

63 the gratuitous apology: The point is El-Abbadi's; he is firmly convinced that the library was a casualty of the war, 1990, 151.

63 "As to the war in Egypt": JC, XLVIII (ML translation).

64 "for whose sake" to "in Caesar's company": Dio, XLII. 44.

64 in C's bed every night: Pelling, 1999, 140.

64 every visitor to Hellenistic Egypt: As Braund (1984, 79) notes: "The wise king was a lavish host when Romans came to visit."

64 "in view of Caesar's favor": Dio, XLII.xxxiv.3.

66 "For the ruler labors": Ibid., LV.xv.5–6.

66 "the first city of the civilized": Diodorus, XVII.52.4. Even Cicero conceded as much, De Lege Agraria, II, XVI, 44.

66 "Looking at the city": Achilles Tatius, V.i.6. He was a native son.

68 "It is not easy": Dio Chrysostom, "The 32nd Discourse, To the People of Alexandria, 20," in *Alexandria: The Site and the History*. Cited in Gareth L. Steen, ed. (New York: New York University Press, 1993), 58.

69 "The general rule": Athenaeus, V.196d.

69 three hundred tons of dinner vessels: Ibid., 453.

69 "ordinary ware": The point is Thompson's, from "Athenaeus's Egyptian Background," in David Braund and John Wilkins, eds., *Athenaeus and His World* (Chicago: University of Chicago Press, 2000), 83–4. See Athenaeus, VI.229d.

69 "a silver platter": Athenaeus, IV.129b.

70 On C's wardrobe: Interview with Larissa Bonfante, February 2, 2009; interview with Norma Goldman, October 19, 2009; Casson, 2001, 24–5; Rowlandson, 1998, 313–34; Stanwick, 2002, 36–7, Dorothy Burr Thompson, *Ptolemaic Oinochoai and Portraits in Faience* (Oxford: Clarendon Press, 1973), 29–30; Susan Walker and Morris Bierbrier, *Ancient Faces: Mummy Portraits from Roman Egypt* (London: British Museum Press, 1997), 177–80; Walker and Higgs, 2001, 65.

70 "prolonged parties until dawn": DJ, LII (translation modified). Similarly Frontinus, Stratagems, I.i.5. Plutarch has CR drinking until dawn in order to ward off assassination attempts, JC, XLVIII.

70 Dionysian procession: For the best dissection of Athenaeus, V.197–203, see E. E. Rice, *The Grand Procession of Ptolemy Philadelphus* (New York: Oxford University Press, 1983). Thompson, "Philadelphus's Procession: Dynastic Power in a Mediterranean Context," in Mooren, 2000, 365–88. Thompson emphasizes that such a procession was meant to unite the populace and promote a sense of civic identity. Arrian, XXVIII, notes the triumph's Dionysian roots.

71 "the shrewdest amasser": Appian, preface, 10. The translation is Macurdy's, 1932, 108.

72 Had Auletes married C to CR: Ptolemy VIII had tried unsuccessfully to woo a (rich) Roman woman, Cornelia, mother of the Gracchi, Plutarch, Tiberius Gracchus, I.

72 "Cleopatra has been able" to "gain Rome": Lucan, X, 359–60.

72 "surrendered to Alexander": *Justin: Epitome of the Philippic History of Pompeius Trogus*, J. C. Yardley, tr.

73 "she had a thousand": Plutarch, MA, XXIX (ML translation).

73 Such an unsociable: Plutarch, "Demetrius," III. By its very definition, empire made a mockery of family relations, inviting "ill-will and distrust."

73 "everything that lifts people": Dio, XXXVIII.xxxix.2.

74 "There is nothing": Lucan, X.189–90. Egypt exerted no less of a spell on the Greeks, before and after C; it was the ultimate land of mystery. See E. Marion Smith, "The Egypt of the Greek Romances," *Classical Journal* 23, no. 7 (April 1928): 531–7.

75 "the father of yellow journalism": Robert Graves, introduction to Lucan, *Pharsalia: Dramatic Episodes of the Civil Wars* (New York: Penguin, 1956), 13.

75 "received with the utmost": Letter of 112 BC, *Select Papyri*, II, 416 (George Milligan translation).

75 The Nile cruise: The dates remain in dispute. Lord, 1930, doubts the cruise altogether.

75 One modern historian goes so far: Heinen, 2009, 127. "It seems as if the author [of *The Alexandrian War*] knowingly sought to deceive his readers, and attempted not only to conceal the Nile journey, but to represent the chronological sequence of events in such a way that this episode could never have taken place."

76 "I gulped down color": Gustave Flaubert to his mother, November 17, 1849. The translation is from Empereur, 2002, 136.

76 The barge: Athenaeus, V.204e–206d. See also Nowicka, 1969.

77 hide supplies: Foertmeyer, 1989, 235.

77 "Once is enough": Cicero to Atticus, 353 (XIII.52), December 19, 45.

77 "floating palace": Nielsen, 1999, 136.

78 The misconceptions: Herodotus for the skull; Diodorus for the primordial half-mice; Strabo for the twins, turtle shells, grass serpents, and astonishing fecundity, XV.I.22–3. Similarly NH, from which come mice walking on two feet and the abbreviated pregnancies, VII.iiiff. Much of this descends from Aristotle (*History of Animals*, vii.4); Aulus Gellius picked up the theme, *Attic Nights*, X.ii. Dio Chrysostom has mythical man-eating mermaids in the desert, half snake, half siren, *Discourse*, 5.24–7. Ammianus Marcellinus, *Roman History*, XXII.15.14ff would marvel over dolphinlike creatures in the Nile, hippopotami that were "sagacious beyond all unreasoning beasts," and the Egyptian ibis, a bird that laid eggs through its beak.

79 "I saw, and I was amazed": Casson, *Everyday Life in Ancient Egypt* (Baltimore: Johns Hopkins University Press, 2001), 142.

79 The Macedonian parallel: Nepos, *Eumenes*, III.4.

80 "and enjoyed himself": Appian, II.89.

80 "She would have": Dio, XLII.45.1.

80 "was neither creditable": Dio, XLII.47.2.

CHAPTER IV: THE GOLDEN AGE NEVER WAS THE PRESENT AGE

Cicero, Pliny, and Plutarch are the invaluable guides to Rome and the Romans. For the trips there I have relied on the wisdoms of Lionel Casson, and especially on *Travel in the Ancient World;* see also Michel Reddé and Jean-Claude Golvin's lavishly illustrated

Notes

Voyages sur la méditerranée romaine (Paris: Actes Sud, 2005). On C in Rome, Erich Gruen's debunking "Cleopatra in Rome: Facts and Fantasies," in *Myth, History and Culture in Republican Rome,* David Braund and Christopher Gill, eds. (Exeter: University of Exeter Press, 2003); Edmond Van 't Dack, "La Date de C. Ord. Ptol. 80–83 = BGU VI 1212 et le séjour de Cléopâtre VII à Rome," *Ancient Society* 1 (1970): 53–67. Eusebius attests to the inevitable retinue, 183.30, as does Horace, in a different way; he regretted the wealthy woman's veritable armature of attendants, Satires I.ii. 95–100.

On the administration of Egypt and the Ptolemaic machine, Bagnall and Derow, 1981, 253–255; Bingen, 2007, 156–255; Bowman, 1986; R. A. Hazzard, *Imagination of a Monarchy: Studies in Ptolemaic Propaganda* (Toronto: University of Toronto Press, 2000); Maehler, 1983; Leon Mooren, *La hiérarchie de cour ptolémaïque* (Leuven, Belgium: Studia Hellenistica 23, 1977); Mooren, 2000; Dominic Rathbone, "Ptolemaic to Roman Egypt: The Death of the Dirigiste State?," in *Production and Public Powers in Classical Antiquity,* Cambridge Philological Society, 26 (2000), 4–54; Geoffrey Rickman, *The Corn Supply of Ancient Rome* (Oxford: Clarendon Press, 1980); Michael Rostovtzeff, *A Large Estate in Egypt in the Third Century BC* (Madison: University of Wisconsin Studies, 1922); *Select Papyri: Public Documents,* II (Cambridge: Harvard University Press, 1995); Raphael Taubenschlag, *The Law of Graeco-Roman Egypt in the Light of the Papyri* (Warsaw: Panstwowe Wydawnictwo Naukowe, 1955); D. J. Thompson, "Nile Grain Transport under the Ptolemies," in *Trade in the Ancient Economy,* Peter Garnsey and others, eds. (London: Chatto & Windus, 1983), 64–75. For a fine, flavorful summary of papyri, ostraca, and inscriptions from C's reign, see Ricketts, 1980, 114–36.

On Rome and its mores: Cicero, Horace, Juvenal, Martial, Pliny, Strabo. Among modern sources: Balsdon, *Life and Leisure in Ancient Rome* (London: Bodley Head, 1969); Casson, *Everyday Life in Ancient Rome* (Baltimore: Johns Hopkins University Press, 1998); Florence Dupont's colorful *Daily Life in Ancient Rome* (Oxford: Blackwell, 1993); Luc Duret and Jean-Pierre Neraudau, *Urbanisme et metamorphoses de la Rome antique* (Paris: Belles Lettres, 2001); Otto Kiefer, *Sexual Life in Ancient Rome* (New York: Dorset Press, 1993); Thomas Wiedemann, *Adults and Children in the Roman Empire* (London: Routledge, 1989); T. P. Wiseman, *Catullus and His World: A Reappraisal* (Cambridge: Cambridge University Press, 1985).

For CR, Matthias Gelzer, *Caesar: Politician and Statesman* (Oxford: Blackwell, 1968); Adrian Goldsworthy, *Caesar: Life of a Colossus* (New Haven: Yale University Press, 2006); Christian Meier, *Caesar: A Biography* (New York: MJF Books, 1982); Stefan Weinstock, *Divus Julius* (London: Oxford University Press, 1971); Maria Wyke, *Caesar: A Life in Western Culture* (Chicago: University of Chicago Press, 2008); Zwi Yavetz, *Julius Caesar and His Public Image* (Ithaca: Cornell University Press, 1983).

83   The golden age: Benjamin Franklin, *Poor Richard's Almanack* (1750).

83   "What excuses": Euripides, "Andromache," in *The Trojan Women and Other Plays,* James Morwood, tr. (Oxford: Oxford University Press, 2001), 85–87.

83   CR's silence: Dio, XLII.iii.3. All in Rome assumed CR would perish at the hands of

the Egyptians, "as, indeed, they kept hearing was the case." Cicero in particular was aware of CR's difficulties extricating himself from Africa.

83–84 On birthing: Soranos, cited in Rowlandson, 1998, 286–9; Joyce Tyldesley, *Daughters of Isis: Women of Ancient Egypt* (New York: Viking, 1994), 70–5.

84 "not be prone to anger": Third-century BC letter, cited in I. M. Plant, ed., *Women Writers of Ancient Greece and Rome* (Norman: University of Oklahoma Press, 2004), 79–80. Given the infant mortality rate, wet nurses were easy to find.

83–85 paternity: For a neat summary of the case against Caesarion, Balsdon, "Cleopatra: A Study in Politics and Propaganda by Hans Volkmann," *Classical Review* 10, no. 1 (March 1960): 68–71. See also Heinen's 1969 response to J. Carcopino's 1937 repudiation of Caesarion, reprinted in Heinen, 2009, 154–75. Here as elsewhere the ancient sources are less than helpful: Suetonius both doubts the paternity and notes that CR allowed the child to be named for him, DJ, LII.

84 volumes of advice: See Keith Hopkins, "Contraception in the Roman Empire," *Comparative Studies in Society and History* 8, no. 1 (1965): 124–51; Angus McLaren, *A History of Contraception* (London: Basil Blackwell, 1990); Sarah B. Pomeroy, *Goddesses, Whores, Wives, and Slaves* (New York: Schocken, 1975), 167–9; John M. Riddle's *Contraception and Abortion from the Ancient World to the Renaissance* (Cambridge: Harvard University Press, 1992). Also Juvenal, Satire 6.595–6; NH, VI.42; Soranus, I.60–65.

86 The swelling Nile: Diodorus, I.36.7. For flora and fauna I have drawn on Poole, 2003. For river conditions, W. M. Flinders Petrie, *Social Life in Ancient Egypt* (Boston: Houghton Mifflin, 1923), 129–68; Amelia B. Edwards, *A Thousand Miles up the Nile* (London: Century, 1982), 319ff.

86 On the birthday gifts: Préaux, 1939, 394. Neal, 1975, suggests that the timing was so perfect that C may have chosen that date on which to announce the birth. She issued gold coins that year, one of only two occasions on which she did so.

86 Isis association: Pelling, 1999, 251–2; Ashton, 2008, 138. See Claire Préaux, *Le monde hellénistique* (Paris: Presses Universitaires de France, 1978), II, 650–5; Sarolta A. Takacs, *Isis and Serapis in the Roman World* (Leiden: E. J. Brill, 1995); R. E. Witt, *Isis in the Graeco-Roman World* (Ithaca: Cornell University Press, 1971). On Isis's fate on the northern side of the Mediterranean, see especially Sharon Kelly Heyob, *The Cult of Isis among Women in the Graeco-Roman World* (Leiden, Holland: E. J. Brill, 1975).

87 The ax-wielding consul: Valerius, 1.3.41.

87–88 Ceremonial attire: O. E. Kaper to author, March 16, 2010.

87 "the queen should have greater power": Diodorus, I.27. On Isis and women: Préaux, 1959, 127–75. Many have pointed to Isis's involvement with the Virgin Mary; Foertmeyer, 1989, 279, notes that as late as the sixteenth century, a French cardinal smashed a statue to pieces on discovering it to be a representation of Isis rather than of the Virgin.

88 On the state and the clergy: Thompson, 1988. Guy Weill Goudchaux, "Cleopatra's Subtle Religious Strategy," in Walker and Higgs, 2001, 128–41. Also E. A. E. Reymond and J. W. B. Barns, "Alexandria and Memphis: Some Historical Observations," *Orientalia* 46 (1977): 1–33. For the grant of asylum, see Kent J. Rigsby,

Asylia: Territorial Inviolability in the Hellenistic World (Berkeley: University of California Press, 1996). On the temple hierarchy, Gilles Gorré, "Les relations du clergé égyptien et des Lagides," in *Royaumes et cités hellénistiques des années 323–55 av. JC,* Olivier Picard and others, eds. (Paris: SEDES, 2003), 44–55.

88 The synagogue grant: Rigsby, 1996, 571–2.

88–89 The flood measurements: NH, X.li.60 on the Nile, V.x.58 on the heights. On the behavior of the Nile, Lewis, 1983, 105–15; Achilles Tatius, IV.11–15. Strabo is otherwise the best river guide.

89 "There was no famine": See Jacques Vandier, *La famine dans l'Egypte ancienne* (New York: Arno Press, 1979), 35ff; as well as Dorothy Thompson, "Nile Grain Transport under the Ptolemies," in Peter Garnsey et al., eds., *Trade in the Ancient Economy* (London: Chatto & Windus, 1983), 64–75. Heinen, "Hunger, Misery, Power," reprinted in 2009, 258–87, notes that the ruling class won points as well for its benevolence and that the crises were often exaggerated. To stress the people's misery was further to extol official munificence.

90 "Anyone familiar": Flatterer, 790A. Centuries earlier Antigonus Gonatas, a particularly clear-eyed Macedonian king, had informed his son that the royalty business was "a glorious state of slavery." Dio, LII.X.2, put it similarly: It was the sovereign's fate to "always and everywhere both see and hear, do and suffer, only that which is disagreeable."

90 the formulaic correspondence: AJ, XII.148, XII.166, XIV.306.

90 lulled an earlier Ptolemy to sleep: Flatterer, 71d. The tutor who slapped the dozing Ptolemy V Epiphanes awake was rewarded with a goblet of poison.

90 crush of business: For the paperwork, see Peter van Minnen, "Further Thoughts on the Cleopatra Papyrus," *Archiv für Papyrusforschung* 47 (2001): 74–80; Peter van Minnen, "An Official Act of Cleopatra," *Ancient Society* 30 (2000): 29–34.

91 "unadultered and without delay": Thompson, 1983, 71; also Christopher Haas, *Alexandria in Late Antiquity: Topography and Social Conflict* (Baltimore: Johns Hopkins University Press, 2006), 40–4. Generally on the functioning of the economy, Rostovtzeff, 1998; Préaux, 1939; Tarn and Griffin, 1959; Thompson, 1988; Dominic Rathbone, "Ptolemaic to Roman Egypt: The Death of the *Dirigiste* State?," *Cambridge Philological Society* 26 (2000): 44–54.

92 "nobody is allowed": Cited in M. M. Austin, *The Hellenistic World from Alexander to the Roman Conquest: A Selection of Source Materials in Translation* (Cambridge: Cambridge University Press, 1981), 561.

93 "knew each day": William Tarn, *Hellenistic Civilization* (London: Edward Arnold, 1959), 195.

93 "cheer everybody up": *Select Papyri,* 1995, II.204.

93 "We may conclude": Dorothy Crawford's illuminating "The Good Official of Ptolemaic Egypt," in *Das Ptolemäische Agypten: Akten des internationalen Symposions 1976* (Mainz, Germany: von Zabern, 1978), 202.

93 "stolen donkeys": John Bauschatz, "Policing the Chora: Law Enforcement in Ptolemaic Egypt," Ph.D. dissertation (Duke University, 2005), 68.

94 They preyed equally: Bingen, "Les tensions structurelles de la société ptolémaïque," *Atti del XVII Conresso Internazionale di Papirologia III* (Naples, 1984): 921–937; Rathbone, 2000.

94–95 On the grievances: Bagnall and Derow, 2004; Bevan, 1968; Maehler, 1983; Rostovtzeff, 1998. And on the benevolence: William Linn Westermann, "The Ptolemies and the Welfare of Their Subjects," *American Historical Review* 43, no. 2 (1938): 270–87.

95 The infirm father: *Select Papyri*, II, 233. The girl had run away with her layabout of a boyfriend and—claimed her father—would no longer provide him with the necessities of life, despite having signed a contract to do so.

95 "come early in the morning": *Select Papyri*, II.266. Translation from M. Rostovtzeff, "A Large Estate in Egypt in the Third Century BC: A Study in Economic History," *University of Wisconsin Studies* 6, 1922, 120.

95 Taxation cases forbidden: Rostovtzeff, 1998, II, 1094.

95 "scalded my belly": Cited in Bagnall and Derow, 1981, 195.

96 "When we inherited": Cicero, *The Republic*, V.I.2. The translation is from Everitt, 2003, 180.

96 On Auletes and the family fortune: T. Robert S. Broughton, "Cleopatra and 'The Treasure of the Ptolemies,'" *American Journal of Philology* 63, no. 3 (1942): 328–32. Here too opinions differ: Maehler, 1983, subscribes to "undisturbed prosperity." Bowman, Casson, Ricketts, and Tarn agree. Rostovtzeff, 1998, is certain of C's personal treasure but less sanguine about the economy under her reign, III, 1548. Thompson, Broughton, and Will see an economy in decline if not disarray. Athenaeus accuses C's father of having dissipated the fortune of Egypt, V.206d. In 63 Cicero found Egypt still a flourishing kingdom, De Lege Agraria, II.XVI.44.

96 On the devaluation and C's coins, see Guy Weill Goudchaux, "Was Cleopatra Beautiful? The Conflicting Answers of Numismatics," in Walker and Higgs, 2001, 210–14. Chauveau, 2000, 86, succinctly terms devaluation "the ancient equivalent of printing money."

97 "the equivalent of all of the hedge fund": Interview with Roger Bagnall, November 21, 2008.

97 palace drinking contest: Athenaeus, X.415. Athenaeus (XII.522) also mentions that a philosopher earned twelve talents a year, which sounds high. The bail is from Casson, 2001, 35; he equates fifteen talents with millions of modern dollars. For the impressive monuments, Peter Green, *Alexander of Macedon* (Berkeley: University of California Press, 1991), 414. Marrinan, 1998, asserts that you could hire an army of 10,000 men for a year with 1,000 talents, 16. Diodorus reports that for a lowly Roman craftsman a talent was the equivalent of seventeen years' wages, Josephus (JW, I.483) that a prince with a private income of 100 talents was a man to be reckoned with. During the honeymoon of Egypto-Roman relations, a visiting Roman dignitary was offered gifts worth eighty talents—so immodest a sum he did not accept (Plutarch, "Lucullus," 2). On a more prosaic level, a talent bought enough wheat to feed a man for seventy-five years. See also Tarn and Griffin, 1959, 112–16.

97 one contemporary list: http://en.wikipedia.org/wiki/Richest_man_in_history.

98 The trip to Rome: This is based on the best educated guess in the business, that of Casson. Interviews, January 26, 2009, and June 18, 2009. See also Casson, 1971; Casson, *The Ancient Mariners* (Princeton: Princeton University Press, 1991); Casson, 1994. He describes the entire arduous system in "The Feeding of the Trireme Crews and an Entry in IG ii2 1631," *Transactions of the American Philological Association* 125 (1995): 261–9; and in "The Isis and Her Voyage," *Transactions of the American Philological Association* 81 (1950): 43–56. Casson to author, December 9, 2008. For comparisons see Philo, "Against Flaccus," V.25ff, "On the Embassy to Gaius," 250–3; JW, 1.280; Horace, Satires, I.5; Germanicus's travels in Tacitus, *Annals*, II.50; Casson on Cicero and Pliny, 1994, 149–53. C may well have docked at Ostia, which Bagnall and Thompson think more likely; Casson preferred Puzzuoli, as there were at the time no docking facilities of any size at Ostia (Casson, 1991, 199). It is not impossible that C embarked or disembarked at Brundisium as would Horace (heading west) and as had Cicero, heading east. From there she would have made the long trek overland through hill country and along the Appian Way. That trip could be done in about seven days (Casson, 1994, 194–6).

98 The risks at sea: Achilles Tatius gives a fine (fictional) account of shipwreck, III.2–6. He washes up at Pelusium.

98 arrival in Rome: Eusebius, 183.3.

98 "like a camel": Dio, XLIII. 23.2–3. See also Strabo, 16.4.16.

99 The advice regarding royal travel: Letter of Aristeas, 249, cited in T. A. Sinclair, *A History of Greek Political Thought* (London: Routledge, 1959), 292.

100 "two chariots": An appalled Cicero to Atticus, 115 (V.1), February 20, 50, translation from Boissier, 1970, 120. Similarly Foertmeyer, 224; Plutarch, "Crassus," XXI.6; Préaux, 1939, 561.

101 On the Rome of foul air and poor hygiene, and on the idyllic Janiculum: Leon Homo, *Rome impériale et l'urbanisme dans l'antiquité* (Paris: Albin Michel, 1951); Dionysius of Halicarnassus, *Roman Antiquities*, III.xlv; Horace, Odes, II.29, 9–12; Martial, *Epigrams*, IV.64. Otherwise Cicero remains the best guide to Rome. The stray hand and ox: Suetonius, "Vespasian," 5.4.

101 "Only the priests": JC, LIX (ML translation).

101 "the only intelligent calendar": O. Neugebauer, *The Exact Sciences in Antiquity* (Princeton: Princeton University Press, 1952), 71. For the Egyptian calendar (twelve months of thirty days, to which were added five days, and at the end of every fourth year six days), see Strabo, 17.1.29.

102 "to make them more desirous": DJ, XLII.

102 "Easier for two philosophers": Seneca, *Apocolocyntosis*, 2.2.

103 On the Roman triumph: Appian, Dio, Florus, Suetonius, and Mary Beard's superb *The Roman Triumph* (Cambridge: Harvard University Press, 2007).

104 "the most fortunate captive": JC, LV.2.

105 "a woman and once considered": Dio, XLIII.xix.3–4.

105 infants or chickens: On the political and legal rights of women, Mary Beard and Michael Crawford, *Rome in the Late Republic* (London: Duckworth, 2005), 41.

106 hundred swordsmen: Cicero to Quintus, 12.2 (II.9), June 56.

107 "Even if his slaves" to "carvers": Juvenal, Satire 9, 100ff.

107 "absolutely devoted" to "bloom of youth": Dio, XLIII.xliii.4.

107 "among the friends and allies": Dio, XLIII.xxviii.1. Gruen, 1984, 259, challenges the date of the statue's installation. He moves it forward by some fifteen years, to make it a tribute not to C but to her defeat.

108 "No one dances": Cicero, *Pro Murena*, 13; translation from Otto Kiefer, *Sexual Life in Ancient Rome* (New York: Dorset Press, 1993), 166. As Athenaeus points out by contrast, "No other people are recorded as being more musical than the Alexandrians" (IV.176e).

108 "You have to be a very rich": Juvenal, Satire 3, 236. The flying pots are also his, Ibid., 270ff.

108 "Otherwise he wouldn't be so good": Plutarch citing Antisthenes, "Pericles," I.5.

108 "not a real man": Athenaeus, V.206d.

109 "superficially civilized": Lucan, in P. F. Widdows's translation (Bloomington: Indiana University Press, 1988), 544.

109 "the last word": Casson, 1998, 104.

109 "idle and foolish": NH, XXXVI.xvi.75. In the Loeb, "They rank as a superfluous and foolish display of wealth."

109 Greek and Latin: Quintilian acknowledges that the world sounded harsher in Latin, shorn as it was of the sweetest Greek letters, with which "the language at once seems to brighten us up and smile" (12.10).

109 word . . . for "not possessing": Seneca, Epistle LXXXVII.40.

109 "gold-inlay utensils": Dalby, 2000, 123. Dalby notes that a Greek accent alone carried with it a whiff of luxury, 122. Similarly Dio, LVII.xv.3; Valerius, Book IX, 1, "Of Luxury and Lust." It seemed impossible to describe excess without recourse to Greek. It is Dalby who observes that "the classic practical manual of sexual behavior was in Greek, 123.

109–111 On the rise of luxury: Livy, 39.6; NH, XXXVI; Plutarch, "Caius Marius," 34; Athenaeus, XII; Horace, Odes II, xv; Dalby, 2000; Wiseman, 1985, 102ff.

110 The stolen napkins: Catullus, Poems, 12 and 25; NH, 19.2.

110 the beautiful vase of poisonous snakes: Saint Jerome, cited in Jasper Griffin, "Virgil Lives!," *New York Review of Books* (June 26, 2008): 24.

111 Women in Rome: Richard A. Bauman, *Women and Politics in Ancient Rome* (London: Routledge, 1992); Diana E. E. Kleiner and Susan B. Matheson, eds., *I Claudia: Women in Ancient Rome* (New Haven: Yale University Art Gallery, 1996); Barbara S. Lesko, "Women's Monumental Mark on Ancient Egypt," *Biblical Archeologist* 54, no. 1 (1991), 4–15; Rawson, 1985; Marilyn B. Skinner's fine *Sexuality in Greek and Roman Culture* (Malden, MA: Blackwell, 2005); Wyke, *The Roman Mistress* (Oxford: Oxford University Press, 2002). Interview with Larissa Bonfante, February 2, 2009.

111 "Hard work": Juvenal, Satire 6, 289ff.

111 "teasing, scolding": Samuel Butler, *The Humour of Homer, and Other Essays* (London: A. C. Fifield, 1913), 60. Edith Hamilton remarks on the absence of deceived husbands in *The Roman Way* (New York: Norton, 1993), 35.

112 "There's nothing a woman": Juvenal, Satire 6, 460–1.

112 even C's eunuchs were rich: Seneca, Epistle LXXXVII.16.

113 The much-discussed pearls: Suetonius, "Caligula," XXXVII; Horace, Satire 2.iii.239; Pausanias, 8.18.6; NH, IX.lviii. C's two pearls—"the largest in the whole of history"—are from Pliny, IX.119–121. Lucan too ropes a fortune in pearls around C's neck and through her hair, X.139–40. See also Macrobius, *The Saturnalia*, 3.17.14. In that much later account C and MA arrive at a wager over the pearl in the course of their extravagant feasting. They are well matched; "It was as the slave of this gluttony that he [MA] wished to make an Egyptian kingdom of the empire of Rome." Plancus good-naturedly umpires the contest. For centuries C's name remained a synonym for extravagance. In the fifth century AD Sidonius (Letter VIII.xii.8) described the most lavish of dinners as akin to "a feast of Cleopatra's."

113 "When I boiled a pearl": B. L. Ullman, "Cleopatra's Pearls," *Classical Journal* 52, no. 5 (1957): 196. See also Prudence J. Jones, "The Cleopatra Cocktail," 1999, http://www.apaclassics.org/AnnualMeeting/99mtg/abstracts/jonesp.html. She finds the pearls do dissolve. Keats included the melted pearls in "Modern Love."

114 "the leaves at the top": Hesiod, *Works and Days*, 680–1.

114 "did not let" to "name to the child": DJ, LII.2.

114 "was her best card": Aly, 1989, 51.

115 needed to press her case: Interview with Roger Bagnall, November 11, 2008.

115 passionate, admiring letters: Dio, LI.xii.3.

115 "A more raffish assemblage": Cicero to Atticus, 16 (I.16.), early July 61. On broadening C's base of support, Andrew Meadows to author, March 5, 2010.

115 On C's concern with the reorganization of the East: Gruen, 2003, 271.

CHAPTER V: MAN IS BY NATURE A POLITICAL CREATURE

Generally on Rome's political climate, Appian, Dio, Florus, Nicolaus of Damascus, Plutarch, Suetonius, and most eloquently, as always, Cicero. On Cicero, Plutarch, and Suetonius: for modern portraits, Everitt, 2003; and Elizabeth Rawson, *Cicero: A Portrait* (London: Bristol Classical Press, 2001). On the rain of honors, Appian, Cicero, Dio. For the geography of unlit Rome, the Janiculum Hill, etc.: Homo, 1951; Aly, 1989. On C and science, Monica Green, "The Transmission of Ancient Theories of Female Physiology and Disease through the Early Middle Ages" (Ph.D. dissertation, Princeton University, 1985), 156–61, 185–9; Albert Neuberger, *The Technical Arts and Sciences of the Ancients* (London: Kegan Paul, 2003); Margaret Ott, "Cleopatra VII: Stateswoman or Strumpet?" (MA thesis, University of Wisconsin, Eau Claire, 1976); Okasha El Daly, "'The Virtuous Scholar': Queen Cleopatra in Medieval Muslim Arab Writings," in Walker and Ashton, 2003, 51–6.

For the traditional Ides: Ovid, *Fasti*, iii, 523; Martial, *Epigrams*, IV.64. For the Ides of 44: Appian, II.111–119; Dio, XLIV; Florus, II.xiii.95; ND, 25.92, Fr. 130.19ff; JC, LXVI–LXVII; Plutarch, "Brutus," XIV–XVIII; MA, XIII–XIV; DJ, LXXXII; VP, LVI.

Cicero provides the earliest details, *De Divinatione*, II.ix.23. See also Balsdon, "The Ides of March," *Historia* 7 (1958): 80–94; Nicholas Horsfall, "The Ides of March: Some New Problems," *Greece & Rome* 21, no. 2 (1974): 191–99.

117 "Man is by nature": Aristotle, *Politics*, I.1253a.

117 "O would that the female sex": Euripides, "Cyclops," in *Euripides: Cyclops, Alcestis, Medea*, David Kovacs, ed., tr. (Cambridge: Harvard University Press, 1994), 185.

117 "I don't know how a man": Cicero to M. Curius, 200 (XII.28), c. August 46.

117 "general perturbation": Cicero to Rufus, 203 (IV.4), c. October 46.

118 "endless armed conflict": Cicero to A. Torquatus, 245 (VI.2), April 45.

118 C's fashion: On the hairstyle, Peter Higgs, "Searching for Cleopatra's Image: Classical Portraits in Stone," in Walker and Higgs, 2001, 203. On contemporary Egyptomania, Carla Alfano, "Egyptian Influences in Italy," Ibid., 276–91. See also Kleiner, 2005, 277–8.

118 "neither a chatterbox": Aulus Gellius, citing Varro, in *The Attic Nights*, XIII.xi.2–5. The translation is from Balsdon, 1969, 46.

118 chicken or the egg: For the dinner discussions, Plutarch, *Table Talk (Quaestiones Convivales)*, II.3 (635)–V.9 (684).

118 "He was not at all concerned": Dio, XLIII.xxviii.1.

119 "a great deal of barking": Ibid., XLVI.xxvi.2.

119 "I knew no security" to "treachery of old ones": Cicero to Cn. Plancius, 240 (IV.14), c. late 46.

120 "of a literary kind": Cicero to Atticus, 393.2 (XV.15), c. June 44.

121 "blood nor spirit": Cicero, *De Lege Agraria*, II.42.xvii (traslation modified).

121 whiff of dishonor: Cicero to Atticus, 25 (II.5), c. April 59.

121 "The arrogance of the Queen": Cicero to Atticus, 393 (XV.15), c. June 13, 44.

121 "a certain foolish vanity": Ibid., 38 (II.17), c. June 59.

121 Plutarch was more explicit: Plutarch, "Demosthenes and Cicero," II.1.

121–122 "He was the greatest boaster": Dio, XXXVIII.xii.7.

122 governed a vast kingdom: MA, LVI.

122 It bothered Cicero: As he put it in a summer 50 letter to Atticus, 117 (VI.3): "I have never put up with rudeness from the most powerful personages."

122 "rescue almost from the brink": Attributed to Sallust, "Letter to Caesar," XIII.5.

123 "was impossible to terrify": Appian, II.150.

123 "encouraged him and puffed him up": Dio, XLIV.iii.1–2.

125 "from one to another": Appian, II.117.

125 "bloodstained and cut": Ibid., III.35.

125 "Run!": Dio, XLIV.xx.3.

125 "the city looked as if": ND, 25.

127 The Helen of Troy comparison: Cicero, "Philippic" 2.XII.55. Nor does C figure on Florus's list of CR's misdeeds, Book II.

127 "because they wished" to "as he pleased": Dio, XLIV.vii.3–4.

127 "for the purpose of begetting": Suetonius, citing an anonymous source, DJ, LII.

127 "taking with him the resources": Ibid., LXXIX.

128 founder of the Roman Empire: Collins, 1959, 132.

128 "silly folk": DJ, LVI.

128 "And so, every kind of man": ND, 19.

129 "proud and thunderous" to "dirge-like": Appian, II.144–6.

130 "almost the whole city": Dio, XLV.xxiii.4–5.

130 bloodthirsty barbarians: For the Roman view of the "facile, fickle" (Dio, LI.xvii.1) Alexandrians, Reinhold, 1988, 227–8. Dio Chrysostom, "The 32nd Discourse"; Polybius, The Histories, XV.33; Philo (himself an Alexandrian), "Flaccus," V.32–35. Philo thought his countrymen unmatched in their insubordination, "being constantly in the habit of exciting great seditions from very small sparks" (Flaccus, IV.16). The emperor Hadrian wrote off the Alexandrians as "a rebellious, good-for-nothing, slanderous people," single-mindedly devoted to lucre. To Florence Nightingale, disembarking in 1849 and not at her enlightened best in Egypt, the Alexandrians were "the busiest and the noisiest people in the world," November 19, 1849, cited in Gerard Vallée, ed., *Florence Nightingale on Mysticism and Eastern Religions* (Waterloo: Wilfrid Laurier University Press, 2003), 144. For the Rome/Alexandria encounter, see also M. P. Charlesworth, "The Fear of the Orient in the Roman Empire," *Cambridge Historical Journal* 2, no. 1 (1926): 9–16; and Jasper Griffin, *Latin Poets and Roman Life* (London: Duckworth, 1985).

130 "for they stood in awe": Dio, XLIV.xv.2.

130 "I detest" to "have a spleen": Cicero to Atticus, 393 (XV.15), c. June 13, 44 (translation modified).

131 "regulations, favours, and gifts": Appian, II.133.

131 "an orgy of loot": Hirtius to Cicero, cited in Cicero to Atticus, 386 (XV.6), c. June 44.

131 "There is a very large element": Dio, XLV.viii.4.

131 "never showing its ordinary radiance": JC, LXIX (ML translation).

132 "Who can adequately express": VP, II.lxxv.

132 Visit of a sovereign: Plutarch, "Lucullus," II.5. Herod too is escorted by the authorities to Alexandria, JW, I.279.

133 "Alexandria is home": Cited in Siani-Davies, 2001, 105 ("Pro Rabirio Postumo," 13.35). Regarding Alexandria, Cicero continues: "It is from its inhabitants that writers of farces draw all their plots."

133 plenty of precedent: For example, Arrian, 6.28.3.

134 "There's a common proverb": Cicero to Plancus, 407 (X.20), May 29, 43.

134 "so utterly unsociable": Plutarch, "Demetrius," III.3.

135 Isis attire: Interview with Norma Goldman, October 19, 2009. Judith Lynn Sebesta and Larissa Bonfante, *The World of Roman Costume* (Madison: University of Wisconsin Press, 2001); Dorothy Burr Thompson, 1973, 30; Elizabeth J. Walters, *Attic Grave Reliefs that Represent Women in the Dress of Isis* (Princeton: American School of Classical Studies at Athens, 1988); Apuleius, *Metamorphoses*, XI.iii–iv.

135 Dendera: Goudchaux, "Cleopatra's Subtle Religious Strategy," 2001, 138–9; Bingen, 2007, 73; Kleiner, 2005, 85–8; Jan Quaegebeur, especially "Cléopâtre VII et le temple de Dendara," *Göttinger Miszellen* 120 (1991): 49–73. Nearly 1,900 years later Florence

Nightingale visited Dendera. Generally she had little patience for the Ptolemies; she remained unimpressed by the "acres of bas-reliefs" and the miles of sculpture. The complex struck her as vulgar. "The earliest name which you find there is of that vile C," she huffed, Vallée, 2003, 397. Nightingale certainly could not miss her; C appears no fewer than seventy-three times on the temple and chapel walls.

135 "I cannot describe": Cited in Michael D. Calabria, ed., *Florence Nightingale in Egypt and Greece* (Albany: SUNY Press, 1997), 31.

136 On the Caesareum: Philo, "On the Embassy to Gaius," C. D. Yonge, tr., *The Works of Philo* (Peabody, MA: Hendrickson Publishers, 1993), 150–1. See also Ferdinando Castagnoli, "Influenze alessandrine nell'urbanistica della Roma augustea," *Rivista di filologia e di istruzione classica* 109 (1981): 414–23; Ammianus Marcellinus, XXII.16.12.

136 intellectual revival: See Gabriele Marasco's fine "Cléopâtre et les sciences de son temps," *Sciences exactes et sciences appliquées à Alexandrie*, Gilbert Argoud and others, eds. (1998): 39–53; Fraser, 1972, I, 87, 311–22, 363, 490.

137 contradicting himself: Seneca, Epistle LXXXVIII.37. See also Athenaeus, IV.139. For the book-forgetter, Quintilian, 1.8.20–1; Ammianus Marcellinus, XXII.16.16; H. A. Russell, "Old Brass-Guts," *Classical Journal* 43:7, 1948, 431–2.

137 "intellectual stimulus": Rawson, 1985, 81.

138 "rubbed until it sprouts": Galen, cited by Ott, 1976, Appendix A, 33.

138 "all sorts of deadly" to "set one upon another": MA, LXXI.

138 "great scientific curiosity" to "an actual embryo": Cited in Ott, 1976, Appendix C, 35. Possibly another Queen C was intended. For C the scientist, see also Plant, 2004, 2–5, 135–47.

138 "that I always used": Cited in Monica Green, 1985, 186. For C's involvement with alchemy, see F. Sherwood Taylor, "A Survey of Greek Alchemy," *Journal of Hellenic Studies* 50, I (1930): 109–39. The word *alchemy*—Arabic in origin—postdates C. It did not help that various alchemists published under the pen name Cleopatra. See Plant, 2004, 145.

139 "magic arts and charms": Plutarch, MA, XXV.4 (ML translation).

139 "general malaise" to "hatred of evil": April 12, 41, cited in Marie-Thérèse Lenger, *Corpus des ordonnances des Ptolémées* (Brussels: Palais des Académies, 1964), 210–5.

140 "No wild beast": Plutarch, "Cicero," XLVI.

140 "what humiliations": Plutarch, "Cato the Younger," XXXV.4 (ML translation).

141 "she had not been terrified": Appian, V.8.

141 "the most aggressive of men": Ibid., II.88. His violent temper was legendary. Appian adds that the Parthian mounted bowmen joined Cassius of their own volition, attracted by his reputation, IV.59.

141 Brutus's stern reminder: Plutarch, "Brutus," XXVIII.

142 "not only ruined everything": Appian, V.8.

142–143 On Quintus Dellius: Seneca the Elder, *Suasoriae*, 1.8; JA, 14.394, 15.25; JW, 1.290; Seneca the Younger, *De Clementia*, I.x.1.

142–143 "had no sooner seen her face" to "kindest of soldiers": MA, XXV (ML translation).

143 Hera in the *Iliad:* It is unclear whether Plutarch or Dellius invokes the Homeric comparison, Ibid.

143 "accompanied by a remarkable crowd": Appian, III.12.

143 "a great halo": Dio, XLV.iv.4.

144 "the butchery" to "craftily and patiently": Appian, III.13–14.

144 "to stand behind me" to "other finery": Ibid., III.15–17.

145 "all the prestige": Florus, II.xv.2.

145 "that you in fact possess" to "good enough for me": Appian, III.18–19.

145–146 The hostilities to be encouraged: Appian, III.21, 85; Dio, XLV.xi.3–4, XLVI.xl.4, XLVI.xli.1.

146 malign, blackmail, slander: Quintus Fufius Calenus, cited in Dio, XLVI.viii.3–4.

146 "I don't trust his age": Cicero to Atticus, 419 (XVI.9), November 4, 44.

147 "my wonderful Dolabella": Cicero to Atticus, 369 (XIV.15), May 1, 44.

147 "No affection was": Cicero to Dolabella, 371A (XIV.17A), May 3, 44.

147 "The gall of the man!": Cicero to Atticus, 373 (XIV.18), May 9, 44.

148 "the systematic organization": Henry Adams, *The Education of Henry Adams* (New York: Library of America, 1990), 13. Adams was speaking of Massachusetts politics.

148 A's carousing wake: Suetonius, "On Rhetoricians," V (29).

148 "He was a spendthrift": VP on Curio the Younger, II.xlviii.4. Translation is from Cicero to Atticus, 14 (I.14), February 13, 61, editor's note.

148–149 "All over the city" to "their legacy?": Appian, III.28.

149 "to set them at odds": Dio, XLVI.xli.

149 provided that Octavian did: Ibid., 29.

149 wildly shouting oath after oath: Appian, III.39; Seneca on Octavian's temper, *De Clementia*, I.xi.1.

149 "On the other hand": Cicero to Atticus, 425.1 (XVI.14), c. November 44.

149 "The man who crushes": Cicero to Plancus, 393 (X.19), c. May 43.

150 "In truth, we ought not to think": Cicero, "Philippic," VI.III.7.

150 "the fume of debauch": Cicero, "Philippic," II.xii.30; "the belching," Cicero to Cornificius, 373 (XII.25), c. March 20, 43; "spewing," Cicero to Cassius, 344 (XII.2), c. late September 44.

150 "It is easy to inveigh": Cicero, "Pro Caelio," xii.29.

150 "And so, if by chance": Ibid., xvii.42.

150 "an air of high": Cicero to Quintus, 21.5 (III.1), September 54.

151 "would prefer to answer": Cicero, "Philippic," VI.ii.4. Why would A do so? Because, volunteered Cicero, "he so enjoys lecheries at home and murders in the forum."

151 "to exchange enmity": Appian, IV.2.

151 "Lepidus was actuated": Florus, II.xvi.6.

152 "their staunchest friends": Dio, XLVII.vi.1.

152 "Extra names": Appian, IV.5.

152 "The whole city filled": Dio, XLVII.iii.1. The heads were delivered for fixed rewards, the rest of the body left to rot in the street. You could tell that the wrong person had

been killed if the corpse retained its head. Appian, IV.15. On the ingenious wife, Appian, IV.40.

153 "his face wasted with anxiety": Plutarch, "Cicero," XLVII.3.

153 On Cicero's death: Appian, IV.19–20; Plutarch, "Cicero," XLVII; Dio, XLVII.viii; Eusebius, *Chronicles,* 184–3; Livy, "Fragments," CXX.

154 On Brutus's death: Florus, II.xvii.14–15; VP, II.lxx; Appian, IV.135; DA, XIII; Plutarch, "Brutus," LII–LIII.

154 "but its results": Dio, XLIV.ii.1.

154 a reputation for invincibility: Appian, V.58.

CHAPTER VI: WE MUST OFTEN SHIFT THE SAILS
WHEN WE WISH TO ARRIVE IN PORT

On A, his women, and his marriages, Eleanor Goltz Huzar's very fine "Mark Antony: Marriages vs. Careers," *Classical Journal* 81, no. 2 (1985/6): 97–111; the indispensable Pelling, 1999, as well as Pelling, *Plutarch and History: Eighteen Studies* (London: Duckworth, 2002). For C's arrival in Tarsus, Plutarch, with a little help from Athenaeus. Appian completes the picture, but without detail; Strabo and Xenophon (*Anabasis,* I.2.23) describe the city. Françoise Perpillou-Thomas gives a vivid idea of Egyptian entertaining, "Fêtes d'Egypte ptolémaïque et romaine d'après la documentation papyrologique grecque," *Studia Hellenistica* 31 (1993). For this and the subsequent chapter, the portrait of Herod is drawn primarily from Josephus, JA and JW. For modern biographies: Michael Grant, *Herod the Great* (London: Weidenfeld, 1971); A. H. M. Jones's excellent *The Herods of Judaea* (Oxford: Clarendon Press, 1967); Samuel Sandmel, *Herod: Profile of a Tyrant* (Philadelphia: Lippincott, 1967).

157 "We must often shift": Cicero to Lentulus Spinther, 20 (I.9), December 54. The (loose) translation is from Boissier, 1970, 223. "Unchanging consistency of standpoint has never been considered a virtue in great statesmen," explained Cicero, justifying his change of horses.

157 "Yet what difference": Aristotle, *The Politics,* II.vi.4–7.

157 seemed uncannily: Appian, IV.129.

158 "had known her" to "intellectual power": MA, XXV.

158 "puts the height of beauty": Pelling, 1999, 186.

158 "the greatest confidence" to "as if in mockery": MA, XXV.4–XXVI.1. The latter from the ML translation, where the Loeb has "she so despised and laughed the man to scorn as to sail up the river." The point is that C was neither cowed nor impressed by A. There is a less strategic explanation for the delay as well: The high priest of Egypt died on July 14. C may have been detained by clerical responsibilities.

159 The trip across the Mediterranean: Again reconstructed with the assistance of Lionel Casson, interview, January 26, 2009. As Casson put it: "The only possible conclusion is that Cleopatra dolled up a local river boat," letter to author, March 22, 2009.

159–160 "She herself reclined" to "good of Asia": MA, XXVI (translation modified).

160 "Affecting the same pursuits": Flatterer, 51e (translation modified). France Le Corsu argues, not altogether convincingly, that C posed in Tarsus as Isis rather than Aphrodite, "Cléopâtre-Isis," in *Bulletin de la Société Francaise d'Egyptologie*, Paris, 1978, no.82, 22–33.

161 "At once, then, wishing": MA, XXVI.4.

161 "a spectacle that has seldom": Ibid., XXVI.4 (ML translation).

161 On the jewelry: Thompson, 1973, 29; O. E. Kaper to author, March 6, 2010.

162 "that all these objects": Athenaeus, IV.147f.

162 "litters and bearers": Athenaeus, 148b.

162 "beggared description": Plutarch, MA, XXVI.4.

162 "Kings would come": Ibid., XXIV.

162 "irresistible charm" to "her discourse": Ibid., XXVII.

163 Proudly she catalogued: "She did not excuse herself so much as present a list of what she had done for him and Octavian," Appian, V.8.

163–164 "was ambitious to surpass" to "rusticity": MA, XXVII.

164 "Perceiving that his raillery": Ibid., XXVII (ML translation).

164 "she wished to rule": Ibid., X.

165 "so that neither the senate": Dio, XLVIII.iv.1.

165 "no mean city": Paul the Apostle, in Acts of the Apostles, 21:39.

166 On the mess made of Tarsus: Cassius Parmensis to Cicero, 419 (XII.13), June 13, 43; Appian, IV.ixiv and V.vii. Dio claims the Tarsans were so devoted to CR that they had changed the name of their city to Juliopolis, XLVII.xxvi.2. See also Dio Chrysostom, "The 33rd Discourse."

166 "bold coquette": Plutarch, JC, XLIX.2.

166 "The moment he saw her": Appian, V.8.

166 "succumbed with good will": Syme, 2002, 214. For Syme's doubts, 274–5. This too is conjecture, though the opposite assertions have been made with equal certainty, concerning both A and CR. See Anatole France's C, in *On Life and Letters* (London: Bodley Head, 1924): "It is certain that Caesar loved Cleopatra" (114) vs. Froude, 1879: "Nor is it likely that, in a situation of so much danger and difficulty as that in which he [CR] found himself, he would have added to his embarrassments by indulging in an intrigue at all" (456). Froude equally doubts C's visit to CR in Rome. Gruen scrubs that stay of all romance.

167 "and yet it was thought": Plutarch, "Alexander the Great," XLVII. He was writing of Alexander's useful marriage to a Bactrian princess.

167 "brought him to fall in love": JA, XIV.324 (in William Whiston's translation [Nashville, TN: Thomas Nelson, 1998]).

168 "not only because of his intimacy": JA, XV.93.

168 a slave to his love: See for example Florus, II.XXI.11.

168 "an ill name for familiarity": MA, VI.5 (ML translation).

168 On the Temple of Artemis: NH, XXXVI.xxi; Livy, *History of Rome*, I.XLIV. Pliny

provides a fine description of the temple construction. So difficult has it been to settle the main lintel into place that the architect contemplated suicide.

168 "Now Cleopatra had put to death": JW, I.360 (Whiston translation). Similarly JA, XV.89. Josephus continues: Having killed off her own family, one after another, until no relative remained, C "was now thirsting for the blood of foreigners."

168 Arsinoe had conspired: See P. J. Bicknell, "Caesar, Antony, Cleopatra and Cyprus," *Latomus* 36 (1977): 325–42, for an elaborate case that Arsinoe had been rehabilitated and set up as a secondary Ptolemaic ruler, a foil to her sister, after the triumph of 46. Green, 1990, subscribes to the theory as well, 669. Strabo indeed has A giving Cyprus to both sisters, 14.6.6.

169 "So straight away": Appian, V.9.

169 "distributing rewards": AW, 65.

169 A's neglect of affairs: Appian, V.10.

170 "He suffered her to hurry": MA, XXVIII.

170–171 "not ruled by himself" to "ordinary person": Appian, V.11.

171 "the sports and diversions": MA, XXVII.1.

171 "The members": Ibid., XXVIII (ML translation).

171 The kitchen chaos: Athenaeus, X.420e.

172 "The guests are not many": Plutarch, MA, XXVIII (ML translation).

172 "It is no easy matter to create harmony": Cicero to Quintus, 1.36 (I.1), c. 60–59.

172 On C as horsewoman: Pomeroy, 1990, 20–3; interview with Branko van Oppen, February 27, 2010. Arsinoe III helped to rally the Ptolemaic army, presumably on horseback, Polybius, V. 79–80.

172–173 "some fresh delight" to "serving maiden": MA, XXIX. There is an alternate explanation for the masquerade. Herod was known to stroll disguised at night among his people so as to gauge the political climate. He was not alone in the practice.

173 "You are forever being frivolous": Dio Chrysostom, "The 32nd Discourse," I.

173–174 "coarse wit" to "comic mask with them": MA, XXIX.

174 "to whom his sojourn": Appian, V.I.11.

174 "was often disarmed by Cleopatra": Plutarch, "Demetrius and Antony," III.3.

175 "Leave the fishing rod" to "kingdoms, and continents": MA, XXIX (translation modified).

175 "For such a rebuke": Flatterer, 61b. Shakespeare packaged the same formula differently: "Other women cloy the appetites they feed, but she makes hungry where most she satisfies."

176 "Although I have made enquiries": Appian, V.21.

176 "so under the sway": Dio, XLVIII.xxvii.1.

176 "for teaching Antony": MA, X.

177 "that he would rather die": Appian, V.55.

177 "that if Italy remained at peace": Ibid., V.19.

177 "because she was angry with Antony": Ibid., V.59.

177 "his passion for Cleopatra": Dio, XLVIII.xxviii.3.

177 "at least an infinitely loyal": Balsdon, 1962, 49.

177 "now rid of an interfering woman": Appian, V.59. Similarly, Dio, XLVIII.xxviii.3–4.

178 "a great and mighty shout" to "necks as they dived": Dio, XLVIII.xxxvii.2.

178 "their ships were moored": Appian, V.73.

179 "A wonder of a woman" to "complete salvation": MA, XXXI. Tacitus suggests that A's marriage to Octavia was a trap from the start, Annals, I.X.

181 an object of gossip: Boccaccio, *Concerning Famous Women* (New Brunswick: Rutgers University Press, 1963), 192.

181–182 "immediately praised to the skies" to "savior gods": Appian, V.74.

182 A's rescue of Octavian: Appian, V.67–8.

183 "rash boy": Ibid., III.43 (Loeb translation).

183 "behaved with excessive sportsmanship": DA, LXXI. Translation from Everitt, 2003, 265.

184 "guardian genius" to "that young man": MA, XXXIII. Similarly Flatterer, "The Fortune of the Romans," 319–320. C is absent from the *Moralia* account, in which Plutarch makes the soothsayer A's friend, "often wont to speak freely to him and admonish him." Surveying A's greater age, experience, renown, and army, the amateur astrologer offers A the same advice concerning Octavian: "Avoid him!" To Neal, 1975, the warning was a veiled one against breaking openly with Octavian. C preferred that A make his name in the east, which would obviate the need for a showdown, 102.

184–185 "lay inside with his friends" to "the ceilings": Athenaeus, IV.148c.

185 "Nearly everything" to "against the Parthians": Dio, XLVIII.liv.7.

186 "lulled to rest": MA, XXXVI. Writing a morality tale, Plutarch had set out to demonstrate "that great natures exhibit great vices also, as well as great virtues," "Demetrius," I.

187 On the coins: Walker and Higgs, 2001, 237; Jonathan Williams, "Imperial Style and the Coins of Cleopatra and Mark Antony," in Walker and Ashton, 2003, 88; Agnes Baldwin Brett, "A New Cleopatra Tetradrachm of Ascalon," *American Journal of Archaeology* 41, no. 3 (1937): 461. As Theodore V. Buttrey notes ("*Thea Neotera*: On Coins of Antony and Cleopatra," *American Numismatic Society Notes* 6, [1954], 95–109), Ptolemaic couples never appear pictured on opposite faces of a coin.

CHAPTER VII: AN OBJECT OF GOSSIP FOR THE WHOLE WORLD

For the best guide to the baroque composition of the East and its colorful parade of dynasts, see Sullivan, 1990. On A's eastern politics, Albert Zwaenepoel, "La politique orientale d'Antoine," *Etudes Classiques* 18:1 (1950): 3–15; Lucile Craven, *Antony's Oriental Policy Until the Defeat of the Parthian Expedition* (Columbia: University of Missouri, 1920); Neal, 1975; A. N. Sherwin-White, *Roman Foreign Policy in the East* (London: Duckworth, 1984). As in the previous chapter, the portrait of Herod is drawn from Josephus's colorful account. On Antioch, A. F. Norman, ed., *Antioch as a Centre of Hellenic Culture as Observed by Libanius* (Liverpool: Liverpool University Press, 2000); Libanius, and Cicero. On C's titles and heritage, "Cléopâtre VII Philopatris," *Chronique d'Egypte* 74 (1999): 118–23. For the Donations, K. W. Meiklejohn, "Alexander Helios and Caesarion," *Journal of Roman Studies* 24 (1934): 191–5.

On Octavian, G. W. Bowersock, *Augustus and the Greek World* (Oxford: Clarendon Press, 1965); Everitt, 2006; Kurt A. Raaflaub and Mark Toher, eds., *Between Republic and Empire* (Berkeley: University of California Press, 1990).

189 "The greatest achievement": Thucydides, *History of the Peloponnesian War*, II.xlv. Translation from David Markson, *The Last Novel* (Berkeley: Shoemaker and Hoard, 2007), 107. Markson notes that Thucydides does women the great favor of mentioning none.

189 "slinked into": Strabo, 16.2.46.

189–190 The inexhaustible Herod: JW, I.238–40, 429–30; the miraculous escape: JW, I.282–4, 331–4, 340–1, among others; astonishing talent: JA, XV.5; Senate confirmation: JW, I.282–85; AJ, XIV.386–7.

191 "noble families were extended": MA, XXXVI.

191 "into his predecessor's bedroom slippers": Everitt, 2006, 148.

191–192 "realms and islands": Shakespeare, *Antony and Cleopatra*, V.2.111–13.

192 "The greatness of the Roman empire": MA, XXXVI.

192 "an army more conspicuous": Ibid., XLIII.

192 "made all Asia quiver": Ibid., XXXVII.

192 "the nobility of his family": Ibid., XLIII (ML translation).

193 no one in the Mediterranean world: Interview with Casson, June 11, 2009. Strabo writes the gift down to cedar, 14.5.3.

193 The disapproving Plutarch: MA, XXXVI.

193 Sixteenth regnal year: By our count it would be fifteen; the ancients had no zero.

194 "It seems to me": Bingen, 1999, 120.

195 Even Plutarch could not call it a mistake: Plutarch, "Demetrius and Antony," I.2. He recoiled from A's marriage to C, "although she was a woman who surpassed in power and splendour all the royalties of her time" excepting only — as Plutarch saw it — the Parthian king.

195 A's attachment to women: Appian, V.76. Dio, XLVIII.xxiv.2–3 has A falling head over heels for C.

197 On Jericho: Strabo, 16.1.15; Justin, 36.iii.1–7; Florus, I.xl.29–30; JW, I.138–9; JW, IV.451–75; HN, XII.111–24; Diodorus, II.xlviii; JW, I.138–9. For incense, balsam, bitumen, and their uses, A. Lucas, *Ancient Egyptian Materials and Industries* (London: Edward Arnold, 1962).

198 "King of a wilderness": JA, XIV.484; similarly JW, I.355.

198 "it would be unsafe": JA, XV.107. Josephus further credits C with the death of Malchus, as with a Syrian king, JW, I.440.

199 "In this way, he said": Ibid., XV.99–100.

199 "laid a treacherous snare": Ibid., XV.98 (Whiston translation).

199 "for she was by nature" to "a slave to her lusts": Ibid., XV.97.

200 "his love would flame up": Ibid., XV.101.

200 "being against such a woman": Ibid., XV.101 (Whiston translation).

200 "one night even forced": JW, I.498. In accusing ND of having recast history, Josephus cites his "false charges of licentiousness" against Mariamme, concocted to justify her unjustifiable murder (JA, XVI.185).

202 "to make one feel": Aristeas, *The Letter of Aristeas*, 99. See also JW, V.231; Philo, "On the Migration of Abraham," 102–5 for the high priest's attire.

202–203 "the offspring of some god" to "she might ask": JA, XV.26–27.

203 "to use him for erotic purposes": Ibid., XV.29.

203 "in slavery and fear" to "she possibly could": Ibid., XV.45–6.

203–204 "it is right for women": From "Helen," in *Euripides II*, 1969, 325.

204 "hatred of him was as great": JW, I.437.

204 palace pool: Nielsen, 1999, on Herod's palaces. Also JA, XV.54–5.

205 "that Herod, who had been appointed": JA, XV.63.

205–206 "it was improper" to "charges against him": Ibid., XV.76–77.

206 "wicked woman": Ibid., XV.91.

206 "There seems to be some pleasure": From "The Phoenician Women," in *Euripides V: Electra, The Phoenician Women, The Bacchae*, David Grene and Richmond Lattimore, eds; Elizabeth Wyckoff, tr. (Chicago: University of Chicago Press, 1959), 200.

206 The fortified Masada: JW, VII.300–1.

206 "a ready ear only for slander": Ibid., I.534.

207 "struck him like a thunderbolt" to "of his life": Ibid., I.440.

207 C's intelligence: According to Cicero, a letter took forty-seven days to travel from Cappadocia to Rome.

208 preparing the silver denarii: Andrew Meadows to author, May 24, 2010.

208 "there is no other medicine": From "The Bacchae," in *Euripides V*, 282–3.

208 "an abundance of clothing": MA, LI. The disgruntled rumor appears both in Plutarch and in Dio, XLIX.xxxi.1.

209 "a yawning and abysmal desert": Plutarch, "Crassus," XXII.4. On the pitiful state of A's men, Florus, II.xx.

209 "For so eager was he": MA, XXXVII; Livy, "Summaries," 130.

209–210 "sharing in the toils": MA, XLIII.

210 "neither reproached him with his treachery": Ibid., L.

210 "called for a dark robe": Ibid., XLIV.

210 "by an extraordinary perversion": Florus, II.xx. See also VP, II.lxxxii, and Dio, XLIX.32.

211–212 "Neither in youthfulness nor beauty": MA, LVII.

212 "her pleasurable society" to "live with him": Ibid., LIII.

212–213 "wearing her life away": Flatterer, 61b.

213 "as long as she could see him": MA, LIII. For C's effect even on A's associates, Dio, L.v.3.

213 a happy subordinate: Dio, XLVIII.xxvii.2.

213 "failed to see": Flatterer, 61b.

213 "it was an infamous thing": MA, LIV.

213 "the passion and witchery": Dio, XLIX.xxxiv.1. For "certain drugs," MA, XXXVII.

215 "In his endeavor to take vengeance": Dio, XLIX.xxxix.2.

215 On Artavasdes: Dio, XLIX.xxxx.1–3; VP, II.82.4; MA, L.6; Plutarch, "Crassus," XXXIII; Livy, "Summaries," 131. On the triumph that was not a triumph, see Beard, 2007, 266–9.

217 C in her Isis regalia: Ashton, 2008, 138–9; Baudoin Van de Walle, "La Cléopâtre de Mariemont," *Chronique d'Egypte*, 24, 1949, 28–9; interview with Branko van Oppen, February 28, 2010.

217 A dressed as Dionysus: VP, II.lxxxii.4.

218 coins minted for the occasion: Buttrey, 1954, 95–109.

218 "the two most magnificent people": Macurdy, 1932, 205. Bevan, 1968, best describes C's golden age: For a second time in a decade, she "saw herself within measurable distance of becoming Empress of the world," 377.

218 The Jews and C's rule: See W. W. Tarn, "Alexander Helios and the Golden Age," *Journal of Roman Studies* 22, II (1932): 142. On the Jews generally in C's time, Victor Tcherikover, *Hellenistic Civilization and the Jews* (Peabody, MA: Hendrickson, 1999).

219 said to be busy: Dio, XLIX.xli.6.

220 "theatrical and arrogant": MA, LIV.3.

221 "a Dionysiac revel": Huzar, 1985/6, 108.

CHAPTER VIII: ILLICIT AFFAIRS AND BASTARD CHILDREN

On the war of propaganda: Dio, Plutarch, Suetonius. Among modern studies of the surviving evidence, M. P. Charlesworth, "Some Fragments of the Propaganda of Mark Antony," *Classical Quarterly* 27, no. 3/4 (1933): 172–7; Joseph Geiger, "An Overlooked Item of the War of Propaganda between Octavian and Antony," *Historia* 29 (1980): 112–4; and Kenneth Scott, "The Political Propaganda of 44–30 BC," *Memoirs of the American Academy in Rome* XI (1933): 7–49. No one makes sense of the battle of Actium, but John Carter and William Murray come closest. See Murray's painstaking and ingenious reconstruction of the events in "Octavian's Campsite Memorial for the Actium War," in William M. Murray and Photios M. Petsas, *Transactions of the American Philosophical Society* 79, no. 4 (1989): 1–172; and Carter, 1970; as well as in Carter's notes on the engagement in *Cassius Dio: The Roman History* (New York: Penguin, 1987), 266. On the battle, the winds, the site, interviews with William Murray, October 14, 2009, and March 3, 2010. See also W. W. Tarn, "The Battle of Actium," *Journal of Roman Studies* 21 (1931): 173–99; Casson, 1991. On ND, Plutarch, *Table Talk*, VIII.iv.723; Bowersock, 1965, 124–5, 134–8; and

Mark Toher, "The Terminal Date of Nicolaus's Universal History," *Ancient History Bulletin* 1.6 (1987): 135–8. Angelos Chaniotis is very good on women and warfare, *War in the Hellenistic World* (Oxford: Blackwell, 2005), 110ff.

For the Greek stay, the work of Christian Habicht, especially "Athens and the Ptolemies," *Classical Antiquity* 11, no. 1 (April 1992): 68–90. Seneca, *Suasoriae,* 1.7, mentions lampoons against A in Athens.

223 "illicit affairs": Lucan, X.76. The translation is from Jones, 2006, 66.

223 "For talk is evil": Hesiod, *Works and Days,* 760. See also Achilles Tatius, VI.10: Virgil's *Aeneid,* IV.240–265: "Slander is sharper than any sword, stronger than fire, more persuasive than a siren; rumor is more slippery than water, runs faster than the wind, flies quicker than any winged bird."

223 "the abundance that flowed": Theocritus, Idyll 17 (translation modified).

224 "galleries, libraries": Philo, "On the Embassy to Gaius," 151. The translation is from Forster, 2004, 133.

224 "if ever that kingdom": Diodorus, XXXIII.28b.3.

224 the kind of man you could rely on: JA, XVII.99–100. Also on ND, Plutarch, *Table Talk,* VIII.iv.723.

225 sea nymph imitation: VP, II.lxxxiii.

225 "All of this I bestow": MA, XXVIII.

225 The basalt inscription: See P. M. Fraser, "Mark Antony in Alexandria—A Note," *Journal of Roman Studies* 47:1–2 (1957): 71–3.

225 The Roman bodyguards: Dio, L.v.1.

225–226 The tax exemptions: See Peter van Minnen, "An Official Act of Cleopatra," *Ancient Society* 30 (2000): 29–34; van Minnen, "Further Thoughts on the Cleopatra Papyrus," *Archiv für Papyrusforschung* 47 (2001): 74–80; van Minnen, "A Royal Ordinance of Cleopatra and Related Documents," Walker and Ashton, 2003, 35–42.

226 "only made them come back": Ibid., 79.

226 "joined him in the management": Dio, L.v.1–2.

226 The young Canidius: Plutarch, "Brutus," III.

227 "disturb the auspicious respect": Appian, V.144. For Sextus Pompey generally, Appian, V.133–45.

228 A's numerous misdeeds: Dio, XLVI.x.3.

229 "good fellowship": MA, XXXII.

229 "a veritable weakling": Dio, L.xviii.3.

229 According to Suetonius: DA, LXIX. Sejanus was much later said to do the same, "for by maintaining illicit relations with the wives of nearly all the distinguished men, he learned what their husbands were saying and doing," Dio, LVIII.3.

230 "invidious wealth" to "solid glory": Cicero, "Philippic," V, xviii.50.

230 "screwing the queen" to "get it up?": DA, LXIX. I have borrowed Andrew Meadows's earthy translation, Walker and Higgs, 2001, 29.

230 "amorous adventures": Dio, LI.viii.2.

231 On Ephesus: Hopkins, *A World Full of Gods* (New York: Plume, 2001), 200–205. Strabo, 14.1.24; NH, V.xxxi.15. Craven, 1920, 22, points out that Ephesus was the seat

of the Roman proconsul in Asia; the public records and treasury were there. It was a logical business address for A.

232 "By certain documents": Dio, L.ii.6.

232 "to sail to Egypt": MA, LVI.

232 Acquiring an empire with money: Plutarch, "Aemilius Paulus," XII.9.

233 "was inferior in intelligence" to "large affairs": MA, LVI.

234 "a rabble of Asiatic performers": MA, XXIV.

234 "And while almost all the world" to "entertainments and gifts": Ibid., LVI.

234 A as Dionysus: On the power of the mythologies, see H. Jeanmarie, "La politique religieuse d'Antoine et de Cléopâtre," *Revue Archéologique* 19 (1924): 241–61.

234 Athenian statue-erecting: Nepos, XXV Atticus, III.2.

235 The Ptolemaic statuary: Pausanias, 1.8.9; Habicht, 1992, 85. NH, 34, 37.

235 "by many splendid gifts": MA, LVII.

235 The Pergamum library: See Casson, 2001, 48–50. Casson has suggested this was a shrewd way of shrugging off a financial burden. There was no real need for the Pergamum library, in Roman hands already for a century.

235 "Many times, while he was seated": MA, LVIII.

235 "wanton bits": Plutarch, "Brutus," V; "Cato the Younger," XXIV.

236 "sprang up from his tribunal": MA, LVIII.

236 kissing his wife in public: Plutarch, "Marcus Cato," XVII.7.

236 "in compliance with some agreement": MA, LVIII.

236 what eunuchs did: Dio, L.xxv.2; Horace, Epodes, IX.

236 The divorce: Neal is especially lucid on the subject, 1975, 110.

237 "which had hitherto veiled": Plutarch, "Pompey," LIII.

238 "required a sober head" to "scurrilities": MA, LIX. For Geminius's heartache, see Plutarch, "Pompey," II.

238 "Treachery," it would be said: VP, II.lxxxiii. For the desertions see also Dio, L.iii.2–3; for Dellius's weakness of heart, Appian, V.50, 55, 144.

238 A's will: Either Dio has his chronology wrong or we all do: He seems to imply (L.xx.7) that Octavian hunted down the will at least a year earlier, before the Donations, which would entirely change the complexion of that ceremony.

239 "should be borne in state": MA, LVIII.

239 "honeyballs of phrases": Petronius, *Satyricon,* I.

239 the Orient and sex: On the "almost uniform association between the Orient and sex," its "sexual promise (and threat), untiring sensuality, unlimited desire, deep generative energies," see Edward W. Said, *Orientalism* (New York: Vintage, 1994), 188; and Flatterer, 56e. For Flaubert in the mid-nineteenth century, the courtesan of old was "the embracing, strangling viper of the Nile."

239 "In his hand was a golden scepter": Florus, II.xxi.11.

240 "bewitched by that accursed woman": Dio, L.xxvi.5.

240 "Then as his love for Cleopatra": VP, II.lxxxii.

240 "melts and unmans": MA, LIII (ML translation).

240 "a slave to his love": Florus, II.xxi.11; "he gave not a thought": Dio, XLVIII.xxiii.2;

"he was not even a master of himself": MA, LX. Plutarch on Omphale, "Demetrius and Antony," III.3.

241 "The Egyptian woman demanded": Florus, II.xxi.11.

241 "For she so charmed": Dio, L.v.4.

241 Reports circulated: Strabo accuses A of pillaging the best art he could find for C, from the temples of Samos and elsewhere, 13.1.30, 14.1.14; also NH, XXXIV 8.19.58.

241 "longed with womanly desire": Eutropius, VII.7.

241 "that the greatest wars": Athenaeus, XIII.560b. He adds that Egyptian women were known to be "far more amorous than other women."

241 "I don't much like": Plautus, "The Pot of Gold," 167–9. The translation is from Skinner, 2005, 201.

242 "Would a woman": Lucan, X.67.

242 A just declaration of war: Livy, 1.32.5–14. On the traditional procedure, Meyer Reinhold, "The Declaration of War against Cleopatra," *Classical Journal* 77, no. 2 (1981–2): 97–103; also R. M. Ogilvie, *A Commentary on Livy, Books 1–5* (Oxford: Clarendon Press, 1978), 127–8; and Thomas Wiedemann, "The Fetiales: A Reconsideration," *Classical Quarterly* 36, no. 2 (1986): 478–90. It is Wiedemann who speculates that Octavian invented the rite.

243 "had voluntarily taken up": Dio, L.vi.1.

243 "What in the world does he mean": Ibid., L.xxi.3.

243 "is at war with me": Ibid., L.xxi.1.

244 "For I adjudged" to "passed against her": Ibid., L.xxvi.3.

245 "as a whole far surpassed": Ibid., L.vi.2–3.

245 "he sought a reputation": Florus, I.xlv.19.

245 "spying upon and annoying": Dio, L.xi.1.

245 The Acropolis statues: Ibid., L.viii.1–5, L.xv.3.

245–246 "Hail Caesar": Macrobius, *Saturnalia*, 2.4.29.

246 "desired to be the ruler": Nepos, "Atticus," XX.4.

246 A's status in Egypt: Generally categories were more fluid in Egypt, where Alexander the Great could become a pharaoh, a female ruler could reign as a king, and the divinities tended to run together. Rome preferred clearer distinctions. Not coincidentally, Latin is "much less hospitable than Greek to compound words and neologisms," Rawson, 2001, 232.

246 One of the greatest twentieth-century classicists: Tarn (and Charlesworth), 1965, 96–7.

247 "we who are Romans": Dio, L.xxiv.3.

247 "for it is impossible": Ibid., L.xxvii.4. He could have been quoting Cicero, who railed against a man "debauched, immodest, effeminate, even when in fear never sober," "Philippic," III.v.12.

247 "are most wanton": ND, Fr. 129. On the costly furniture, DA, LXX.

247 in such a contest: Dio, L.xxviii.6.

248 "this pestilence of a woman": Dio, L.xxiv.5 (Penguin translation).

248 "to conquer and rule" to "equal to a man": Ibid., L.xxviii.3–4.

248 "What is there dreadful in Caesar's": MA, LXII.

248 What does our history mean: Propertius, *Elegies,* 3.11.47–68. On C as a paltry triumph, *Elegies* 4.6.64–6. Nourse, 2002, 128, notes that the Greeks perceived "woman as dangerously emotional and destructively petty when allowed access to power." The magistrate who faces off against Lysistrata in Aristophanes makes a different point. "But men must never, ever be worsted by women!" he cries, handing the baton directly to Lucan and Propertius.

249 infinitely more suitable as a battle site: Dio, L.xii.8.

249 The color of the Actium camp: For the Median vests, Plutarch, "Paulus," XVIII and XXX–XXXII; the Ptolemaic military cloak comes from Athenaeus, V.196f. According to Sallust, the Armenian army was famed for its gorgeous armor. The decorated arms, Mayor, 2010, 11–12, 206; Walker and Higgs, 2001, 264. Plutarch supplies some description of a military camp in his life of Brutus; Josephus vividly evokes its precision in JW, III.77–102. There is some debate about the *Antonia's* purple sails, despite NH, XIX.V, and Casson's conviction about them, interview of January 26, 2009. William Murray believes they may constitute a literary flourish; interview of March 3, 2010. In any event the ship would have been magnificently carved.

249 "For extravagance in other objects": Plutarch, "Philopoemen," IX.3.7.

250 some familiar advice: JW, I.389–90.

250 "May your Lordship": Cited in Antonia Fraser, *The Warrior Queens* (New York: Knopf, 1989), 190.

250–251 A's officers on C: Suetonius, "Nero," III; Appian, IV.38.

251 Ahenobarbus and A in Parthia: MA, XL.

252 eating stale bread: Plutarch, "Caius Marius," VII. He was meant as well to sleep on a simple pallet, which A surely did not do with C in camp.

252 "his ears, it seems": JW, I.390.

252 "abused by Cleopatra": MA, LVIII.

253 "The chief task of a good general": Plutarch, "Agesilaus and Pompey," IV.

253 A's distrust of C: NH, 21.12.

254 Dellius's desertion: VP, II.lxxxiv; Dio, L.xiii.8.

255 blundered grievously: Plutarch, "Pompey," LXXVI; Appian, II.71. The results were pitiful, JC, XLV.

255 "I have chosen to begin": Dio, L.xix.5.

255 "For in general": Ibid., L.iii.2–3.

255 "in miserable logs" to "conquer our enemies or die": MA, LXIV.

255 "better endowed": Ibid., XL.

257 "Since, then, they admit": Dio, L.xxx.3–4.

258 Dio suggests that A fled: Ibid., L.xxxiii.3–4.

258–259 "he went forward alone" to "eat and sleep together": MA, LXVII. It is entirely possible that Plutarch invented the sulk, or introduced it prematurely. It may equally well have been retrofitted to the story, along with C's treachery. See also VP, II.lxxxv.

259 purple and gold spangles: Florus, II.xxi.

260 The floral decorations: Dio, LI.v.4.

260 scale of his victory: Murray, 1989, 142, persuasively argues that before and after Actium Octavian captured some 350 ships, including several equally as large as C's flagship.

For C's final days we are almost exclusively alone with Dio and Plutarch; Eusebius, Eutropius, Horace, Suetonius, and Velleius make ancillary contributions. On Plutarch's approach to C's death, Pelling, 2002, is particularly fine, 106ff. See also J. Gwyn Griffiths, "The Death of Cleopatra VII," *Journal of Egyptian Archeology* 47 (Dec. 1961): 113–8; Yolande Grisé, *Le suicide dans la Rome antique* (Montreal: Bellarmin, 1982); Saul Jarcho, "The Correspondence of Morgagni and Lancisi on the Death of Cleopatra," *Bulletin of the History of Medicine* 43, no. 4 (1969): 299–325; W. R. Johnson, "A Quean, A Great Queen? Cleopatra and the Politics of Misrepresentation," *Arion* VI, no. 3 (1967): 387–402; Gabriele Marasco, "Cleopatra e gli esperimenti su cavie umane," *Historia* 44 (1995): 317–25. Francesco Sbordone, "La morte di Cleopatra nei medici greci," *Rivista Indo-Greco-Italica* 14 (1930): 1–20; T. C. Skeat's ingenious chronology of C's end, "The Last Days of Cleopatra," *Journal of Roman Studies* 13 (1953): 98–100; Tarn, 1931. On the fates of C's children, Meiklejohn, 1934.

For a nuanced account of the triumph and the fallout from Actium, see Robert Alan Gurval, *Actium and Augustus: The Politics and Emotions of Civil War* (Ann Arbor: University of Michigan Press, 1998).

For C's enduring, evolving image, or how she entered into modern mythology: Mary Hamer, *Signs of Cleopatra* (London: Routledge, 1993); Lucy Hughes-Hallett, *Cleopatra: Histories, Dreams and Distortions* (New York: Harper & Row, 1990); Richardine G. Woodall, "Not Know Me Yet? The Metamorphosis of Cleopatra" (PhD dissertation, York University, 2004); Wyke, 2002, 195–320.

261 "The wickedest woman": Cecil B. DeMille, cited in Michelle Lovric, *Cleopatra's Face* (London: British Museum Press, 2001), 83.

261 "I was equal to gods": Euripides, "Hekabe," in *Grief Lessons: Four Plays by Euripides*, Anne Carson, tr. (New York: New York Review of Books, 2006), 371–2.

261 Misfortune, went the saying: Euripides, "Heracles," in *Euripides II*, 560.

261 She did not care to watch them: Dio, LI.v.5.

262 "a most bold and wonderful" to "war and slavery": Plutarch, LXIX (ML translation). For an intriguing take on A and C's post-Actium plans, see Claude Nicolet's "Où Antoine et Cléopâtre voulaient-ils aller?," *Semitica* 39 (1990): 63–6.

262 the monstrosity of a vessel: Athenaeus, V.203e–204d.

262 The Nabateans: Strabo extends their territory from southern Jordan to the head of the Gulf of Eilat, 16.4.21–6.

263 "every bit of his soul": JA, XV.190. Similarly if less dramatically, JW, I.388–94. Herod's

cozying up to Octavian looked nobler in retrospect: "And when war had been declared by the Romans on all the monarchs in the world, our kings alone, by reason of their fidelity, remained their allies and friends," explains Josephus, *Against Apion*, II, 134.

263 "the new Hannibal": On Sertorius, Plutarch, "Pompey," XVII–XIX; Plutarch, "Cato the Younger," LIX; Dio, LI.viii.6.

265 "without having accomplished anything": Dio, LI.v.6.

265 Octavian's assassination: Ibid., LI.vi.4.

265 A's modest hut: Strabo, 17.1.9.

265 "for he himself also had been wronged": MA, LXIX.

265 Dio slips in a bitter note: Dio, LI.vii.2–3.

266 "at such a time there is no use": Flatterer, 69a.

266 "irresistible courage": Appian, IV.112.

266 "set the whole city": MA, LXXI (ML translation).

266 "to continue the struggle": Dio, LI.vi.1.

266–267 Caesarion was hailed as pharaoh: Walker and Higgs, 2001, 175.

267 "for she hoped that even if": Dio, LI.vi.6.

267 "amorous adventures" to "might be saved": Ibid., LI.viii.2–3.

267 rank and file in check: Ibid., LI.iii.4.

268 "a woman who was haughty": MA, LXXIII.

268 "thought it her due": Dio, LI.viii.7. To C's list of Roman conquests, Plutarch offhandedly and illogically adds Cn. Pompey, MA, XXV.4.

268 "to hang him up": MA, LXXII.

269 "suited to her fallen fortunes" to "went away rich": Ibid., LXXIII (ML translation).

269 "splendor, luxury, and sumptuosity": Ibid., LXXI (ML translation).

270 "surpassingly lofty": Ibid., LXXIV.

270 "that Antony and Cleopatra learned": Dio, LI.v.2.

270 "realm was far too" and the welcome: JW, I.394–6. See also JA, XV.199–202.

270 "strange, wild life": Macurdy, 1932, 221.

271 The account of C's bribery: MA, LXXIV.

271 Octavian storming Pelusium: Dio, LI.ix.5.

271 "she expected to gain": Ibid., LI.ix.6.

272 "Then, exalted by his victory": MA, LXXIV.

272 "a mummy and a nothing": Ibid., LXXV.

273 "that Cleopatra had betrayed": Ibid., LXXVI (translation modified).

273 Now in a panic, the city: Paulus Orosius, *The Seven Books of History Against the Pagans* (Washington, DC: Catholic University of America Press, 1964), 274.

273 "yet in his infatuation": Dio, LI.x.5–6; Livy, 133.30; MA, LXXVI.

274 "O Cleopatra": MA, LXXVI (translation modified).

275 "Never" to "speedier release": Ibid., LXXVII.

275 On Gaius Proculeius: A may not have been entirely misguided about him; Proculeius displayed a remarkable generosity with his brothers, Horace, Ode 2.2. Tacitus (*Annals*, IV.40) further testifies to his character; Juvenal (Satire VII.94) mentions him as a patron of the arts.

276 "a man who had been his relation" to "in his replies": MA, LXXVIII.

276 Burning A's letters: Dio, LII.xlii.8.

276 "add greatly to the glory": MA, LXXVIII.

276 "yet he was unwilling": Dio, LI.xi.3.

277–278 "Wretched Cleopatra" to "ease and pleasure": MA, LXXIX (translation reworked).

278 "in order that she should entertain": Dio, LI.xi.5.

278 The massive Caesareum wall: Goudchaux estimates they were between 2.5 and 3.5 meters thick, "Cleopatra's Subtle Religious Strategy," in Walker and Higgs, 2001, 136.

278 For more on the ritual lamentations, Branko Fredde van Oppen de Ruiter, "The Religious Identification of Ptolemaic Queens with Aphrodite, Demeter, Hathor and Isis." (PhD dissertation, The City University of New York, 2007), 274–370.

278–279 "in sumptuous and royal" to "regarding her children": MA, LXXXII.

279 "by far the richest": Orosius, 1964, 274.

279 "inflict any irreparable injury": Dio, LI.xvi.3–4.

280 "Her hair and face": MA, LXXXIII.

280 "wonderfully became her": Dio, LI.xii.1.

280 "for he was well worth beholding": ND, 5.

280 "To be so long prey": Cicero to Atticus, 206 (X.14), May 8, 49.

280–281 "she would lament and kiss" to "even in Hades": Dio, LI.xii.3–7.

281 "to necessity and fear of Antony": MA, LXXXIII.

282 throwing herself vigorously at all kinds of feet: Dio has her casting herself at Octavian's knees, but then again Florus has the same in 48, on CR's arrival, II.13.56, and again at Octavian's, II.21.9.

282 "The charm for which she was famous": MA, LXXXIII.

282 "musical accents" and "melting tones": Dio, LI.xii.4.

282 "stealing away" to "more gentle?": MA, LXXXIII (translation reworked).

283 "worse than a thousand deaths": Dio, LI.xiii.2.

283 "more splendid treatment" to "deceived by her": MA, LXXXIII.

283–284 "a certain tenderness" to "apart from you": Ibid., LXXXIV (translation reworked). Cornelius Dolabella may have been the son of P. Cornelius Dolabella, C's near-ally of 44–43, *Prosopographia Imperii Romani*, 2nd edition.

285 "The mischief": MA, LXXXV. For more on the asp, Nicander, *Poems and Poetical Fragments* (London: Cambridge University Press, 1953).

285 "her most beautiful apparel": Dio, LI.xiii.5. Descriptions of the couch and royal emblems, O. E. Kaper to author, March 18, 2010. The crook and flail, interview with Roger Bagnall, May 3, 2010.

285 "A fine deed" to "so many kings": MA, LXXXV.

285 "Valor in the unfortunate": Plutarch, "Aemilius Paulus," XXVI.12. As was said of Alexander the Great's mother—another suicide—the greatness of the son could be read in the death of the mother.

285 On the psylli: Lucan, IX.920–38; NH, VII.ii.13–5. Also Plutarch, "Cato the Younger," LVI.3–4; Dio, LI.xiv.4.

285 Even Strabo: Strabo, 17.1.10.

286 "The truth of the matter": MA, LXXXVI.

286 "sharp-toothed serpents": Horace, Ode I.37.

287 "Cleopatra cheated the vigilance": VP, II.lxxxvii (translation reworked).

287 both the date and the time: DA, L.

289 Instead he boasted: AA, 4.

289 "vexed at the death" to "lofty spirit": MA, LXXXVI.

289 "excessively grieved": Dio, LI.xiv.6.

289 "No craven woman": Horace, Ode I.37 (Louis E. Lord translation).

290 "with royal splendor": MA, LXXXVI (Modern Library translation).

290 The statues of Iras and Charmion: Lindsay, 1998, 337.

292 Cleopatra Selene's crocodiles: NH, 5.51.

292 Ptolemy's murder: Suetonius, "Caligula," XXXV; Dio, LIX.25. For an intricate, speculative account of the death, Jean-Claude Faur, "Caligula et la Maurétanie: La fin de Ptolémée," *Klio* 55 (1973): 249–71.

292 The death of A's associates: Orosius, 1964, 274.

292 On Caligula's alternate views: Dio, LIX.xx.1–2; Suetonius, "Caligula," XXIII.1.

293 devotion was the talk of Alexandria: See Hölbl, 2001, 249.

293 Octavian and the Alexander mummy: DA, XVIII; Dio, LI.xvi.5.

294 "the common terror": Gallus dedication of April 15, 29, cited in Robert K. Sherk, *Rome and the Greek East to the Death of Augustus* (Cambridge: Cambridge University Press, 1993), 94.

294 "in costliness and magnificence": Dio, LI.xxi.7–8. On the children, Eusebius, 187–94.

295 a lumbering hippopotamus: Gurval, 1998, 29.

295 "the Roman empire was enriched": Dio, LI.xvii.8. NH for the obelisk, XXXVI. xiv.70–1.

295 On the Egyptomania: Carla Alfano, "Egyptian Influences in Italy," in Walker and Higgs, 2001, 286–8. Earlier, Cicero (*De Legibus*, II.2) had heaped scorn on Rome's fashionable faux-Egyptian landscapes. Future Roman emperors would embrace Egyptian culture as Octavian did not; see René Preys, "Les empereurs romains vus de l'Egypte," in *Les Empereurs du Nil* (Leuven, Belgium: Editions Peeters, 2000), 30–3.

295 a golden age of women: See Reinhold, 1988, 72; Kleiner and Matheson, 1996, 36–9.

295 Livia's status: Dio, LVII.12. For good modern accounts, Anthony A. Barrett, *Livia: First Lady of Imperial Rome* (New Haven: Yale University Press, 2002); Ruth Bertha Hoffsten, "Roman Women of Rank of the Early Empire in Public Life as Portrayed by Dio, Paterculus, Suetonius, and Tacitus" (PhD dissertation, University of Pennsylvania, 1939). On Livia's staff, Balsdon, 1962, 93, 276. Kleiner, 2005, 251–7, has Livia deliberately modeling her ascent on C.

296 The melted tableware: DA, LXXI. And, professes Dio, Octavian kept none of C's furnishings save for "a single agate cup."

296 "For it is fitting": Dio, LII.xxx.1–2. C was even outdone as a consumer of pearls.

Lollia Paulina, Caligula's third wife, was said to have appeared at a banquet "covered with emeralds and pearls interlaced alternately and shining all over her head, hair, ears, neck and fingers, the sum total amounting to the value of 40,000,000 sesterces." That was four times the price of C's pearl, and Lollia stood ready to offer up the receipts to prove it, NH, IX.lviii.

296 the whisper about Livia: Tacitus, *Annals*, I.10.

297 "that no high position": Dio, LV.xv.1–2.

297 "Validity was restored": VP, II.lxxxix.

297 "from a most grievous danger": J.H.C. Williams, "'Spoiling the Egyptians': Octavian and Cleopatra," in Walker and Higgs, 2001, 197.

297 Tiberius's scoff: Dio, LVII.xviii.2.

298 "How much more attention": Brutus to Cicero, 25 (I.16).

298 "A man who teaches a woman": Menander, cited in Lefkowitz and Fant, 1992, 31.

299 "ancient writers repeatedly speak": The author of the pornographic piece is uncertain, Hughes-Hallett, 1991, 68.

299 "she often played the prostitute": Propertius, *Elegies*, 3.11.30. Skinner points out that the famous prostitute, denounced for her greed and celebrated for her wit, already constituted a familiar trope in history and biography, 2005, 167.

299 "many men bought nights": Aurelius Victor, *De Viris Illistribus*, 86.2. With "Egyptian Nights," Pushkin enthusiastically took off from there.

299 "a dazzling piece of witchcraft": Anna Jameson, *Memoirs of Celebrated Female Sovereigns* (New York: Harper, 1836), 55.

299 "that disgusting Cleopatra": Nightingale's January 1850 letter, cited in Vallée, 2003, 244. C's crime was to have immortalized herself—and Caesarion—with the carvings at Hermonthis. In *The Way We Live Now*, Trollope's irrepressible Matilde Carbury airily sums up C's career with "What a wench she was!" Lady Carbury is energetically flogging her new volume, *Criminal Queens*.

299 "How would you like": Cecil B. DeMille, in Lovric, 2001, 83.

299 "wily and suspicious": Plutarch, "Pompey," LXX.4 (translation reworked). The marriages are "tricks of state" in the ML edition, "suspicious and deceptive" partnerships in the Loeb. As Alexander the Great's repeatedly wed father had discovered, marriage was much cheaper than war.

300 "who had already ruined": MA, LXVI. She comes in for the worst abuse from Josephus, who nearly hyperventilates enumerating her crimes, *Against Apion*, II, 57–9: C "committed every kind of iniquity and crime against her relatives, her devoted husbands [sic], the Romans in general, and their emperors, her benefactors; who slew her innocent sister Arsinoe in the temple, treacherously assassinated her brother, plundered her country's gods and her ancestors' sepulchers; who, owing her throne to the first Caesar, dared to revolt against his son and successor, and, corrupting Antony by sensual passion, made him an enemy to his country and faithless to his friends, robbing some of their royal rank, discharging others, and driving them into crime."

300 mother of Christ: See Jack Lindsay, *Mark Antony: His World and His Contemporaries* (London: Routledge, 1936), 231.

300 "the most illustrious and wise": *Chronicle of John, Bishop of Nikiu*, 67.5–10. Cited in Lindsay, 1998, 333. He nominates C as the greatest of the Ptolemies, though also credits her with achievements not her own.

300 a rollicking tribute to guilt-free middle-aged adultery: René Weis, *Decoding a Hidden Life: Shakespeare Unbound* (New York: Holt, 2007), 355–8. Weis notes that Shakespeare was forty-three while working on the play. So is A as the curtain rises.

300 Blame Shakespeare: *Antony and Cleopatra* was itself written off as indecent through much of the nineteenth century. Although it includes what many consider Shakespeare's best female role, the play is famously lacking in fine productions and in admirers. In 1938 Somerset Maugham offered an explanation for its unpopularity: "Audiences have felt that it was contemptible to throw away an empire for a woman's sake. Indeed if it were not founded on an accepted legend they would be unanimous in asserting that such a thing was incredible" (*The Summing Up* [Garden City: Doubleday, 1938], 138–9). A and C's grand and hopeless passion is lost on the British, who were "not an amorous race," and generally, in Maugham's view, one disgusted by sex. They did not ruin themselves for a woman. Which may or may not explain why the play was the favorite of Emily Dickinson; see Judith Farr, "Emily Dickinson's 'Engulfing' Play: *Antony and Cleopatra*," *Tulsa Studies in Women's Literature* 9, no. 2 (1990): 231–50. Samuel Johnson and William Hazlitt too gave the play mixed grades; Johnson found it overblown and carelessly constructed. It gave George Bernard Shaw dyspepsia. Coleridge alone ranked *Antony and Cleopatra* among Shakespeare's greatest.

301 "What woman, what ancient succession": Cited in Hebert W. Benario, "The 'Carmen de Bello Actiaco' and Early Imperial Epic," *Aufstieg und Niedergang der römischen Welt* II, 30.3 (1983): 1661. For more on that fragment, see Bastien Pestel, "Le 'De Bello Actiaco,' ou l'épopée de Cléopâtre" (MA thesis, Université de Laval, 2005).

302 "What is it to lose" to "worse than people say": Euripides, "The Phoenician Women," in *Euripides V*, 388–90.

302 "who destroyed the Egyptian monarchy": Athenaeus, VI.229c (translation reworked). A generation and a half after C's death, Philo reflected on the impermanence of wealth and power. His own country offered a prime example, *On Joseph*, 135–6: "Egypt had once the supreme authority over many nations, but now it is a slave.... Where is the house of the Ptolemies, and the glory of the individual successors of Alexander which at one time shone over all the bounds both of earth and sea?" C had been the last of that line.

Selected Bibliography

Ashton, Sally-Ann. *Cleopatra and Egypt*. Malden, MA: Blackwell, 2008.

Bagnall, Roger S., and Raffaella Cribiore. *Women's Letters from Ancient Egypt: 300 BC–AD 800*. Ann Arbor: University of Michigan, 2006.

Bagnall, Roger S., and Peter Derow, eds. *Greek Historical Documents: The Hellenistic Period*. Chico, CA: Scholars Press, 1981.

———. *The Hellenistic Period: Historical Sources in Translation*. Malden, MA: Blackwell, 2004.

Beard, Mary, and Michael Crawford. *Rome in the Late Republic*. London: Duckworth, 1999.

Bevan, E. R. *The House of Ptolemy*. Chicago: Argonaut, 1968.

Bianchi, Robert S., and others. *Cleopatra's Egypt: Age of the Ptolemies*. New York: The Brooklyn Museum, 1988.

Bingen, Jean. *Hellenistic Egypt: Monarchy, Society, Economy, Culture*. Berkeley: University of California Press, 2007.

Bouché-Leclercq, Auguste. *Histoire des Lagides*. 4 vols. Aalen, Germany: Scientia Verlag, 1978.

Bowman, Alan K. *Egypt After the Pharaohs*. Berkeley: University of California Press, 1986.

Braund, David. *Rome and the Friendly King*. London: Croom Helm, 1984.

Braund, David, and John Wilkins, eds. *Athenaeus and His World: Reading Greek Culture in the Roman Empire*. Exeter, UK: University of Exeter Press, 2003.

Burstein, Stanley. *The Reign of Cleopatra*. Norman: University of Oklahoma Press, 2004.

Carter, John M. *The Battle of Actium*. New York: Weybright and Talley, 1970.

Casson, Lionel. *Ships and Seamanship in the Ancient World*. Princeton: Princeton University Press, 1971.

———. *Travel in the Ancient World*. Baltimore: Johns Hopkins University Press, 1994.

Chamoux, François. *Hellenistic Civilization*. Oxford: Blackwell, 2003.

Chauveau, Michel. *Cleopatra: Beyond the Myth*. Ithaca: Cornell University Press, 2002.

————. *Egypt in the Age of Cleopatra*. Ithaca: Cornell University Press, 2000.

Everitt, Anthony. *Augustus: The Life of Rome's First Emperor*. New York: Random House, 2006.

————. *Cicero: The Life and Times of Rome's Greatest Politician*. New York: Random House, 2003.

Foertmeyer, Victoria Ann. "Tourism in Graeco-Roman Egypt." PhD thesis, Princeton University, 1989.

Fraser, P. M. *Ptolemaic Alexandria*. 3 vols. Oxford: Oxford University Press, 1972.

Grant, Michael. *Cleopatra*. Edison, NJ: Castle Books, 2004.

Green, Peter. *Alexander to Actium: The Historical Evolution of the Hellenistic Age*. Berkeley: University of California Press, 1990.

————. *The Hellenistic Age: A Short History*. New York: Modern Library, 2007.

Green, Peter, ed. *Hellenistic History and Culture*. Berkeley: University of California Press, 1993.

Gruen, Erich S. *The Hellenistic World and the Coming of Rome*. 2 vols. Berkeley: University of California Press, 1984.

Heinen, Heinz. *Kleopatra-Studien: Gesammelte Schriften zur ausgehenden Ptolemäerzeit.* Konstanzer Althistorische Vorträge und Forschungen. Vol. 49. Konstanz, Germany: UKV, Univ.-Verlag Konstanz, 2009.

Hölbl, Gunther. *A History of the Ptolemaic Empire*. New York: Routledge, 2001.

Huzar, Eleanor Goltz. *Mark Antony: A Biography*. Minneapolis: University of Minnesota Press, 1978.

Jones, A. H. M. *The Greek City: From Alexander to Justinian*. Oxford: Clarendon Press, 1984.

Jones, Prudence J. *Cleopatra: A Sourcebook*. Norman: University of Oklahoma Press, 2006.

Kleiner, Diana E. E. *Cleopatra and Rome*. Cambridge, MA: Belknap Press, 2005.

Lewis, Naphtali. *Greeks in Ptolemaic Egypt*. Oxford: Clarendon Press, 1986.

————. *Life in Egypt under Roman Rule*. Oxford: Clarendon Press, 1983.

Lindsay, Jack. *Cleopatra*. London: Folio Society, 1998.

Macurdy, Grace Harriet. *Hellenistic Queens*. Baltimore: The Johns Hopkins Press, 1932.

Neal, Linda Ricketts. "Cleopatra's Influence on the Eastern Policy of Julius Caesar and Mark Antony." MA thesis, Iowa State University, 1975.

Pelling, C. B. R., ed. *Plutarch: Life of Antony*. Cambridge: Cambridge University Press, 1999.

Pomeroy, Sarah B. *Women in Hellenistic Egypt*. Detroit: Wayne State University Press, 1990.

Préaux, Claire. *L'Economie royale des Lagides*. Brussels: Édition de la Fondation Egyptologique Reine Elisabeth, 1939.

————. *Les grecs en Égypte, d'après les archives de Zénon*. Brussels: J. Lebegue & Co., 1947.

Rawson, Elizabeth. *Intellectual Life in the Late Roman Republic*. Baltimore: Johns Hopkins University Press, 1985.

Reinhold, Meyer. *A Historical Commentary on Cassius Dio's Roman History.* Atlanta: Scholars Press, 1988.

Ricketts, Linda Maurine. "The Administration of Ptolemaic Egypt Under Cleopatra VII." PhD thesis, University of Minnesota, 1980.

Rostovtzeff, M. *The Social and Economic History of the Hellenistic World.* 3 vols. Oxford: Clarendon Press, 1998.

Rowlandson, Jane, ed. *Women and Society in Greek and Roman Egypt: A Sourcebook.* Cambridge: Cambridge University Press, 1998.

Sacks, Kenneth S. *Diodorus Siculus and the First Century.* Princeton: Princeton University Press, 1990.

Shipley, Graham. *The Greek World After Alexander.* London: Routledge, 2000.

Sullivan, Richard D. *Near Eastern Royalty and Rome: 100–30 BC.* Toronto: University of Toronto Press, 1990.

Syme, Ronald. *The Roman Revolution.* New York: Oxford University Press, 2002.

Tarn, William W., and M. P. Charlesworth. *Octavian, Antony and Cleopatra.* Cambridge: Cambridge University Press, 1965.

Tarn, William W., and G. T. Griffith. *Hellenistic Civilization.* London: Edward Arnold, 1959.

Thompson, Dorothy. *Memphis under the Ptolemies.* Princeton: Princeton University Press, 1988.

Tyldesley, Joyce. *Cleopatra: Last Queen of Egypt.* London: Profile Books, 2008.

Van 't Dack, E., ed. *Egypt and the Hellenistic World: Proceedings of the International Colloquium, Leuven, 24–26 May 1982.* Studia Hellenistica 27. Leuven: Studia Hellenistica, 1983.

Volkmann, Hans. *Cleopatra: A Study in Politics and Propaganda.* New York: Sagamore Press, 1958.

Walbank, F. W. *The Hellenistic World.* Cambridge; MA: Harvard University Press, 1981.

Walker, Susan, and Sally-Ann Ashton. *Cleopatra Reassessed.* London: British Museum, 2003.

Walker, Susan, and Peter Higgs, eds. *Cleopatra of Egypt: From History to Myth.* Princeton: Princeton University Press, 2001.

Whitehorne, John. *Cleopatras.* London: Routledge, 1994.

Will, Edouard. *Histoire politique du monde hellénistique.* Paris: Seuil, 2003.

Index

Timon of Athens, 265
Troy, fall of, 79
Twain, Mark, 5, 109

Ullman, B. L., 113n

Velleius Paterculus, 240, 297
Vestal Virgins, 238
Virgil, 182, 191, 286, 297–98
Virgin Mary, 88, 301, 319n

women
  education of, 35–36, 312n

Egyptian women's reputation, 241,
  338n
Euripides on, 4, 203–4, 206, 212
Greek attitudes toward, 289, 339n
and power, 4, 301
pregnancies in Egypt, 78, 81, 317n
of Ptolemies, 21, 23
roles in Egypt, 24–25, 35, 87
Roman attitudes toward, 24, 35n,
  72–73, 72n, 105, 111, 111n, 112, 121, 177,
  236, 241n, 247, 248, 289, 295,
  298, 339n
and wet nurses, 84, 319n

Illustration Credits

Endpapers: Nimatallah / Art Resource, NY

Watercolor of the Canopic Way: Jean-Claude Golvin

Watercolor of Alexandria: Jean-Claude Golvin

The world as Cleopatra knew it: Cram's 1895 Universal Atlas

Possible Cleopatra, in Parian marble: Sandro Vannini / Corbis

Possible Cleopatra, with tight chignon: Bildarchiv Preussischer Kulturbesitz / Art Resource, NY

Possible Cleopatra, without a diadem: © The Trustees of the British Museum

Possible Cleopatra, with pronounced cheekbones: © Hellenic Republic / Ministry of Culture / Delos Museum

Women playing knucklebones: © The Trustees of the British Museum

Girl with writing tablet: Erich Lessing / Art Resource, NY

Ptolemy Auletes: Courtesy of the Brooklyn Museum

Ivory game piece depicting Ptolemy XIV: Bibliothèque nationale de France

Likely Caesarion, in granite: Araldo de Luca

Granite Cleopatra as Isis: © Musée royal de Mariemont

Bust of Ptolemy Philadelphus: Jack A. Josephson

Basalt statue of Cleopatra: Image courtesy of the Rosicrucian Egyptian Museum, San Jose, California

Likely Alexander Helios: Photo © The Walters Art Museum, Baltimore

Cleopatra stela: Louvre, Paris, France / Lauros / Giraudon / The Bridgeman Art Library

Bust of Caesar: Scala / Art Resource, NY

Buchis bull stela: Cairo, Egyptian Museum

Chalcedony intaglio of Caesar: Bibliothèque nationale de France

Bust of Mark Antony: akg-images

Red jasper intaglio of Mark Antony: © The Trustees of the British Museum

Bronze Cyprus coin: © The Trustees of the British Museum

ABOUT THE AUTHOR

STACY SCHIFF is the author of *Véra (Mrs. Vladimir Nabokov)*, winner of the Pulitzer Prize; *Saint-Exupéry*, a Pulitzer Prize finalist; and *A Great Improvisation: Franklin, France, and the Birth of America*, winner of the George Washington Book Prize and the Ambassador Book Award. Schiff has received fellowships from the Guggenheim Foundation, the National Endowment for the Humanities, and the Center for Scholars and Writers at the New York Public Library. The recipient of an Academy Award in Literature from the American Academy of Arts and Letters, Schiff has contributed to *The New Yorker*, the *New York Times*, and the *Washington Post*, as well as many other publications. She lives in New York City.